HOW TO GROW A PLAYSPACE

How to Grow a Playspace takes you through a global perspective of the different stages of child development and the environments that engage children in play around the world. From the urbanity of Mumbai; to rainbow nets in Japan; nature play in Denmark; recycling waste in Peru; community building in Uganda; play streets in London; and gardens of peace in Palestine, it proves that no matter where play occurs, it is ubiquitous in its resourcefulness, imagination and effect.

Written by international leaders in the field of play including academics, designers and playworkers, *How to Grow A Playspace* discusses contemporary issues around children and play, such as risk benefit in play, creativity and technology, insights into children's thinking, social inclusion and what makes a city child-friendly.

With its own 'Potting Shed', this text is also a practical guide to support playspace projects with advice on teams, budgets, community engagement, maintenance and standards. *How to Grow a Playspace* is a comprehensive 'go-to' guide for anyone interested or involved with children's play and playspaces.

Katherine Masiulanis (AILA) is a registered landscape architect based in Melbourne, Australia. She is the Director of Leaf Design Studio, which specialises in combining landscape architecture with interpretive design. Having started her career as an industrial designer, she has a broad base of design skills. Katherine has worked on the design of play environments since 1998 in various capacities, allowing her to complete many award-winning designs. She has a particular interest in the enrichment of play with sculptural and artistic elements, and in creating sites which relate their unique stories.
www.leafdesignstudio.com.au

Elizabeth Cummins is a qualified landscape architect (Bachelor of Design 1st Class Hons, RMIT 2001) and educator (Diploma of Teaching Early Childhood, Monash University 1989). Beginning her professional life as an early childhood teacher in the early 1990s, Elizabeth has worked as both a pre-school and primary educator in Australia, the UK and Japan. After qualifying as a landscape architect, Elizabeth worked professionally with

Jeavons Landscape Architects for almost six years and has lectured and tutored at RMIT University, Melbourne. Elizabeth has also spent many years working in and for local government. In 2011 Elizabeth branched out to take her own creative project direction, called Bricolage Design. Bricolage specialises in design and strategic planning, particularly for children's environments. Elizabeth is a founding coordinator of the Creative Cubby Project, a local initiative to encourage creative play for children by building temporary cubby houses using cardboard boxes and recycled materials. Elizabeth is also a passionate advocate for quality play and the right of children to be independently mobile and able to freely and actively explore and engage in their local neighbourhoods. She is a member of Play Australia and in 2015 co-authored their guide to risk benefit assessment, 'Getting the Balance Right'. Elizabeth blogs regularly on play and projects for children. **www.bricolagedesign.com.au/leafgenius**

'*How to Grow a Playspace* draws on the experience of Elizabeth Cummins and Katherine Masiulanis, two inspiring Australia-based landscape architects with a passion for creating outdoor playspaces for children. This book includes contributions from current world leaders in playspace development and design, challenging perceptions of the importance and complexity of play. *How to Grow a Playspace* uncovers the possibilities of designed and appropriated environments for play. More than just a reference guide, readers can come back to this book again and again for inspiration, enjoyment and support to create dynamic and engaging playspaces that children love.'

Barbara Champion, Executive Director – Play Australia

HOW TO GROW A PLAYSPACE

Development and Design

Edited by Katherine Masiulanis and Elizabeth Cummins

LONDON AND NEW YORK

First published 2017
by Routledge
2 Park Square, Milton Park, Abingdon, Oxon OX14 4RN

and by Routledge
711 Third Avenue, New York, NY 10017

Routledge is an imprint of the Taylor & Francis Group, an informa business

© 2017 selection and editorial matter, Katherine Masiulanis and Elizabeth Cummins; individual chapters, the contributors

The right of Katherine Masiulanis and Elizabeth Cummins to be identified as the authors of the editorial material, and of the authors for their individual chapters, has been asserted in accordance with sections 77 and 78 of the Copyright, Designs and Patents Act 1988.

All rights reserved. No part of this book may be reprinted or reproduced or utilised in any form or by any electronic, mechanical, or other means, now known or hereafter invented, including photocopying and recording, or in any information storage or retrieval system, without permission in writing from the publishers.

Trademark notice: Product or corporate names may be trademarks or registered trademarks, and are used only for identification and explanation without intent to infringe.

British Library Cataloguing-in-Publication Data
A catalogue record for this book is available from the British Library

Library of Congress Cataloging in Publication Data
Names: Masiulanis, Katherine, editor. | Cummins, Elizabeth, editor.
Title: How to grow a playspace : development and design / edited by Katherine Masiulanis and Elizabeth Cummins.
Description: Abingdon, Oxon ; New York, NY : Routledge, 2017. | Includes bibliographical references and index.
Identifiers: LCCN 2016035261| ISBN 9781138906549 (hdk : alk. paper) | ISBN 9781138907065 (pbk : alk. paper) | ISBN 9781315695198 (ebk)
Subjects: | MESH: Environment Design | Play and Playthings--psychology | Child Development | Child Classification: LCC GV425 | NLM WS 105.5.P5 | DDC 711/.558--dc23 LC record available at https://lccn.loc.gov/2016035261

ISBN: 9781138906549 (hbk)
ISBN: 9781138907065 (pbk)
ISBN: 9781315695198 (ebk)

Typeset in Bembo
by Fakenham Prepress Solutions, Fakenham, Norfolk NR21 8NN

CONTENTS

Dedication and acknowledgements   xi
List of contributors   xii

Part I: GROUND

    An introduction   3
    Elizabeth Cummins & Katherine Masiulanis

Part II: SOWING

1. A history of playspaces   13
   Dr Carla Pascoe

2. Fundamental perceptions of and ingredients for play: Having fun, opening up and letting go   21
   Elizabeth Cummins

3. Insights into the mind of the child   27
   Tracy R. Gleason & Becky L. Geer

4. Play environments and affordances   37
   Elizabeth Cummins & Zahra Zamani

5. Chaos and confusion: The clash between adults' and children's spaces   49
   Katherine Masiulanis

vi Contents

   6 City play   55
       Elger Blitz & Hannah Schubert

   7 Of agency, participation and design: Two contrasting play scenarios
      in Indian cities   65
       Mukta Naik

   8 Designing inclusive playspaces   73
       Katherine Masiulanis

   9 Glenallen School   79
       Mary Jeavons

Part III: SEEDLINGS

  10 Child development   97
       Elizabeth Cummins & Katherine Masiulanis

  11 The natural environment as playspace   105
       Helle Nebelong

  12 Planting for children's play   115
       John Rayner

  13 Introducing water play environments to Early Years settings   129
       Theresa Casey & Margaret Westwood

  14 The development of forest school in the UK   137
       Christina Dee

  15 Children's gardens: A tale of two cities   147
       Andrew Laidlaw

  16 Reflections on designing Lafayette Park playground   155
       Jeffrey Miller

Part IV: SPROUTS

    17 Child development   167
          Elizabeth Cummins & Katherine Masiulanis

Playspaces and art

    18 Colours and materials   175
          Katherine Masiulanis

    19 Embedded art in playspaces   181
          Dorelle Davidson

    20 Child led creativity   189
          Matthew Shaw

    21 Art as playspace   195
          Interview with Toshiko & Charles MacAdam

Schools

    22 Quintessential play patterns in schools: The interface of space, materials and play behaviour   207
          Mary Jeavons

    23 When is a slide not a slide? (Or what if we think differently about and beyond design?)   219
          Dr Wendy Russell

    24 'This place is like a building site… .'   227
          Judi Legg

    25 The stepping stones to many playgrounds   235
          Carla and Tom Gill

Part V: SAPLINGS

    26 Child development   251
          Elizabeth Cummins & Katherine Masiulanis

27 Beyond 14+ years 257
    Gabrielle McKinnon & Alasdair Roy

28 Technology in playspaces: A snapshot 265
    Katherine Masiulanis

29 Lima and the ever-postponed electric train 267
    Basurama

30 Be not afeared: Embracing the need for risk in play 275
    Bernard Speigel

31 Not in my front garden! Play Streets: A doorstep controversy 287
    Paul Hocker

32 We are such stuff as dreams are made on: Paraphrased conversation with Mark Halden, Senior Playworker, Glamis Adventure Playground 297
    Penny Wilson

Part VI: THE POTTING SHED

33 The team 311
    Katherine Masiulanis

34 Tin tacks – budgeting and resources 313
    Elizabeth Cummins

35 Social and environmental responsibilities 317
    Katherine Masiulanis

36 Site analysis and opportunities for play 321
    Katherine Masiulanis

37 Playspaces and community engagement 323
    Elizabeth Cummins

38 Insight into playground manufacturers 327
    Katherine Masiulanis

39 Staging 329
    Elizabeth Cummins

40 Planting maintenance 331
    Katherine Masiulanis

41 Maintenance and longevity 333
    Elizabeth Cummins

42 Supporting infrastructure 335
    Katherine Masiulanis

43 Standards and regulations (general and best practice principles) 337
    Paul Grover

    Conclusion 341
    Elizabeth Cummins & Katherine Masiulanis

Index 343

DEDICATION AND ACKNOWLEDGEMENTS

KM – For Rhys and your future

EC – To my kinder teacher, Mrs Raguse, for inspiring my love of play

The contributing editors wish to thank all our contributing authors, artists and photographers for their time and patience and for the wealth of knowledge they bring to this book. We would also like to thank Athi Kokonis and Robert Morden for their support and editorial assistance.

LIST OF CONTRIBUTORS

Basurama are an art and architecture collective that focus their field of study and action in the city and the complex processes that coexist in it. Basurama use trash in its broadest meaning as a starting point, as a tool as an excuse to think, reflect and build new possibilities. Basurama believe that networking, active participation, enhancement of local resources and creativity are the keys to develop projects of social transformation.

Elger Blitz is founder and senior designer at Carve. He accidentally got involved in designing playgrounds in the early 1990s, which gives more than 25 years of experience in relevant projects in public space. His cross-disciplinary and renewing approach to designing urban spaces from the perspective of play has been proven to anticipate actual demands and trends, with a result that extends beyond the relevance for urban spaces for children and youngsters alone. He handles design tasks in a very integral manner, switching easily between different scales and disciplines. His unconventional approach and distinctive ideas on designing for kids and teenagers makes him a guest lecturer at different universities in the Netherlands and abroad.

Theresa Casey is an independent play consultant, specialising in play environments, children's rights and inclusion. Theresa was the consultant to OPAL Water Play, providing support to settings. With a strong interest in advocacy, she was elected President of the International Play Association: Promoting the Child's Right to Play in 2008.

James Cattell was born in 1954 in New Zealand, where he studied law, history, philosophy, literature and art. For the first ten years after moving to Australia as a young man, he worked as a puppeteer and street performer and lived surrounded by dusty sculptures and paintings. After becoming a parent in 1988, he and his partner, Dorelle Davidson, started an art business, Honeyweather & Speight, producing murals and mosaics, children's books and site-specific sculptural works. This experience has evolved into a particular specialty producing interactive artworks for children's playgrounds.

Elizabeth Cummins is a qualified landscape architect (Bachelor of Design 1st Class Hons, RMIT 2001) and educator (Diploma of Teaching Early Childhood, Monash University 1989). Beginning her professional life as an Early Childhood Teacher in the early 1990s, Elizabeth has worked as both a pre-school and primary educator in Australia, the UK and Japan. After qualifying as a landscape architect, Elizabeth has worked professionally with Jeavons Landscape Architects, lectured and tutored at RMIT University, Melbourne, as well as worked for local government. In 2011 Elizabeth formed Bricolage Design, specialising in design and strategic planning, particularly for children's environments. She is a founding coordinator of the Creative Cubby Project, encouraging creative play for children by building temporary cardboard box cubby houses. Elizabeth is also a passionate advocate for quality play and the right of children to be able to freely explore and engage in their local neighbourhoods. She is a member of Play Australia and in 2015 co-authored their guide to risk benefit assessment, 'Getting the Balance Right'. Elizabeth blogs regularly on play and projects for children at www.bricolagedesign.com.au/leafgenius.

Dorelle Davidson started her working life as a primary school teacher, but was lured away by overseas travel and the fancy-free life. After returning to Australia, she studied and worked in the Interior Design industry until she had children with her artist partner, James Cattell. Together they decided to merge their skills in a business, Honeyweather & Speight, producing artworks and created many fantastic things from giant tennis balls to muralised swimming pools. These days, most of their work turns up in children's playgrounds.

Christina Dee is the Director of Forest School Learning Initiative Limited; she has been a fully qualified forest school leader for 16 years and has established nationwide forest school training. As a consequence, FSLI is the largest and most successful forest school training company in the UK. Chris has been a practicing forest school leader throughout, leading sessions for children between 2 years and 16 years old, including those who have special needs. Chris facilitates the provision of forest school to 300 children per week through FSLI. Before FSLI, Chris was a Senior Manager in the Health Service and completed her MBA in 1991. After having her children, Chris became a Lecturer in Child Care at Evesham and Malvern Hills College on a variety of programmes from Foundation to Degree level courses. Chris is particularly passionate about developing and delivering forest school to areas where Outdoor Learning is not a way of life, such as inner city areas in London. Chris has particular strengths in working with people and prides herself on her inspirational approach to forest school.

Becky Geer is Interim Educational Director of the Wellesley College Child Study Center and Adjunct Faculty in Early Childhood Education at Great Bay Community College. She earned a Master's degree in Education from Lesley University (2004). Becky's interests include social development and supporting interactions between children and nature.

Tom and Carla Gill founded East African Playgrounds in 2009 when they met at the University of Leeds. With Tom's vast travelling experience and his 'nothing is impossible' attitude and with Carla studying Childhood, Education and Culture and having been a play worker since she played as a child, building playgrounds in East Africa was the perfect match.

As the founding directors they both enjoy life between the different worlds of Uganda and the UK with the vision spreading the joy of play further and wider.

Dr Tracy Gleason is a Professor of Psychology at Wellesley College and Psychological Director of the Wellesley College Child Study Center. She received a PhD in child psychology (1998) with certification in early childhood education from the Institute of Child Development at the University of Minnesota. She primarily researches imagination and friendship in young children.

Paul Grover is a Civil Engineer and founder of Play DMC, a Melbourne-based consultancy specialising since 2001 in playspace assessments from concept design through to construction and ongoing site inspections. While assessments are often focussed on safety and Standards requirements, Play DMC recognises that play is essential for the physical, social, intellectual and emotional development of children; and that children want and need to take risks to develop. Play DMC uses practical experience and theoretical knowledge of benefits of play, risk and Standards to assist in the provision of exciting, attractive and ultimately fun environments for play.

Mark Halden is a Senior Playworker at Glamis Adventure Playground in Shadwell, London, in the UK. Glamis Adventure Playground is an award-winning community project and best practice model for playwork in the UK. Aware of the children's needs for activity, fresh air, less TV and computers and a generally less sedentary lifestyle, Glamis Adventure Playground focusses on healthy eating and exercise, especially outdoor activities.

Paul Hocker is London Play's Director and is also chair of the England, Wales and Northern Ireland branch of the International Play Association. Paul is the creative lead on many of London Play's groundbreaking initiatives, designed to bring play and active recreation to London's 1.8 million children, their families and communities. Paul's experience includes his appointment as a London Leader for the Mayor of London's Sustainable Development Commission, pioneering play streets in the capital, writing for children's television (BBC, Discovery) and lecturing in play and playwork for the University of East London's degree course.

Toshiko Horiuchi MacAdam is a graduate of both the Tama Fine Arts University and Cranbrook Academy of Art. She has taught at Columbia University Teachers College, Haystack Mountain School, the University of Georgia, Bunka Institute (Tokyo) and the Kyoto Junior College of Art. She also currently teaches textiles part-time at the Nova Scotia College of Art & Design. A highly skilled textile artist, she has exhibited her work in museums and galleries in the US, Europe, Japan and Southeast Asia. Her first large playspace for children was created for the Okinawa Memorial National Park in Japan in 1979. Her husband, Charles MacAdam (an NSCAD alumnus), joined her in 1990 to establish Interplay Design & Manufacturing Inc. Together they have created 'public art for kids' in Japan, Singapore, China, Korea, the US and Spain over the past 40 years. Other notable projects include Knitted Wonder Space I (1981) and II (2009) for the Hakone Open Air Museum in Japan and Harmonic Motion, initially commissioned for Enel Contemporanea in Italy in 2013 and later exhibited at the Toledo Museum of Art in Ohio, USA in 2015.

Mary Jeavons is the Principal of award-winning landscape architectural practice Jeavons Landscape Architects based in Melbourne, Australia. Jeavons Landscape Architects are known for their high quality, detailed and customised landscape design – especially in natural environments, parks, children's spaces, sensory gardens and other sites in the public domain. Mary has worked for 25 years planning and designing children's spaces of all kinds, particularly those which are accessible to children and adults with disabilities. Mary has carried out important research and advocacy in the field and has written, published and spoken widely in forums in Australia and overseas. She also has a particular niche in strategic planning for open space, parks and play areas for local government and developers, Australia wide.

Andrew Laidlaw is a qualified landscape architect and horticulturalist with over 30 years of experience in the industry. Andrew is well known for his in-depth knowledge of plants, his mastery of design and his unique, innovative approach to design. Andrew is most widely known for his long standing role as the landscape architect at the Royal Botanic Gardens Melbourne. In this position he has designed and developed many projects including the Ian Potter Foundation Children's Garden, Guilfoyle's Volcano and the Fern Gully rejuvenation. Andrew has taught Landscape Design at the University of Melbourne's Burnley campus (previously VCAH) for over 25 years, teaching many of Australia's gardeners and designers, and he is a regular presenter on ABC 774's Saturday morning gardening programme. Andrew founded Laidlaw & Laidlaw Design in 2004 with his wife Sarah, and has undertaken a range of domestic and public projects while continuing his work for the Royal Botanic Gardens Melbourne. Andrew's love of plants and nature began in childhood and was inspired by his father's love of the gardens. The childhood memories of playing free in the bush and connecting with nature have inspired Andrew's lifelong passion to not only work with nature, but to help others learn, enjoy and find their own connection with the natural world.

Katherine Masiulanis (AILA) is a Registered Landscape Architect based in Melbourne, Australia. She is the Director of Leaf Design Studio, which specialises in combining Landscape Architecture with Interpretive Design. Having started her career as an Industrial Designer, she has a broad base of design skills. Katherine has worked on the design of play environments since 1998 in various capacities, allowing her to complete many award-winning designs. She has a particular interest in the enrichment of play with sculptural and artistic elements, and in creating sites which relate their unique stories. www.leafdesignstudio.com.au.

Gabrielle McKinnon began her career as a lawyer and advocate for children and young people involved in the criminal justice system. She has a strong interest in the human rights of children and young people, and worked as the Director of a Linkage project at the Australian National University examining the impact of Australia's first legislative bill of rights. Since 2009 Gabrielle has worked as a human rights legal adviser and senior adviser to the Children & Young People Commissioner in the ACT Human Rights Commission.

Jeffrey Miller, ASLA, LEED AP BD+C, is the principal and founder of Miller Company, a licensed landscape architect and landscape contractor with over 35 years of experience designing and building. He is recognised as a leader and expert in the realm of green schoolyard design and development. Committed to the idea that landscape architecture is a powerful vehicle for addressing community needs, Miller has spent much of his career working with neighbourhood groups, schools and service organisations designing landscapes that naturally enhance and support the social context in ways that strengthen the potential for delightful, open and safe interaction. Under his direction, Miller Company has provided numerous design solutions for community projects creating native, edible and recreational gardens in formerly abandoned urban spaces. Jeffrey has collaborated with artists to create expressive landscapes for healthcare facilities, arts centres and libraries. Miller innovates for constructed sustainability in all of his projects. He has lectured widely, highlighting strategies targeting the reduction of potable water in the landscape, promoting designs for the capture and use of stormwater. He is known for his 'hands on' involvement in the implementation of Miller Company designs, and is committed to the idea that it is important to be engaged at the moment when a design becomes a physical reality.

Helle Nebelong is a Danish Landscape Architect and Master of Public Management with a special focus on spaces for children and how to adapt and improve the city for everyday life. A key pioneer of the natural playground movement, which advocates for using local materials, Nebelong is internationally recognised for this special philosophy. Helle has presented numerous keynote lectures and publications, and playspace designs, such as 'The Garden of Senses' and the 'Nature Playground' in Copenhagen. For more than ten years Nebelong was employed by the City of Copenhagen (1994–2006), leading the Technical and Environmental Administration's strategy 'City for All – Improving the accessibility of the Urban Spaces in Copenhagen'. Between 2004 and 2014 she was president of the Danish Playground Association. Since 2007 she has been a member of the Nature Action Collaborative for Children Leadership Team representing Europe in the design and planning field. www.hellenebelong.com

Dr Carla Pascoe is an Australian Research Council DECRA Fellow at the University of Melbourne and an Honorary Associate at Museum Victoria. Her research focusses on histories of children and women in twentieth-century Australia, with a special interest in historical geographies of childhood, the cultural heritage of children, the cultural history of menstruation and the changing experience of motherhood. Publications include *Spaces Imagined, Places Remembered: Childhood in 1950s Australia* (2011), *Children, Childhood and Cultural Heritage* (2013, co-edited with Kate Darian-Smith) and articles in leading Australian and international journals.

John Rayner is Director of Urban Horticulture and Senior Lecturer at the University of Melbourne, Australia. John's research and teaching interests include landscape plants, planting design, green roofs and walls, children's gardens and therapeutic landscapes. He is a passionate and award-winning educator, publishes widely across industry and scientific journals and regularly consults in the horticultural and landscape industries. John has worked collaboratively with different organisations and on specific projects involving planting and plant selection in children's landscapes. Over the last decade he has been instrumental in helping to develop the multi-award-winning 'Learning Landscape' at The Patch School in the Dandenong Ranges, Victoria.

Alasdair Roy has worked with children and young people for over 25 years, and was the ACT Children & Young People Commissioner between 2008 and 2016. Alasdair is committed to supporting and enhancing the rights, interests and well-being of children and young people, including, in particular, the right of children and young people to have a say about issues which affect them. As Children & Young People Commissioner, Alasdair spoke regularly with children and young people about a wide range of issues, from the practical – such as their views on parents smacking children, or participation in Family Court proceedings – to the philosophical – such as what makes a happy childhood, or the best and worst things about being young. While Alasdair has played a key role in improving service delivery for children and young people, his proudest achievement has been increasing the participation of children and young people in government decision making.

Dr Wendy Russell is Senior Lecturer in Play and Playwork at University of Gloucestershire (UK). She has worked in the play sector for 40 years, initially on adventure playgrounds and then in development, research, education and training. She has worked with local authorities, the private sector and local, national and international voluntary organisations.

Hannah Schubert is an Associate at Carve. While she studied urban planning, Hannah's interest in architecture, landscape and the design of public space grew. After some time in Germany and England to do research on globalising cities, she returned to the Netherlands to become a landscape architect. Hannah is particularly interested in urban landscapes, the contribution of public space to local communities and, at the higher scale level, how this fits into city regeneration processes.

Matt Shaw has been a professional artist for over 15 years. He originally trained as an engineer but decided instead to follow a career in sculpture. Taking an MA in sculpture at Winchester School of Art and subsequently becoming artist in residence at Whitnash Nursery has led to his involvement in numerous creative play projects throughout the UK and overseas. Working in collaboration with schools, galleries and communities, he has created many large-scale structures, objects and environments that provoke participation and enquiry into creative processes. The use of simple but open-ended materials has supported these processes and is an important part of encouraging children and adults of all abilities and ages to play, explore and create freely.

Bernard Spiegal is an author, advocate and director of PLAYLINK, a multi-disciplinary practice in the United Kingdom focussed on securing children and teenagers' freedom to play in a variety of settings including, importantly, within shared communal (e.g. social housing) space and the wider public realm. If he had to say why he believes play is so significant, both for the individual and for wider society, it is because he values play as an initiation into, and embodiment of, the idea and practice of freedom. Thus, for him, promoting play – *free* play – is a moral and political stance ultimately indifferent to the sort of 'evidence' conventionally thought to justify its importance. He wishes that advocates of play would more vigorously make the case for play as intrinsically worthwhile, this being the only ground that, in his view, can ultimately secure its flourishing. Bernard, with Professor David Ball and Tim Gill, co-authored Play England's seminal *Managing Risk in Play Provision; an implementation guide* in 2007 and the UK Play Safety Forum's guide to Risk-Benefit Assessment both of which highlight the need for a more balanced approach to risk in play. Bernard is an advisor to the UK Play Safety Forum. Bernard is a regular blogger and, once a week, sells raw honey at a market.

Margaret Westwood is Senior Play Development Officer for the City of Edinburgh Council with strategic responsibility for Play. She has 25 years' experience in managing children's play projects and in developing play partnerships with the voluntary sector. She leads Edinburgh's Outdoor Play and Active Learning projects.

Penny Wilson is a playworker – one of a group of professionals who facilitate children's play in adventure playgrounds, parks and other settings, principally in the United Kingdom. Wilson grew up in the Southeast of England and spent much of her childhood playing on the coast near her family home. She studied illustration in art school, settled in London's East End and came to playwork through a community programme for children with disabilities. Over the course of two decades, she has earned distinction for helping such children play with their peers. She worked for the Play Association at Tower Hamlets (PATH), a second-tier, not-for-profit organisation and play provider, for twelve years. Currently she works as a part of the team of Glamis Adventure Playground establishing a children's community cafe.

Zahra Zamani received her Bachelor's degree in Architecture and Master's in Landscape architecture from the University of Tehran, Iran. For her Master's thesis, she explored eight primary schoolyards of Tehran for their physical environment qualities. To fulfil her passion for knowledge, in 2010 Zahra decided to continue her education with a PhD degree in Design from North Carolina State University. For her dissertation, Zahra compared natural, mixed and traditional outdoor preschool environments' physical qualities and children's cognitive play. Currently, she is working as a postdoctoral scholar at Ball State University, exploring how playing in forests promotes children's attention spans.

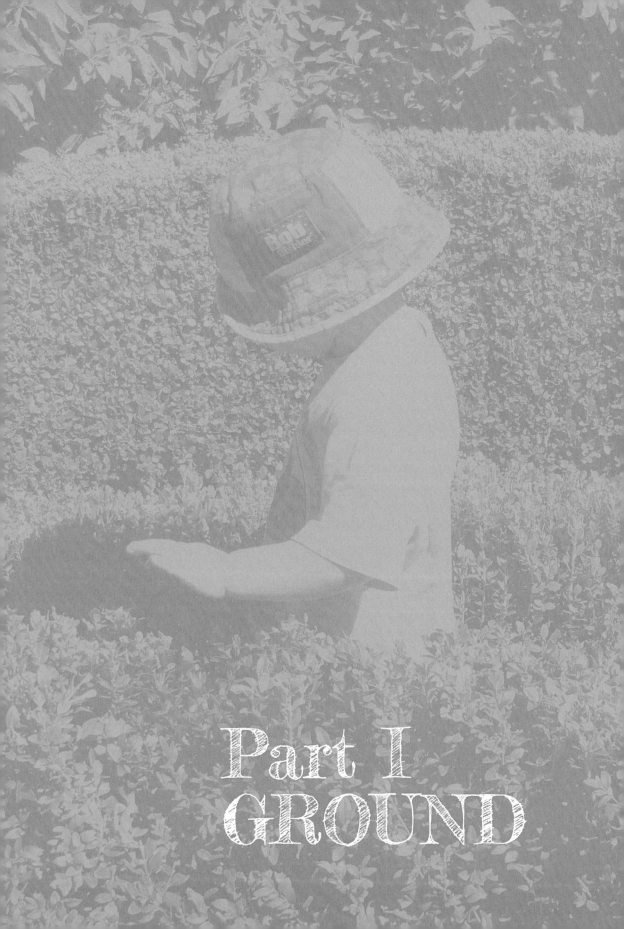

Part I
GROUND

AN INTRODUCTION

Elizabeth Cummins & Katherine Masiulanis

The ground is a place of beginnings. Plant life, which feeds so many other forms of life, must have soil to grow. We build upon the ground, and rely on it for support. The ground is also a place where we can establish deep roots. In the context of this book, and 'growing a playspace', the ground is a commitment to recognising the importance of play, and our role in influencing the quality of play. Great thinking is rich soil.

If you are searching for a simple formula for a playspace, you will not find it here. There are no diagrams telling you where to put the swings. What you will find in these pages will open your eyes to the complexity of designing playspaces. In many ways, they are some of the most complex landscape projects undertaken. Designing playspaces requires an understanding not just of aesthetics, materials and construction, but also of children's changing developmental needs; an ergonomic, social and cultural sensitivity; an assessment of risk and challenge; and an openness to spaces being used in ways beyond their design. A strong understanding of the importance of play, and the reasons behind the need to provide fantastic playspaces, give us the motivation to investigate, research, design and carry through a project which will enrich lives in the same way as any bountiful harvest from the soil.

In our adult world, play is sometimes dismissed. In our serious, goal-driven, time-managed lives, play can seem to be 'just messing about', and the real importance of play in developing complete human beings is lost. However, if we want children to know what their bodies can really do; to have strong imaginations and creative minds; and to get along with one another, it is crucial that they are given the opportunity for as much good, fulfilling play as possible.

Article 31 of the United Nations Convention on the Rights of the Child (1989) states:

> Every child has the right to rest and leisure, to engage in play and recreational activities appropriate to the age of the child and to participate freely in cultural life and the arts.
>
> That member governments shall respect and promote the right of the child to participate fully in cultural and artistic life and shall encourage the provision of appropriate and equal opportunities for cultural, artistic, recreational and leisure activity.

Adopted by the United Nations in 1989, this convention is remarkable in being the most widely ratified of any human rights treaty in history, with 192 countries signed up as state parties as of 2005. It clearly speaks of strong international support for the right of all children to play.

Knowing that providing valuable environments for play is important for children, we need to examine why this is so. How can we go about this effectively? What exactly makes play valuable for life and a playspace valuable for play?

Play is the opportunity for children and young people to engage in spontaneous activity and exploration, a chance to make friends, discover new places, learn new skills and build a picture of the world. Play, in short, is the opportunity to practise 'life' and the **playspace** a microcosm of the world in which that practice takes place. The form of a playspace may change from country to country, but the objective remains the same. Children, no matter where they live, what abilities they have, what language they speak or the particularities of their culture, will inherently seek opportunities to play, either individually or together.

Play may teach children a scientific concept, help them to make a new friend, encourage them to create something, or build up muscle strength and balance by climbing up high. Play is important as *'a scaffold for development, a vehicle for increasing neural structures and a means by which all children practice skills they will need later in life'*.[1] The neurological importance of play is investigated in later chapters.

It is worth recognising that there is much we can learn from the natural world and what it provides for play. Natural settings *'provide a variety of loose parts that enable children to shape their environment, developing their creative and constructional, cognitive abilities'*.[2] Allowing children to move and build with real elements like seed pods, flowers, rocks and so on enriches not only the sensory nature of play, but also the precious ability to manipulate the world in ways that may not be available to children as adults.

To provide some context, we will look at the history of play and the rise of the 'designed' or 'created' playspace from its beginnings in the natural world. This book will seek to examine the full circle of approaches to play within the last 200 years, as styles and thinking about play have changed. This includes the more recent return to 'nature play' led in part by greater cultural sensitivity to increasing urbanisation and the fragility of our environment.

It is important to understand that the physical playspace in itself does not entirely hold the key to play. The decks, mounds, rocks, logs, climbing frames, slides, swings, sand, water and plants are merely the physical stage on which the 'play' occurs. Just like a theatre set, they support the action, but the story is created by the children themselves. What is critical is *how* children are able to interact with the playspace, as the freedom to explore and experience challenge adds richness to play. A great playspace will stimulate children's imaginations and creativity, giving them the gift of a world in which anything can happen. The opportunity to play together with others and make friends is fundamental to social inclusion and self-confidence. This is a crucial factor when designing places for people of all abilities.

Play is ubiquitous, it happens everywhere, though is most likely to be seen in homes, schools or early childhood centres, in local neighbourhoods or public places. It is important to understand that play does not just occur in designated playspaces, nor do designated playspaces provide the only opportunity for valuable play. This book focusses specifically on play that occurs in public or programmed places, as *'for many children designed environments are their main opportunity for play'*.[3]

So what makes a great playspace?

No doubt there are many answers to this, depending on your perspective.

We feel that a playspace should support children to play at a level and in a way that they feel comfortable. This includes providing safe spaces (in the sense of not being unnecessarily frightening) and developmentally appropriate, and which offer the opportunity for children to stand back and observe the play if they do not wish to directly participate. Practical issues such as shade, shelter and good maintenance are also important in allowing everyone at the playspace to feel comfortable.

That said, there should also be enough complexity, challenge and intrigue to allow children to take risks, learn and become completely involved in their play. A space which is completely 'safe' can easily become simply dull. It has been said that the happiest people are those who achieve 'flow'[4] – the sense of complete immersion in a task so that time seems irrelevant – and children deeply engrossed in their play certainly achieve flow.

Arguably, a great playspace should also develop some importance to children. Many of these spaces are not designed at all, and often look uninviting to adults. For example, Richard Louv, who coined the term 'Nature Deficit Disorder' in his book *Last Child in the Woods*,[5] talks with nostalgia about his childhood playspaces, which were the fields and wood behind his house in Independence, Missouri. Sometimes these spaces can be a small clearing in a shrubbery, which contains a boulder which makes a perfect seat; or the corner of building with special nooks in the crumbling brickwork. It is not always possible to predict which spaces will appeal, but it is possible to avoid designing a space which is bland and in which there are no surprises. Sometimes playspaces can become important to children because they contain a particularly memorable feature such as intriguing artwork, or because of the community and family activities which happen in that place.

Every playspace is different, and those which respect the nature of their setting have an immediate point of difference. For example, existing trees may be used for shade and to climb, or natural mounds to shape the space. Look at the opportunities for play which already exist on the site and consider building upon those. It has been said that the primary difference between landscape design and architecture is that buildings may sit just as well in many places around the world, but landscape must be designed on its own merits.[6] Allow the character of the place to colour the design and it cannot help but be special.

Great playspaces also need to consider the hard wear of play. Children use spaces with intensity, and this needs to be considered in the initial design, or the space will not remain a good place to play for very long. Some spaces are designed to have short lives, others to last decades. Either way, the materials and maintenance should be appropriate and planned.

Of course, the most important element in designing a great playspace is that it invites play! They should be attractive and fun, but also make it clear that it is acceptable to 'mess about'. In many cultures, most spaces are adult-dominated, and children are not allowed to play freely. A place where children are allowed to do what they please – run, shout, move things around, pretend – is precious.

Even when a space has been allowed especially for children, sometimes adult thinking can intrude. Children and adults see the world quite differently and as such understand the value of a playspace quite differently as well.

It has been emphasised that places for children are not the same as children's places, and that the latter does not always fit with the perspective of planners and other adults who affect children's physical environments.[7]

This book seeks to understand and explain playspaces as a child might and from there develop an understanding of the opportunities that lie within an 'affordance', such as the quality of a surface or the ergonomics of a structure. An 'affordance' is an opportunity, and many of these only become apparent when children are let loose, to appropriate their environment and make it become whatever they need to support their play. This is perhaps most evident in school grounds, where every inch is intensively used over a period of years, and a rich diversity of games and legends arise in particular places.

By exploring the details of child development, this book will lead the reader through how these stages have intrinsic links with play, and how they can be supported in a range of different playspaces. Bear in mind that these stages should be seen as a general guide only: every child develops at their own rate, and with interests and skills in different areas. The aim of these sections is to broaden the understanding of what might best support children's various play needs, including their social development and relationships with their peers and carers. By understanding the usual patterns of development, designers can better accommodate the elements which encourage aspects like growing independence, the need for challenge and the rich, imaginative world of children, as well as the physical needs most commonly catered for in traditional playspace design.

Intended less as a glossy picture book and more as a 'nuts and bolts' guide to thinking about playspaces, this book uses the analogy of the plant and its growth cycle to discuss play at different stages of childhood. Practical issues such as planning, developing and constructing a project are explored and real life examples of unique projects from around the world are presented to inspire. Areas of specific interest have been written by leading practitioners and academics in those fields. As there are various schools of thought, you may sometimes find contradictions. This book is not intended as a manifesto: it is a holistic toolkit to arm you with the information you need to form your own opinion.

So how do you go about designing a real playspace?

We recognise that in the real world, inspiration itself is not enough. As a provider of play, whether that be as a manager, designer or educator, responsibility lies with you to ensure that the play you provide is of benefit to children and your community.

Resources, time and space are not infinite, so concentrating your efforts to design and build a space which permits the best quality of play possible is important. Undertaking a playspace project can be a daunting task in itself, so this book explores the principles of preparation and planning for your project, such as engaging design teams, involving children and your community, planning requirements and the need for technical drawings and specifications.

Finally, before you commence reading we would like to remind you that all playspaces, big or small, should always be fun, inspiring and encourage interaction and use in ways never thought of before. The value of play is in the lessons learnt in childhood. Confidence, judgement, resilience, innovation and well-being can all be successfully shaped in a playspace through this practice of 'life' we call play.

Notes

1 Joan Packer Isenberg & Nancy Quisenberry, Play: Essential for All Children. *Childhood Education* 79(1): 33–39, 2002.
2 Robin Moore & Herbert Wong, *Natural Learning: The Life History of an Environmental Schoolyard*. Mig Communications, 1997.
3 Sports and Recreation Victoria, *Good Playspace Guide: I Can Play Too!* 2007. Available online at: http://sport.vic.gov.au/sites/default/files/Good-Play-Space-Guide_2011_0.pdf.
4 Mihaly Csikszentmihalyi, *Beyond Boredom and Anxiety: Experiencing Flow in Work and Play*. Jossey-Bass, San Francisco, 1975.
5 Richard Louv, *Last Child in the Woods: Saving Our Children from Nature Deficit Disorder*. Atlantic Books, Great Britain, 2010.
6 Tom Turner, *British Gardens: History, Philosophy and Design*. Routledge, Taylor & Francis, Oxford, 2013.
7 Marit Jansson, Children's Perspectives on Public Playgrounds in Two Swedish Communities. *Children, Youth and Environments* 18(2): 88–109, 2008.

Part II
SOWING

Introduction

In this section, we lay the groundwork of some different and more holistic ways to think about play and playspaces. These seeds of wisdom will hopefully inform the choices that are made about your playspace. To give some perspective on the field, we start with a historical view. Following this are several pieces exploring what it is to play, children's psychology and also the means we can provide to enhance particular types of play. Taking a different tack, we then look at urbanism and play – the interaction between our cities and children's needs and desires. Finally, the important area of inclusive play, to allow everyone to play equitably and in line with their own development needs.

In this section you will find:

1. **A history of playspaces – page 13**
   Provides an insight into the developing philosophy of playspaces from the seventeenth century to the present day.
2. **Fundamental perceptions of and ingredients for play: Having fun, opening up and letting go – page 21**
   A perspective on playing for all ages, and the need to change our attitudes and approach to this important activity.
3. **Insights into the mind of the child – page 27**
   A psychological discussion about children's cognitive development from a child's perspective.
4. **Play environments and affordances – page 37**
   An evidence based investigation of how scale, shape and form influence play.
5. **Chaos and confusion: The clash between adults' and children's spaces – page 49**
   Investigates the potential for spaces which appeal to both adults and children.
6. **City play – page 55**
   A series of case studies of projects from Carve, which focus on play as an urban intervention.
7. **Of agency, participation and design: Two contrasting play scenarios in Indian cities – page 65**
   A discussion of two very different play scenarios in urban India, and the implications for urban planners and designers.
8. **Designing inclusive playspaces – page 73**
   Some suggestions on how to design both physically and socially inclusive playspaces for children with disabilities.
9. **Glenallen School – page 79**
   Case study of designing an outdoor play environment for children with disabilities.

1

A HISTORY OF PLAYSPACES

Dr Carla Pascoe

Children's play has existed across every human culture and time period.[1] However, the history of play spaces specially designed for children is relatively short. The idea that children need separate places for their games is a modern notion, virtually unknown before the nineteenth century. Archaeologists struggle to recreate a detailed sense of children's lives in the pre-written past.[2,3] Where traces of ancient children's history have been uncovered – such as objects presumed to be toys – there has been no corresponding evidence that children's play was restricted to certain areas.[4] Visual evidence from the medieval period in Europe reinforces this sense that children played anywhere and everywhere.[5] Anthropological studies from non-urbanised communities and pre-twentieth-century societies record the omnipresence of children's play. These children appropriated their own play spaces that were informal, fluid and seasonal, like the nineteenth-century New Zealand youth studied by Brian Sutton-Smith.[6]

A seismic shift in the way children are defined and understood changed all that. Spaces for children emerged in the nineteenth century once a concept of childhood had developed in the western world.[7] Before the seventeenth century, children in the west were viewed as miniature adults, capable of adult responsibilities such as work and marriage. Over the next few centuries, children gradually came to be seen as vulnerable, innocent and dependent.[8] Alongside this changing definition of the child, anxieties about the ill effects of industrialisation and urban growth combined to generate concern about children living in cities.[9] Before this, most western children used public spaces like the street for their play. But from about 1800, middle-class adults increasingly restricted the play of privileged children to the home environment and became concerned about the street games of working-class children.[10]

Trans-national movements emerged in cities across North America, Europe, Australia and New Zealand that lobbied for special play spaces for children. The play movement developed early in Germany, where outdoor gymnasia and sandpits were created to increase the physical fitness of the German people and reduce disease.[11] From the second half of the nineteenth century their influence spread, buttressed by the writings of people like the German Frederick Froebel and later the American John Dewey, who argued that play was

FIGURE 1.1 Image of seventeenth-century Dutch children at play entitled 'Kinder-spel' (Children's play) by an unknown artist, from the book *Houwelyck* (1618) by Jacob Cats. Courtesy of The Strong National Museum of Play, Rochester, New York.
Source: http://www.museumofplay.org/blog/play-stuff/2011

critical to child development.[12] These play associations had links to early forms of urban planning and other reform movements aimed at children, such as child labour legislation, compulsory education, medical programmes in schools and recreational organisations like the Boy Scouts and Girl Guides.[13] Middle-class reformers believed staunchly in the benefits of fenced, supervised playgrounds segregated according to gender and age. They wanted to steer children's play off the streets and into safe, orderly areas.

Some of the first public play areas were the 'sand gardens' from Germany and were quickly copied in the United States in the 1880s before spreading to other parts of the globe In

FIGURE 1.2 A group of children playing in a sand pit at a new playground in South Australia, circa 1918. Courtesy of the State Library of South Australia PRG 280/1/17/329.
Source: http://images.slsa.sa.gov.au/searcy/17/PRG280_1_17_329.htm

the late nineteenth century 'model playgrounds' began to develop in US parks and schools, but remained uncommon until the early twentieth century. The Playground Association of America was founded in 1906, and similar organisations soon followed in other countries. During the early twentieth century, ideas about the importance of providing public playgrounds for children travelled the globe, resulting in remarkably similar play equipment springing up in places as far flung as Australia,[14] Palestine[15] and the United Kingdom. In the United States, only 41 cities had playgrounds in 1906; however, that number had increased to 872 by 1928.[16] These early twentieth-century playgrounds were fenced areas including running tracks, sports fields and even community buildings like libraries or clinics. A section called the 'apparatus' or 'gymnasium' most resembled a modern playground, with seesaw, giant stride, monkey bars, rings, slides and ladders. They often included lighting so that adults could use the equipment at night.[17]

Although reformers were well intentioned and concerned about issues such as the high mortality of children playing on streets, their actions have since been criticised as a middle-class attempt to mould working-class and immigrant children into physically fit, morally upright, obedient citizens.[18,19,20] Once begun, the momentum of the playground movement was irresistible. The desire to create safe and contained play areas for children continued to grow in western, developed countries throughout the twentieth century, finding expression in municipal, school and kindergarten playgrounds.

FIGURE 1.3 Children playing on swings at Wicksteed Park in 1923, Kettering, Northamptonshire, United Kingdom

Courtesy of Wicksteed Park

Playground development slowed during the 1930s and 1940s due to the Great Depression and World War Two. In the United States the government attempted to remedy Depression-era unemployment with public works programmes that included the creation of parks and playgrounds. By the 1930s most playgrounds were designed solely for children's recreation. Instead of a single structure with many parts like the early apparatus, designs began to favour separate pieces of equipment such as swings, seesaws, slides, sand boxes and climbing frames. Public authorities preferred playgrounds with minimal maintenance, so they were generally constructed from undecorated metal, with wooden seats for the swings and seesaws.[21]

The eruption of global warfare in 1939 shifted the priorities of many nations. Parks in North America, Australia and New Zealand fell into disrepair as raw materials and human resources were diverted to the war effort. In Europe, the hardships of war produced a new type of playground. Danish landscape architect Carl Theodor Sorensen created a 'junk playground' in German-occupied Copenhagen in 1943. Inspired by the observation that children would raid construction sites, garbage dumps and derelict places for supplies to build their play spaces and hideouts, Sorensen's junk playground provided fragments of wood, metal or masonry and the tools to put them together. His concept included trained play leaders who would facilitate juvenile construction.[22,23]

The idea soon spread across Europe, North America and the Asia-Pacific. For some, these play areas were a backlash against overly regimented playgrounds where the space dictated the types of games possible. Instead, junk playgrounds were a kind of junkyard of leftover bits and pieces that placed children in the role of designer and builder. Lady Allen of Hurtwood dubbed them 'adventure playgrounds', establishing several in post-war UK.[24] By 1970 she had created an adventure playground for disabled children in London.[25] Adventure playgrounds continued to be built in the UK into the 1970s, but since 1980 their numbers have halved due to fears of legal liability in the event of accidents.[26]

The first American adventure playground opened in Minneapolis in 1950. They enjoyed an era of popularity in the 1970s when they operated in many US states, but most survived for only short periods due to concerns about their dishevelled appearance, a fear of possible injuries, lack of funding and a shortage of play leaders. One of the few still remaining opened in Berkeley, California, in 1979, where children build their own playground under loose supervision amidst wooden boards, spare tyres, telephone poles and mud.[27]

Playground design and construction flourished after the end of war in 1945 as many countries entered a period of economic prosperity and increased leisure opportunities. Playground historian Joe L. Frost calls the 1950s to 1970s the era of 'novelty' playgrounds, as designers departed from traditional equipment and introduced shapes such as rockets, vehicles and animals. These colourful, imaginative forms were influenced by the popularity of television, space travel, westerns and Disneyland.[28]

Architects and landscape architects became involved in designing playgrounds, many of them looking for engaging ways to join pieces of equipment together to create seamless play experiences.[29] Thus trends in art and architecture began influencing playground design in the mid-twentieth century. In the Netherlands, Aldo van Eyck designed over 700 playgrounds in Amsterdam between 1947 and 1978.[30] He preferred minimalist equipment so that play possibilities were left open-ended and situated his playgrounds at in-between points in the urban landscape.[31] Connections between playgrounds and sculpture were explored by artists like Japanese-American Isamu Noguchi, who designed a series of innovative playgrounds. Most were never constructed, as his concepts were too radical a departure from traditional playgrounds for decision makers.[32] For example, his 1933 design Play Mountain called for tilting and excavating a New York City block. Similarly his 1951 plan for a playground at the United Nations in New York involved moulding or sculpting earth rather than traditional equipment. Neither was ever built.[33]

While Noguchi's ideas were too revolutionary for some, New York's Museum of Modern Art actively encouraged such experiments, holding exhibitions on playground design in the 1950s.[34] Creative Playthings was a commercial firm which also perceived an artistic potential in play equipment. Established in 1951 to manufacture toys with modernist designs, the company started a division called Play Sculptures in 1953, employing sculptors from around the world to design play equipment for production. In 1954 Creative Playthings co-sponsored a 'Play Sculpture Competition' with *Parents* magazine and MoMA.[35] Despite the mixed reaction to Noguchi's ideas, during the 1960s a number of New York playgrounds were designed by landscape architects such as Richard Dattner and Paul Friedberg.

However, it was during the 1960s and 1970s that playgrounds became big business; less likely to serve artistic purposes and more likely to fulfil commercial imperatives. Four large

FIGURE 1.4 Novelty era play equipment
Courtesy of Joe Frost

companies came to dominate equipment production in the US, mass-producing designs on a large scale to minimise costs. The result, according to some, was playgrounds that were less diverse and less interesting.[36,37] Historian Susan Solomon argues that part of the fault lies with McDonald's, which built nearly identical playspaces in its thousands of restaurants across the US and eventually the world.[38] Another compelling reason for more homogeneous play equipment was a rise in safety concerns and an accompanying fear of litigation.

From the 1970s national standards for playground equipment safety were adopted in many wealthy countries such as the United States, the United Kingdom and Australia (though internationally many nations still lack such standards in the twenty-first century).[39] Playgrounds changed partially in response to heightened fears of potential injuries and the growth of a litigation culture where schools, councils and other bodies were held legally responsible for juvenile accidents at playgrounds. This resulted in the standardisation of equipment into what has been dubbed 'the four S's': swings, slides, see-saws and superstructures.[40] Such concerns are not entirely new: as early as 1915 the parents of an American boy sued their school board over an injury he sustained falling from a swing, and there were discussions about safe surfacing in 1917.[41] However, the release of the Handbook for Public Playground Safety by the US Consumer Product Safety Commission in 1981 is regarded as a turning point in expectations about play equipment safety. The late twentieth and early twenty-first century has witnessed the development of measures to not just design playspaces for children, but to actively discourage play in non-designated spaces, such as steel protrusions on public surfaces to deter skateboarding.

Research into play and playgrounds has grown in the last few decades. Whilst many kindergartens, schools and parks still feature traditional apparatus, there has been an increasing trend to diversify playgrounds. Recent playgrounds often include natural features such as plants, sand, water, rocks and even animals. In response to concerns that some urban children suffer from 'nature deficit disorder',[42] playground designers are incorporating garden elements for nature-starved city kids. Frost concludes that 'the term "playground" is taking on even broader meanings to include people of all ages (intergenerational playgrounds), natural and built (integrated playgrounds), provisions for people of all abilities (accessible or inclusive playgrounds) and electric powered (cyber playgrounds)'.[43]

Overall, the historical trend across the twentieth century in the west has been to increasingly shepherd children off the streets into playgrounds and to progressively make these safer. For example, Sanford Gaster's study of New York City children from 1915 to 1976 identified a decrease in the number and diversity of places children were allowed to access and an increase in adult supervision of play.[44] Lia Karsten identified a similar trend in Amsterdam from the 1950s, finding that whilst streets used to be child spaces for play, they have been taken over by adults, primarily through increased car usage.[45] There have been many criticisms of this trend to restrict children's play to isolated pockets and attempt to remove all dangers from their lives. Tim Gill argues that a culture of risk aversion has developed in countries like the UK, with adults unwilling to let children learn through mistakes and develop resilience.[46] Yet Gill and a host of media commentators seem unaware that adult fears for children are not new: they have a very long pedigree and can be clearly discerned by the mid-twentieth century.[47,48]

Some researchers into children's use of space argue that children do not need adult-designed playgrounds.[49] Cities should be designed so that the whole environment is accessible to children, rather than deliberately separating the activities of children and adults.[50,51] Research into children's play spaces has consistently affirmed that throughout history, children have delighted in appropriating their own places. Young Australians from the late nineteenth to mid-twentieth centuries skilfully colonised a range of urban spaces, including streets, laneways and building sites.[52,53] German, Dutch and Italian youths in the mid-twentieth century were attracted to urban wastelands because their behaviour and activities could not be controlled by adults.[54] Kevin Lynch's 1977 UNESCO study of young people in Argentina, Australia, Mexico and Poland also identified the allure of wastelands and found that the street was more appealing than parks designed specifically for recreation.[55] Tellingly, Kim Rasmussen found a disparity between the places which adults created for Danish children and the places which children themselves preferred, often seeming disorderly, dirty or dangerous to adults.[56] This had led some researchers to argue that children need spaces they can adapt, create and control themselves, rather than adult-designed playgrounds.

It is easy to forget that such debates are culturally specific. In fact, the ready availability of well-built playgrounds is a marker of privilege by global standards. The early history of playground construction has been strongly associated with developed countries, whilst only gradually appearing in developing nations. Many poorer communities around the world continue to view safe, appealing playgrounds as a luxury; valuable spaces where children can play free from fear of danger, traffic or conflict. They are a 'luxury' in the sense that land allocated to public playgrounds has no direct economic benefit to its custodians (although parks and playground do contribute to the value of surrounding real estate by increasing the desirability of certain suburbs[57]). Researchers have found a lack of local playgrounds in many communities around the world, including Poland[58] and Iran.[59] Some communities are so bereft of playgrounds that they have become the focus of charitable efforts by not-for-profit organisations, such as East African Playgrounds, which works in Uganda, or the KidsFirst Foundation, which builds playgrounds for orphans in Russia.[60,61] Even where playgrounds do exist, they are not necessarily safe. Numerous hazards have been detected, including lead-based paint throughout South African playgrounds;[62] high levels of air pollution in Turkish playgrounds;[63] dangerous metals in Brazilian playground soil;[64] and a general lack of safety standards in Chinese play spaces.[65]

Where space is not at a premium and nature is freely accessible, children arguably do not require adult assistance to create spaces for play. However, as more of the planet's population squeezes into cities and urban density increases, preserving pockets of land for play is increasingly vital to safeguard children's well-being. The critical importance of childhood play has now been enshrined in international human rights law, under Article 31 of the United Nations Convention on the Rights of the Child. Whilst the concept of leaving children to create their own playspaces may be appealing to some commentators, cities are changing in the twenty-first century, with fewer in-between or neglected spaces for children to colonise. In studying children's behaviour and preferences outdoors, Robin Moore and Donald Young discovered that children use playgrounds more in high-density areas because there is nowhere else to play.[66] Moore emphasised that whilst experts disagree about the value of playgrounds, they have a high social value to children and are crucially necessary in cities to ensure adequate space for play.[67]

One thing this historical overview makes clear is that playgrounds have never been simply passive pieces of metal, wood or plastic. Wherever they have been built, they reflect prevailing cultural concepts, whether that be British colonial ideals about education in Indian schools;[68] racial segregation in the United States;[69] attempts to promote harmony between Arabs and Jews in Palestine;[70] Fascist aspirations for healthy youth in 1930s Italy;[71] or simply dominant expectations of childhood (dis)ability in a given era. As Susan G. Solomon explains: 'Playgrounds were, and remain, microcosms of the values and interests of a country at a particular time.'[72] Look closely enough at any playground and one can discern an entire world of cultural values frozen at a specific moment in time.

2

FUNDAMENTAL PERCEPTIONS OF AND INGREDIENTS FOR PLAY

Having fun, opening up and letting go

Elizabeth Cummins

Introduction

It is my firm opinion that we don't give ourselves enough credit for our resourcefulness in creating opportunities for play, wherever we are. Here I focus on the 'practice' of play rather than the 'setting' for it, as play is something that I suspect occurs in big or small ways in every corner of the globe every day. The material point is a direct and purposeful 'interaction' between the mind and the physical world, and in my experience that is not entirely restricted to children. Adults too, in their own particular way, engage in play. They appear to spend less time doing so, however, as culturally play is not seen as an acceptable way for an adult to spend their time.

I imagine the majority of the population to be in agreement about the need for children to play (although in some cultures and historically in western culture this has not always been the case). One must remember that the concept of leisure time has only existed since the twentieth century for most. What is puzzling to me is that in practice we don't seem to value its capacity for play to influence our own lives and often see it as a frivolity, something not to be taken too seriously unless it has academic or health imperatives Why do we feel this way? Do we in some way feel a sense of guilt about 'having fun', about 'opening up', about 'letting go'?

Play occurs best when:

- there are NO boundaries – it can happen anywhere, and I mean anywhere!
- it is spontaneous and fluid – don't interrupt, unless you're invited in.
- there are lots of things to move around – you can never get enough of them in play, they just keep giving and giving.
- there are no timeframes – it can be over in the blink of an eye or continue forever. Always allow time for play to take its course.
- we are brave and trust. You and the kids in your care have much better judgement than you think – fight that urge to intervene no matter how well intentioned it is.

FIGURE 2.1 Left: Opening up involves developing confidence in your skills and Right: Cubby zone, a great insight into what children can achieve when given the freedom to play. Creative Cubby Project – Ballarat Begonia Festival 2015
Photo: Talina Edwards

- we realise we are resourceful and imaginative. Ergonomics, textures and spatial qualities all do play their part, but literally anything can be appropriated for play.

Having fun

As humans we look for the means to justify our ends, as if something only has inherent value when it is quantified. For example:

play = learning = educational outcomes; or
play = physical activity = health benefits.

What if play in its essence is just play, something that occurs naturally across all cultures in children and sometimes as leisure time in adulthood. Something which is driven by our desire for pleasure?

Play is industrious, there is no doubt about that, but what if the primary function of play is nothing more than just having fun and all the other mantles we attach are merely incidental benefits? How would that affect the value we place on play? Would our time allocated to it be reduced? Would the spaces we build for it be different? These are all interesting points to ponder.

I used to have the opinion that 'play' is just children's work, the function of which is to give children a non-threatening setting to practise adult scenarios and social interactions that they observe in real life. I have, however, come to realise that it is far more earthy than that, possibly having its basis in very early childhood where we curiously seek out interactions and sensations that delight and satisfy us. This is, after all, what really contributes to our sense of well-being. As children mature into teenagers, then adults, the play becomes more sophisticated as their understanding of the world, both concrete and abstract, expands. At the heart is the one common thread about play as an end goal of 'having fun'. From a baby mouthing a toy it has picked up off the floor, to an adult feeling the wind in their hair as they sail on a yacht, play allows us to physically embody the emotion of 'pleasure'.

In some parts of the world, childhood ends at a very early age, as the need for survival forces children to become adults before their time. The United Nations Convention on the Rights of the Child states '*That every child has the right to rest and leisure, to engage in play and recreational activities appropriate to the age of the child and to participate freely in cultural life and the arts*'.[1] This particular article is aimed at committing UN member states to childhood improvements around the world. It is a step in the right direction in making sure that as many children as possible are given the opportunity for time and space to play so they can 'have fun'. The critical point to make here is that fun through play in any cultural context is not better or worse, and that having built or designed equipment doesn't necessarily result in better play than only having a tree and a patch of dirt.

Sometimes play can make adults feel uncomfortable. An example of this is children engaging in seemingly politically incorrect play that involves toilet humour and fighting. This is not the '*behaviour of polite society*'[2] as Jane Austen may have put it. Viewing children in our care as carefully observed reflections of our own behaviour, we don't like what we see here. These types of play, however, are a vehicle for children to disseminate their understanding of the world and their emotional selves. Even games where children might rough and tumble or use sticks as swords or guns are valid play and in fact often are extremely fun to the children participating. If we value play, we need to respect these play choices.

Opening up

Children are naturally curious, and at an early age this overrides any fears we may have surrounding new experiences. On the contrary, curiosity encourages our pursuit of new experiences. I would like to talk about the concept of 'opening up' to opportunities for play

FIGURE 2.2 Left: The joy of cubby world, Creative Cubby Project – Ballarat Begonia Festival, Ballarat, Australia 2015 and Right: Children's inventiveness knows no bounds! Creative Cubby Project – Ballarat Show, Ballarat, Australia 2014

Photo: Talina Edwards

across both time and space, as this is imperative to making the most of what the experience has to offer.

Play can happen anywhere, and there are no boundaries. The smallest of interactions with the physical world constitutes play. Play doesn't just occur in designated settings such as playspaces or school grounds or at designated times, as our regulated world would sometimes like. This is why there has been such consternation about the loss of childhood mobility in local neighbourhoods in the western world as we shuffle around in cars from destination to destination. Play as simple as avoiding the cracks in the pavement on the way to school is a pleasurable act and one where the child itself observes and engages with the differences and irregularity of the world around them. It is not an experience that can be replicated on a virtual screen.

Restricting children to particular environments on a daily basis, to those that are purpose built or perceived as safe (like our homes), denies them the opportunity for different interactions. Even the fencing of playspaces and the uplifting of trees for perceived safety reasons denies children the broader benefits an environment such as a park can provide. Teaching children the extents of their environment, building better and more engaged neighbourhood connections and trusting children's judgement to seek adult assistance when required is part of 'opening up' better opportunities for play.

Spontaneous and fluid, it becomes challenging to find valuable space for play in a world that is governed by overriding needs and time constraints. The adult carer is often under the pressure of meeting the commitments of home and work and not able to 'stop and smell the roses', to use an old analogy. Unfortunately, by doing this, a child's carefree time is lost. The opportunity to immerse themselves in an imaginary world, or dance wildly, or play a game with another child in the supermarket queue, is replaced by the need to move on to the next task in hand. Considering how many adults in the western world suffer from mental health issues, I think we need to look at the pace of the routine of our lives particularly in urban settings and how much free time we allow each day for children to be spontaneous in their play.

Fluidity in play occurs as the course of one interaction morphs into another. This can happen in a matter of minutes to weeks. Never expect play to stay the same. Props for play are integral to its fluidity. Never underestimate the importance of an old, rotten piece of timber to a particular game. The flexibility of an environment allows the same concrete elements to be re-invented over and over again until they either fall apart or something new takes their place. Allowing children to leave their props in situ where they can return to play is equally important as giving children loose materials that they can move around to play with.

Letting go

At the heart of all of this is 'freedom'. Play is fundamentally about letting go and experiencing the liberation of freedom. Adults in western countries are particularly afraid of this concept, because it makes us feel that we aren't performing our duty of care towards children or being as responsible as we should. The truth is freedom is behind the breakdown of any form of control or power, and that's what scares us. Freedom, however, is key to our joy of living.

FIGURE 2.3 Left: Blake letting loose in the cubby and Right: Creativity at play in the cubbies, Creative Cubby Project – Ballarat Show, Australia 2014
Photo: Talina Edwards

I have already talked about politically incorrect play that makes adults uncomfortable. Our need to regulate play is where I believe we most need to be mindful of our own behaviour and trust the judgement of children. The opportunity for encouraging children to feel confident about risky behaviour in play is central to this. Children need to challenge themselves, learning to make judgements about what they haven't experienced and to be innovative and circumspect. Play offers many opportunities for this, in small and non-threatening ways, building confidence and leadership skills in children.

As the freedom to experience and explore is integral to play, so too is failure, frustration, disappointment and embarrassment. Adversity is something adults look to protect children from, but letting go of our desire to intervene, to make things easy and safe, is very powerful in terms of building a child's future capacity for resilience and determination. The world is not an easy or straightforward place, and whilst we don't wish to throw our children to the wolves, we need to accept that the age old saying 'learning from our mistakes' is actually true, even if it involves bumps and bruises along the way.

The 'bubble wrapping'[3] of playspaces in recent years has served no purpose other than to teach our children that we will always fix things for them, we will always make things right and keep things safe. This is an impossible reality, one we can never live up to and one that will more than likely harm our children more than help them. There have been too many instances of beloved play equipment being removed from play spaces because it didn't comply with Playground Standards or some well-meaning person thought it looked unsafe. What then follows is a replacement by a banal and simple item of equipment, innocuous and unchallenging.

We need to ask ourselves why we provide for play and who is this experience really for? Not the local councillor or school principal, not the designer or play equipment manufacturer, or even the parent. The play experience is for the child. The conundrum is that this experience is usually decided upon by adults' values, rather than the child's values.

Summary

Observing children and trying to step inside their shoes a little more, to see the world and the opportunities it offers for play through their eyes, before we make decisions surrounding their spaces for play is important. Be a little more patient in terms of time and space, allow for play and enable and encourage children to play without intervening (unless invited in).

If we trust ourselves by trusting our children a little more, their play will become richer, and our society will be better for it in the long run.

3

INSIGHTS INTO THE MIND OF THE CHILD

Tracy R. Gleason & Becky L. Geer

Over the years, developmental psychologists have explored how children's thinking differs from that of adults. In some domains, such as attention, memory, and processing speed, children's thinking resembles adults', but is immature.[1] In other domains, such as problem solving, children seem to think fundamentally differently than adults.[2] For instance, children make greater use of their bodies and senses in their thinking in comparison to adults, so much so that many textbooks on child development have chapters that combine physical and cognitive development.[3] For example, a child will physically manipulate puzzle pieces to get them to fit, whereas an adult will often do so mentally. A child might imagine different outcomes to a scenario by acting them out, while an adult might picture each possibility in the mind. These cognitive differences influence the ways that children and adults function in and process the physical world – a fact with significant implications for designers and educators interested in facilitating children's learning.

Three principles help explain how children's thinking interacts with their functioning in the physical world. First, cognition occurs through exploration. Especially prior to formal schooling, children's physical and social exploration interacts with innate capacities to provide the basis for cognitive development.[4] Second, cognitive development is a function of challenge and risk. As children explore, the objects and social situations that provide the most cognitive change are those just beyond what the child has already achieved.[5,6] Third, the context of cognitive development is social interaction. Other people are, of course, a significant source of information, but interactions are also the environment in which children learn abstract concepts, such as ownership and justice, as well as cultural scripts that guide human behaviour. Indeed, children's experience of the world is governed at every level by caregivers and other adults and is influenced by the presence of others of all ages.[7]

Cognition occurs through exploration

The single most important principle for understanding cognition in the early years is the central role of exploration. Initially, exploration is largely sensory. Children begin learning the minute they open their eyes and encounter the sights, sounds, smells, tastes, and feel of the world around them. Within the first year, they begin developing an understanding about different types and categories of objects by manipulating them,[8] they learn language by listening to sounds humans utter and noticing which co-occur frequently,[9] they discover the differences between animate and inanimate motion,[10] and they learn about self and other by gradually becoming aware of the effects (or lack of effects) of their own actions on others' behaviour.[11] These abilities are facilitated by steady, gradual increases in attention and memory that eventually enable children to recognise environments encountered earlier in exploration and to generalise from one situation to another.

By the time children reach early childhood, the variety of experiences has increased exponentially, and their repertoire for acquiring new information has also expanded. With development, they are also capable of greater physical exploration because of their ability to walk, run, reach high shelves, and manipulate small objects without accidentally dropping or crushing them. These abilities facilitate children's pursuit of knowledge of interest to them, as they are no longer limited in their exploration to the objects, people, and environments within immediate reach or sight. Environments that allow for and encourage these adventures are enticing to children.

Over the course of early childhood, exploration expands to include the internal as well as the external world. A significant achievement, children's ability to imagine objects, people, and situations not actually present opens a new dimension in cognition.[12] This form of exploration might initially be manifested in pragmatic ways, such as children's understanding that objects still exist even when out of sight, or their realisation that certain sounds (i.e., words) are symbols for particular objects. Rapidly, though, symbolic representation evolves to include exploration of imagined environments, roles, and behaviours. While exploration of the physical world continues, exploration of imagined worlds encourages and eventually facilitates the development of the abstract thought processes.[13]

When children first engage in symbolism, as in early pretence, they begin to use toys as representations of real objects, such as a toy phone as a real phone or a doll as a real baby. At first, young children do not see that a stick could be a magic wand or a pirate's sword, but gradually, as their experience and repertoire of behaviours increase, they make creative use of objects that have fewer defining features.[14] Moreover, the stipulations (e.g., declaring a block is a piece of cake) and transformations (e.g., pretending to pour tea) of symbolic pretend play are important practice for adult behaviours, such as using a map or a metaphor.

The context for all of this exploration – whether external, in the physical world, or internal, in the imagined one – is the behaviour we refer to as play. Although hard to define, play is usually characterised by enjoyment and pretence.[15] While playing, children gather information about the world (real or imagined), conduct experiments, practice their symbolic skills, and satisfy their own curiosity.[16] The best environments for children, then, are those in which exploration is encouraged through play.

An environment that encourages exploration and play has three characteristics. First, because of young children's reliance on physical and sensory exploration (relative to adults), materials that include a variety of textures, smells, and visual stimulation provide good fodder for play. For infants, whose exploration is focused on the environment within reach, a variety of surfaces, such as carpet, hardwood floors, and cushions indoors and grasses, mosses, and non-toxic, low plants (e.g., pansies) outdoors, provide a range of colours and textures to

Insights into the mind of the child   **29**

FIGURE 3.1 Symbolism in Action. Wellesley, Massachusetts, USA 2015
Photo: Wendy Gonsenhauser

explore. Herbs in particular integrate a variety of sensory opportunities, including taste. For older children, sand, mulch, gravel, rocks, and grass all provide a variety of safe textures to explore and manipulate, as do plants, from rough evergreens to fuzzy lambs-ears.

Second, because imaginative, representational play is a large part of early exploration,[17] materials that can be gathered, "mixed," or "cooked," like play-dough, sand, dirt, grasses, and water, encourage play that uses children's budding sensory and transformational skills. Similarly, children are attracted to what they perceive as "real" tools,[18] which are often forbidden to them. Items like child-sized garden tools, nets, hammocks, and ropes offer older children opportunities to imitate and replicate adult behaviours in outdoor settings.

Lastly, because cognition is built on the incorporation of new information into existing organisational structures,[19] children are attracted to spaces that are novel, but resemble familiar environments. For example, teepees and tents are much like ordinary rooms with walls and a floor, but their small size and different shape provide interesting variation.

Outdoor playspaces with many natural features, such as trees and other plants, water, and muddy or sandy areas, become entirely new spaces for exploration in climates with changing seasons, or even on rainy versus sunny days. Whereas adults understand that stones are essentially the same whether wet, dry, or snow covered, young children's mental organisation of information categorises these conditions not so much as variations on a theme as different objects altogether. Their exploration of these three "different" stones is what teaches them about what is constant (stone) and what changes (wet/dry/snowy).

Cognition is a function of challenge and risk

Developmental theorist Lev Vygotsky[20] introduced the notion of the "zone of proximal development" to emphasise and explain how exploration and learning co-occur in cognitive development. According to Vygotsky, for a child to acquire new skills or absorb new information, the novel processes must be presented at a level that is just beyond the child's current capabilities or knowledge. With support from the environment (often including an individual who is more competent than the child), children can accomplish tasks slightly beyond what they can complete independently. Such supported practice slowly translates into the acquisition of skills or knowledge, as when a child completes a difficult puzzle with strategic suggestions from a parent. Moreover, learning in a social context also means the child might receive emotional support for persistence and the management of frustration, which can foster enthusiasm and enjoyment for both the learner as well as the teacher.

The concept of the zone of proximal development is important in cognition, as it emphasises two features of the environment that support children's development. First, challenges must be developmentally appropriate, precisely within the zone.[21] Indeed, when children are confronted with completely novel information, they have difficulty processing and remembering it without adult assistance.[22] Second, cognitive (and other) challenges must include a component of risk, meaning the opportunity for failure. Even within the zone of proximal development, new skills and knowledge are not automatically acquired; they are

FIGURE 3.2 Modification of familiar setting. Wellesley, Massachusetts, USA 2008
Photo: Becky Geer

sometimes only won after many attempts. Mistakes are typically discussed in education as learning opportunities, and research in many specific domains of cognition, including math,[23] analogical reasoning,[24] and language,[25] has demonstrated the importance of making mistakes to conceptual development. Indeed, some learning paradigms depend upon testing children's mistaken theories to teach certain concepts.[26]

In the context of playspaces for children, challenge and risk can come in multiple domains, such as in intellectual, social, and physical development. An example of an element of play environments that affords challenge for all these domains is moveable parts, such as stones, rocks, logs, tree cookies (3–4" thick slices of logs), bamboo, pine cones, leaves, sticks, sand, and water. Intellectually, these materials afford planning and organisation for children of a wide range of ages to decide how to interact with them. Physically, children can move these materials independently, although not all of them with ease. A heavy log might encourage social challenge through cooperation and coordination – or a physical challenge through multiple tries may cause development. As with all materials, as children explore them, adults can gauge the appropriate level of challenge in each domain. When children are taught and then trusted to handle these responsibilities, they can be surprisingly safe with all sorts of materials.

The context of cognition is social interaction

The bulk of children's development occurs in a social context, and cognition is no exception. Fundamentally, children learn by asking questions and discussing their discoveries with adults or each other. Similarly, the role of adults in assisting young children to organise and remember new information through conversation is well-documented,[27] as is the role of adults in scaffolding new experiences. But the importance of social interaction for cognitive development moves well beyond the idea that other people are resources for information and its organisation. The fact is, children's most important thinking is the thinking that they do about other people's thoughts, emotions, motivations, desires, and behaviours.[28]

A critical tool in deciphering the code of human behaviour is imagination. The ability to transcend one's own thoughts/feelings/desires so as to consider those of another person is a significant achievement in cognition that emerges over many years from early childhood through adolescence.[29] Initially, children are not even cognisant of their thoughts as "theirs." But as the sense of self develops and is distinguished from others, children begin to respond to others' needs – albeit often from their own perspective, such as when a young child provides a distressed adult with a comforting blanket or teddy bear.[30] Over time, children begin to realise that others' thoughts do not mirror their own, and even that others could hold thoughts that children themselves know to be wrong. With this realisation comes the understanding that other minds are not, in fact, knowable, but also the motivation to try to interpret others' thoughts by observing their behaviour.

As children start to develop what is called "theory of mind" – the knowledge that other people have their own minds with their own contents – imagination becomes a critical tool in learning how to decipher the social world. Imagination allows children to ask questions such as, "What are the responsibilities of a parent?" or "How does a superhero feel?" By taking on roles, whether realistic or fantastic, children experiment with identity, meaning that these roles can give children an easily accessible entrée into the world of adults. By imitating grown ups, children get a sense for the feelings associated with adulthood, such as power, duty, and concern for others' safety and comfort. Perhaps more important, pretend play also affords safe opportunities for experiencing strong emotions, such as exasperation with misbehaving children, bravery and courage in the face of evil, or even the forbidden feelings associated with perpetrating evil.[31]

An important context for pretend play is, of course, the social version. When children engage in imaginative play with other children, they can experience not only alternate identities, but relationships associated with those identities. After all, what is a parent without a baby or a superhero without a villain? These social contexts, in which children take on related roles in pretense, offer myriad opportunities for children's budding cognition. For example, children often enact scripts in social pretend play, such as "visiting a restaurant," in which one child plays the patron and the other the server. By using imagination and memory to imitate adults they have seen in these roles, children portray the norms that govern these interactions. In other instances, particularly as they age, children embark on pretend play scenarios that are not script-based, meaning that they must engage in a great deal of discussion about the play in addition to enacting it. In communicating their ideas and desires with regard to the pretend play storyline, children gain experience in negotiation, compromise, and the construction of narratives – all skills requiring sophisticated cognition and associated with social competence.[32]

FIGURE 3.3 Three-person spot for play. Wellesley, Massachusetts, USA 2009
Photo: Jennifer Clifton

For young children, trying to understand other minds and coordinate play is hard work. Children in child care, for example, are sometimes expected to spend long hours accommodating their behaviour to the needs of the group – a significant challenge. Consequently, although fostering social interaction is a priority, optimal playspaces for children also provide opportunities to be alone. Indeed, spaces for quiet reflection, resting, and reading a story can be constructed indoors or out. As such, playspaces, both indoors and out, can nurture a child's spirit and imagination as well as social life.

Contrary to popular belief, outdoor playspaces can allow for but do not need to centre on high-energy active play; they are not places for children to simply burn off energy. For many, the outdoors is the perfect environment for solitary play or making a social connection with a single friend. Smaller spaces, like mud holes for two, can encourage children to play alongside each other, or even cooperatively. Ladders and slides built to accommodate two children side by side also encourage but do not require social connections between children.

As children examine social relationships, spaces that foster pretend play will facilitate their social cognition. Spaces resembling homes, cars, boats, restaurants, or other familiar areas are particularly appealing for two reasons. First, these spaces encourage children to imitate the goings-on in these venues, and such spaces offer unacquainted children a shared knowledge base to begin play. Second, child-sized versions of familiar places are appealing and manageable to children in ways that the adult-sized world is not. A small house feels safe and

FIGURE 3.4 Negotiation of Dramatic Play. Wellesley, Massachusetts, USA 2011
Photo: Jennifer Clifton

secure to children in that everything is nearby and within reach – they need not depend upon mental maps to think about finding bedrooms that are out of sight or remember in which of many cupboards the dishes are kept. What is more, a small house is likely to accommodate a small number of family members, meaning that negotiation of roles and coordination of behaviour will remain at a level that is manageable for small children – whether alone or with adult support.

Functioning in the physical world: children's interpretation of space

Geography

An important task of early childhood cognition is understanding geography. For example, children must learn where to find the bathroom in their homes and at school and where the front door is. Because young children's representational skills are still developing, they are aided by concrete geographic signals such as landmarks much more so than abstract representations such as maps. In addition, even if capable of making a mental map of a novel space, children are often unable to do so as they are too small to see across areas such as classrooms and playgrounds full of equipment. Creating geographically interesting play spaces with easily identifiable landmarks is thus helpful for children's navigation of these areas. Outdoors, a grove of trees, a water fountain, or a wooden stage are easily discernible and distinguishable landmarks. Landmarks like a stick stack, rock garden, or brick pile also convey a sense of organisation, or how to "clean up." Indoors or out, a well-used, central pathway can provide an anchor for separating areas and linking smaller paths to "hidden" spaces, such as the enclosure under a loft or the space beneath a willow tree. Moreover, because young children's concepts of distance and scale are typically inaccurate, spaces that are around a corner may feel private and comfortable, but those more than a metre or two off the beaten path may feel isolated and less secure.

Messages of space

Because of the nature of their cognition, children receive different messages than adults do from the spaces they encounter. Although capable of considering other people's perspectives by the end of the preschool years, young children's focus is often limited to what is before them – the concrete rather than the abstract. Thus, the young child who comes upon an unattended pile of blocks or sticks tends to think about what s/he might do with those items rather than the intentions of the person who made the pile or abstract notions of property rights. Another way to think about children's orientation toward space is via Gibson's[8] concept of perceptual affordances, or the realisation of how an object or place can be used. To young children, a long, straight path affords running, a low stone wall affords a place to walk and balance, and shallow water affords wading or at least splashing one's hands. These messages of space, often unintended, might foster behaviours that adults find inappropriate or even irritating – but we have only ourselves to blame. By using children's perspectives to analyse spaces, adults can design spaces to elicit or inhibit certain behaviours and provide clarity and guidance to children entering that space.

Spaces that are not meant for children are easily perceived – they have adult-sized furniture, high countertops and tables, an absence of books, toys, or equipment for children, and they are often sterile and austere. In contrast, spaces that have furniture and equipment sized for children, low shelves, and materials like children's books and toys send clear messages that children are welcome. But the organisation and choice of materials within spaces for children also sends important messages. A space with two identical sets of materials invites a dyad to play, but discourages play among three children unless use of the materials can be successfully negotiated. A space in which materials can be moved around invites open-ended, varied play in contrast to an arrangement in which equipment is all firmly rooted in place.

Lastly, because young children must always be supervised, spaces for children must include spots where adults feel comfortable as well. Benches, logs for sitting, and gliders can be adult-sized spaces that are simultaneously landmarks and places for adults to observe or be with children. Areas with differently sized seating or materials invite collaboration between children and adults or between children of different ages. Additionally, spaces where adults can "peek in," but not necessarily play, balance children's need (and desire) for supervision with the illusion of playing independently. For example, a small enclosure without a roof can give children a feeling of privacy while still allowing for adult observation, and a low hedge resembles a solid wall to a child without blocking an adult's view. Such spaces provide balance for young children to explore and discover, seek out new challenges, and engage with others, even as they remain emotionally tethered to the adults in their lives.

4

PLAY ENVIRONMENTS AND AFFORDANCES

Elizabeth Cummins & Zahra Zamani

Play is a complex matter that appears so simple and naïve from the outside, yet also surreal and abstract at times. Representing a snapshot of the world, play is in effect the coming together of the physical world and the cognitions or thinking that the physical world prompts.

This chapter is in two parts. The first part seeks to simply deconstruct the meaning of affordances and their relationship to play. The second part examines research undertaken in the USA of environmental affordances and play in an early childhood setting and conclusions drawn through observation.

What are affordances, and how do they relate to play?

Affordances, first identified by an American named JJ Gibson in the 1970s, *define the physical qualities of objects and elements in relation to their use or possible use*.[1] In effect that means that their ergonomics allow or 'afford' the user particular opportunities for interaction. Gibson developed this concept to refer to the action possibilities of any given environment. Gibson argued that environments consist of affordances and that these action possibilities are the primary objects of perception, that is that we perceive the environment in terms of what behaviour it affords (i.e. a floor affords walking, a chair affords sitting).

In Gibson's view, 'people and animals do not construct the world that they live in, but are attuned to the invariants of information in the environment'.[2]

This is particularly important in the world of children's play, which is an open-ended continuum of interaction within the physical world, where a child responds and creates purely in relation to the spatial and physical boundaries in which he or she is moving (i.e. a mound affords viewing out, a tunnel affords hiding or crawling). More interestingly, the range of possible affordances any one element can give in terms of play is based on children's imagination and the fact that this affordance is often only temporary (i.e. today a bench seat is a boat, tomorrow it is spaceship). Note in both cases the role of the bench is to keep the child off the ground, in the case of the boat play 'out of the water' and in the case of the spaceship play 'outer space'. In both cases the role is as refuge despite the changing scenario. Likewise the interaction of elements, structures, spaces or terrain throws up multiple affordances (i.e. a raised log with an open grassed area in front will not only afford elevation for presenting, but a space for an audience to sit and listen).

Many practitioners only see affordances reflected in movable, natural materials. It is important to note that while these materials do provide many opportunities to support play, affordances are not exclusively natural nor movable. A collection of concrete blocks or plastic pipes may be just as useful in facilitating construction, for example, and a paved asphalt surface is necessary to afford many ball games. Affordances also are not stand alone; rather, one enacts another. 'Affordances can be regarded as graded property rather than one which belongs to an either-or category.'[3]

The different levels of affordances are: potential, perceived, utilised and shaped affordances. For example, a tree has the 'potential' for climbing; it is therefore 'perceived' by the child as being useful in structure for this purpose and may then be 'utilised' for that purpose. Finally (and this applies particularly to flexible and loose materials or objects) it can be 'shaped' as an affordance, meaning that by bending branches, pruning branches or combining other materials such as timber planks, etc. the affordance of the original object, element or structure can change.

In the following paragraphs I will refer to affordances as 'objects', 'elements', 'structures', 'spaces' and 'settings' in relation to the environments for children's play. In effect the meaning of these terms centres on their capacity for interaction, use and the reaction they evoke in terms of play.

Objects

Objects are moveable physical parts for play (manufactured ones like a 'ball', to collected or found ones like a 'rock' or 'stick'). Objects are usually small in size and lightweight, making them easy to be collected and stored (sometimes in multiples), and they can usually be carried easily in a child's hand. Objects are used as 'currency' for play, something that can afford different uses depending on the play, but more often than not brings inanimate structures and spaces to life during the play ritual.

Elements

Elements are more natural in foundation and state and may not have a solid presence at all, but operate within the play ritual as a different form of 'currency'. Water is probably the best known element in this context.

Structures

Structures are larger pieces, sometimes fixed (such as a 'log' or 'low wall' or 'climbing frame') and sometimes movable. These are of varying sizes and orientations, affording physical movement in different ways based on height differentiation.

Spaces and terrain

Refers to the spaces 'between' structures where movement takes place. These can be small or large depending on the boundaries of the setting. Smaller, more intimate 'nook spaces' will produce different responses to a wide open 'field' for example, as the physical space for movement is increased, thus affording running, ball games and rough and tumble play.

Settings

Settings differs from the other classes in that they are more esoteric, rather than measurable. They bring socio-cultural meaning to the afforded play ritual within a particular environment. Of course this doesn't happen independent of a combination of the previously discussed types, rather it constitutes a layering of associated meaning to the environment as part of play.

FIGURE 4.1 A good example of the urban fabric affording children space to crawl through and play. Queen Victoria Market, Melbourne, Australia 2014

Photo: Courtesy of Mary Jeavons

An example of this would be a forest clearing where there are many trees and logs (structures), pine cones (objects), dirt (elements) and of course the clearing itself (spaces). All of these come together with a learnt understanding from fairy tales, films and stories around mythical creatures and so on to encourage children to become involved in a whimsical imaginary play scenario involving 'hobbits' or 'fairies' or 'ewoks'. The physical elements guide the children's movements, but the setting evokes meaning. This coming together of imagination through the physical environment is the basis of open-ended play.

Children's imaginations are very powerful and move beyond the setting to inspire play. There are many examples of children converting a completely foreign setting into something quite the opposite in play through suspended reality. This demonstrates the beginnings of abstract thought.

Settings in the following research project are discussed using the following terms: natural settings, mixed settings and manufactured settings. This further breaks down the nature of each setting in relation to the objects, elements, structures, spaces and terrain of which they are made.

The importance of open-ended play for all ages

Imagination and open-ended play bring the affordances to life. Children perceive objects, elements, structures, spaces and terrain in relation to how they can be physically utilised and through movement and perception incorporate them into interactions for play.

Children's capacity to suspend reality 'affords' different scenarios for play to occur. These may be drawn from recent experiences or observations made about the world, or from stories heard, read or seen; or purely from the opportunity to express emotions such as joy or anger. Regardless, they are central to a bond of social interaction between children. The beauty of open-ended play is that it can be re-invented within the same environment again and again, sometimes daily within the same setting.

Open-ended play is often boxed within the bounds of the pre-school years, with a societal expectation that the older the child becomes the less opportunity there should be in daily life for this freedom to occur. The capacity to dig deep for this skill therefore weakens over time in most individuals.

The role of anthropometrics

Anthropometrics is the science that deals with the measurement of size and weight of the human body, particularly in a comparative sense. Whilst I do not want to reduce play to a science, the role of anthropometrics in relation to affordances does play a strong part in the capacity for movement and physical skill in any given human. This is based on their height, weight and physical proportions. For example, how wide any given hand span is affects the child's capacity to grip certain objects effectively; this in turn then affects climbing, pulling oneself up or what can be picked up and moved around, thus structuring the options for play.

Anthropometric data across different age ranges are discussed and diagrammed at the beginning of each of the chapters for Seedlings, Sprouts and Saplings.

How can affordances be used in design thinking for play environments?

It is important to note that a play environment is made up of a complexity of affordances that act alone or in combination, forming further opportunities.

When designing or programming play environments it is important to consider the impact bringing varieties of elements together in a designed sense has on play. Rather than 'engineering' interactions, think about possible opportunities, as children, though often returning to a common base in play, will always surprise as to what they will invent and how they will use and adapt their surrounding physical environment.

A clearer understanding of children's interactions with their environment through observation is useful in terms of designing for them for play. What appears interesting for play to an adult may not necessarily constitute an interesting interaction to a child. Children's responses to their environment are far more intuitive and primal than adults', who tend to overthink and often bring value judgements around elements based on past experiences and cultural knowledge.

It is also important to consider the different viewpoints and anthropometrics of an adult to a child. Critical to an engaging play environment is the scale and location of elements, which are different when seen and interacted with from a child's height.

Play affordances at a North Carolina pre-school – a case study

This section examines the results of a combined qualitative (information about the qualities of play, that cannot be measured) and quantitative (numerical information or data about the volume of play) study that explored young children's cognitive play behaviours within an outdoor pre-school in North Carolina.

The data collection involved behaviour mapping from 36 children, and photo preferences, drawings and interviews from 22 four-to-five year olds. Behaviour mapping was employed as a quantitative method for recording observed cognitive play opportunities within settings. Additionally, the study relied on qualitative methods to describe and understand the complex interaction between the environment and young children.

The outdoor pre-school included three playground settings: manufactured, mixed and natural. At the time of data collection, the outdoor pre-school provided 24 behaviour settings and 23 types of elements.

The 'Play Observation Scale'[4] classifies cognitive play behaviours as:

Functional: involves simple or repetitive motor behaviour that can include objects, such as jumping, climbing, etc.
Constructive: involves manipulating and shaping an already familiar material with a direct goal in mind.
Exploratory: involves examining the qualities of objects to gather visual data about their physical features.
Dramatic or imaginary: involves playing the role of someone, engaging in a pretend activity with an object or someone or assigning life to an inanimate object.
Games with rules: involves employing a sense of competence with peers while creating regulations for games.

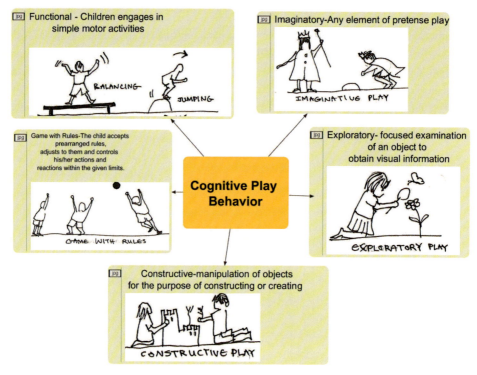

FIGURE 4.2 Cognitive Play Behaviours diagram
Original Diagram: Zahra Zamani

Environmental design researchers in various fields have applied the concept of *behaviour settings* to evaluate the level of use and future design approaches. Behaviour settings are defined as subspaces of the physical environment with boundaries and locations in time and space that integrate events and processes and predict future behaviours.[5] Evolving this concept further, the outdoor pre-school environment can be divided into its functional units as behaviour settings and categorise them based on the proportion of natural to manufactured components.[6] This classification is explained as:

Natural: These are settings mostly composed of organic materials in their original configuration (i.e. water, boulders, sand, trees, shrubs, etc.). Natural settings stimulate children's imaginations, while allowing them to experience all their senses and interpret the natural world.

These settings can be further sub-classified as 'Loose' and 'Fixed', differentiating those objects/elements that are flexible, manipulative and portable, from those permanently fixed in a particular location.

Manufactured: These are purposefully fabricated settings that include fixed and synthetic elements (i.e. play equipment, shade structures, etc.) and mostly support children's physical activity and movement opportunities.

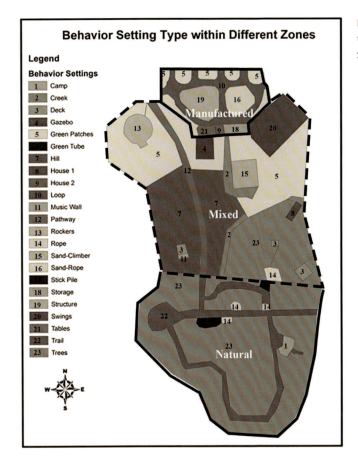

FIGURE 4.3 Map of behaviour type with setting
Source: Zahra Zamani

As with Natural Settings, these can be further sub-classified as 'Loose' and 'Fixed', differentiating those objects/elements that are flexible, manipulative and portable, from those permanently fixed in a particular location.

> **Mixed:** These environmental-behaviour units encompass a balanced proportion of natural and manufactured elements (i.e. pathway, sand-climber, etc.), offering the challenging and control quality of manufactured materials combined with the diversity and variety of natural elements.

Natural settings and play affordances

Complex and exciting interactions present in natural settings promoted higher levels of cognitive play behaviours. The characteristics of natural settings, such as topographic change, distinct and challenging features and manipulative props, inspired children to build, discover, imagine and invent games.

1) **Hills:** Slopes supported fast movement and challenging behaviours, such as sliding, walking, rolling, running, as well as role-play, and games with rules. Children favoured topographic variations that provide challenging opportunities. The hill setting included

scattered shrubs with loose elements that inspired symbolic and constructive play. Bushes provided places to hide, imagine or build shelters. Children enjoyed examining the bushes for creatures, such as bees, bugs or worms. Bushes also created boundaries for imaginary territories and private spaces for children's dramatic play. The available toys, such as balls or Frisbee, stimulated children's functional or games with rules play behaviour in this setting.

2) **Camp:** This behaviour setting includes tree logs, small stones and trunks arranged in a circle. Children enjoyed gathering and engaging in dramatic play through available natural loose elements ('turning on the fire', 'putting poison sparkles', etc.). They also favoured balancing on rocks or logs, demonstrating functional play behaviour.

3) **Stone-lined swale:** Combining rocks, dirt, mud (after rain) and vegetation inspired explorative and imaginative play. Encouraging functional and game play, children enjoyed walking on bridges, as well as balancing, running or jumping on the rocks that sometimes developed into games with rules. Children enjoyed exploring creatures, such as worms, ants or bugs. They learned about small transformations, creatures and novel experiences through the natural ecosystem. Children were interested in moving rocks to 'see what is underneath'. This excitement and curiosity encouraged dramatic play, such as seeking 'dinosaur bones' or 'finding the worm's mommy'.

4) **Stick pile:** Sticks are ample, accessible loose elements for creating games. Encouraging constructive and dramatic play, children created special places in natural playgrounds through collecting sticks, leaves and logs. Stick pile settings encouraged constructive play behaviour in which children collected sticks and logs and stacked them. The pile supported continuous activities of building a 'fort' or a 'house', developing a sense of place. This building process promoted dramatic play, where children imagined becoming 'builders' or 'decorating home'. The setting provided a small place for children to hide and imagine being in a 'prison' or a 'haunted house'.

5) **Trail:** Trails are naturally designed pathways in natural playgrounds. This setting encouraged running, chasing and jumping behaviours. The trails connected diverse natural settings, intrigued children to explore plants, tree barks or creatures. The surrounding trees also increased the sense of mystery and discovery, encouraging children to engage in dramatic and exploratory play. The existing tree trunks, logs and trees, combined with the ambiguity of the woods along the trail, promoted children's games.

6) **Trees:** Tree settings included elements such as trees, rocks, logs, creatures, leaves and dirt that inspired diverse opportunities for functional, dramatic and game behaviours. Children enjoyed the functional, challenging and fast movement opportunities, such as 'climbing', 'hanging', 'jumping over the logs'. Trees supported the evolution and development of many ecosystems that inspired children's exploratory play and curiosity about the natural environment. Children used sticks to dig holes in the tree trunks or the soil, to find ants or bugs, encouraging exploratory play. The existing natural loose elements inspired dramatic play scenarios, such as creating 'houses', 'being in a forest', 'chasing animals', or playing 'Star Wars'. This setting encouraged games with rules, such as hide and seek.

Mixed settings and play affordances

The combination of loose and fixed elements in mixed settings promoted a variety of dramatic play behaviours. In mixed settings, children enjoyed collecting manufactured loose and natural loose elements and arranging them in these semi-enclosed, private spaces. The following describes the cognitive play affordances in mixed settings.

1) **Pathways:** The hard surface of pathways supported functional play behaviours, including riding bikes and scooters, running and walking. The circular design supported continuous activities. Playing with the bikes also afforded dramatic play where children imagined 'driving a truck'. These settings afforded games with rules, such as chasing or rolling tires.
2) **Sand:** Combining sand, toys, rope or climbing structures enticed children to many dramatic and functional play behaviours. Sand was mixed with liquids and shaped, poured, moulded or moved with play toys, affording constructive and dramatic play chances. Including a small climber afforded refuge, lookout or hiding opportunities that encouraged children's dramatic play and functional play through climbing, jumping or balancing affordances. In addition, children employed toys in their constructive, exploratory and dramatic play (for instance, when digging or creating music).
3) **Ropes:** Ropes tied to trees challenged children to balance, walk, climb, jump and swing. Affording functional play, the swinging opportunity inspired children's functional and dramatic play. They imagined themselves as 'swinging monkeys' or 'jumping off a pretend volcano'. Children enjoyed holding trees and climbing on ropes to balance or walk on the rope. This challenging arrangement stimulated children's games with rules. Climbing on ropes, children enjoyed the lookout opportunities that ropes afforded.
4) **Manufactured tube:** Within a natural context the tunnel afforded the most dramatic play opportunities. In addition, the existing natural loose props surrounding the tube developed children's sense of imagination and creativity. The interior space of the tube provided a popular, protected and safe boundary in which children retreat, socialise and explore their surroundings. The overlook and hiding quality of the tunnel afforded dramatic and game opportunities.
5) **Play houses:** The play house in a natural context afforded dramatic play, such as cooking, cleaning, playing family roles or repairing the roof. Children also enjoyed the sense of privacy and refuge afforded by houses. These small-scaled spaces created 'nooks and crannies' that develop a sense of belonging.[7] The availability of tables, and natural and manufactured loose elements near houses encouraged dramatic play.
6) **Green patches:** This setting consisted of bushes, grass and scattered tyre tube elements. Bushes afforded hiding games as well as natural props. The natural loose props afforded exploratory, dramatic and construction play. Children enjoyed collecting, mixing and arranging leaves and flowers for dramatic play. The grassed area afforded many functional play behaviours through providing running and walking opportunities. Tyres offered hiding spaces for retreat and solitude that encouraged dramatic play, such as 'Transformers', 'unicorns', 'shooting', 'house', 'pool', 'animals' and 'princess'. In addition, children enjoyed climbing and jumping from tyres, which can inspire games. The hiding quality of tyres also inspired games, such as hide and seek.

FIGURE 4.4 Play house with dramatic play affordances. North Carolina, USA 2013
Photo: Zahra Zamani

Manufactured settings and cognitive play behaviour affordances

Manufactured settings mostly afforded functional play behaviours. Compared to other settings, manufactured settings rarely offered high ranges of cognitive play behaviour. Access to natural loose and manufactured loose elements in these settings improved chances of dramatic play. The following describes the cognitive play affordances in manufactured settings.

1) **Tables:** Adjacent to a playhouse setting, tables promoted children's dramatic play in the manufactured playground. Children employed sand and mulch elements in plates and utensils, and organised them on the tables during their dramatic play. Fixed benches and movable plastic chairs afforded seating and dramatic play around this setting.
2) **Swing:** Swings afford high levels of functional play behaviour compared to other settings. Children perceived swings to afford exciting experiences, such as a sense of 'flying', 'jumping' or 'doing back flips'.
3) **Rockers:** The rockers mostly afford functional play associated with the existing rocking apparatus. They can also encourage dramatic play, such as riding a 'horse' or 'super heroes'. Providing child-scaled shelters and circular design features in these settings around the rockers offered a sense of enclosure and promoted dramatic play. The manipulative and transformable quality of mulch inspired children to incorporate mulch in their games with the rockers, such as 'Catch the Mulch'.

4) **Music wall:** A setting with attached musical elements afforded constructive and exploratory play behaviour. Positioning a wooden stage in this behaviour setting encouraged dancing, sitting and gathering.
5) **Gazebo:** The wooden surface of the gazebo encouraged children to sit, crawl and mix loose elements to represent symbolic objects. The wooden surface afforded rope games such as jumping, as well as singing.
6) **Platform:** Small platform settings inspired children to create imaginary play (i.e. ship or a performance stage). Platforms defined a perimeter and landmark for children's games. Platforms afforded sitting and gathering opportunities that facilitated games.
7) **Play structure:** Children enjoyed the complex play structure that afforded functional play, such as climbing, sliding, hanging down, jumping, balancing, running and balancing. They also enjoyed the observing opportunities that the structure afforded. The void space under the structure encouraged hide and seek games or a private area for dramatic play activities. Accessible natural loose and manufactured loose elements around the play structure also inspired children's dramatic play.

Summary

Based on the findings, a combination of elements and behaviour settings were found to be most supportive for different cognitive play types. For example, if there are swings, ropes, bikes and pathway settings, chances of functional play increase.

In summary, children's cognitive development is supported by play behaviours when diverse settings and elements are provided in the outdoor pre-schools. Children have greater opportunities for problem solving abilities, decision making, executive functioning and interaction with peers in settings that integrate both natural and mixed settings.

Now that we have an understanding of the importance and role of play, and some of the elements which encourage certain types of play, we will take a look at the broader context. How do we determine where play can occur? How do we design our world to allow for play?

5

CHAOS AND CONFUSION

The clash between adults' and children's spaces

Katherine Masiulanis

It is hard to tie down an exact name, or even a distinguishing feature, of contemporary design. It has been suggested that Landscape Architecture is in a phase of Sustainable Postmodernism,[1] but whatever we call it, I think it is fair to suggest that designers of public spaces have come to appreciate clean lines, order and comprehensibility. Upon those bones, there are layers of narrative, green principles and social ergonomics which tissue-paper over the structure, but we feel that for a space to be great, it must be pleasingly organised.

This is all very well for adults. Time poor and overloaded with information, we need a space we can 'scan' and understand easily. As Alain de Botton suggests:

> We require consistency in our buildings, for we are ourselves frequently close to disorientation and frenzy. We need the discipline offered by similarity, as children need regular bedtimes and familiar, bland foods. We require that our environments act as guardians of a calmness and direction on which we have a precarious hold.[2]

I'd like to look at whether this model of public space design works for children, any more than bland foods really do.

At the heart of this is a concern that by designing places which impose adult ideals and aesthetics over those of our children, whether consciously or otherwise, we send messages about their importance to us. To put it another way: 'Landscape design conveys the values of a community and ultimately impacts on whether individuals are welcomed or excluded from a space. Designed spaces can profoundly affect individuals, communities, and society at large.'[3]

Generally, it has been assumed that children value formal order less than adults – but is this true? Children do seem to benefit from the stability of a predictable routine. Structuring of time appears to give children a confidence and security that allows them to explore the world at their own pace.[4] However, I think it is worth distinguishing between the 'routine' of time, and the 'regularity' of space. Any visitor to a typical early childhood centre at the end of the day will find what appears to be a messy space, with materials, toys and other apparent 'junk' strewn about. However, to the child's eye, this is often a rich environment, with a density of things to do and explore.

I think there may be two things at play here: scale and description. Do you remember a place from your childhood, which when revisited was so much smaller than you recall? For me, the steps in my grandfather's house were quite a challenge – they had open, slippery timber treads, and it felt like bridging a chasm to step from one to another. Coming back to the same house as an adult, they are nothing out of the ordinary. How then must a large paved plaza space at a town centre seem to a child?

The other difference in perception is in how we see the world from a functional perspective. To quote Maria Kylin:

> Children, especially in urban areas, live and act in environments planned and monitored by adults. Adults, planners not excepted, describe and plan these environments through an adult and professional perspective using cognitive and physical classifications. However, children mostly describe the same environment in terms of activity and meaning.[5]

That is, adults create abstract justifications and satisfactions to a place: whereas children are more grounded in the significance of a place, and what they can do there. It is becoming widely recognised that children learn by doing, not just by observing.[6]

To be able to appreciate a space for its abstract qualities, there is a clear developmental stage that we all need to go through, starting with the sorting of objects into different categories, usually in the preschool years. The ability to generalise about an object's characteristics (for example, these are all blue: even though they may be all shades from sky to navy) is the precursor to mathematical principles, and may be the seed of an appreciation of the platonic forms (cones, spheres and other 'perfect' forms) which underpins much modern design. As Le Corbusier said:

> These things are beautiful because in the middle of the apparent incoherence of nature or the cities of men, they are places of geometry, a realm where practical mathematics reigns ... And is not geometry pure joy?[7]

Children, however, need the opportunity to explore and investigate things, rather than just look at them. By creating places where the range of allowed activities is prescribed, we may limit their ability to learn about the world, although children are very skilled at subversion. If children need surprise and challenge to learn, then an ordered and predictable space presumably offers decreased opportunity for this to occur.

Arguably, adults (perhaps particularly those who manage the risks associated with public open space) have a deep-seated sense of caution about allowing this to happen. Mess makes us uncomfortable – wary even. As documented in other sections of this book, a creeping malaise of risk aversion has inclined us to design spaces which seem safer, but are also more open to inappropriate use, and perhaps duller for everyone.

As far back as 1972, Simon Nicholson identified this dilemma in his *Theory of Loose Parts*, which states: 'In any environment, both the degree of inventiveness and creativity, and the possibility of discovery, are directly proportional to the number and kind of variables in it.' He suggests that our society allows the designers, architects and builders to have all the fun, leaving everyone else feeling as if they are too incompetent to create something – but also identifies how much people would love to interact with the world, given the opportunity.

In 1970, the Institute of Contemporary Art in London held an interactive exhibition called 'Play Orbit', which was soon followed by work 'parts' by the artist Robert Morris at the Tate Gallery. A contemporary critic noted that, 'the public got into the party spirit – a somewhat overzealous participation. They were jumping and screaming, swinging the weights around wildly – the middle aged in particular. The children were the most sensible of all the visitors.'

Research suggests that more creative children are those who are given choices about their environment, and creative problem solving is also enhanced by physical environments designed to stimulate the senses. It might be supposed that chaos is then inherently connected to creativity, but this is not necessarily the case. As children develop, a more systematic and structured method of problem solving has been observed to occur. Having a structure and framework allows an idea to be maintained, tested and creative approaches developed, much in the way that an artist working through a particular phase in their career would. Perhaps the most famous example of this, Picasso, went through many different phases of his career – blue, rose, cubist, neo-classicist, surrealist and so on – and could very well be described as playing with each of these within a distinct structure.

So, given that our understanding of what children really require in a space is limited, and by imposing planned spaces we also may be restraining their creative potential, is designing children's spaces counterproductive?

There are certainly some who would say so. Proponents of true adventure playgrounds, which are usually defined places in which children can build with real materials, often speak about the real delight children take in constructing their own environments.

Erin Davis, who made a film about *The Land* adventure playground in Wales, suggests:

> It's really more about child-directed play than 'risky' play, per se. When a child chooses the content and direction of an activity, it's likely that eventually something about it will make adults cringe. Committing to support child-directed play means relinquishing control and managing your own feelings of discomfort. At its core this is an act of deep respect for the child and their experience. … So ultimately I think it's about control and power. People who have power over others – in this case, adults over children – are often reluctant to share it.[8]

Likewise, studies into cubby or den building suggest that adults are not always welcome in these activities. Given the opportunity, children will carefully select an area of vegetation which has a degree of concealment, but also with space defining qualities that allow them to observe the world in privacy. One of the main reasons given for abandoning a favourite haunt was that it was no longer secret.[9]

Although it may be possible to consider giving over some land and control to children, ultimately our public environments are ones we must share. I would suggest two strategies to improve them for us all.

The first of these is embedding complexity. By this, I do not mean chaos, fuss or frivolous levels of ornament for its own sake. It is possible to create rich and interesting spaces which are still easy to interpret and navigate. Building in delight, surprise and change takes a playful attitude to design, and may be assisted through the clever use of materials, inclusion of artwork, consideration of scale and careful choice of seasonal planting. People are, after all, highly complex and varied – why then should we think that we will all find pleasure in an expanse of grey concrete? William H. Whyte once said: 'It is difficult to design a space that will not attract people. What is remarkable is how often this has been accomplished.'

Simplicity in design is surely one of the most difficult of all aspects to achieve, although this may come as a surprise to many outside the profession. The temptation to keep playing, to keep solving problems, to keep tinkering without integration into an overriding scheme is sometimes overwhelming, particularly when there are many different stakeholders. However, this does not create complexity, but chaos. As Terence Conran says:

> Simplicity, however, should not be confused with simplistic. … Simplistic does not rule out precision, craft or finesse.[10]

Think, for example, of a beautifully crafted handmade object – perhaps a Japanese ceramic bowl. There is a richness of patina, of shape, of imperfection, which is brought about quite deliberately, and is yet contained within a very simple and clean shape. There is the potential for different layers of interaction with such a piece. I would suggest that by incorporating this level of thought and sensory detail into our public spaces, we have a greater chance of making spaces which have interest for children at the smaller scale at which they perceive things, and yet the modernity and legibility adults crave.

The second strategy to improve public space is to wholeheartedly embrace play. As discussed in relation to the notorious 'Play Orbit' exhibition, adults also appreciate the opportunity to be allowed to play. They may not wish to squash down a fibreglass slide, but there are many examples where we are invited to play. On the banks of the Yarra river in Melbourne, Australia, a giant musical Theremin was installed for a while, which sang to passersby depending on their movement past it, and allowed up to eight users to interact polyphonally.[11] The Theremin's creator, Robin Fox, notes: 'The project was a lot of fun and led to some surprising public interactions ranging from Tai Chi groups gathering around it in the mornings to groups of young BMX'ers jumping in sonic loops off the face of the works.'

Likewise, playful spaces – not necessarily 'playgrounds' as such – can enliven our cities and bring communities together, whilst subliminally giving the idea that children and young people are actually welcome in our public spaces. For example, the Sculptural Playground in Schulberg, Germany, has been described as:

> a crafty alternative to the simply green-play lawn or deconstructivist forest type of urban park. The central idea of reclaiming an area in the name of play has given this city centre a fun gathering space. A giggle instead of a hiccup along the medieval streets and town squares.[12]

Chaos and confusion 53

FIGURE 5.1 Both adults and children interact with the Giant Theremin by artist Robin Fox on the banks of the Yarra River

Courtesy of City of Melbourne

FIGURE 5.2 Sculptural playground, Schulberg. Image courtesy Annabrau, Architektur und Landschaft, Berlin

Courtesy of Annabrau

6
CITY PLAY

Elger Blitz & Hannah Schubert

Ours is the first period in human history in which the majority of people live in urban agglomerations, and this percentage is expected to rise to 70% around 2050. Without doubt this affects the way our children grow up. We do not want to discuss here whether the city is going to be our natural habitat soon, or if it already is. But we cannot deny any longer that our kids, and their kids, are more likely to grow up between buildings than between trees.

As a result, playgrounds have been growing in importance; playgrounds are the unnatural policy for the loss of natural grounds to play on and with. Less than a century ago the act of playing was something in which adults were not involved, as playing was a self-organised outdoor activity. Increasing urbanisation, welfare and free time have turned playing more and more into an age-defined and regulated activity – and the majority think that this activity needs to be planned, designed and organised.

Because playing in general is integrated into our lives, any type of play, in any type of surrounding, is natural. 'Natural play', as a result, can be understood as unconditioned play, non-restrictive and non-directed, although others may take it to mean only play in outdoor settings such as forests and meadows. A playspace is a secure place where kids can play with light spirits, sheltered from the hectic reality of the cityscape they live in. A place to explore and discover, a space that encourages children to practise social, motor and cognitive skills, without preconceived rules. Hence, we would like to suggest a different kind of definition of 'natural' play, and also a different approach to the realisation of playgrounds in our cities; playgrounds that are just as valuable.

From public to private

The above – the unconventional, the free and the non-directive – is exactly what's missing in most of today's playgrounds, and particularly those we plan in cities. It intrigues us to think of strategies to develop playgrounds with a 'natural playing competence' which can be incorporated in today's cities and in city kids' lives. We think it is all about recognising opportunities, stretching the borders of the conventional.

Seeing opportunities or even creating them is, obviously, not easy. As cities are increasingly focussed on transport, infrastructure dominates the public space; from parking spaces in historic towns to highways, connecting offices and shopping malls. Furthermore, public space is being directed and exploited by municipalities as an important source of income; the limited available space is developed for more housing, hotels and offices. This is an ongoing chain reaction, leaving only little space for the unplanned and the unconventional. Generally speaking, we might conclude that our priorities are formed purely by commercial values rather than on cultural, social and educational values.

Simply said, there is not much space left for such a thing as a playground in our growing, densifying cityscapes, because a playground means investing in values that cannot easily be calculated in economic terms.

This sounds gloomy, and on one hand it is; but it has also led to a new playground phenomenon. In our congested cities, large shopping malls are popping up everywhere. Fighting for the grace of their consumers they are trying to make their investments profitable. One solution they have discovered is reinvesting in playgrounds; after all, kids are tomorrow's potential customers, and even more importantly – they play a deciding role in choices parents make.

Almost all shopping malls or fast food chains have a playground nowadays, but most of them are pre-fabricated and ordered from a catalogue – the same everywhere. In a bid to attract clients, however, shopping malls have started to invest in larger, more bespoke playgrounds, making them more appealing destinations for kids and families.

FIGURE 6.1 Zorlu Centre playground is an island of colour and relaxation in the heart of Istanbul
Photo: Orguz Meric

We can criticise this, but we can also embrace this trend, regardless of any ethical doubts; some truly amazing playscapes have already been built in shopping malls all over the world. One of them is the Zorlu Centre in Istanbul, Turkey. The city of Istanbul is congested, developing at a high speed – parks are scarce, let alone for public playgrounds. This is the perfect example of a commercial party stepping in and contributing to city life. The Zorlu playground is publicly accessible, and although the main motive may be commercially driven, in fact the mixed-use development of Zorlu truly gives something back to the citizens of Istanbul. It is a unique and custom-designed playspace that not only makes up for ten years of building activities, but also provides a place where the youngest generation can play freely, unhindered by traffic and the buzzing city life.

This idea of developing something site specific and customised is key to our philosophy, as is the idea of ambiguous play opportunities. We consider playgrounds an integral part of public space, and strive for them to be inviting places to be discovered; providing room for different groups and ages, and several forms of use. Faced today with too many age-restricted areas which are filled with prefabricated furniture, directive as well as limited in terms of use, Carve's leading motive is to create space for play that fosters possibilities.

Instead of making use of archetypical playground-equipment, which can be pretty directive on what to do and how to play, we prefer to work with more general objects, playable landscapes or multi-use interventions. In the design for the Zorlu playspace, we have embraced these principles to create an important space for the people of Istanbul.

This shows that while (local) governments have stepped out, either by selling (former play)grounds to real estate developers, or removing them due to decreasing budgets for

FIGURE 6.2 Spaces of different scales are important
Photo: Marleen Beek

FIGURE 6.3 Challenging climbing structures echo the surrounding city buildings

Photo: WATG

maintenance, private parties and companies sometimes step in, filling the gap. This is the outcome of our money-driven society, fitting perfectly in our new city-lives. Ideal for busy families with kids, perfectly accessible by car – but is it really what we want?

Recognising opportunities

Probably most of us wouldn't. Luckily, we still can find solutions to incorporate a playful environment, even in a dense city. How can we develop ideas to let these places contribute to people's lives, and become hubs of different activity types? And, on a macro-level, how can playgrounds become an urban catalyst for change? The following examples show our way of thinking, providing unconventional solutions for limited spaces within the city of Amsterdam, the Netherlands.

How to turn a street into a playscape

One of the projects that beautifully illustrates the possibilities and – self-created – limitations of a playground in a dense historic city is Potgieterstraat. The project is located in a context of nineteenth-century buildings dating back to the first major enlargement of Amsterdam. The architectural and planning style of that time appears to be a disadvantage in today's public

FIGURE 6.4 Reforming the urban landscape of Potgeiterstraat
Source: Carve

life, since the inner courtyards of these blocks are not open for public use and the streets were never designed for today's traffic. There is a lack of public squares and public green space: streets are dominated by cars and although bike lanes are a traffic solution, unfortunately they claim the little available space from adjacent side walks. Furthermore, public sidewalks are prone to the never-ending need for outdoor terraces in an over-gentrified area, and are 'sold out' by the municipality for extra income.

The district as a whole was in need of a refreshing new strategy for children and pedestrians to strengthen and revitalise the public realm. Dutch governments are keen on participation processes. In the case of Potgieterstraat, local inhabitants were asked to agree upon and formulate new guidelines in one such participatory process, and were involved in the selection of an architect to execute their ideas. One of the desires was the creation of more playing space in a neighbourhood where how best to use the scarce space is a hot topic. A problem was born.

In this particular situation, Carve suggested closing down one of the streets entirely to car traffic in order to re-dedicate that street space to citizen utilisation. Potgieterstraat's function was changed from traffic and parking into an urban design which included meeting and pausing places, a playground for children, an upgrading of the landscaping and, overall, a positive urban beacon for the district.

Carve's intervention aimed to rethink the street into a play street, accessible only to bicycles and pedestrians. The existing trees were kept and new ones added. Into that clearance, we designed a mogul landscape with integrated play objects, set in abstract black rubber. The play objects vary from interactive elements to water sprayers. The rubber can be used as a drawing surface, and is an invitation to jump, run and fall. It combines a soft feel while also reducing noise levels. However, the true benefit of this design is not obvious on a first glimpse. It is rather the reclaiming of the local urban realm by its community. Parents, as well as citizens without children, interact and relax here on wooden benches and around a little kiosk. The location becomes an anchor for neighbourhood interaction and interlocks with the surrounding blocks, as well as helping to get together people of different backgrounds and ages.

Where normally participation is seen as a process in which all stakeholders are positively involved, this wasn't the case in this particular situation. The participative processes were characterised by conflict rather than by cooperation. Conflicts with the city council, which had the ambitious demand that by written survey 70% of all residents in the housing blocks should agree to the plan; conflicts with residents that didn't want their acclaimed public parking places to be moved around the corner; conflicts with local retailers; and a new political administration that changed plans that had already been agreed on by residents and the former administration. On top of that, there was a lack of cooperation between the different city departments, which only further delayed the project.

Interestingly, these conflicts resulted in improved social bonding before the realisation of the plans, due to the residents' perseverance. The success of this playful public domain is an important side product of the design. The main attraction is surely the exciting, unique playground, which excels in attracting a large number of locals: the community is no longer anonymous, as the space stimulates chats between neighbours. Literally, whenever the weather allows for it, one can witness children and adults claiming this street; Potgieterstraat illustrates urban revitalisation.

The alternative city-square

The Van Beuningenplein is a project of a completely different scale, but in a similar setting. The former Staatsliedenbuurt is an early twentieth-century extension of Amsterdam. In recent years this area has undergone an extensive urban renewal process. Social houses are

FIGURE 6.5 Left: Play environments embedded in the urban fabric and Right: Multipurpose playing surfaces, serving different people at different times
Source: Carve

renovated and partly sold to stimulate diversity among the inhabitants. A lot of emphasis is put on upgrading the public space's quality. Gentrification has started but not as rapidly as seen in other parts of the city built in the same era. In the vicinity of the Van Beuningenplein the population consists of people with low imcomes and immigrant backgrounds. The Van Hallstraat, which passes one side of the Van Beuningenplein, is the demarcation line for this poorer neighbourhood, which lacks public facilities.

The Van Beuningenplein was hidden from view by cars, fencing and poorly maintained green space, isolating a former play and sport area from its surrounding context. As a result, this hidden square became a hang out place for teenagers, and vandalism was an ongoing issue. Residents living around the Van Beuningenplein were strictly opposed to the removal of any old trees, although they didn't make use of the square since it was perceived as a no-go area. The district decided to construct a parking garage at Van Beuningenplein from the revenues of the paid parking spaces. Although the underground parking did not add any parking spaces to the area, parked cars were removed from the street, creating more open space. This was the start for a new Van Beuningenplein.

The square had to introduce a new positive liveliness into the district, this time for everyone. It had to be safe at night, inviting children to play and citizens to find their personal place to pause and relax. It needed to be a space where there was room to engage, interact and allow for the unforeseen. The most important demand was to keep all existing large trees around the square. The new parking garage had to be carefully fitted in, leaving more space on street level for public use.

From a theoretical point of view, at Carve, we believe that playing is the cheerful development of physical and social skills. In that sense 'play' is a necessity for children to grow up – but play isn't limited to any one age. Playfully preparing and mastering skills is an argument for the mingling of different ages and groups, providing them with a space alongside each other – to create their own community. We endeavoured to combine groups in areas in a logical lay-out eluding strict borders, making 'transition' zones playable as well. By providing a non-prescriptive play environment, we permit teenagers places to understand their limits and identity, and adults to engage in play, learn new skills and stay young.

This follows in the footsteps of the best Dutch traditions, as initiated by twentieth-century architect and urbanist Aldo van Eyck. Although radically different in its urban positioning and implications, it shares a focus on local initiatives and community, far outstretching the relevance of space (to play) for children.

The Van Beuningenplein site was designed in a collaboration between three offices, each bringing in their special expertise. The buildings were designed by Concrete Architectural Associates, the landscape concept came from Dijk & Co and the inner courts of the square, leisure areas, the playground and sports fields were designed by Carve. Bringing together three disciplines reacting to each other's perspectives certainly added to the quality of the plan. Collaborative processes with residents and engaging experts with their particular knowledge, including disabled people, local kids, city ecologists and the Association to Preserve Amsterdam Trees, provided further enrichment.

Along the edges of the square, façade gardens, benches and hedges are placed in strategic locations, creating intimate green rooms for locals to sit and relax. Where cars used to be parked, front doors are now directly connected to the square. By doing this, the previous harsh boundary between private and public space has become less rigid. It now is a colourful, lively zone in the new green frame of the Van Beuningenplein, in which there is still space for resident initiatives.

The central surface is designated for sports and play. Two adjacent playing fields allow for a variety of sports, like soccer and basketball. One of them is sunken into the ground, its concrete edges designed for skaters. This field can be flooded to freeze naturally and become an ice rink in wintertime. In summer, its water features turn the same field into a water playground. The Krajicek Foundation donated funds for the realisation of the plans, on the condition that a weekly active sports programme was run for children on the square. The wavy surface hosts a variety of playing towers, especially designed for Van Beuningenplein, to offer playing challenge to all ages, alongside other playing elements spread throughout the square.

The buildings added to the square are multifunctional. One grants access to cars into the parking garage, the other one holds a workplace for a playground generator, supervising the security of the square. Teenagers can find a place to hang out in a youth centre located on the square, and a public tea-house with a roof terrace is also housed here – attracting residents, and also people from outside the district.

Reflecting on the project, we have learnt the following: the Van Beuningenplein successfully bridges the former barrier of Van Hallstraat between two neighbourhoods that have very different demographics. The small, commercially operated tea-room is large enough to make a difference but too small to dominate the square, hence contributing as a catalyst in this meeting of neighbours. Van Beuningenplein has stimulated public life in the wider neighbourhood in a remarkable way. Different groups, ages and backgrounds gather on the square, using the many functions it offers. Social cohesion of the neighbourhood is thoroughly strengthened, throughout the whole day. Whatever time of the day, the square is buzzing with life and children: many different ages and user groups have learned to use this square jointly, sharing the space.

Finding new pockets

The last example we would like to present is about finding smart solutions for impossible requests – or, in other words, 'finding new pockets'. Laan van Spartaan is a classic contemporary example. A playground situated on the little space that's left, because the rest has been

City play 63

FIGURE 6.6 Laan van Spaartan playspace is sandwiched between a bike path and high density housing
Photo: Rob van Dijk

FIGURE 6.7 Challenging climbing structures at Laan van Spartaan
Source: Carve

densely built. The solution is simple; just like dense cities tend to develop vertically, our design for the playground did, too.

Laan van Spartaan is a new city development just outside the ringroad of Amsterdam. On the former site of the football club VVA Spartaan and Sportshall Jan van Galen more than 1,000 housing units will be built by 2016. Renowned architects designed the housing blocks, a new sports hall, offices, a school and community facilities.

The dike along Laan van Spartaan, on the Willem Augustinstreet, was designated as a play zone. The 200 metre long strip, however, is squeezed in by a bike path and a lowered road, so that the site could not contain any play equipment wider than 1.50 metres plus the mandatory safety zones.

We took the limitations of the location as a starting point for the design. By raising the play objects, increasing the height and giving them a minimal footprint, the most was made of the limited space. Three zones offer play options for different age groups. The northern space is designed especially for younger children, while the middle zone – with play houses and hammocks – attracts older children. The southern and most challenging play zone contains a climbing garland, which curls up to more than 5 metres high, offering a panoramic view on the whole strip. Whilst the initial concept of the playstrip was there at the very beginning – and didn't change much during the process – the technical engineering turned out to be a great challenge, due to all the different angles, heights and cantilevers.

We found that a community that does not yet have roots greatly benefits from spaces where children can play together and parents can meet. Laan van Spartaan fulfils this role with fervour. Furthermore, the visibility of the climbing objects from afar contributes to the discovery of this playspace by children from surrounding neighbourhoods.

Conclusion

These projects illustrate the concept of 'natural play' as we understand it, and as it exists in modern, urban lives. Each of these varied sites takes advantage of opportunities that were based on restrictions, but moreover they are designed around the social aspects and the limitations that we encounter in our cities. They are an addition to the public realm – and leave room for the unexpected.

7
OF AGENCY, PARTICIPATION AND DESIGN

Two contrasting play scenarios in Indian cities

Mukta Naik

India is a young country. As per the 2011 census, 39% of India's population is below 18 years of age. Of its 472 million children, about 27% live in urban India.

In India, children and youth are seen as important to the country's economic future: a demographic dividend available to reap. India's policy climate therefore focuses on education and skill development for children and youth. On the other hand, children are also seen as helpless and without agency; as a weaker section of society who are disproportionately impacted by poverty, disaster and poor governance. Infant mortality and malnutrition among the youngest children are particularly recognised as serious threats to India's human development. As such, the mental and physical development of children as well as their health and nutrition are seen through the two lenses of economic development and rights-based frameworks.

That play is critical for the enhancement of physical, psychosocial and cognitive skills in children is well accepted by child psychologists.[1] Adult attitudes to play, however, are often detrimental to the interests of children. Adults tend to see play as a recreational rather than a holistic activity. Studies have found that parents and teachers in the Indian context tend to see play and learning as a dichotomy such that children are either playing or learning,[2] not both. Adults often interpret play as time taken away from 'useful' activities like learning and working.

As India experiences significant urbanisation, deteriorating urban environments and shrinking spaces for play threaten the well-being of its 128 million urban children. For instance, children in Delhi cannot access school playgrounds post school hours, 80% of the city's population has no access to public sports complexes and the majority of the city's 15,000 parks are in degenerate condition or have been encroached upon.[3]

To add to this, urban planners, urban designers and architects who actively shape playspaces for children are not party to – nor interested in – the specialised knowledge of child psychologists about the interconnections between space design and a child's well-being. Further, adults' misguided attitudes about play shape the thinking of those – whether experts or non-experts – who influence the 'physicality' and 'temporality' of playspaces. These two words are used deliberately here because play environments are shaped equally by physical characteristics of size, shape, access and urban form, as they are by the activities that occur in and around these spaces at various times of the day.

Two specific play scenarios in urban India

While the modern ideal for Indian cities emerges from ideas of planning and order – as evidenced by the Government of India's commitment to building smart cities – very few Indian cities have genuinely benefited from spatial planning.

Planned residential areas in Indian cities have traditionally been plotted developments with single-family homes, but scarcity of land has meant the mid- and high-rise housing condominium is increasingly visible in urban India. However, the majority of children in urban India live in what is colloquially termed 'the slum' but which is, in reality, a wide variety of dense, informally created living environments. Even in India's capital city Delhi, a study found that inadequate planned housing supply resulted in over 70%[4] of its residents living in incrementally built informal and quasi-legal settlements like unauthorised colonies that spring from illegally plotted agricultural land, slums that develop as squatters occupy undeveloped land within the city and urban villages.

Given this background, we will focus on two distinct scenarios of play from India's urban life. One scenario is that of playspaces in the increasingly popular gated enclaves where the middle and upper classes live. These are part of the planned city, where specific spaces are allocated for parks and sports centres, recreation and greenery. This is a scenario that isn't hard to conjure for readers familiar with the formal language of urban planning. However, the experience of childhood in these gated neighbourhoods is another story, a reality quite distinct from the order and design of the spaces they play in.

Scenario two examines the playspaces of children in the informal, incrementally built neighbourhood. Here, play areas are rarely segregated from other uses; children inhabit spaces that are able to transform by the time of the day, by season and by occasion. These areas sometimes change their nature to become something quite different on festivals or special occasions like marriages.

In both scenarios, we will examine the role of the planner and designer, and also to what extent children are allowed any agency in the decision making about their own playspaces.

Contestation over recreational space in the middle class gated enclave

Safety concerns, especially freedom from crime, are the driving force behind the wide-scale adoption of the gated enclave in Indian cities, which is a reflection of growing class segregation.[5] Particularly attractive is the idea that children will be able to access play spaces safely, interact with a controlled group of peers and adults and be restricted from wandering out of the boundaries of the enclave.

Ironically, however, children are often prohibited from playing in the very parks and playgrounds that have ostensibly been designed for their safety and convenience. Playgrounds become contested spaces and powerful groups within the community, usually Resident Welfare Associations (RWAs) controlled by the elderly, envision parks as spaces of beautification and repose. They perceive children as the spoilers of these pristine, green patches, and access is often restricted (for example, limited timings, or the prohibition of ball games) or denied.

In 2013 in Mumbai, kids filed a police complaint against their elders for prohibiting play in the park.[6] In Delhi, an RWA went to court[7] in 2011 to uphold their right to fence off a neighbourhood park so that they could prevent/control the use of the park as a children's play area and by adults to play volleyball. They suggested in their plea that these sports and play activities were causing "damage to trees and plants in the park and fear of injury to those walking near (the play area)". Justice Endlaw, who heard the case, quashed the plea, saying that "complaints of nuisance if any caused from certain players in the park cannot be a ground for prohibiting (play)". He upheld the rights of not only children, but even adults to play, and laid the blame for inadequate play spaces on the lack of city planning. "During the hearing I had repeatedly asked the counsel for the petitioner as to where else can the children or the adults indulge in such activity. The city has not made many provisions for such activities," he said in his judgement.

FIGURE 7.1 Sign typical of parks in planned enclaves in urban India

Photo: Mukta Naik

Further, Justice Endlaw recalled an earlier Supreme Court judgement dating back to 1991[8] that says open spaces and playgrounds are "required to protect the residents of the locality from the ill effects of urbanisation and to ensure a place where children can run about and the aged and infirm can rest". In referring to parks as "a gift from people to themselves", this older SC judgement, however, places citizens responsible for the appropriate usage of public spaces.

Despite the deliberate inclusion of open space and play areas in Delhi's gated enclaves, a variety of adult protagonists, especially the elderly, deny children the space for play. While toddlers are better tolerated largely because adults accompany them, the discrimination is particularly harsh against older children playing sports like cricket and football. The presence of cars parked around play areas, landscaped areas and seating spaces for the elderly commonly inhibits sport in open areas, and children are involved in daily conflicts with adults.

Decisions on how neighbourhood parks are used evolve through discussions and debates among adults, and children have very little say. At present, children have very little recourse when adults do not support them in their pursuit of play spaces. A wider policy discourse on the Right to Play is only beginning to emerge in India. India is under obligation to protect children's right to play as a signatory of Article 31 of the United Nations Convention on the Rights of the Child (UNCRC) 1974, and a National Charter on Children 2004 has already promised suitable arrangements for promotion of play. However, in reality much more needs to be done in this regard.

The slum as a site for spontaneous, creative and risky play

In the mixed-use, incrementally built and relatively dense neighbourhoods that are common to Indian cities, children rarely have the luxury of designated playspaces like parks. In these relatively lower-income neighbourhoods, the street is the hub of social interaction. This is where women talk and buy wares from vendors; this is where adults interact; this is even where children play, as family members can keep a watch on them easily. Gully Cricket evolved from these narrow city streets.

In a slum redevelopment project in East Delhi, the design team from micro Home Solutions found that women were not interested in the idea of a tot-lot for young children, preferring them to play in the street outside their home where they could watch them while they worked. Home-based work like stitching, craft and manual assembly for industrial purposes is a common occupation for women and an important supplemental income for households in these neighbourhoods. For example, in Sundernagari, 70% of the community voted for a car-free design that recreated an ordered network of multi-level streets, allowing young children to play outside their homes.[9]

These spaces – the street, the corridor and the courtyards – are used in multiple ways by adults and children. "Big events like a gathering for a festival or marriage take place within the streets and courtyards by simply demarcating space with a bamboo structure covered in sheets," writes Architect Sourav Kumar Biswas,[10] as he underlines the flexibility of space in settlements like Dharavi in Mumbai. Moreover, in the absence of strict 'do's and don'ts', he observes that children are able to convert any available space, like the area around the community toilet or an empty parking lot, into a space for play. Because the informal

FIGURE 7.2 Gully cricket in Varanasi

Photo: Rajarshi Chowdhury

FIGURE 7.3 Slum children at play in the streets

Photo: Mukta Naik

settlement has less resources for community (or private) use, spaces change use temporally and the community shares common spaces by keeping their use as flexible as possible.

Architect and urban designer Sudeshna Chatterjee, who heads the Delhi-based Action for Children's Environments (ACE), finds that the type of play that children indulge in is also qualitatively different in these spaces. In a 2011 intervention,[11] she found that children in Delhi's Khirkee urban village played over 40 innovative games (as opposed to 16 in an adjacent middle-class area) that went beyond traditional sports like cricket and football, often using whatever was available to them, including scrap materials.

However, even as the above description paints a rosy picture, the truth is that while children in the informal city make the best of what they have, several studies show they do seek natural spaces away from the slum[12] to play and interact with friends.

In general, city development plans for Indian cities lack a child-oriented approach and there is a particular need to pay attention to integration while designing urban slum redevelopment projects or public space projects.[13]

Children as agents of change

Sadly, play is not the highest priority for slum children, who feel strongly about shortage of resources in their communities. As such, they outline adult problems with an uncanny clarity. Says Preeti Prada, National Head, Humara Bachpan, "Children in the slum often prioritise infrastructure and amenities in their mapping exercises. Inadequate water supply, poor sanitation, lack of public toilets, no streetlights, these are the things they really worry about. Playspaces are important to them, but with the poor quality of life they have, they come much lower on their list of priorities."

Humara Bachpan's focus on child-led planning is a step forward in helping children articulate their priorities through tools like mapping. Further, attempts to take children's voices to city planners and policymakers have met with some success. In a slum in Bhubaneshwar, a young mapmaker succeeded in outlining her inability to attend night tuition classes because of poor street lighting and brought the ward official's focus on this pressing issue in her neighbourhood. In Mumbai's Gautam Nagar slum, members of a child club met with their municipal representative and successfully sought his assistance in cleaning an open area of pipes and debris so that they could use it to play in.

Role for planners, designers and adults-at-large

It is clear that participatory approaches, such as the ones outlined above, could be used effectively to improve planning interventions in favour of better urban playspaces. However, participation is also a necessary element for designers to keep in mind.

"Designers need to listen to children, ask children how they want their spaces to be,"[14] advises Meera Oke, Child Development Consultant with the Dublin-based Portobello Institute. "Children who are allowed to play by themselves with less adult supervision develop better play skills," she explains, pointing to the need for designers to balance the need for safety with that for opportunities for risky and exploratory play. Playspaces can also be a way for designers to create experiences that urban children are missing out on. For instance, spaces that use natural materials and are akin to landscape settings can address the increasing disconnect of urban children from nature.

Key to addressing safety concerns is the design of inclusive and mixed public spaces, rather than segregated spaces. A diversity of classes, genders and age groups can be achieved through design elements like outdoor gymnasiums, walking and cycling facilities, sports complexes and so on that are easily accessed by residential neighbourhoods. In this, it is possible to align the agenda of child-friendly recreational spaces with other citizens' priorities like walkability.

The highly successful Raahgiri programme co-ordinated by EMBARQ India, a division of World Resources Institute (WRI), is a good example of this, in which certain streets of the city are declared car-free on Sunday mornings. Initiated by citizen groups in a bid to promote non-motorised transport, sustainable living and road safety, Raahgiri has proved to be particularly attractive to children across income groups as a safe space to participate in activities, engage in sports and interact with friends. Raahgiri is currently running in several Indian cities including Gurgaon, Delhi, Chandigarh and Bhopal.

Finally, there are several small but strategic interventions that can improve children's access to urban playspaces. For example, in a study brought out by NGO Butterflies,[15] children make several suggestions. Better integration of sports and physical development in the school curriculum would offer children from disadvantaged backgrounds a chance to play, especially girls who are not allowed the freedom to leave the home to play. Local governments could offer incentives for schools to leave playgrounds open until sunset. Efficient neighbourhood level garbage collection systems, even a well placed dustbin, could prevent littering in parks so that these spaces are available for children to play in once again.

Making Indian cities more child-friendly and specifically encouraging play, demands a range of creative solutions from everyday interventions in communities to citywide and national strategies. At the core is the need to reinforce to adults that play is integral to child development. Adults who influence children's lives need to prioritise play over supervised alternatives like hobby classes in the case of the elite, and over household or wage work in the case of the poor.[16] Only with the support of adults and civil society organisations that help bring the voices of children to the fore is it possible to change the conversation so that policymakers, planners and designers can seek creative and strategic solutions[17] to improve urban play.

Recognising the need for adults to permit children to play, and the spaces in which to do so, is an important part of the battle. Recognising that all children, regardless of their abilities, need to play is the second step. Next, we look at playspaces for children with disabilities: both where they can play equitably in public spaces, and an example of how to design a truly enriching educational environment.

8
DESIGNING INCLUSIVE PLAYSPACES

Katherine Masiulanis

As a Landscape Architect working in the field of play, briefs often come to me with the phrase "design a playground for all ages and abilities". In this section, I'd like to discuss some of the considerations in designing a playspace which really does provide an inclusive and engaging environment for as wide a cross-section of our community as possible.

Crucially, I think it is most important to recognise that children with disabilities are children first. Their disability comes a distant second. All children enjoy play of one sort or another, and benefit enormously from it, physically, emotionally and socially. Secret spaces, high spaces, elements which challenge a child, elements which capture a child's interest in its sensory detail or which capture their imagination are just as important for a child with disabilities as for any other child. Equally, dull, repetitive or condescending playspaces do not serve either group.

Be aware that some of the barriers to children with disabilities may already be in the head of the designer or the commissioning organisation. To quote Alison Lee:

> One of the most important considerations … when caring for a disabled child and providing for their play and learning activities is to never make assumptions! It should not be assumed that a child who wears a leg calliper cannot climb, or that a child in a wheelchair will not enjoy feeling the sand between their toes. … it is absolutely crucial that you do not discriminate against a child with disabilities because you assume they cannot do something or will not enjoy it as a result of their disability.[1]

The phrase 'children with a disability' (itself somewhat contentious, but used here with no intended offence) covers a very wide range of impairments, including physical disabilities of varying degrees, intellectual and learning issues, sensory disabilities (such as degrees of deafness, blindness or a combination of the two) and behavioural disabilities (such as autism). Although children in wheelchairs are the ones people most often consider when thinking about accessibility, this is actually the least common type of impairment,[2] although one which requires the most careful consideration of the physical environment. If a new playspace is to be in a public environment, it is particularly important to design for carers who may have disabilities also.

Some of the most rewarding design projects are for Special Needs and Specialist Schools, which cater for a distinct group of children. In this case, staff (including all the specialist staff such as Physiotherapists, Occupational Therapists, Art and Music teachers), parents and often the children themselves are able to be quite specific about their particular desires, needs and challenges. The most important part of designing play environments for these schools is to listen to the wealth of knowledge that these people have.

Sometimes the playspace will provide exactly the same challenges, sensory richness and equipment that any other space would. At other times, fascinating possibilities are opened for the designer to embrace elements which, for example, catch and enhance the temperature changes of the weather, or increase the focus on linking pattern throughout a space, and will be of particular benefit to this group of children.

One special school I worked with catered primarily for children and young adults with moderate to severe intellectual disabilities. There was a perception in the wider design team that it would be good to have a 'visually and physically permeable' boundary to the school, to encourage interaction and acceptance with the wider community: a seemingly well intentioned and worthwhile approach. The staff were firmly against this idea, noting that their students needed privacy. If a student was 'acting out', which at times included undressing, staff needed to be able to retreat to ensure that the behaviour was not reinforced through attention, whilst knowing that the student was safe, and their personal dignity maintained. Likewise, staff at a school for deaf and deaf-blind children enlightened me to the hazards of plastic slides for their students. The static electricity built up by the slides can disable the mapping of deaf children's cochlear implants. In a neighbourhood playspace, the need to turn off their implants to avoid this can lead to isolation from their peers.[3]

Examples like this point to the necessity of taking a broader view when designing for a more general public space. One of the most important aspects of playspace design in this context has to be social inclusion. To quote Keith Christensen:

> Designers need to understand the difference between accessibility (the removal of physical barriers), and inclusion (the removal of social barriers).

In my work, I have often come across well intentioned people who work specifically in the Accessibility field who do not understand that physical access at the cost of social inclusion is of dubious value. It has been noted that the most common effect of any child's disability is peer isolation. As designers, we are able to design spaces which promote social inclusion and interaction with other children, but it is harder to buy this kind of space 'off-the-shelf'. It is also necessary to recognise that in the real world, where budgets and space are not infinite, it will probably not be possible to make every element in a playspace accessible to everybody: but that is no excuse not to provide a good range of play experiences that each person can access.

Research suggests that there are multiple benefits beyond enjoyment when a child can choose where they play, as "when children with disabilities gain greater independent mobility, they also show improved social, cognitive and language development".[4]

Removal of physical barriers is a necessary and important part of the design of inclusive playspaces, but not simply so that a child or carer can get to all areas and pieces of equipment. For example, some standard play equipment is provided with 'transfer decks', which theoretically allow a child in a wheelchair to slide across from their chair on to the equipment. However, if the child is then forced into the humiliating position of needing to crawl around the structure, this is a very poor example of social inclusion.

It has been suggested that one of the keys to successful interaction between children with and without disabilities is the ability for the child with a disability to participate in an activity without drawing unnecessary attention to their impairment.[5] Two examples of this spring to mind. The first is the ability to use a shop counter or sand play table 'front-on'.[6] Children in wheelchairs, pushers or who use walking aids need to be able to access these types of activities in the same way as everyone else: face on. This means, for example, that the counter or table needs to be of a suitable height, and also that there is room for their aid underneath the structure.

The second example is multi-level structures which for one reason or another (such as budget or extreme level change) cannot be accessed at the upper level, unless one is able-bodied. In this case, if a child with a disability is still able to be at the centre of the action, and able to participate in play on the upper level, whether through interactive elements, talk tubes or periscopes, then some opportunity for social inclusion remains. Interactive activities should highlight the similarities between children if there is to be a chance of them playing together.

That said, I question the value of providing play elements which can be accessed by children with a disability, but which exclude able-bodied children, as this too can lead to social isolation. A shop counter, for example, which is 700mm/2.3 feet or more high to allow a child in a wheelchair to access it front on, will be too high for a toddler who may wish to use this item. Specific wheelchair swings, which are locked and fenced from the rest of the playground, risk being labelled as 'for the disabled kids', whereas another item which is open to use by everyone is more likely to provide interaction and friendship between children.

My feeling is that if budget and space allows, it is always better to provide multiple options for the same activity, or spaces which have the possibility of being changed from day to day.

Likewise, it has been recommended that overly diligent application of some disability Standards can be confusing and exclusive in a play setting. For example, widespread use of TGSIs (Tactile Ground Surface Indicators) can be more confusing than otherwise for a child with a vision impairment in the complex environment of a playspace, although of course they should be used where a serious danger exists, as presented under the various Building Codes.[7] However, more subtle elements like using highly visible edges to steps will probably be useful to many people who use the space. If in doubt, there are many good Access Consultants who will be able to advise on the most legible way to delineate a play environment.

Often, a playspace has one or more structures, and I'd like to offer a few pointers when designing these for children in wheelchairs and with mobility aids, who, as I have said earlier, require the most substantial alterations to 'standard' play equipment. If these structures are to be not just accessible, but also worthwhile play pieces, the designer needs to consider a few additional aspects. Clearly the first is whether the child can reach the structure: seamless access. Perhaps this sounds obvious, but many times I have seen ramped structures in the middle of a loose surface such as timber mulch which is hard to traverse, or even with a step at the bottom of the ramp!

Head height is also a hidden barrier. Often the under deck space is underutilised, and could be a fantastic place for imaginative and complex inclusive social play. However, a child in a wheelchair will find it difficult to access these places if they are simply too low. I would suggest that an absolute minimum of 1600mm/5.25 feet is required to allow the majority of children to use these spaces. There also needs to be room to move and manoeuvre in a space. Typically a wheelchair can pass through a gap as narrow as a doorway, but will need much more (at least 1800mm/6 feet of clear space) to be able to turn around.

Ramps should be designed with care and attention. There are great advantages in allowing a child to be higher than everyone else, which is a particularly unusual experience if you are always seated. However, some ramps can be a very long road to that high place. Each country has standards of some sort describing the requirements for maximum grades, required landings and handrails. Consider using the landform of your site to circumvent some of the height gain, for example by accessing what is effectively the top of a retained space. Think hard about what the play experiences are on the way up. Is there a play activity on each landing, for example, interaction between levels, or are there manipulable elements on the handrails? When the high place is finally reached, ensure that there is something exciting a child with a mobility aid can use, and also the space to turn around or proceed on another journey.

Providing options when it comes to play is terribly important, as it allows children to choose the equipment or space which best suits their development at any particular time. Children with an intellectual disability, for example, may wish to play with equipment which is usually designed for younger, and hence smaller, children. Including elements like large swing seats not only allows these children to play, but also parents and carers to play alongside their children. Playspaces with options for both active play and respite in quieter, more sheltered spots allow children to choose when and whether they participate with a larger group, which can be particularly important for children with autism. Naturally, both of these strategies broaden the play opportunities for all children and members of the public.

When evaluating a design, step into the shoes of those who will be using it. If you are sighted, consider what it would be like to walk around the space blindfolded: would there be a clear logic to the space, edges to follow or other sensory cues to guide you? If you used a wheelchair, could you move easily from wherever you arrive in the space to a range of interesting activities, and use them as other children do? We can never replicate the experience of a person with a disability, but that does not remove our obligation to consider their perspective.

Fencing is an issue that is often raised in relation to accessible playspaces, and one which needs to be carefully considered. Research has proven that a very high percentage of children with autism spectrum disorder wander from places of safety, and this is obviously of great concern in public places.[8] If there are several playspaces in your neighbourhood, at least some of them should be fully fenced. However, be aware that fencing can also absorb large parts of the available playspace budget, and so perhaps this should be done strategically so those spaces that offer the best play opportunities for these children are treated in this way. The fence need not be a tight collar around the equipment, no child likes to feel that they are in a cage, but should encompass some areas where natural play is available, and also if possible picnic areas or places to kick a ball. Fencing may also be made less formidable by softening it with planting, or including playful elements within its structure.

There are many aspects to designing great accessible playspaces, but a few points to consider may include:

- Providing spaces with a sense of enclosure, like cubbies, tunnels and under deck areas.
- Many children who use mobility aids love to gain elevation, as they rarely have this advantage over others.
- Respite spaces and seating (which need not be formal: rocks, logs or art elements can be just as suitable as a park bench).
- If providing an activity in which a smaller child who uses a wheelchair may be lifted out of their chair to participate (such as a basket swing), ensure that there is room to 'park' the mobility aid without being in the way of other users.
- For children who cannot sit unaided, a spot where a carer can sit against a backrest with a child in their lap can be most helpful (such as at the edge of sandpits).[9]
- A range of stepping opportunities, of different sizes and grades, can be useful practice for the 'real world', but should be integrated into the playspace, so that they become part of the play, rather than a physiotherapy exercise.
- Accessible sandplay tables with a way for children to independently access the sand if possible (through conveyors, bucket and pulley or chutes) are popular with all children as they provide a 'special' place to build.
- Shade is important for all children, but can be particularly so for children who may become involved in the play in one area for a long time (such as sandpits), particularly if their medication makes them photosensitive.[10]
- A legible path and accessible system between different activity areas, whilst retaining some surprise and sense of adventure when encountering new opportunities. Sometimes it can be valuable to provide a 'tactile plan' in a key location within the playspace if it is large or complex. Otherwise, ensuring that there are distinct 'feelings', scents or colours can aid with orientation. Consider the inclusion of scented planting at particular places, the feelings that arise through being in an open space or surrounded by structure, the sounds of wind through the leaves, musical elements or the grind of gravel under your feet. All these experiences will assist a child with a vision impairment to know where they are within a familiar play environment.
- The amenities and infrastructure which socially support a playspace, such as seamless access into the site, accessible toilets and drinking fountains at different heights.[11]

One of the most valuable experiences provided for any child is that of 'free play'. This most often occurs in a natural environment, where there is access to loose parts, which a child may choose or use as they wish. Free play "establishes children's disposition to take risks and to believe that they are competent, capable learners".[12] During free play, children play at their own discretion, making up games and activities, without a structure imposed by adults. This can be of particular importance to children with a disability, as they tend to spend more time indoors, in schools and other places where play is structured and organised.

It is often more difficult for children with a disability to independently access natural materials, which can be hard enough for any child in an increasingly programmed, risk-averse, urbanised landscape, as will be discussed in more detail in other sections of this book. However, the potential benefits are enormous. To quote again, "Research shows, too, that children who have behavioural or learning difficulties often perform much better in an outdoor setting".[13] This appears particularly relevant to children with ADHD, who find that natural environments allow them to slow down and benefit from improved attention span.

One study of summer camps with extensive access to nature in America has shown that people with disabilities "seek risk, challenge, and adventure in the outdoors just as do their contemporaries without disabilities",[14] and that by doing so, they gain positive body image, as well as improved initiative and self-direction. It seems a shame to limit anyone's access to experiences with these benefits, which is obtained so easily through the provision of a playspace with natural and challenging elements. I suspect that often it is simply easier to turn to what has been replicated in a hundred other places than to consider the individual merits and possibilities of a site.

Sometimes parents, school or council staff have concerns about providing these types of loose materials, as they fear that their use will reduce the safety of children in the playspace. Sticks may be used as 'swords', and rocks and sand may be thrown. This is to some extent true, but also true of many other things commonly available to children, should they choose to use them in that way. To quote a head teacher who introduced loose materials into their school ground, "If we take away all risk, children will never learn anything".[15] In another study involving introducing 'Play Pods' to schools, the rate of accidents, incidents and unwanted behaviour substantially decreased when loose materials were introduced, as children were actively and positively engaged in play, rather than being bored. Children were also much more likely to be co-operative and inclusive with their peers: one of the keys to social inclusion of children with a disability.

This is surely one of the best ways a designer or Landscape Architect can contribute to the quality of the play experience in a truly inclusive playspace, as we work with the whole setting. In the place of a piece of plastic play equipment, neatly edged and fenced in the middle of an area of grass, we can encourage better integration into the natural environment, where children can take advantage of the existing features of the site, such as trees, mounding or boulders. We can then enhance this space with planting that encourages free nature play, having flowers, leaves or bark which are attractive to children. Logs and boulders become private seating spaces, castles or spaceships, as they do not have the prescriptive quality of much manufactured play equipment. Sensory details such as pebbles, sand, mulch and the sight, smell and texture of plants all contribute to the richness of this environment.

Most importantly, by providing these sorts of experiences in connection with some of the other physical and social accessibility measures mentioned above, we can design playspaces which are better for every child, in all their varied and developing abilities, sizes and tastes.

"It is not always the amount of money that makes the best play environments, but the quality of time and energy in planning for play opportunities."[16]

9
GLENALLEN SCHOOL

Mary Jeavons

Glenallen School, located in the eastern suburbs of Melbourne, Australia, provides individual learning programmes for students with physical disabilities and health impairments requiring paramedical support. The students are aged between five and eighteen years. The student population includes students with complex, severe and multiple disabilities. The previous junior school playground was not suited to the needs of these students and did not allow these students to actively interact with the environment. It also had a level change of close to 3m/10 feet over a short distance.

To address this lack of appropriate outdoor play environments, we were engaged to design a new play area that would cater for the needs of both mobile students and those with physical challenges. The design of an accessible inclusive play space that enables these students to play out of doors requires a high level of detailed design. Critical to the project was the strong relationship established between the school community (especially the specialist teachers and therapists) and the designers.

Collaboration

Jeavons Landscape Architects collaborated closely with school educators, therapists and students in order to understand the needs of the students, the benefits they sought from their play environment and how to best meet their complex needs.

Consultation sessions included meetings with staff and conversations with students about their play. These findings were supplemented by research, technical investigations and observations of the students outside at lunch time and breaks.

Principles

The following fundamental principles underpin this project, above and beyond children's right and need to play:

- Outdoor play is fundamentally important to the development of all children.
- Play is a critical tool in learning and development and has intrinsic value.
- Children with disabilities are often highly disadvantaged in accessing quality play opportunities. However, their need for play is equal, if not greater, in overcoming the effects of their disabilities.
- Play environments can also be successfully used for therapeutic and adult directed teaching purposes, but these are not their only purpose.
- For children with severe physical and intellectual disabilities, the concept of free play has to be negotiated, as many children need help to initiate and sustain play.

Functional requirements

The Glenallen outdoor space needed to meet multiple complex needs for children of a very wide range of physical and intellectual ages and abilities. As a basis, the space had to remain physically and universally accessible to children, some of whom are ambulant and some of whom use mobility aids such as walking frames, wheelchairs and beds.

Beyond physical access, it also needed to cater for the school's social, teaching and psychological requirements. These can be broadly divided into independent play and therapeutic requirements, and extend well beyond the traditional physical characteristics of designed play environments.

For example, to support the students' free time play, it was desirable for the space not only to be visually appealing, but also to encourage social interaction, imaginative/role play and learning by children who typically do not easily engage with their peers. Closely related to this type of interactive behaviour, the playspace also needed to encourage communication between children, as a tool within each child's communication strategy. From a therapeutic perspective, the outdoor area ought to be a space where therapy can be playful and willingly undertaken. Staff should be able to utilise the outdoor spaces in individual student teaching and learning programmes, while also providing for rest and respite in an attractive natural setting. In addition, the school identified some highly specific therapeutic needs such as:

- Learning to walk
- Encouraging specific physical movements
- Engaging with music and sound
- Integrating the senses and overcoming sensory aversions
- Encouraging abstract and imaginative play and thinking, and
- Engaging with sensory and loose materials in a creative way.

The design outcome

As a teaching, learning and therapeutic space (as well as a free play area), the new physical environment of this outdoor play space is fully integrated with the learning programmes of the school. The new outdoor play space not only fulfils the brief, but also includes art works and a gathering place for the school community. It includes a range of zones with particular play purposes that are discussed below.

Glenallen School   **81**

FIGURE 9.1 The outdoor play environment at Glenallen integrates natural and built form
Photo: Andrew Lloyd

Themed role play areas

Many children with an intellectual/cognitive disability have trouble in initiating imaginative/ role play and the intention was to assist with this process and stimulate play, communication, interaction and learning. The space is therefore less abstract than other play settings should typically be.

The space is divided into a number of themed outdoor zones. The themes were developed in collaboration with the children and staff. They are intended to build on concepts that the children may be familiar with such as a camping space and teepee, helicopter, train, touchy-feely/sensory spaces, a play stream with a water pump and an 'underground' tunnel.

Highly detailed art works and tuned musical instruments add sensory layers to all areas. The helicopter and the train have wheelchair accessible control panels for role play. The teepee is located at the back of the space on a higher level and provides a good getaway and social space for the older children.

Terrain for walking, wheeling and elevation

Some major constraints in terms of site levels became an advantage and were carefully incorporated into the space's design. A wheelchair accessible graded walking track around the perimeter passes through planted areas and under some beautiful pre-existing eucalyptus trees. The trail encourages movement around the site, and connects onto an elevated bridge and structure, allowing a great opportunity for overlooking. For children who use wheelchairs and are usually physically looked down upon by others, this is a good opportunity to in turn look down upon others, and indeed over a whole space.

The graded terrain and elevated structures provide height that supports accessible climbing and sliding activities, and includes easy stairs to encourage this skill for those who can manage stepping. The gentle ramped access from both sides allows a full circuit without having to turn and return the same way. The ground level terrain has flat sections and undulating areas that require children to learn to negotiate a world that is not flat.

Walking pod

Learning physical movement and communication, with a goal towards independence, is an important theme in this project. The 'assisted walking pod' is an example.

The design team worked with the physiotherapists to design a 'pod' where students are encouraged to move out of their mobility devices (wheelchairs and walking frames) into a safe space; pull themselves up to a standing position; and then use a rail to help them move independently around the circular space. Whilst this is hard work for the students, they are motivated by the beautiful ceramic artworks by James Cattell of Honeyweather and Speight.

These ceramic works are incorporated into a semi-circular wall with a child height railing. All along the wall, detailed and intriguing miniature space people float through a sky of ceramic stars and moons, and there are little niches children can look into and see other figures. The wall demands further investigation.

Swinging and rocking play equipment

Movements such as swinging and rocking are valued for play and also have therapeutic value to develop children's vestibular sense and improve balance. The existing wheelchair accessible Liberty Swing was retained, as was a large spring rocker that offers back support for users. A new swing with a large bird's nest style seat allows children many options for sitting or lying on their own, or with others, as they swing or rock.

FIGURE 9.2 Walking pod details. Constructed by Honeyweather and Speight
Photo: Mary Jeavons

Music

Musical instruments by Herbert Jercher provide opportunities for engagement with music and sound for even the least able children. The musical sculptures produce a variety of sounds, invite engagement, provide a response (cause and effect connection) and do not require fine motor skills or co-ordination. They add to the rich sensory opportunities in the play setting.

Sensory tunnel

An important part of the design brief was to incorporate a wheelchair accessible tunnel that could be darkened and used for sensory development with specially designed lighting. The tunnel also has textured ceramic details along its wall that encourage touch and feeling. The tunnel proved to be difficult to make dark enough for the lighting to be effective, but the enclosed space nonetheless forms a useful contrast to the open areas in the play space.

Gathering/performance space

These sheltered structures provide social/gathering spaces at lunch time and recess, as well as a stage and opportunities for performances, dancing and impromptu play. The window openings allow for puppet type shows.

Sand

An extensive sand play area provides access both at ground level and to elevated areas for children in wheelchairs. Children can enter the ground level sand pit easily using walking frames or crawling. Set with a beached edge flush with the surrounding surface there are also synthetic grass mounds to provide support for lying. The sand play area is protected by a large roof, and has proved to be a highly successful focal point for the whole space.

One of the unexpected benefits arose when children started to use the rails of an adjacent ramped boardwalk to slide along, holding onto the rails and then throwing themselves back into the soft sand, laughing together. The children's therapists noted that this sideways sliding movement is important as a therapy but usually hard to persuade children to do. The space has encouraged them to do it voluntarily.

Gardens and planting

We deliberately selected a wide range of plant materials to maximise the sensory interest and tactile values of the space without sensory overload. This requires a fine balance. Robust native and indigenous plantings with low water requirements are balanced with exotic plants to give highlights of colour and strong textures to stimulate children with high sensory thresholds.

Post-occupancy evaluation

No matter how thorough the detailed design of a space, there will always be elements which cannot be fully understood until they are in use. It was always the intention of the design

84 Mary Jeavons

FIGURE 9.3 Children at Glenallen school using the hand rail along the ramp as a playful element that also delivers therapeutic movement

Photo: Mary Jeavons

FIGURE 9.4 The raised sand pits at Glenallen; the modified trays allowing wheelchair access are visible on the left in the background

Photo: Andrew Lloyd

to provide full access to the sand play areas for children using all mobility aids, including wheelchairs.

The initial design of the raised sand pit proved to be difficult to use for many children with mobility aids, as they range enormously in size, from small walking frames to large electric powered wheelchairs for older children. There proved to be insufficient overhang, and children couldn't effectively reach the sand.

Following the post-occupancy evaluation, the sand pit edges were modified to provide much more depth and space under the edge for front wheels, and a greater range of heights to accommodate different sized children and chairs. The resulting changes with a range of different elevations and profiles allowed all children to play in the sand successfully.

Conclusion

In conclusion, this project demonstrates the benefits of a quality outdoor play environment to all children and in particular to children with severe disabilities. Consulting children and their teachers always proves beneficial, as does a post-occupancy evaluation. The Glenallen School project shows how very fine details are critically important to get right, as they ultimately determine how accessible or inclusive or functional any particular design will be.

Staff report that the whole school community still enjoy the space, which was completed in 2012.

Notes

Chapter 1

1. Factor J. *Captain Cook chased a chook: children's folklore in Australia*. Ringwood, Victoria: Penguin; 1988.
2. Baxter JE. *The archaeology of childhood: children, gender, and material culture*. Walnut Creek, CA: AltaMira Press; 2005.
3. Sofaer Derevenski J, editor. *Children and material culture*. London and New York: Routledge; 2000.
4. McBride A. Where are all the ancient playgrounds? Toronto: Public places past and present; 2014 [6 January 2015]. Available from: https://publicplacespastpresent.wordpress.com/2014/05/27/where-are-all-the-ancient-playgrounds/.
5. Ariès P. *Centuries of childhood: a social history of family life*. New York: Knopf; 1962.
6. Sutton-Smith B. *A history of children's play: New Zealand 1840–1950*. Philadelphia: University of Pennsylvania Press; 1981.
7. Adams A, Van Slyck AA. Children's spaces. In: Fass PS, editor. *Encyclopedia of children and childhood in history and society*, 1. New York: Thomson Gale; 2003. p. 187–94.
8. Cunningham H. *Children and childhood in Western Society since 1500*, 2nd ed. Harlow, England: Pearson/Longman; 2005.
9. Tuan Y-F. Children and the natural environment. In: Altman I, Wohlwill JF, editors. *Children and the environment*. New York and London: Plenum Press; 1978. p. 5–32.
10. Adams A, Van Slyck AA. Children's spaces. In: Fass PS, editor. *Encyclopedia of children and childhood in history and society*, 1. New York: Thomson Gale; 2003. p. 187–94.
11. Wassong S. The German influence on the development of the US playground movement. *Sport in History*. 2008;28(2):313–28.
12. Frost JL. Evolution of American playgrounds. *Scholarpedia*. 2012;7(12):30423.
13. Cavallo D. *Muscles and morals: organized playgrounds and urban reform, 1880–1920*. Philadelphia: University of Pennsylvania Press; 1981.
14. Gatley J. Giant strides: the formation of supervised playgrounds in Adelaide and Brisbane. *Journal of the Historical Society of South Australia*. 2001;(29):34–46.
15. Shehory-Rubin Z, Shvarts S. Teaching the children to play: the establishment of the first playgrounds in Palestine during the Mandate. *Israel Studies*. 2010;15(ii):24–48.
16. Howell O. Play pays: urban land politics and playgrounds in the United States, 1900–1930. *Journal of Urban History*. 2008;34(6):961–94.
17. Solomon SG. Foreword. In: Biondo B, editor. *Once upon a playground: a celebration of classic American playgrounds, 1920–1975*. Lebanon, NH: University Press of New England; 2014.
18. de Coninck-Smith N. Where should children play? City planning seen from knee-height: Copenhagen 1870 to 1920. *Children's Environment Quarterly*. 1990;7(4):54–61.
19. Goodman C. *Choosing sides: playground and street life on the Lower East Side*. New York: Schocken Books; 1979.
20. Kernan M. Developing citizenship through supervised play: the Civics Institute of Ireland playgrounds, 1933–75. *History of Education*. 2005;34(6):675–87.
21. Solomon SG. Foreword. In: Biondo B, editor. *Once upon a playground: a celebration of classic American playgrounds, 1920–1975*. Lebanon, NH: University Press of New England; 2014.
22. Kozlovsky R. Adventure playgrounds and postwar reconstruction. In: Gutman M, de Coninck-Smith N, editors. *Designing modern childhoods: history, space and the material culture of children*. New Brunswick, NJ: Rutgers University Press; 2008.
23. Solomon SG. *American playgrounds: revitalizing community space*. Hanover, NH: University Press of New England; 2005.
24. Highmore B. Playgrounds and bombsites: postwar Britain's ruined landscapes. *Cultural Politics*. 2013;9(3):323–36.
25. Solomon SG. *American playgrounds: revitalizing community space*. Hanover, NH: University Press of New England; 2005.
26. Peterson GT. 'Playgrounds which would never happen now, because they'd be far too dangerous': risk, childhood development and radical sites of theatre practice. *Research in Drama Education*. 2011;16(3):385–402.
27. Clendaniel M. Fall down, go boom. *Education Digest*. 2009(6):31–6.

28 Frost JL. Evolution of American playgrounds. *Scholarpedia*. 2012;7(12):30423.
29 Solomon SG. Foreword. In: Biondo B, editor. *Once upon a playground: a celebration of classic American playgrounds, 1920–1975*. Lebanon, NH: University Press of New England; 2014.
30 Solomon SG. *American playgrounds: revitalizing community space*. Hanover, NH: University Press of New England; 2005.
31 Oudenampsen M. Aldo van Eyck and the city as playground. In: Méndez de Andés A, editor. *Urbanacción 07/09*. Madrid: La Casa Encendida; 2010, p. 25–39.
32 Pursell C. The safe and rational children's playground. *History Australia*. 2011;8(3):47–74.
33 Solomon SG. *American playgrounds: revitalizing community space*. Hanover, NH: University Press of New England; 2005.
34 Pursell C. The safe and rational children's playground. *History Australia*. 2011;8(3):47–74.
35 Solomon SG. *American playgrounds: revitalizing community space*. Hanover, NH: University Press of New England; 2005.
36 Clendaniel M. Fall down, go boom. *Education Digest*. 2009(6):31–6.
37 Pursell C. The safe and rational children's playground. *History Australia*. 2011;8(3):47–74.
38 Solomon SG. *American playgrounds: revitalizing community space*. Hanover, NH: University Press of New England; 2005.
39 Christiansen M. Playground safety around the world. *Parks and Recreation*. 2001 April:72–7.
40 Frost JL. Evolution of American playgrounds. *Scholarpedia*. 2012;7(12):30423.
41 Frost JL. History of playground safety in America. *Children's Environments Quarterly*. 1985;2(4):13–23.
42 Louv R. *Last child in the woods: saving our children from nature-deficit disorder*. Chapel Hill, North Carolina: Algonquin Books; 2005.
43 Frost JL. Evolution of American playgrounds. *Scholarpedia*. 2012;7(12):30423.
44 Gaster S. Urban children's access to their neighbourhood: changes over three generations. *Environment and Behaviour*. 1991;23(1):70–85.
45 Karsten L. It all used to be better? Different generations on continuity and change in urban children's daily use of space. *Children's Geographies*. 2005;3(3):275–90.
46 Gill T. *No fear: growing up in a risk averse society*. London: Calouste Gulbenkian Foundation; 2007.
47 Pascoe C. Be home by dark: childhood freedoms and adult fears in 1950s Victoria. *Australian Historical Studies*. 2009;40(2):215–31.
48 Pooley C, Turnbull J, Adams M. Kids in town: the changing action space and visibility of young people in urban areas. In: Schildt A, Siegfried D, editors. *European cities, youth and the public sphere in the Twentieth Century*. Aldershot, Hampshire: Ashgate; 2005. p. 90–109.
49 Chawla L. Childhood place attachments. In: Altman I, Low SM, editors. *Place attachment*. New York and London: Plenum Press; 1992. p. 63–86.
50 Hart R. Containing children: some lessons on planning for play from New York City. *Environment and Urbanization*. 2002;14(2):135–48.
51 Ward C. *The child in the city*. Harmondsworth, Middlesex: Penguin; 1979.
52 Pascoe C. *Spaces imagined, places remembered: childhood in 1950s Australia*. Newcastle upon Tyne, UK: Cambridge Scholars Publishing; 2011.
53 Sleight S. *Young people and the shaping of public space in Melbourne, 1870–1914*. Surrey, UK: Ashgate; 2013.
54 Dienel H-L, Schophaus M. Urban wastelands and the development of youth cultures in Berlin since 1945, with comparative perspectives on Amsterdam and Naples. In: Schildt A, Siegfried D, editors. *European cities, youth and the public sphere in the Twentieth Century*. Aldershot, Hampshire: Ashgate; 2005. p. 110–33.
55 Lynch K, editor. *Growing up in cities: studies of the spatial environment of adolescence in Cracow, Melbourne, Mexico City, Salta, Toluca, and Warszawa*. Cambridge, MA: The MIT Press; 1977.
56 Rasmussen K. Places for children – children's places. *Childhood*. 2004;11(2):155–73.
57 Howell O. Play pays: urban land politics and playgrounds in the United States, 1900–1930. *Journal of Urban History*. 2008;34(6):961-94.
58 Pawlikowska-Piechotka A. Urban outdoor recreation: children's playgrounds in Warsaw. *Studies in Physical Culture and Tourism*. 2010;17(4):375–84.
59 Gharahbeiglu M. Children's interaction with urban play spaces in Tabriz, Iran. *Visual Studies*. 2007;22(1):48–52.
60 Gill T, Gill C. Our story. Leicestershire, UK: East African Playgrounds; 2015 [30 July 2015]. Available from: http://eastafricanplaygrounds.org/story/.

61 Johnston L, Marker M. WestPoint Financial Group donates $32,000 during National Adoption Month to build playground for Russian orphans. Indianapolis, IN: *KidsFirst Foundation*; 2008 [30 July 2015]. Available from: http://www.kidsfirst-foundation.org/press/pressrelease_1108.pdf.
62 Mathee A, Singh E, Mogotsi M, Timothy G, Maduka B, Olivier J, et al. Lead-based paint on playground equipment in public children's parks in Johannesburg, Tshwane and Ekurhuleni. *South African Medical Journal*. 2009;99(11):819–21.
63 Ozdemir H, Mertoglu B, Demir G, Deniz A, Toros H. Case study of PM pollution in playgrounds in Istanbul. *Theoretical & Applied Climatology*. 2012;108(3/4):553–62.
64 Figueiredo AMG, Tocchini M, dos Santos TFS. Urban environmental pollution 2010: metals in playground soils of São Paulo city, Brazil. *Procedia Environmental Sciences*. 2011;4:303–9.
65 Keon-ha L, Young-eun K. A study on the play space of residential complexes for children in Hefei, China. *Architectural Research*. 2012;14(2):57–65.
66 Moore R, Young D. Childhood outdoors: towards a social ecology of the landscape. In: Altman I, Wohlwill JF, editors. *Children and the environment*. New York and London: Plenum Press; 1978. p. 83–130.
67 Moore RC. *Childhood's domain: play and place in child development*. London: Croom Helm; 1986.
68 Kumar N. Lessons from contemporary schools. *Sociological Bulletin*. 1998;47(1):33–49.
69 Wolcott VW. *Race, riots, and roller coasters: the struggle over segregated recreation in America*. Philadelphia: University of Pennsylvania Press; 2012.
70 Shehory-Rubin Z, Shvarts S. Teaching the children to play: the establishment of the first playgrounds in Palestine during the Mandate. *Israel Studies*. 2010;15(ii):24–48.
71 Dogliani P. Environment and leisure in Italy during Fascism. *Modern Italy*. 2014;19(3):247–59.
72 Solomon SG. American playgrounds: revitalizing community space. Hanover, NH: University Press of New England; 2005.

Chapter 2

1 Article 31 General Comment. United Nations, 'Convention on the Rights of the Child.' 2012.
2 Jane Austen depicts a society which, for all its seeming privileges (pleasant houses, endless hours of leisure), closely monitors behaviour. http://www.bl.uk/romantics-and-victorians/articles/jane-austen-and-social-judgement.
3 'Bubble wrapping' is a coin termed by American Lenore Skenazy who is a contemporary advocate for free ranging children, and the author of *Free Range Kids*.

Chapter 3

1 Kail RV. Longitudinal evidence that increases in processing speed and working memory enhance children's reasoning. *Psychological Science*. 2007;18(4):312–13.
2 Woodward A, Needham A. *Learning and the infant mind*. New York, NY, US: Oxford University Press; 2009.
3 Lightfoot C, Cole M, Cole S. *The development of children* (7th ed.). New York, NY: Worth; 2012.
4 Carey S. *The origin of concepts*. New York, NY, US: Oxford University Press; 2009.
5 Rhodes M, Wellman H. Constructing a new theory from old ideas and new evidence. *Cognitive Science*. 2013;37(3):592–604.
6 Vygotsky LS. *Mind in society: The development of higher psychological processes*. Cambridge, MA: Harvard University Press; 1978.
7 Nelson K. Narrative practices and folk psychology: a perspective from developmental psychology. *Journal of Consciousness Studies*. 2009;16(6/8):69–93.
8 Gibson EJ. Perceptual learning in development: Some basic concepts. *Ecological Psychology*. 2000;12(4):295–302.
9 Saffran JR, Aslin RN, Newport EL. Statistical learning by 8-month-old infants. *Science*. 1996;274(5294):1926–8.
10 Spelke ES, Phillips A, Woodward AL. Infants' knowledge of object motion and human action. In: Sperber D, Premack D, Premack AJ, editors. *Causal cognition: a multidisciplinary debate*. New York, NY, US: Clarendon Press/Oxford University Press; 1995. p. 44–78.

11 Bowlby J. *Attachment and Loss. Vol. 1: Attachment*. New York: Basic Books; 1969.
12 Harris P. *The work of the imagination*. Oxford: Blackwell; 2000.
13 Taylor M. *Imaginary companions and the children who create them*. New York: Oxford University Press; 1999.
14 McLoyd VC. The effects of the structure of play objects on the pretend play of low-income preschool children. *Child Development*. 1983;54(3):626–35.
15 Smith PK, Takhvar M, Gore N, Vollstedt R. Play in young children: Problems of definition, categorization and measurement. *Early Child Development and Care*. 1985;19(1–2);25–41.
16 Engel S. *The hungry mind: the origins of curiosity in childhood*. Cambridge, MA, US: Harvard University Press; 2015.
17 Harris P. *The work of the imagination*. Oxford: Blackwell; 2000.
18 Montessori M. *Dr. Montessori's own handbook*. New York: Schocken Books; 1965.
19 Siegler RS. Children's learning. *American Psychologist*. 2005;60(8):769–78.
20 Vygotsky LS. *Mind in society: the development of higher psychological processes*. Cambridge, MA, US: Harvard University Press; 1978.
21 Rhodes M, Wellman H. Constructing a new theory from old ideas and new evidence. *Cognitive Science*. 2013;37(3):592–604.
22 Boland AM, Haden CA, Ornstein PA. Boosting children's memory by training mothers in the use of an elaborative conversational style as an event unfolds. *Journal of Cognition and Development*. 2003;4(1):39–65.
23 Muldoon KP, Lewis C, Berridge D. Predictors of early numeracy: Is there a place for mistakes when learning about number? *British Journal of Developmental Psychology*. 2007;25(4):543–58.
24 Ball LJ, Hoyle AM, Towse AS. The facilitatory effect of negative feedback on the emergence of analogical reasoning abilities. *British Journal of Developmental Psychology*. 2010;28(3):583–602.
25 Bosco FM, Bucciarelli M, Bara BG. Recognition and repair of communicative failures: a developmental perspective. *Journal of Pragmatics*. 2006;38(9):1398–429.
26 Kloos H, Van Orden GC. Can a preschooler's mistaken belief benefit learning? *Swiss Journal of Psychology/Schweizerische Zeitschrift für Psychologie/Revue Suisse de Psychologie*. 2005;64(3):195–205.
27 Boland AM, Haden CA, Ornstein PA. Boosting children's memory by training mothers in the use of an elaborative conversational style as an event unfolds. *Journal of Cognition and Development*. 2003;4(1):39–65.
28 Reis H, Collins WA, Berscheid E. The relationship context of human behavior and development. *Psychological Bulletin*. 2000;126(3):844–72.
29 Astington J, Jenkins J. Theory of mind development and social understanding. *Cognition and Emotion*. 1995;9:151–65.
30 Zahn-Waxler C, Radke-Yarrow M, Wagner E, Chapman M. Development of concern for others. *Developmental Psychology*. 1992;28(1):126–36.
31 Singer D, Singer J. *The house of make believe*. Cambridge: Harvard University Press; 1990.
32 Doyle A-B, Connolly J. Negotiation and enactment in social pretend play: Relations to social acceptance and social cognition. *Early Childhood Research Quarterly*. 1989;4(3):289–302.

Chapter 4

1 Greeno JG. Gibson's Affordances, *Psychological Review*. 1994;101(2):336–42.
2 Gibson JJ. *The Ecological Approach to Visual Perception*. Boston: Houghton Miflin; 1979. Greeno 1994. Kytta, M. Affordances of children's environments in the context of cities, small towns, suburbs and rural villages in Finland and Belarus. *Journal of Environmental Psychology*. 2002;22(1):109–123.
3 Greeno JG. Gibson's Affordances, *Psychological Review*. 1994;101(2):336–42.
4 Rubin KH. *The Play Observation Scale (POS)*. University of Maryland: Center for Children, Relationships, and Culture; 2001.
5 Barker R. On the nature of the environment. In: Proshansky H, Ittelson W, Rivlin L, editors. *Environmental psychology: People and their physical settings*. New York: Holt, Rinehart and Winston; 1976.
6 Cosco NG. Motivation to move: Physical activity affordances in preschool play areas. Edinburg: Heriot Watt University; 2006.
7 Moore R, Wong H. *Natural learning: the life history of an environmental schoolyard*. Mig Communications; 1997.

Chapter 5

1. Tom Turner, 2013, *British gardens: History, philosophy and design*. Oxford, Routledge, Taylor & Francis.
2. Alain de Botton, 2006, *The architecture of happiness*. Australia, Penguin Books.
3. Diana Witcher, 'Isamu Noguchi's utopian landscapes.' *Journal of Student Research*, p. 76.
4. Dr. Laura Markham's website: Aha! Parenting. Accessed: December 2014. http://www.ahaparenting.com/parenting-tools/family-life/structure-routines
5. Maria Kylin, 'Children's dens.' *Children, Youth and Environments*, Vol 13, No.1 (Spring 2003). http://www.colorado.edu/journals/cye/13_1/Vol13_1Articles/CYE_CurrentIssue_Article_Dens_Kylin.htm. Accessed: December 31, 2014.
6. Alison Lee, *Childminder's Guide to Child Development*, p. 65.
7. Le Corbusier, 2006, quoted in Alain de Botton, *The architecture of happiness*. Australia, Penguin Books.
8. 'Inside a European Adventure Playground' by Kasia Cieplak-Mayr von Baldegg – *The Atlanic* http://www.theatlantic.com/education/archive/2014/03/europes-adventure-playgrounds-look-way-more-fun/284521/. Accessed: June 30, 2015.
9. Maria Kylin, 'Children's dens.' *Children, Youth and Environments*, Vol 13, No.1 (Spring 2003). http://www.colorado.edu/journals/cye/13_1/Vol13_1Articles/CYE_CurrentIssue_Article_Dens_Kylin.htm. Accessed: December 31, 2014.
10. Terence Conran, 1996, *Terence Conran on Design*. London, Conran Octopus.
11. http://robinfox.com.au/projects/giant-theremin/. Accessed: June 30, 2015.
12. 'Didactic Discourse Blog.' Sculptural playground, Schulberg, Location: Wiesbaden, Germany. https://didacticdiscourse.wordpress.com/2011/10/27/sculptural-playground/. Accessed: May 18, 2015.

Chapter 7

1. Rubin, K.H., Fein, G., Vandenberg, B. (1983) 'Play,' in P.H. Mussen (ed) *Handbook of Psychology*, Vol. 4, pp. 693–755. New York: Wiley.
2. Malayankandy, Usha Ajithkumar (2014) 'Perceptions of Parents and Teachers in India on Play and Child Rights: A Comparative Study,' Human Rights Education in Asia-Pacific—Volume Five, Asia-Pacific Human Rights Information Center, Osak, p. 223–242.
3. Butterflies (2010) 'Conditions, attitudes and resources: A study collating information pertaining to state of "play" in the city of Delhi.'
4. Delhi Urban Environment and Infrastructure Improvement Board, 2009.
5. Brosius, Christiane (2010) *India's Middle Class: New Forms of Urban Leisure, Consumption and Prosperity*. New Delhi: Routledge.
6. 'Denied access to playground by elders, Mumbai kids complain to cops,' *First Post*, 10 July, 2013. Accessed at http://www.firstpost.com/india/denied-access-to-playground-by-elders-mumbai-kids-complain-to-cops-944059.html on 4 June, 2015.
7. Rajinder Nagar Welfare Association … vs Mcd And Ors on 26 April, 2011, WP(C) NO.13516/2009. Accessed at http://indiankanoon.org/doc/633727/ on 5 June 2015.
8. Bangalore Medical Trust Vs. BS Muddappa (1991) 4 SCC 54.
9. Mehra, Rakhi., Naik, Mukta., Randolph, Gregory (2012) 'Traditional Livelihoods and Community Centred Urban Development,' *Context* 9(2), 85–90. Micro Home Solutions (2011) 'Self construction: Enabling safe and affordable housing in India,' New Delhi.
10. Biswas, Sourav Kumar (2013) 'PLAY! Tactics & strategies for public spaces in Mumbai's informal city,' Observer Research Foundation, Mumbai.
11. http://timesofindia.indiatimes.com/city/delhi/Play-space-shrinking-but-slum-kids-are-game/articleshow/9391139.cms\.
12. Banerjee, Kanchan, Driskell, David D. (2002) 'Tales from Truth Town,' in L. Chawla (ed) *Growing up in an urbanising world*, pp. 135–160. London: Earthscan.
13. Chatterjee, Sudeshna (2015) 'Making children matter in slum transformations: Lessons from India's National Urban Renewal Mission,' *Journal of Urban Design*. DOI: 10.1080/13574809.2015.1044506

14 Oke, Meera, Khattar, Archna, Pant, Prarthana, Saraswati, T.S. (1999) 'A profile of children's play in urban India,' *Childhood* May 1999 vol. 6(2), 207–19.
15 Butterflies (2010) 'Conditions, attitudes and resources: A study collating information pertaining to state of "play" in the city of Delhi.'
16 An analysis of government data by NGO Child Rights and You (CRY) shows that child labour in urban India has increased by 53% in the period 2001–2011. Accessed at http://www.cry.org/about-cry/media-center/press-releases/child-labour-in-india-decreasing-at-a-snails-pace.html on 29 June 2015.
17 Naik, Mukta (2013) 'Building safe playgrounds where all kids can play,' *The Alternative*, http://www.thealternative.in/society/building-safe-playgrounds-where-all-kids-can-play/ Accessed at http://www.thealternative.in/society/building-safe-playgrounds-where-all-kids-can-play/ on 1 June 2015.

Chapter 8

1 Alison Lee, *Childminder's guide to child development*. Continuum, London, 2009.
2 Keith M. Christensen, Creating inclusive outdoor play environments: Designing for ability rather than disability, *MLA, The Journal of Eyewitness in Special Education*, 910 (Sept-Oct 2006): 48–55.
3 Yael Bat Chava and Elizabeth Deignan, *Peer relationships of children with cochlear implants*. Oxford University Press, Oxford, 2001.
4 P. Rosembaum, Physical activity play in children with disabilities: A neglected opportunity for research? *Child Development*, 69 (1998): 607–608.
5 Keith M. Christensen, Creating inclusive outdoor play environments: Designing for ability rather than disability, *MLA, The Journal of Eyewitness in Special Education*, 910 (Sept-Oct): 48–55.
6 Sue Elliott (ed), *The outdoor playspace naturally, for children birth to five years*. Pademelon Press, Australia, 2008.
7 Information from Murray Mountain, Director of Access Design Solutions, Brighton, Victoria, 2012.
8 Connie Anderson, J. Kiely Law, Amy Daniels, Catherine Rice, David S. Mandell, Louis Hagopian, Paul A. Law, occurrence and family impact of elopement in children with autism spectrum disorders, *Pediatrics*, 130, No. 5, (November 1, 2012): 870–877.
9 Sue Elliott (ed), *The outdoor playspace naturally, for children birth to five years*. Pademelon Press, Australia, 2008.
10 Ibid.
11 Information from Murray Mountain, Director of Access Design Solutions, Brighton, Victoria, 2012.
12 Keith M. Christensen, Creating inclusive outdoor play environments: Designing for ability rather than disability, *MLA, The Journal of Eyewitness in Special Education*, 910 (Sept-Oct): 48–55.
13 Ibid.
14 Richard Louv, *Last child in the woods: Saving our children from nature deficit disorder*. Atlantic Books, London, 2010.
15 Marc Armitage, *Play pods in schools*, An independent evaluation (2006–2009), Playpeople.
16 Keith M. Christensen, Creating inclusive outdoor play environments: Designing for ability rather than disability, *MLA, The Journal of Eyewitness in Special Education*, 910 (Sept–Oct): 48–55.

Part III
SEEDLINGS

Introduction

Understanding some of the issues which affect playspace design broadly, such as the history of playspaces, urban design and inclusion, we can start to focus in on the design features which best serve various age groups. This is not to say that a public space should necessarily segregate age groups: children should be able to choose how and where they play whenever possible, and will find different ways of engaging with a space at each level. However, by providing this division, we can deal with the specific needs and interests which are likely to be exhibited by each group. In this section, we look at children between birth and 5 years old.

These children are often heavy users of designed playspaces, partly because they lack the independence to select where they play. Getting the social dynamics and dimensions right is key to this age group.

In this section you will find:

10. **Child development – page 97**
    A discussion of the physical, emotional and social development of children between birth and 5 years old, including relevant ergonomic information.
11. **The natural environment as playspace – page 105**
    Discussing the values and qualities of natural playspaces, and their potential to deeply engage children with nature through play.
12. **Planting for children's play – page 115**
    A detailed discussion on Planting Design and Selection for play environments, including special applications, horticultural and maintenance considerations.
13. **Introducing water play environments to Early Years settings – page 129**
    Case study of a programme to introduce water play in Early Childhood settings in Scotland.
14. **The development of forest school in the UK – page 137**
    Looking at the forest school programme, which allows children to play freely in a natural outdoor place. Includes case studies of disadvantaged urban children and children with disabilities.
15. **Children's gardens: A tale of two cities – page 147**
    A designer's perspective on the design and operation of the Ian Potter Children's Garden in Melbourne Botanic Garden, Australia, and the parallels between this site and the proposed Global Garden of Peace in Gaza.
16. **Reflections on designing Lafayette Park playground – page 155**
    Understanding the design process behind a large public playspace in San Francisco.

10

CHILD DEVELOPMENT

Elizabeth Cummins & Katherine Masiulanis

Developmental stages

Physically and mentally speaking, children go through the most dramatic changes of their lives between the ages of 0 and 5. The speed with which children go from tiny babies, unable to roll over, to running, jumping and climbing is quite astonishing.

Humans have been described as having 'sensitive periods', which are when we are particularly open to developing in a certain way, such as language acquisition. That is not to say that this skill will not develop anyway if the stimulation is missed during the sensitive time, but it may be slower.[1] Hence, providing multisensory and engaging environments is particularly important during early childhood when so many fundamental skills are being established. As the focus of this text is on playspaces, it would be foolish to assume that any playspace can provide a completely fulfilling environment on its own, especially given the social needs of infants and toddlers. They can, however, provide a terrific range of opportunities and sensations which are not always readily available in the home.

Gross motor skills (those which control large movements of the body) undergo the most development during this period, as does 'prioperception' – that is, the awareness of where different parts of the body are in relation to each other and the world. Fine motor skills (smaller and more controlled movements) follow from these. The first two years of life are all about the development of *voluntary* motor control. Anyone watching a tiny baby trying to grasp a dangling object will appreciate how difficult it is to get the hang of these skills which an adult takes for granted.

Crawling usually happens somewhere in the first year of life, and is an important milestone, as the world opens up to independent exploration. Often play spaces are not really designed for this age group, and yet there are many simple ways that play can be supported for infants in an outdoor setting. There is more detail on these opportunities in the Affordances section.

Infants progress from the core outwards: first lifting the head, shoulders and trunk. Control comes over the legs and arms, but only as a whole limb. Afterwards, control spreads from the whole arm, to the elbow, to the fingers. Walking, which usually occurs between 10 and 18 months, frees the hands to do other things, such as collecting, carrying and pushing or pulling.

Designers need to note when creating spaces for infants that children up to the age of about 3 may still 'mouth' objects, although the tendency is generally highest up until the age of 2. This is an important sensory way for children to learn about the world. However, we must be aware of potential choking hazards, which are generally regarded as anything small enough to fit into an old fashioned film canister.

Toddlers are busy and active children, who work hard at learning new concepts, often through repetition and experimentation. Rapid brain development occurs during this time. For this reason, multisensory environments are particularly important at this age, although they are of benefit at every age. More is said about this in the Colours and Materials chapter of this book.

Fine motor skills start to become slightly more refined, although skills like drawing take some mastering. Part of the reason for this is purely physical. For example, an adult wrist has 9 bones, but a 1 year old has only three. Typically all 9 bones can be seen (but not necessarily fully formed or articulated) by the age of 51 months in girls, and 66 months in boys, so that girls are often more advanced at writing and drawing.[2]

Generally, a normally developing child will be able to walk up steps one foot per step, skip on both feet, pedal and steer a tricycle by age 4, and walk on tiptoe or along a thin line by 6. They may also be able to catch and throw a ball. What has been termed 'exercise play' – that is, rough-and-tumble, and rushing around physical play – peaks at about 4–5 years old.

Between 3 and 5 years old, the imagination becomes particularly active and vivid, and this can be well supported in the design of playspaces. Spatial concepts also start to have more meaning at about this age. About half of toddlers this age know the function of a map, but most have trouble interpreting the content. This is an important consideration when thinking about wayfinding in a playspace.

Observable patterns and interests

Patterns are particular sequences of developmental events experienced by most children as they grow. Interests refer to objects, situations and interactions that typically spark children's interactions. This section will address some of the typical patterns and interests that occur, as many are interrelated and are relevant to understand the kinds of play environments we can provide.

As development between 0 and 5 years is exponential and diverse, I have further divided the age range 0–3 into the sub-age ranges 0–6 months, 6–12 months, 12–18 months, 18–24 months, 2–3 years. Please note that children develop at different rates and that whilst this represents the norm it is not representative of all children.

0–6 months

The first 6 months of life are characterised by discovery and 'firsts'. Children begin by recognising the sounds of the world around them and their capacity to interact with that world by crying, laughing and smiling. They listen to voices and watch faces intently. They also begin to discover their hands and feet as an extension of themselves and enjoy holding, grabbing and manipulating objects. The first 6 months is a very oral stage of discovery, as everything within their grasp is put into their mouths and sucked. Increasing strength in their arms and shoulders enables them to master rolling from back to stomach, followed by raising themselves up on their forearms and finally raising their heads.

6–12 months

The second 6 months of life involves observe and respond behaviour, and mimicking noises. Children learn that life has a routine and begin to anticipate events, in particular developing expectation around familiar events (such as feeding times). Life is marked by an increasing drive and independence from carers, as they begin taking pride in their first personal accomplishments. An interest in performing develops and the first understanding of social approval and disapproval. Body awareness grows as they learn to identify and point to different body parts. Physically they move through the stages (not always sequentially) of sitting independently, crawling, standing assisted, before finally walking independently. Hand-eye coordination increases as children enjoy practising repetitive manipulative activity such as packing and unpacking and nesting or stacking objects.

12–18 months

Age 12–18 months is a period of development in children marked by increased memory functioning, as they learn and remember faces and routines. They begin to respond to simple requests and learn to make choices between clear alternatives. Physically they begin walking confidently (even while holding an object) and learn to throw a ball. Rapidly developing fine motor skills enable them to pick up small objects with their pointer finger and thumb (pincer grip), which gives them greater control when building block towers or turning the pages of a book. Socially they begin to show an interest in cause and effect scenarios, often enjoying anticipated outcomes (block tower falling over). Emotionally they often will exhibit stubborn and possessive behaviour, sometimes demonstrated through an unwillingness to share.

18–24 months

Children of 18–24 months clearly demonstrate developing confidence and independence from carers. This period is marked by a rapid increase in concept acquisition. Children learn to sort shapes and colours, and begin to take an interest in the size and weight of objects they are playing with. They are also able to point to and name objects. Mimicking adult behaviour, they are able to refer to themselves by name and learn new skills by working alongside (helping) adults. Physically they are now confident enough to run, kick their legs backwards and forwards and stand and balance on top of objects. They develop increasingly complex fine motor skills such as drinking from a straw or drawing simple scribbles. Emotionally they begin testing the limits of acceptable behaviour, sometimes showing pride or embarrassment. Socially they begin to engage with other children in parallel play (playing side by side) and whilst social interaction in their play has not quite developed as yet, they are able to begin to demonstrate an understanding of others, by showing some empathy. Children of this age also begin to engage in simple imaginative play.

2–3 years

Age 2–3 years is a period of increased concentration and marked independence. Children often become adamant about dressing themselves, as they learn to manipulate zips, buttons and fasteners. They commence toilet training and develop the physical capacity to control bodily functions. They have a really strong sense of ownership, particularly over possessions, which extends to people as they begin to develop 'preferred' friends. Their play now includes cooperative and symbolic play with others. They also begin to understand time sequence and more complex concepts around size, shape and colour. Fine motor and manipulative skills are now expanded to include threading beads, feeding themselves using cutlery, cutting with scissors and holding a pencil correctly. Physically they can now walk backwards, as well as forwards, and balance on one foot. Emotionally they develop the capacity to understand and think about consequences. They begin to take an interest in television characters, dinosaurs, robots, cars, trucks and trains. They enjoy dressing up, having stories read to them and simple, short games.

3–5 years

The period 3–5 years is marked by a development in social interaction, as children enjoy playing with other children more and more. At this age sex roles become more marked. They begin to express anger more dramatically, alongside a developing sense of 'fairness' (justice). They learn to make situation judgements, to take turns and begin negotiating with others. Conceptually they develop a more complex sense of time and space, beginning to use the terms 'in-front', 'behind', etc. They can rote count (sequentially recite numbers) and begin to understand simple maths concepts. With an acute memory, children of this age are able to recall main details in stories and follow simple instructions and directions. Their continually improving fine motor skills allow them to draw with a pencil correctly, copy a simple design, use scissors confidently and complete simple puzzles. Physically they can hop on one foot, skip and jump. During this period they learn to catch a ball or bean bag with two hands. Play includes dolls, make-believe, running and chasey and using manipulative or loose materials to create and build. Interests include caring for animals (pets), gardening, insects and the natural world, as well as TV, computer games and creative activities (making and building). Children's humour also becomes more sophisticated with a great enjoyment particularly of 'toilet and bodily functions'.

Social ergonomics

We use the term 'social ergonomics' to describe the way that children comfortably relate to other people. Ergonomics is the study of what makes a chair supportive, a shaft graspable or a light noticeable. In the same vein, there are certain relationships with other people and spaces which are right and comfortable for most people at a certain stage of development.

In the case of young children, their primary play is with a few important adults. Adults are of course caregivers, but they also provide intellectual and social 'scaffolding'. This has been described as providing structure of children's thinking, which stretches their abilities just far enough to master new skills.

As children get a little older, they start to participate in 'parallel play': that is, not with other children, but alongside them, mirroring their activities. For this reason, it can be good to have more than one opportunity for the same type of toddler play, particularly if it is of an attractive or engaging sort, such as sensory play with sand or water. As they grow, they start to be more comfortable with interacting with other children.

By the age of 2, children may have started to play with their peers, but relationships can be stormy. Learning to share and take turns, learning that others have desires contrary to your own, are important lessons of the 3rd year. By about the age of 3 or 4, half will have at least one mutual friendship. As a general rule, the smaller the children, the smaller the group in which they will play. By peers, we are not necessarily talking about children of the same biological age, but those of the same developmental level. 'Theory of mind' – that is, the realisation that others think differently to yourself, and also that they do not always know what you are thinking – usually comes between the ages of 3 and 5, but not with the same finesse of understanding as an adult.

Between 18 months and 3 years, two stages occur which are fundamental to the way in which children interact with the world and others. Firstly, there is a strong desire for increasing independence, and playspaces play an important role in allowing them to develop skills of which they are proud. Secondly, language develops. Not only does this allow for much more complex interactions with adults and peers, but also allows a child to be clearer about their preferences. About the age of 2, 'Language becomes intellectual and thinking verbal'.[3] The explosion of imagination from this time is a reflection of this leap to abstract thought.

It is important to note that children of this age cannot understand the complex rules of games. However, they are learning all the other important, unspoken rules of life: right and wrong; about sex roles; social actions and the effect of aggression. For this reason, socio-dramatic play is a large part of the play of small children. Imaginative role play and symbolic play allow children to investigate these complex areas in a safe way. Hence, allowing children to play with others is important, as there is a crucial difference between a child's position in a peer–peer relationship, and that in an adult–child relationship. Ultimately, adults always have the last say, whereas between children the power balance is more even.

Common affordances for play

This section covers the translation of knowledge on child development to the physical play environment. This is to support many of the developmental milestones discussed earlier through play. In the construction of any given play environment particular ergonomics of structures, surfaces and combinations can afford particular responses through play. This varies from age group to age group.

0–6 months

Children of this age enjoy secure, observable spaces and surfaces, as they are less independent of their carers and not yet mobile. They have a great interest in hanging and moving objects (such as mobiles), mirrors and music. Their favourite toys are strong, textural objects they can mouth. They get a great deal of value out of floor coverings including mats, rugs, cushions or mattresses.

6–12 months

As children of this age become more mobile, flat, solid and smooth surfaces as well as low, secure furniture such as coffee tables, chairs and boxes become useful in assisting movement. Boxes, screens and curtains are highly valued by children for imaginative play and interactive games such as 'hide and seek' where they can be comfortably concealed. Soft tunnels are also valued for crawling through, and mirrors or windows to observe themselves and others. Large, smooth strong parts or toys that can be stacked or pulled apart are important as well. Bench seats or low ledges, seats or rocks for sitting with children of this age while they play are valuable for promoting adult/child interaction.

12–24 months

An interest in more manipulative and sensory materials and surfaces marks this period. Children of this age enjoy engaging in water play, sand and dirt. Simple steps and inclines, including low step decks and slides, are important. Children continue to enjoy tunnels, with greater confidence in using other hidey-holes and boxes. Sofa cushions are very valuable for creating soft cubby spaces. Preferred toys include blocks, fixed manipulative objects (handles), noise-makers (keys) and, as they become more mobile, pushing or riding on wheeled toys or trolleys.

2–3 years

Common affordances for play for this age group builds on the previous stage. Physical play is built around mounds, hills, more complex steps and platforms and structures that can be used as cubbies. Cubbies become more important as stages for imaginative play. Children get great enjoyment out of digging or pouring implements, such as shovels, spades, diggers, containers and jugs, during sand or water play. Open space areas (grass or paved) become more useful for children's games and physical activity, in particular path surfaces of different textures. Seats are important for interaction with peers and adult carers, particularly for storytime and eating.

3–5 years

This age group needs quite complex, sensory environments to support all types of play. Flexible elements such as rocks, logs, branches, screens, loose objects including leaves, twigs, sand and dirt support diverse, child-directed play. Collecting objects or materials is part of the play ritual. A balance of hard surfaces for balls, cycling or scootering and chalk drawing is also important. Waterplay is valuable either as an activity in itself or in combination with sand or dirt. For physical play ladders, logs and rocks, beams, nets and slides are all important for climbing, as are look-outs and challenging heights. Imaginative play uses concrete and abstract props such as platforms, windows, screens and roofs which children enjoy. An interest in the natural world including trees, shrubs, plants, insects and animals increases during this period. They also enjoy more sophisticated noise-making through different objects or tuned percussion. Above all else social interaction should be supported in the environment through seats and decks for gathering, eating outside and storytime with friends.

Ergonomics

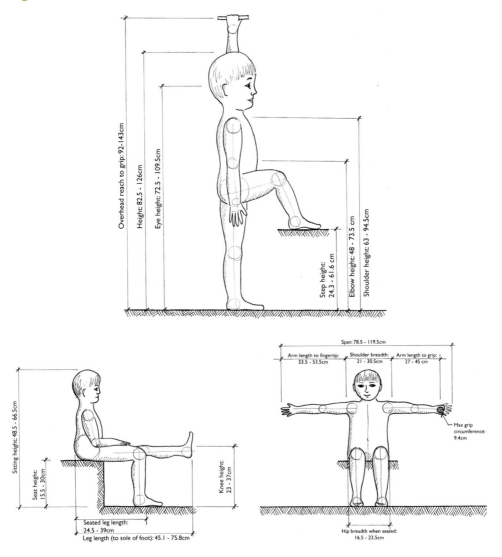

FIGURE 10.1 Ergonomic data of 5th percentile 2 year olds to 95th percentile 5 year olds
Data from: Beverly Norris & John R. Wilson, Consumer Safety Unit, Childata, The Handbook of Child Measurements and Capabilities: Data for Design Safety, Institute for Occupational Ergonomics, Department of Manufacturing Engineering and Operations Management, University of Nottingham

Figure 10.1 shows some of the physical limits which a designer might expect in children aged 2–5 years old. These dimensions represent the 5th percentile of 2 year olds – that is, a working estimate of the smallest 2 year olds – and the 95th percentile of 5 year olds – that is, a working estimate of the largest 5 year olds. By limiting ourselves to these extremities of the probability bell curve, we focus on what might reasonably be expected. These dimensions are based on measurements made of many children, and are of great help when designing spaces and objects for children. However, a word or two must be said about their use.

Firstly, they do not replace dimensions required by Playground Standards. If required to use the Standards, then sizes required to avoid entrapments (for example of the head or fingers) will be stipulated. These may have been based on younger children (data is not provided for children under 2 years old in these tables), or on the full population. Note that before age 2, children vary very widely, and their growth can come in unpredictable spurts which sees them appearing small for their age at one time, and large the next time they are measured. After 2, development starts to become more predictable, so that a small child is more likely to stay in the lower percentiles. However, this means that ergonomic data is not generally available or reliable for infants.

Bear in mind also the studies from which the dimensions are drawn. While comprehensive, they are based on studies of children in the UK and Germany at a certain time, and other populations of children may vary from this, either through natural genetic differences, cultural differences or the apparent tendency for humans to become larger as nutrition improves throughout the world. Use them as a guide, not as a scripture.

It is also necessary to consider which dimension is the most appropriate for your particular use. For example, if designing a tunnel, consider the largest child that might try to wiggle through: for a shop, perhaps consider whether the smallest child would be able to see over the counter.

In many cases, it is the dimensions of play equipment which will limit its use by certain children, more than their enthusiasm for trying a certain type of play. For example, very often we see equipment with small slides which would be attractive to pre-school aged children, which are accessed by climbers that they cannot physically manage. Rungs are spaced too far apart, or the distance from a deck to the climber much longer than their limbs. Children are remarkably adept at tackling these challenges, but when they have been designed inadvertently, it says more about the designer than the users. They create unplanned hazards.

A beautifully designed playspace considers the real dimensions of children: how high a comfortable seat is; how far they can reach to grip; what they can peek over. They are a powerful and subtle tool which differentiates a place that children will genuinely love, and one which just looks the part.

In the next few sections, we look at natural playspaces – the philosophy behind them, how to design planting for all types of playspace and also some case studies which focus on play with natural materials, at different scales and in different settings.

11
THE NATURAL ENVIRONMENT AS PLAYSPACE

Helle Nebelong

'Green is good for the eyes' says the mother duck in Hans Christian Andersen's fairytale 'The Ugly Duckling',[1] and science has proved that being out in nice green woods, parks and well-designed green spaces influences the human mind positively.[2]

American scientists Stephen and Rachel Kaplan developed the 'Attention Restoration Theory' regarding two kinds of human attention. *The involuntary attention* is the instinctive, automatic attention, which appears when we are under influence of sounds, smells, visual impressions and changes of temperature in nature and natural environments. It demands no special mental effort. *The directed attention* is one that uses energy; one we devote lots of hours to daily, when we force ourselves to eliminate unnecessary noises that interrupt our concentration on, for instance, specialised work. Directed attention has limited resources and, according to Kaplan's theory, we will collapse mentally if we go beyond the limit, trying to solve more and more complex problems. When we collapse mentally we need to recreate ourselves in peaceful green spaces to gather new strength.[3]

After years of work with children's outdoor spaces, I have observed that children have this instinctive, automatic attention and an inner urge to explore and try out things. Children experience and acquire knowledge by seeing, hearing, smelling, tasting, feeling and moving. They linger mentally with nature and we – the grown-ups – are the ones to ensure that children are given these experiences, so that they will be familiar with nature. In my opinion it is of great importance that children from their early childhood have the right to experience nature and play outside every day. Exploring nature takes time – lots of time – and children should have plenty of time to explore. Everything should not be demystified beforehand!

It is a misguided, but well-meaning, adult idea that everything for children must be openly amusing and painted in bright colours. Play is much more than fun. Play is essential for developing skills and learning how to manage life in general. Through my experiences I have seen again and again how children calm down when they go out to play. Nature's own colours are good for their eyes and relaxing to their minds – perfect for the playspace and they may be spiced up here and there with a few artistic colour splashes.

Things will happen

The playspace is an important place for children's development. It is a stage where they rehearse different roles and find their own identities through meeting others. The playspace scenery and content have a big influence on the quality of children's play. Natural materials like little stones, big boulders, logs and tree trunks, earthworks, water and plants are perfect elements for versatile play, and a hilly terrain motivates children to run up and down. Bringing in natural elements and minimising the amount of fixed equipment forces children to use and develop their own imagination and be the ones who give colour to their play and make things happen.

The risk issue

Risk is a matter that needs to be considered when designing playspaces. All countries have safety requirements that should be combined with a common sense approach. Sometimes the safety requirements go too far and the child's real needs for play and development set aside by well-meaning adult intentions. These intentions sometimes do more harm than good.

I am convinced that standardised playspaces are problematic, because of their limitations. When the distance between all the rungs in a climbing net or a ladder is exactly the same, the child has no need to concentrate on where he puts his feet. Standardisation is problematic because play becomes simplified and the child does not have to worry about his movements. This lesson cannot be carried over to all the knobby and asymmetrical forms in the world. The ability to concentrate on estimating distance, height and risk requires a lot of practice and is necessary for a person to be able to cope successfully with life. The focus on safety is important but must not lead one to forget to care about design and atmosphere.[4]

If we protect children with bubble-wrap, we prevent them from real life learning that sometimes hurts both physically and mentally. Sometimes children get dirty when they are playing. Sometimes children get scrapes and recognise that they have blood flowing under their skin! That's it! That's a natural part of childhood. It teaches children to take care of themselves, be aware of risks and estimate challenges.

FIGURE 11.1 Left: View from one of the many hillocks, 2008; Right: Bicycling on the 210 meter circular bridge that floats above the ground, 2007

The Nature Playground in Valbyparken, Copenhagen, Denmark. Photo: Helle Nebelong

A Danish approach to children's play

Denmark has a long-standing reputation for promoting the child's right to free play in natural surroundings. Invented by the Danish landscape architect Carl Theodore Sorensen (1893–1979) in 1931, the first junk playspace was opened in 1943 in the Emdrup district in Copenhagen and is still in existence today. Today junk playspaces are called adventure playspaces or constructing playspaces.

The concept is to teach children how to manage all sorts of things like using knives and tools, and how to make a bonfire. They also grow flowers and vegetables. By practicing skills and learning to master a lot of different things, children gain self-confidence and strengthen independence.

The Danish Playspace Association was founded in 1961. Sorensen was the first president. International Play Association (IPA), promoting the child's right to play, was founded in Denmark in 1961.

Sorensen inspires me in my work. Especially his approach to children's play and their needs for outdoor play:

> For outdoor play children should be given three kinds of landscapes: The beach, this should be a connection between sand playspaces and water play, but this seems a more insoluble problem than creating a spaceship. The meadow, surfaces of grass to play on, this should be an easy thing to do. Clumps, like little woods, this can be done, but unfortunately it lasts long till the trees are big enough for climbing and play.[5]

Experience of designing children's outdoor spaces – with a focus on nature experiences

When I design playspaces for children I get inspiration from natural themes such as running brooks, the beach, the woods, the wilderness, a wide meadow or the high mountains. I scale it into a size that fits into the place, targets the users and is suitable for the budget.

I always work with asymmetrically shaped elements that force children to develop the kinesthetic sense for moving the body in space, estimating distance, height and risk. I also shape the landscape into a hilly terrain with robust plantings, logs and boulders and different beautiful surfaces of bricks and granite or other aesthetic tactile materials. A good mixture of these arranged in a thoughtful way will enable children to play, run, jump and move around. Physical movements are good for a child's concentration span and give a feeling of having control of one's movements. The child should also be encouraged to meet challenges, through trying and overcoming them.

Designing playspaces for children is to me a question of designing accessible environments that work for all children, irrespective of abilities and skills. All children wish to be treated like other children and as such should be given the same opportunities and not feel excluded.

We are living in a global era fascinated by technology, but it is essential to stay connected with nature. Nature offers us a primordial force and has so much to give. Referring again to Kaplan and Kaplan's 'Attention Restoration Theory', nature gives us strength to cope with the daily pressures of our modern life, where lots of 'disturbing' things happen that need our directed attention and steal our energy.

Good design is a key issue

The senses are our key to connect with the world around us. We learn a lot when we open our eyes, prick up our ears, widen our nostrils and give full rein to our curiosity. A playspace abundant with nature and natural elements appeals to children's curiosity and synergy with nature, and makes it possible for them to explore the seasons' changing wonders. Like plants and all living creatures on Earth, children need good conditions to grow up robust and socially balanced.

Playspaces at early childhood centres

Playspaces located at childcare centres and schools should assist in supporting children's play, development and culture and should be challenging to a diversity of children. Children are individuals with different needs for physical, mental and social stimuli, and the playspace can encourage a child's potential for independence as well as support and develop the child's belonging to a group.

The playspace should be a place where a child can experience wonder, and feel excitement and curiosity. The physical frame of a playspace should support the pedagogical praxis for a child's optimal development. The outdoors are as important as the indoors, and the design imperative to what occurs in those spaces.[6]

The primary function of a playspace is to offer children a free open air space, where play and rest can take place, where creativity will develop and where the seasonal changes can be studied. A carefully shaped playspace strengthens a child's development and learning and gives teachers many different possibilities to work with.

Open-air shelters where children can have a nap and a shed to keep toys, different props, tools and equipment for the bonfire are important but will not be discussed in this chapter.

Play and movement

The pleasure of using and challenging your body begins in childhood. The outdoors should stimulate the child's innate desire to be physically active. Through play and movement both the fine and gross motor skills are strengthened, and that gives the child an experience of self-esteem and self-confidence when he feels his competences grow. *I feel fine, my body feels good, I can manage this!*

All places are unique

Every design task is different. The place, the target group and the budget differ. The context is new each time. Before I start sketching a new playspace, I always visit the place, find out about the history and analyse the qualities already there. This can be a part of a building, an old tree with character, something that happened at the place, an old sculpture or something else. All places are different and all places are unique. I therefore try to find the spirit of the place, the *genius loci*,[7] and use it as a good starting point for the overall plan of how the area should be organised and developed.

Masterplan and maintenance

The overall plan for the playspace – either located at a daycare centre, a school or in a public park – should be divided into different zones, and aesthetics should be an integrated part of the whole design and the chosen materials.

The space close to a building is an obvious location for activities that normally take place indoors but could be moved outside when the weather is fine. Tables and benches should be placed here and big, organically shaped areas with sand where the youngest children can play in a more quiet way. A tap close to the sand spaces is an essential for sand play and watering plants. If there's an outdoor kitchen water access is also required and should be connected to raised beds planted with herbs and edible plants.

The space farthest from the building is suitable for wilder activities to unfold with hilly terrain and wilderness, climbing nets and swings, and driving paths for moon-cars (Danish play-cars) and tricycles. If the space is big enough there could even be a little fenced space for ball games.

The intermediate area should be designed as a zone of plantations, a zone where the terrain differs or something else, that can at the same time divide and connect the different play activities.

The main path

A winding path of soft curves going through the whole playspace and connecting the different zones and activities is like a common thread, and it's my experience that this functions well. The main path itself could have plenty of play value. It should be given a solid surface like asphalt or hard, compact gravel. There could be little side paths with more complex, challenging, rough and bumpy surface materials. Paths meant for bicycling should be constructed so that they can function without colliding with places meant for more quiet and peaceful play.

Spaces and frames

The playspace should be divided into different spaces in different sizes by establishing 'walls' that could differ in height, width and materials. Wild plantations or cut hedges, raised beds, pergolas and woven willow fences can help vary the spaces.

Separation of outdoor spaces can also be achieved by shaping terrain. This may be in the form of little hillocks and banks, or by making borders of boulders, brick walls or fixed fences. A change in surface materials also marks that you are entering a new part of the playspace.

Surface textures

The outdoor spaces can be divided into areas with hard surfacing like asphalt, concrete and hard gravel, and smaller spaces with rubber surfacing and loose materials like sand and pebble stones. In addition there are spaces with garden beds: grass, bushes, herbs and perennials and wood like wilderness.

FIGURE 11.2 Left: A natural play icon with a wide variety of surfaces and plantings, 2005; Right: Water play

Murergarden Daycare Centre, Copenhagen, Denmark, 2007. Photo: Helle Nebelong

Paths for biking and driving in moon-cars function best with an asphalt surface bordered with cobblestones against areas with grass, gravel, sand and soil. The track should be shaped with loops and the terrain going up and down. Asphalt surfaces and concrete flagstones are also good for chalk drawing.

Play equipment

The range of play equipment is enormous: play houses, swings, slides, trampolines and climbing features are only some of the elements you will find in most playspaces. The standardised equipment has limited play value, though, when it comes to children's greater capacity for free and flexible play and imagination. It is therefore important to shape the landscape into a more challenging topography with lots of garden beds and beautiful nature elements that will sustain children's interest longer over time.

Loose materials

Children can influence the changing shape and form of the playspace if there are plenty of loose materials to build with and move around; if there are places where they are allowed to dig holes in the soil; places where rain water can stay for a while to make puddles and mud holes. At daycare centres old pots, pans, flower containers and so on are most popular among children when playing versatile role games.

Nature integrated in the playspace

A playspace at a daycare centre or a school or in a public park should be designed with as many plants and nature elements as possible to stimulate children's senses and give them opportunities to learn about nature. Nature is widely defined as the broad spectrum of effects that can be created when using plants, water, boulders, tree trunks and shaping the terrain. A place for a bonfire and playing with water should be considered as well as raised beds where children and teachers can grow some vegetables and herbs, and why not grow a sunflower fort?

FIGURE 11.3 Copenhagen school gardens
Photo: Helle Nebelong

A diversity of plants makes it possible to study natural phenomena and notice that some plants attract butterflies, bees and other insects while others attract birds and squirrels. This variety opens up a multi-faceted conversation, building language proficiency. Children can learn about the names of the plants, the colours of flowers, and put down artistically on paper the nature phenomenon they have experienced. To a child it could be a revelation to recognise that one single sunflower seed can grow into a large plant with hundreds of new seeds in a very short time. This is knowledge learned through observation and experience.

Trees and shrubs help to create shade and humidity during hot summers. Depending on the size of the area, wilderness, shrubs and ground-cover should be established using robust indigenous species and avoiding poisonous or allergenic species. It's a good idea to protect the plantations with low barrier fences, so that children don't trample them with tricycles, yet are able to climb over the fence and play and hide in the greenery. In the garden beds there could be little paths of stepping stones that can direct children and protect the plants.

A diversity of species provides seasonal changes and sensory experiences with the different flowers, foliage, fruits, berries, cones and seeds. Choose familiar plants that smell good, that can be eaten directly on location or picked and used in the kitchen. Finally don't forget to encourage children to stop and smell the flowers!

Involve parents, children and teachers in an annual planting day when new trees and bushes are planted, and show children how to take care of and water plants. The teachers and children can make their own herbarium – a collection of plants or leaves and flowers that are collected in the field, pressed flat and dried between newspapers. The herbarium could be enriched with photos of the plants at different seasons, so children get to know about the cycles of nature throughout the year.

Early childhood teachers should not just feel like doing something with the kids. They are committed to learn the most basic natural phenomena or else we are guilty in stopping children's developing.

Brita Fabricius, principal of The Integrated Daycare Centre Murergarden, Copenhagen

Sustainability and recycling

Generally the outdoor spaces in daycare centres and schools are small, and it is therefore important to design and choose robust materials that age beautifully and can take a lot of wear and tear from everyday use. The local community may already have a material yard with old materials that could be reused.

Rain water can be percolated through the soil and some of it could be collected for watering plants. The maintenance of the playspace should be considered thoroughly when design details are decided. Sustainability and recycling in the outdoors can contribute to an understanding of the environment for both children and staff.

The beach, the woods, the wilderness. It's that simple!

When we design playspaces for children, it is not necessary to turn to catalogues of fine, colourful playspace products. Today's institutionalised children are bombarded with colours and colourful interiors in daycare centres, schools and at home. TV and computers also serve to engage them in fantasy worlds that are not their own.

The playspace should appeal to children's imagination and give them the opportunity to shape and colour their own individual play in a way that suits their ages and stage of development. A child's natural urge to explore and investigate the world with all their senses should be stimulated through the playspace's design.

When designing or working with outdoor areas for children it is important to consider the innate curiosity and desire children have to explore and use natural materials to play and build with.

We should not demystify everything but rather allow children the freedom to have their own imaginary worlds. When children play in natural playspaces with boulders, terrain, vegetation and water, it is their own imagination they use to be creative. In nature they are also challenged physically, mentally and socially, whilst they develop a relationship with nature. This relationship helps them to understand and respect nature.

Natural spaces and materials stimulate children's limitless imaginations and serve as the medium of inventiveness and creativity.

Robin C. Moore

Children have the potential to be more resilient, capable, creative and able to learn than we give them credit for. Yet their lives are becoming ever more scheduled, controlled and directed.

Tim Gill: No Fear: Growing up in a Risk Averse Society

FIGURE 11.4 A view from the pram up into the green treetop, 2014
Photo: Martin Nebelong

My childhood memories

As a child I remember fondly the secret garden in my local neighbourhood. It was a place where no grown-ups ever went. An unkempt garden, where everything had grown wild because there was no maintenance. It was a true children's space and we were allowed to do anything there. There was no control, no-one watching us, and nothing was forbidden. Children of all ages came from all over the neighbourhood. We played everything and built dens and huts in the old apple trees. There were lots of left over materials. It was sometimes very tough; we often had tears running from our eyes, scrapes, bruises and holes in the knees of our pants, but we learned a lot about life!

Plasters, iodine and splinters were everyday occurrences, and we got quite dirty. At the same time the garden was a familiar, safe and homely place. It was somewhere we faced the big world and got a small taste of what our future adult life might bring. It was wonderful to come back home in the evening with my sister, dirty and tired we were … though incredibly enriched for the experience.

12

PLANTING FOR CHILDREN'S PLAY

John Rayner

Plants are critically important elements in a playspace. Where built structures are static, plants are living and dynamic, and provide endless opportunities for play. Their lifecycles, growth features and seasonal changes, big and small, provide new sensations and experiences. As a source of sensory interest, colour and loose materials for play, they cannot be matched by anything man-made.

In a well-designed playspace, plants provide richer and more engaging play opportunities and may help develop more positive relationships to the natural world. As we have seen in other sections, playing in highly sensory environments has many benefits for children's development. Plants facilitate opportunities for creative, dramatic and cognitive play,[1] and have also been shown to increase the range of children's play behaviours and physical activity.[2]

Despite these enormous benefits, there is often some resistance to the inclusion of plants in playspaces. It is important to have a clear picture of these concerns, and how to address them, prior to designing your space.

Safety concerns

In recent years rising concern around personal safety has led to the application of Crime Prevention Through Environmental Design (CPTED) principles in public landscape projects. In playground design this has been applied through increasing site visibility and surveillance, having readily designated entry and exit points, clear identification as a single purpose zone and designing with materials that are less prone to vandalism.[3]

While some of the hard landscape solutions sought through CPTED might be welcome, the results of this for planting design and play are more contentious. These can result in more open and transparent landscapes; produced through the use of higher canopy trees and low growing turf and groundcovers; at the exclusion of shrubs and hedges.[4] This absence of vegetation in the 1 metre/3 feet to 2.5 metre/8 feet height range is often coupled with a loss of vegetation density, leading to sterile plantings lacking interest and diversity. In turn, this can reduce play outcomes that are afforded from more 'natural playspaces' which have richer and more complex planting.

Solutions can be found with more thoughtful plant selection, plant placement and selective pruning to achieve greater visibility and surveillance outcomes. High quality maintenance, supervision and management are also important in landscape crime prevention.[5] Plant and vegetation maintenance in particular signals that there is activity and occupation in a landscape, identifying it as a 'purpose zone'. Clearly a balance is needed between applying CPTED principles and planting design in a playspace, which should be developed independently for each project.

Maintenance

Planted landscapes, just like any playspace, do require maintenance. One of the crucial inputs into any planting design is determining the true level of available maintenance. Realistically deciding at the outset what can be achieved over the long term is a fundamental step in designing for play. Some plant groups also require significant labour and skills during both establishment and recurrent maintenance, such as food gardens, hedges, annual flowers and living structures. Planning for this is crucial for long-term success.

The main resource inputs required post-planting include weed control, nutrition and irrigation, but this is dependent on the vegetation type, soil and seasonality. The water needs of large plants, particularly trees, can be significant post-planting and should be factored into establishment maintenance. Wherever possible, mulches should be used around individual trees and plantings. Mineral, organic and synthetic mulches all provide benefits to soil health, site aesthetics and plant growth. However, not all mulches are equal in terms of performance and effectiveness,[6] and they should be selected carefully.

Ultimately, and particularly for larger sites, a landscape management plan and maintenance schedule should be prepared. This should encompass the planting objectives, plus the relevant tasks, frequency and standards for maintaining vegetation. Clear communication and planning ensure that the planting continues to afford the play and amenity for which it was originally designed.

Planting design

Designing and selecting plants for any landscape can be challenging. Planting design is defined as selecting and arranging a composition of plants, based around inter-related functional, ecological and aesthetic outcomes. Plant *selection*, on the other hand, is the choice of species against design objectives using specific selection criteria.[7] In practice, there is a complex relationship and iterative process between the two, one that involves trade-offs between proposed design outcomes and a chosen plant palette to arrive at a final planting plan.

Planting design in a playspace needs to balance multiple issues. Site and maintenance considerations provide both opportunities and limitations for planting and can be difficult to evaluate. Plant selection is influenced not only by planned design outcomes, but also by the influence of play itself on plant performance.[8] User issues also require assessment, particularly as the features which children and adults value in landscapes frequently differ.[9,10] Engaging children in the planning, design and management process is critical for ongoing success. Garden projects which actively engage children in design have been shown to foster an interest in gardening generally,[11] with children more inclined to care for plants in the resultant landscape.[12]

Plant selection principles

Most approaches to selecting plants involve measuring plants against specific selection criteria, generally using a matrix for analysis and evaluation. The criteria used should encompass outcomes from site analysis, proposed design outcomes and available resource and maintenance inputs (over time) as discussed earlier.

For professional plant users there is a paucity of independent, high quality, performance-based information to assist decision making. The main information sources used tend to be amateur gardener literature sources and nursery catalogues, while the more quality sources, such as online databases, professional user guides and experimental studies (peer-reviewed literature), are less frequent and available.[13] Personal experiences and observations of plants are particularly useful, although successful performance in one location does not automatically ensure success elsewhere. For any source of information, the audience and context of the information needs to be considered along with the content, to determine its usefulness to a design setting. Indicators of quality sources of information typically include comparative descriptions of and/or data of plant performance across climates, geography and sites, sometimes described as plant environmental tolerances.

Children's playspaces can be hostile places for plants. Many suffer from issues associated with use, including plant wear and tear and soil compaction. Some can also be subject to environmental stress, such as drought, low temperatures, soil waterlogging; or from changes in use, maintenance or resource inputs. These can lead to plant failure, often resulting in landscape redesign, renovation or replacement. Having a better method for plant selection in the design process can greatly improve the success of plants and is critical to developing landscapes that can be managed more efficiently, economically and sustainably.[14]

Some general principles include:

Select for multi-functionality

Ideally, individual plants are selected for multiple outcomes, thereby providing for different uses. This is particularly crucial where the size of the site or other constraints limit the type and range of plants that can be used. Some examples of multi-functionality in plant selection include choosing shade trees that also have attractive fruits that can be used for play or art pieces (e.g. *Acer* spp., Maples); hedging plants with sensory features (e.g. *Rosmarinus officinalis*, Rosemary); screening plants that can be selectively harvested for play and cubby making (e.g. *Phyllostachys* spp., Bamboo); or robust shrubs, with edible fruits (e.g. *Acca sellowiana*, Pineapple Guava).

Select for user needs

Plant selection should be influenced by children's ages and abilities, particularly the placement, dimensions and types of plants. Selecting user-appropriate and 'child-sized' plant materials is

FIGURE 12.1 Plants harvested for cubby making, The Patch Primary School
Photo: John Rayner

sometimes overlooked. Very young children often have a greater capacity to respond to more tactile elements than older children and adults. Examples include finer textured materials, such as ornamental grasses (leaves, flowers, seed heads) or smaller, decorative flowers, such as daisies (e.g. *Aster, Brachyscome*).

Select for diversity and variation

Where there is greater variation of plants in the landscape, young children show increased and more varied play behaviours.[15] They also make more use of and have higher values for these landscapes, when compared to less varied spaces.[16] Increased variation can be achieved by choosing plants with differing traits and attributes, such as contrasting leaf textures, plant forms, plant sizes and shapes.[17] Diversity can also be reflected through spatial design, by inclusion of different sized areas in the landscape, and contrasting enclosure (ideally using hedges or screening plants) with larger, more open spaces.

Select for seasonality

Seasonal changes bring focus to the natural world. Seasonality has been observed to result in distinct changes in play behaviours,[18] and hence an extension of the interest available in any planted playspace. The cyclical nature of the seasons can also be used to fascinate and foster greater engagement with children (e.g. winter-flowering bulbs) and to afford greater learning opportunities (e.g. germinating Sunflower seeds).

Aspects of seasonality of use include plant growth traits (e.g. deciduous vs. evergreen), leaf growth and form (e.g. new spring growth vs. leaf fall) and reproductive features (e.g. flowering and fruiting traits). Plants that have strong cultural and social associations with seasonal change through flowering (e.g. flowering cherries) or harvest (e.g. pumpkins) can be particularly meaningful. Seasonality can also be explored through growing, with short life-cycle annual plants, such as vegetables and flowers, especially useful.

Select robust, durable and resilient plants

As noted, playspaces can be tough places and choosing robust, durable and resilient plants is essential for success. This is particularly important in projects where issues of poor site preparation and low maintenance dominate. Here robust and durable plants are those that tolerate the specific site issues, climate and soil conditions, have minimal resource inputs and are easy to cultivate.

'Resilience' in this context refers to plants that can recover from severe environmental stress events, such as drought and waterlogging. It also refers to plants that can recover from accidental damage or from deliberate harvesting. Such plants will have a combination of traits including non-brittle or flexible stems, rapid basal shoot regrowth ('coppice' properties) or strong, flexible thickets.[19] Examples include suckering shrubs (e.g. *Acacia, Cornus, Plumbago*, etc.); perennial herbaceous plants (e.g. *Erigeron, Lomandra, Phormium*, etc.) and evergreen climbing plants (e.g. *Muehlenbeckia complexa, Tecoma capensis, Trachelospermum jasminoides*).

Select plants for amenity values

In many landscapes, plants provide a critical contribution to amenity, particularly improving human comfort through modifying microclimate. In warmer climates and during summer this can include using plants that provide shade and screening, in turn reducing wind and heat exposure. In cooler, temperate climates, or over winter, plants can be selected to increase the available light. Unlike a built structure for the same purpose, plants will change with the season. Both situations require selection of specific plant traits around life cycle, habit and form. These include canopy architecture (shape and dimensions), foliage characteristics (leaf density, branching, shoots, size and type), plant growth rate and longevity.

A further consideration to site amenity is the use of vegetation to assist wayfinding in the landscape. Plants can be used to define spaces, direct circulation and facilitate movement in a much more sensory and interesting way than through the use of constructed barriers or fences. Examples of suitable plants include Bamboos (e.g. *Bambusa multiplex* cvs.), clumping ornamental grasses (e.g. *Calamagrostis x acutiflora*, Feather Reed Grass) and shrubs, particularly hedges (e.g. *Choisya ternata*, Mexican Orange Blossom; *Lavandula angustifolia*, Lavender).

Avoid hazardous plants

Needless to say, landscapes for children's play should avoid the selection of hazardous plants. This includes both those with poisonous, toxic or allergenic properties and those that could cause physical injury. Poisonous plants include a large group with toxic properties harmful through ingestion, inhalation or skin contact. This group includes plants that are well known and reported, such as Poison Ivy (*Toxicodendron radicans*); but it also includes little-known plants, such as Grevillea species, where foliage exposure can cause contact dermatitis. Hazardous plants could also include those that can produce individual allergic reactions to pollens, a potentially large group of plants. This could become more important as the number of allergy-responses in childhood increases, especially in developed nations.

Plants causing physical injury, such as those with sharps, spines, thorns and barbs, should also be avoided in these landscapes. In many species these properties are produced, or become more developed with age, as plants move from their juvenile stage to maturity or visa-versa, such as the thorns produced on Bougainvillea (*Bougainvillea glabra*).

While there are texts that cover lists of poisonous or hazardous plants,[20,21,22] and websites, these are limited and cannot cover all possible plants for use. For any project, current local information should be sourced in respect to hazardous plant properties before selection and use.

Avoid using weeds

Plants that are known weeds should not be selected for use in children's playspaces. This includes plants that have official weed status (i.e. 'Declared' or 'Noxious' weed categories) and cannot be legally sold or grown. It also includes plants sometimes referred to as 'Environmental weeds', those that are locally invasive, spread readily by seed or vegetative parts and can become serious plant pests. Seeking high quality and local information about plant choices will avoid choosing plants that are weeds.

Planting themes

Specific themes can be developed for planting design in playspaces, giving a space character and special play opportunities. To aid in the detailed development of these themes, emphasis is made in this section on two inter-related factors: plant traits and plant uses.

Plant traits are the properties or characters that contribute towards overall plant morphology (i.e. its form, shape and structure); such as leaf, stem, root, flower, reproductive features, etc. How these plants are utilised in the landscape is referred to here as **plant uses**; such as ground cover, hedging, screening, shading, display values and so on. While plants are obviously versatile in terms of how and what they can be used for, the success of this will largely be dependent on the traits they possess and how they are maintained in the landscape.

Examples of planting themes discussed here include refuge; climbing; mazes and patterns; art and sculpture; food plants and gardens; and sensory plants.

Spaces for refuge

In this context, refuge spaces are shaped and defined by plants, and may be plant structures, 'cubbies' or 'dens'. They provide opportunities for retreat, enclosure, cover and shelter, but also can have access, permeability and the capacity for changeable dimensions. These can be important locations for children's play and are generally absent in more formally designed playgrounds. The variable textures and qualities of plants used, plus the complexity and subtlety of children's social activities, make these highly attractive spaces for children.[23] Some studies have found that 47% of all play was in 'refuge' structures of some kind.[24] Design parameters influencing child behaviour included the type and number of access points in the structure, the presence of a ceiling, the ability for it to function as a hide, the complexity and scale in each refuge and the plasticity and potential movement of loose parts.

For a successful refuge, plant traits of importance include suitable foliage properties (size, dimensions, etc.), suckering and re-sprout capacities (for regrowth after harvest or damage) and the presence of robust, durable and flexible stems (for harvesting or weaving). Cultivation and maintenance is crucial in these types of installations, to ensure aspects of structure, dimensions and plant growth are sustained.

Refuges made from living plant structures, such as domes, tunnels and related structures, are widely used in cooler, temperate climates. Lengthy, lateral shoots, harvested from managed stock plants, are struck directly into the ground over winter to create a living and growing structure. While Willow (*Salix* spp.) is the most dominant plant used for this purpose, other deciduous trees, such as Alders (*Alnus* spp.), Hazels (*Corylus* spp.) and Poplars (*Populus* spp.) are used and may be more appropriate in some sites.

Climbing plants can be used to create similar structures by growing them on permanent or semi-permanent supports, such as 'teepee' or 'igloo' shapes. Enclosures can also be created in mass plantings, where spaces are made through careful cultivation and selective pruning to allow access. Suckering shrubs, tall ornamental grasses and bamboos can be used for this purpose, but must be sufficiently 'permeable' and robust in growth to afford access and movement.

Constructed (rather than growing) cubbies or dens are another form of refuge space for play. Made from a variety of plant props and loose parts, they provide significant creative play opportunities for children. Plant parts can include plant stems and branches, with larger leafy materials particularly useful. Plants can be grown on site for the harvesting of plant parts (often by coppicing or pollarding), but will need to tolerate this type of hard pruning to be successful.

FIGURE 12.2 Willow cubbies are deciduous living structures
Photo: John Rayner

Plants for climbing

Given opportunity and availability, children will climb trees. Apart from being dominant elements in the landscape, they also provide unique refuge and vantage points for children. Good selection requires consideration of any site issues and provision of high quality maintenance. Small trees, providing they are safe and well established, can be used by children for climbing with provision of suitable soft-fall beneath. Suitable trees will be those with a strong limb structure, bendable (non-brittle) branches and no hazardous properties. Examples include flowering trees (e.g. *Cercis canadensis*, Eastern Redbud) and even small fruiting trees (e.g. *Malus* spp., Apples).

However, in many playspaces, the best choices for climbing won't be trees but shrubs. Particularly for young children the best choice will be tough, robust shrubs, ~3 metres in height, with strong, flexible branching. Those that sucker (e.g. *Acacia boormanii*, Snowy River Wattle; *Allocasuarina paludosa*, Scrub Sheoak; *Buddleja salviifolia*, Sagewood; *Viburnum opulus*, Guelder Rose) are particularly useful.

Mazes and related patterns

Planted mazes and labyrinths are fascinating spaces for children to explore. Hedge mazes are the most common choices, particularly using evergreen, small-leaved shrubs such as *Buxus sempervirens* (Common Box). Flowering and grey-foliage shrubs provide a useful alternative, however, as they can add seasonal and sensory elements to a playscape. Examples of suitable plants include *Escallonia* ('Pink Pixie'), *Santolina chamaecyparissus* (Lavender Cotton), *Veronica* spp. (Hebes) and *Westringia* spp.

Other plant groups can also be used successfully to create mazes and related patterns, including tussock-forming grasses (e.g. *Pennisetum* spp.; *Poa* spp.) and upright herbaceous perennials (*Dianella* spp., Flax Lilies; *Kniphofia* spp., Red-hot Pokers). For young children hedges will be lower than for adults; a hedge height of 1.5ft/50cm may be sufficient to provide both viewing access and concealment. Further interest can be created through contrasting pathway surfaces, using different gravels, sands, sawdust or grit.

A simpler technique to create ground patterns is turf mazes or through 'differential mowing'. Here regular, repeated mowing of turf at different heights creates a distinctive design. Turf mounds and level changes can also be used to make interesting spaces for active play. However, sloped surfaces can be almost impossible to maintain under conditions of high foot traffic and use. Appropriate turf grass species selection is important, along with high quality maintenance.

Art and sculpture

Art is essential in playspaces. Plants can be shaped through topiary to create spectacular living structures and artforms. Topiary is the frequent pruning of small-leaved climbers or shrubs, either grown freely or on pre-shaped wire frames. Tree shaping, or arborsculpture as it is sometimes described, is similarly used to create spectacular clipped and often grafted living tree sculptures.

Planting for children's play   **123**

FIGURE 12.3 Hedges need not be tall to enclose small children
Photo: Katherine Masiulanis

FIGURE 12.4 Plants can be used to create surprising living artwork – Caterpillar at New York Botanic Gardens
Photo: John Rayner

Plant sculptures can also be made with harvested plant materials. This can include use of long, woven stems and leaves, sphagnum moss, recycled materials, found objects and more to create art pieces in situ. These can also be augmented with easy to grow plants, such as annuals and succulents, grown in organic or foam-based growing media to create 'living structures'. One of the simplest structures can be made by weaving long lateral branches repeatedly in a pattern circle on the ground to gradually form a 'nest'.

Having access to and a suitable supply of plant materials can be a challenge. This can be aided by plants on site with multiple usable features, particularly those able to regrow rapidly after pruning. Materials can also be accessed through local garden maintenance in your community. Long, lateral stems, colourful twigs, shoots and bark, large textured leaves, interestingly shaped buds and flowers and decorative fruits of all kinds, both soft and dry, are particularly useful plant traits for making art.

Food gardens

Much of the recent expansion of children's gardens across the globe has been driven by kitchen or productive food gardens, particularly in schools. These gardens can directly improve children's health by encouraging positive eating behaviours.[25,26] Many food gardens also deliver unique educational opportunities, especially when linked directly to learning and curriculum. For example, plants can be established around themes such as cooking (e.g. pizza garden), culture (e.g. indigenous food plants) and seasonality or lifecycles (e.g. pumpkins and autumn harvest).

As they are maintenance and resource intensive, food gardens require good planning and design to be successful, particularly around the ongoing commitment of adults to care for them. Many vegetables benefit from deep, fertile soil and having some form of raised bed aids plant growth and accessibility. Most productive gardens are managed 'organically', meaning weeds, pests and diseases will need to be controlled carefully. Harvesting can also sometimes be a problem in temperate climate school gardens, when school holidays coincide with an abundance of produce!

Sensory plants

All plants provide sensory opportunities through sight, touch, taste, sound and smell and have been shown to be highly attractive to children. An investigation of children's nature experiences in botanic gardens found that sensory experiences were one of the three dominant themes, with novel sensory experiences fostering interest in nature.[27] Sensory plants have also been shown to be particularly beneficial to children with special education needs,[28] including improvements in independent wayfinding and more social engagement with peers. Sensory elements can both stimulate and arouse, but also produce unpleasant or negative reactions. Either can be useful responses. Within the playspace, it is almost impossible to avoid sensory planting, but it can also be enhanced through sensory trails, or careful planting along paths.

Visual properties of plants are often the most obvious, particularly colour, form and texture. While flowers tend to be the main consideration, fruits, foliage and stems can also provide strong visual interest.

The touch and feel of plants can be equally significant for children, more so for those who have a vision impairment. The shapes and surfaces of leaves, stems and trunks can provide for a variety of textural experiences, including smooth, rough, hairy, warm, cold, heavy, light, wet and dry sensations.

The natural noises produced by plants can provide unique sensory experiences for children, particularly when coupled with wind and water. Hollow stems and dry fruits can be harvested to make 'sound sculptures', while wind movement through leaves, stems and grasses has a natural sound all of its own.

For many children it is the taste of plants that is of interest, especially those that are known in their processed or cooked form but unknown in their raw state. Closely related, scent can surprise and engage. While flowers generally advertise scent well, leaves do less so. Crushing foliage to produce strong, pungent smells or sweet, perfume-like fragrance can be a memorable experience.

Some of the more useful groups of sensory plants include 'indestructible' flowering annuals (e.g. *Helianthus annuus*, Sunflower), 'showy' perennial daisies (e.g. *Rudbeckia* spp., Coneflowers), seasonal flowering bulbs (e.g. *Tulbaghia violacea,* Society Garlic), tough succulents (e.g. *Sedum x rubrotinctum*, Jellybean Sedum) and pungent, edible herbs (e.g. *Mentha* spp., Mint; *Petroselinum crispum*, Parsley).

Horticultural considerations

Horticultural issues can significantly affect the performance and long-term success of any plantings in a playspace. These should be considered carefully during design development and documented to provide guidance and support to any later decision making and/or problem-solving.

Site analysis

There is some discussion of general site analysis in the Potting Shed section of this book. A horticulturally focussed site analysis is a fundamental building block in planting design. The process should begin with a survey and inventory of existing vegetation. Soils, topography, drainage, temperature, precipitation, orientation and aspect, light and shade, wind and related microclimate data should be included and interpreted carefully to determine their relative significance and inter-relation. Often this requires specialist input. By bringing all this

FIGURE 12.5 Sunflowers can be used to investigate the growth cycle, but also as charming mazes, Emerald, Victoria

Photo: John Rayner

information together, it is possible to see whether the desired planting design objectives align with site realities,[29] and plant selection criteria can be developed accordingly.

Trees

Existing vegetation on a site, particularly trees, should always be assessed for retention. Trees deserve a special mention in playspace design. Many are significant elements in the landscape, providing shade, shelter, the possibility of climbing and nature play. In any project, trees on site should be identified and assessed by a qualified arborist during the design phase. Where significant trees are present, no-access zones can be established to assist in their ongoing health and protection.

For most projects where trees are present, some form of protection is needed, and there are good guides available which determine the required protection zone based on trunk diameter. These areas are called Tree Protection Zones (TPZ). Damage to trees most commonly occurs during construction works, particularly from soil compaction, through traffic, machinery and excavation works, including alterations in soil levels. Even changes in microclimate around a tree, such as new buildings that reduce light, can affect tree health. Popular misconceptions about tree roots include deep 'tap roots'. In fact, most tree roots are laterally-spreading and are located in the top 600 mm of the soil profile.[30]

Site preparation

To determine the horticultural preparations required, sites and soils need to be properly assessed by a specialist during project planning. This advice may continue into construction. The physical properties of the soil (texture, structure, organic matter, infiltration and drainage) and chemical properties (pH, nutrient analysis, salinity) are of particular importance. In some cases biological properties (pathogens) may also need evaluation. Weed treatment and some form of cultivation will generally be needed prior to planting, and an expert can advise on the best means to achieve this.

The preservation and use of any local topsoil is important, particularly for later reuse. Construction works should be supervised to ensure that no topsoil is damaged or removed from site, and that it is stockpiled appropriately. Different soil blends, amendments and composts can be used to ameliorate specific soil problems and to support specific planting outcomes (e.g. annual vegetable gardens). However, these should be used sparingly and should meet relevant soil or compost standards. These products should also not be used where they could exacerbate any existing soil problems (e.g. the addition of deep, organic composts to underlying poorly drained clays for tree and shrub plantings).

Many sites, particularly clay soils, can be severely compacted during landscape construction, especially where heavy machinery has been used. Compaction can severely compromise plant performance, particularly shrubs and trees,[31] and is not easy to remedy subsequently. Solutions include specialised deep cultivation before planting and the use of suitable mulches to relieve compaction.[32] In some playspaces, soil compaction from foot traffic alone is significant and can severely compromise tree performance. In these conditions, 'structural soils' can be used to support trees successfully over time.[33]

Plant establishment and maintenance

While issues of plant quality, planting hole construction and post-planting establishment are important in any planting project, they become critical the larger the container and type of plant being installed. Trees should be inspected carefully to ensure they are of an appropriate quality, using reference quality specifications or standards wherever possible. Inspection of both above and below ground parts of a plant can be important determiners of quality.

As a general rule, smaller plants will establish more rapidly on a site than larger plants.[34] That said, if planting cannot be protected for some reason, plants do need to be large enough that they are obvious to children, or they will be trampled unintentionally. Plants are generally regarded as 'established' on site when they are growing successfully with some new growth evident. Plant establishment can take considerable time and should be factored as part of project design and management. In particular woody plants, such as trees, palms and shrubs, can take several years to establish successfully. Wherever possible, planted areas should be mulched and fenced to exclude access and use until plants are established or at a suitable size and maturity.

Summary

Plants add to a playspace in so many ways – aesthetically, in terms of comfort and amenity, and even to the safety of a site, by marking it out as a place which is used and cared for. Most importantly though, plants offer an incredibly rich opportunity for free play and engagement with the real world that is not provided by standardised play equipment. With horticultural advice, good ongoing maintenance and most importantly great planting selection and design, planting can be so much more than just window dressing. It can form the essential backbone of play.

13

INTRODUCING WATER PLAY ENVIRONMENTS TO EARLY YEARS SETTINGS

Theresa Casey & Margaret Westwood

The OPAL Water Play project aimed to improve outdoor play spaces so that young children could enjoy the elemental, scientific and sensory qualities of water throughout the year. While we felt that children should have experience of water's practical uses such as watering plants, quenching thirst, cooling and moving things, we also wanted to highlight water's engaging magical, aesthetic and sensory qualities. This should become an everyday kind of play, whether that was guddling in puddles, damming rivulets in mud, experiencing the crispness of frost or the warmth of summer showers.

By the conclusion of the project, 40 of the City of Edinburgh's Early Years settings had introduced a range of new features, most of which staff, children and parents had been involved in designing and building themselves. They had created 'dry riverbeds', introduced water pumps, sand and boulders, made mounds and paths, started to harvest rain water and created 'water walls'. Perhaps most importantly OPAL Water Play conveyed the basic message that it is okay for children to get wet and muddy.

Origins of the project

The Water Play project came out of Edinburgh's OPAL programme, which aims to introduce an Outdoor Play and Active Learning approach to Early Years (playgroup, nursery and early primary school) settings in the city. The development of outdoor play in Early Years settings is also a part of the City of Edinburgh Council's Play Strategy (2008).

Inspiration for water play was found when the Council's Senior Play Development Officer made a visit to Berlin in 2005 as part of the International Play Association (IPA) Triennial World Conference and saw how schools there made use of natural landscapes and water to enhance children's play. In 2012 the national school grounds charity, 'Grounds for Learning', offered the opportunity for Edinburgh to send a representative to visit Berlin schools, where they had a 10 year plan – *'Grun macht schule'* – to improve city-centre play spaces for young children. The Senior Education Manager who participated was impressed by this approach and wished to support it in Edinburgh.

FIGURE 13.1 Children elaborate on the water play environment, Hope Cottage Nursery School, Edinburgh, Scotland 2013

Photo: City of Edinburgh Council

In the City's Early Years Team, there was a recent history of working to build practical skills and confidence in relation to outdoor spaces amongst Early Years practitioners (those educators working directly with young children). We had run annual workshops, which introduced simple design skills and easily achieved projects such as building sandpits, earth mounds and dry riverbeds. Various training and continual professional development opportunities focused on Nature Play, Elemental Play and Space for Play.

These and the City's Early Years and Play Policies provided the context in which OPAL Water Play was given the go ahead as a city-wide project with a budget of £40,000 including consultancy fees.

Introducing water play environments to Early Years settings **131**

Overall approach

In previous years OPAL had provided small grants to settings to promote outdoor play and, while useful, there was a tendency for this money to be spent in ways which did not appreciably add to play value (for example, when it was used to buy one-off pieces of equipment straight from catalogues).

Rather than take this approach, we decided to go down a different route with OPAL Water Play. The aim became to both:

- improve the physical spaces
- and increase practitioners' awareness of the value of play with water, along with their skills and confidence in creating and supporting play with water.

This was achieved by working with each setting to bring their own ideas to life rather than providing something ready-made to them. A play consultant supported each of the settings, helping them to draw up simple site plans, develop their ideas, source materials and plan build days. A builder was available to assist on these build days when staff and volunteers worked together to make their new play features.

FIGURE 13.2 Staff and volunteers enjoy a sense of achievement on a 'water play' build day, Leith Primary School Nursery, Edinburgh, Scotland 2013

Photo: Theresa Casey

Water play environments

OPAL provides a focus on outdoor environments, and the theme of water proved to be one with plenty of room to move round in. Many of the new features were relatively simple and low-key but seemed to out-perform in terms of the play opportunities they supported.

In the course of the project we made a number of 'dry riverbeds', simple pebbly channels that are inspired by the idea of the bottom of a stream. We made these trickling down slopes, some with small 'islands', others including boulders; we added mosaics, local beach pebbles and 'sea glass'; we introduced planting, stepping stones and bridges.

The 'dry river beds' allowed children to play with moving water and watch how it moved between cobbles. They could float feathers along it and stand well back to watch birds coming to drink. The 'riverbeds' frost up nicely in winter and sometimes have little pools of ice, while in summer the stones feel warm under a little foot.

We spent a lot of time thinking about where the water would come from and many of the settings started to harvest rain water. The fact that there wasn't a limitless supply of water was seen as a benefit and on a purely practical level it stopped the play areas becoming uncontrollably flooded. It was also felt important for children to understand the cycles through which we have water and that our supply shouldn't be taken for granted. Many of the settings chose to have opening celebrations for their new water play projects and used them to raise funds to donate to the charity Water Aid.

Water pumps were both a plus for the project and an enormous headache. We found some 'village' style iron hand-pumps on barrels which used a small reservoir of water (not plumbed into the mains water supply). These were wonderful while they worked but didn't stand up to prolonged playing. We discovered that whereas adults use an up-and-down motion to work the pumps, children tended to use a side-ways motion and this caused them to wear and break.

Although a disappointment, it also illustrated the interaction between the physical opportunities available and the attitude of practitioners. For some settings, if the pump broke down it wasn't an insurmountable issue and they recognised that children loved transporting water in buckets and barrows from barrels and taps. Especially wonderful for children engaged in transport 'schemas', the transporting of water seems to be a big element of playing with water as it sloshes around in buckets, drips from leaky containers and overflows when the tap isn't turned off in time.

On some occasions, however, the adults seemed to get fixated on the mechanics of the pump and forgot there were plenty of other ways to introduce water. In the end the best pumps we found were plastic ones which could be attached to large water cooler bottles. These were a very flexible, inexpensive and popular option and allowed to children to understand the cause and effect of the pumping action.

We also learned quite a bit about volumes of water children seemed to enjoy. This particular project didn't set out to create paddling pools or use large quantities of water, it didn't create ponds or fountains of water, all of which would give different experiences of water. We did discover that children sometimes really just needed a very small amount of water to have satisfying play, not especially wanting more. For example, we observed the fascination to be found in tiny rivulets of water barely wide enough for little fingers to block and unblock; or trickles of water changing the colours in a handful of pebbles. A puddle would emerge where children guddled in mud but they didn't need that puddle to get bigger and bigger. It satisfied as it was.

Many of the projects branched out into complementary features while they had a focus on the outdoors and created sand play areas, little hills and grassy mounds, tunnels and water 'walls' (pipes, funnels and guttering attached to fences for directional play with water). The results were fascinating to observe and 'transforming' was a word used many times by practitioners reflecting on children's play and adult practice. It seemed that it wasn't just the introduction of a new feature that made the difference, but the range of experiences they supported and the change in the adults' approach to playing outdoors.

Staff have noted how children were immersed in sustained play for longer periods and were delighted by the wide ranging use of language it provokes. The water play features support exploration of a natural element; support observation of natural properties and seasonal changes; and encourage interaction with other children in cooperative play and using communications skills.

> The children have loved the opportunity to experience outdoor water play. The feature has opened up a whole range of new play opportunities for the nursery garden – a place to find materials, for bridges and dams or a simple fishing rod. It's been fantastic to watch them invent so many different ways to use it.
>
> *Early Years Centre Deputy Manager*

> It's amazing, the children play in a completely different way now.
>
> *Nursery Practitioner*

The project has had the additional benefit of engaging with parents and community members who had not previously been involved. Fathers and grandfathers, in particular, seemed to enjoy being able to contribute to the child's nursery in a very practical way with many reporting that when they came to help in the build days, it was the first time they had been involved with anything at the nursery.

> I didn't want to come this morning but I'm so glad I did. It's the first time I've been to my son's nursery but I will come back.
>
> *Father volunteering at a 'build day'*

OPAL water play steps – how we carried out the project

In total 40 settings were involved. Twenty of these received one day's training, a Water Play Folder and a small grant and were then responsible for taking their own ideas forward in their setting. A further 20 settings also received direct support from a play consultant in order to develop their ideas and to implement their plans. This support was roughly equivalent to four half days per setting in the course of the project.

The project had a number of elements which supported and enabled new features to be introduced within five months, from start to finish. Although a successful strategy for assisting

FIGURE 13.3 Getting down close. Gilmerton Early Years Centre, Edinburgh, Scotland 2013

Photo: City of Edinburgh Council

a large number of settings, the time frame proved to be a challenge not helped by days of heavy rain and winter snow falls.

Elements of the project

1. **Training:** To introduce the project, provide some basic skills and to inspire ideas. From the outset we promoted the idea of creating imaginative water play environments, suitable for the location and context of the settings. There are many ways experiences with water can be achieved, and we hoped to spark creative approaches.
2. **Support:** Extra support was provided by the consultant who visited each establishment, listened to the team, helped to make drawings and advised on considerations for implementing the project. Different settings needed different types and levels of support which we envisaged as a 'menu'.
3. **Menu of support:**
    - Adding value to the project through use of natural, recycled and found materials
    - Adding value through involvement of the community of the establishment
    - Inclusion of children's views and their practical experience
    - Translating ideas into actual designs
    - Sourcing, estimating and ordering materials
    - Help with organising 'build days' when staff, parents and/or children built and created water play environments (or elements of them)

- Risk-Benefit Assessment
- Communicating play value with parents and colleagues
- Troubleshooting (from countering resistance amongst adults through to physical design and practical arrangements).

4. **Participation:** Practitioners and parents/carers (and janitors, grandparents, aunts and uncles) were involved in most of the 'build days' and without them this project would not have achieved its aims to anything like the extent that it did. This also really encouraged conversations about the value of outdoor play between staff and the children's families.
5. **Documentation:** We provided large scrapbooks to each of the settings as a way of recording the process and capturing early ideas, emerging designs, children's participation, problem solving, building and playing. Where the idea of using scrapbooks was embraced, it proved to be a great way to share and reflect on the process as well as the end results.
6. **Water Play Folders, handouts and ideas sheets:** We wanted to provide back-up to the key contact person in each setting to make it easier for them to take the project back to their team, talk to colleagues and bring it to life. We did this through Water Play lever-arch Folders which contained information and advice (Health and Safety Briefing Notes, Build Day Planners, Sources of Materials) and plenty of visual materials ('Ideas Sheets', Getting into Water Play Leaflet) which we produced especially for the project. We found that our 'Ideas Sheets' were particularly effective as a starting point for conversations as the visuals were appealing and made it easy to talk about what might be achieved.

Concerns about managing risk were addressed through training and the folders which contained Health and Safety Briefing Notes. We emphasised that practitioners themselves were in a position to make good judgements about risk and challenge in play environments and highlighted the Risk-Benefit Approach as the most appropriate method to use.

Lessons we've taken to the next OPAL project

We learned the way of working, coupling support with information, advice and a budget, was far more effective and long-lasting than a budget alone.

We felt that it was really important to demonstrate to practitioners in each of the settings that the play environment is their resource to use and develop. Most would feel confident in reorganising the indoor play spaces but were hesitant outdoors. We surmised that sometimes this is due to having less of a feeling of ownership outdoors than in – were they allowed to dig up the grass or plant a tree, for example? Often the practitioners and children had great ideas but were uncertain about the steps to achieving them. OPAL Water Play helped to overcome these hurdles. Informal observation suggests that subsequent to the project, more and more small projects have taken place independently in settings across the city.

We learned that quite low-key physical changes do have the potential to bring about quite significant changes to children's play opportunities. The project highlighted that Water Play includes experiments and experiences with frost, snow, ice and slush as well as with running water or pools; being alive to the loveliness of dew on the grass or sparkling early morning cobwebs as well as the fun to be had moving water; being alert to glittering snail trails across pebbles and small birds bathing in puddles as well as splashing in puddles ourselves.

The emphasis on participation paid off in fresh thinking, creative approaches and new ways to solve design problems. For example, some settings discovered offers of professional skills amongst their parents so that various combinations of architects, roofers, landscape gardeners, bakers, botanists, joiners, builders and artists mucked in together in their children's play space project. Donations of old roof slates added character to a number of projects and others received lovely weathered old stone. Many of the settings worked in advance with their children to decorate stones to embed in the rivers while others benefitted from more fully realised planting schemes using the expertise of parents.

The majority of settings receiving consultancy support carried forward and enhanced their projects for outdoor play and learning opportunities after the initial support concluded, whilst a slightly smaller number of self-managed projects continued to develop further. It was found that the drive for improvement and sustainability came from key staff engaged in the project.

We discovered that successful collaboration can be supported by working through the whole plan, design, build, review process together and trying as much as possible to build skills and confidence amongst practitioners for whom the play space is their everyday working environment. And most of all, of course, we were reminded of the joy children find in playing with water.

14

THE DEVELOPMENT OF FOREST SCHOOL IN THE UK

Christina Dee

The Forest School Movement originated in Scandinavia in the 1950s. The Scandinavians developed 'Nature Nurseries' where children learned through play in child-led learning environments set in the outdoor natural world. In these countries, being in the outdoors is a more cultural way of life. In 1993 a group from Bridgewater College visited Denmark and observed children playing outside in woodlands, in a child-led learning environment. They were so inspired that, upon their return to the UK, they developed what is now known as forest school, beginning within the Early Years setting.

Forest schools have progressively expanded across the UK and now staff within Early Years, primary and secondary schools are becoming more interested in the benefits of forest school for their pupils. Amongst these are schools with disaffected young pupils who find the structure and confines of the classroom difficult to deal with. Many schools for children with special needs are also implementing forest school programmes to support the development of independence and confidence in these children.

To educate and support these programmes, several training providers have been established to train leaders to facilitate forest school sessions and there are now over 8,000 Level 3 qualified forest school leaders in the UK.

What is forest school?

Forest school is a long term holistic learning process that aims to raise self-awareness and self-esteem in participants. Regular sessions take place in a woodland environment, where the landscape itself adds to the experience of learning.

Qualified practitioners, trained in child development, self-esteem and learning theories, facilitate sessions to gain personal outcomes for each participant. Forest school can be applied to all age groups and abilities, and can be linked to the UK National Curriculum and Early Years Foundation Stage (EYFS).

Forest school England definition

Forest school is an inspirational process that offers children and young people opportunities to achieve, develop confidence and self-esteem, through hands on learning experiences in a local woodland environment.

Forest school England principles

- Forest school is for all children and young people.
- Forest school builds on a child's innate motivation and positive attitude to learning, offering them the opportunities to take risks, make choices and initiate learning for themselves.
- Forest school is organised and run by qualified forest school leaders.
- Forest school maximises the learning potential of local woodland through frequent and regular experiences throughout the year, not a one-off visit.
- Forest school helps children to understand, appreciate and care for the natural environment.

Sessions of forest school are child/learner-led to accommodate individual learning styles and schemas. Children/learners are encouraged to make choices, and follow their own learning. The forest school leader acts as a facilitator, using observation to assess the children/learners and guide development through the programme.

Teacher's learning support staff and child care workers involved with children/learners who undertake forest school report significant improvements in independence, self esteem, social skills and concentration levels in children participating in these programmes. Parents of children involved in forest school have also reported changes in independence, self-esteem and their child's social outlook.

Where can forest schools take place?

The ideal location for forest school is a large, natural forest woodland, because of the associated wellbeing benefits of being within in a natural environment. For some schools, however, this may not be possible due to access, cost and lack of transport available. Many settings may use their garden, local park, school playing field or allotment areas. The most important aspect of a forest school area is to be able to risk-manage the hazards that may be present, such as rubbish, public access and dogs as well as many others. It is important that a non-woodland forest school has some trees (as a minimum), and potential to plant and develop the area; this may mean bringing in some natural materials such as logs, sticks and leaves.

Who carries out forest school and why?

In the UK, forest school is led by a Level 3 qualified forest school leader. Training of a forest school leader involves studying the History of Forest School and Health and Safety Management. Trainee leaders also study Child Development and Learning Theory with a link to forest school context. Finally practical skills such as tool use, fire lighting and shelter building are taught with a particular focus on children. Most people undertaking the training are qualified teachers or child care professionals as they can apply their knowledge taken from their professional training.

Two forest school case studies

Through the following two case studies, I would like to demonstrate firstly why urban forest schools can be just as successful as those in more rural locations, and secondly the importance and value of forest schools to children with special needs. The first case study examines the forest school programme established for the Old Church Nursery School in Tower Hamlets in London's inner-east. The second is a forest school programme established for the Welcome Hills School in Stratford-upon-Avon, Warwickshire.

Urban forest schools (Old Church Nursery School, Tower Hamlets)

The UK has seen a cultural shift from outdoor play being a part of every child's life pre-1970, to children and families having increasingly less access to and use of the outdoors to play and learn.

The United Kingdom statistics[1] are as follows:

- 28% girls and 22% boys aged 2–10 are obese; this has doubled since 1998
- 52% primary children walked to school in 2008, as opposed to their parents' generation where it was 77%.

Perhaps the most significant factor in changing public perceptions is media coverage, which, for example, promotes the outdoors as dirty and 'full of germs', and public parks and spaces as high-risk areas because they attract 'undesirable' people. We live in a risk-averse society – particularly related to children – where the impact of working parents and lack of time, plus the use of TV, computers and other digital media to entertain children, all play a role in the limited opportunities many children have to experience the outdoors.

Can forest school really work in an inner city urban area?

Almost every time we introduce the idea of urban forest school, the first response from teaching staff is 'Where would the children go?' and this might be followed up by 'There are no green spaces' and 'It couldn't be a "real" forest school'. It's also not unusual to hear comments like: 'The urban green spaces are too dangerous with high risk people there and savage dogs.'

These are just some of the typical perceptions and reasons people give to explain why urban forest school is impossible to implement. The evidence says otherwise, however, as there are more than 1,000 forest schools currently taking place in inner city London.

The Forest School Learning Initiative has been developing forest schools in London for the past 13 years, training forest school leaders, working with local parks and their staff to identify green spaces, working with local community groups and working with Early Years and schools teams in eight London boroughs.[2]

This case study focusses on an East End Borough. Some of the significant demographic details of this Borough are as follows:[3]

- In 2012, 89% of the school population were classified as belonging to an ethnic group other than white British, compared to 26% in England overall
- Furthermore, English is an additional language for 74% of pupils
- There are high levels of poverty with 46.4% of primary age pupils eligible for free school meals in 2011
- Although prevalence of childhood obesity in Year 6 has plateaued for the last three years, with the current rate at 25.6% for 2011/12, it is the 2nd highest in London
- The last available School PE and Sport Survey (2009/10) showed that children in Tower Hamlets take part in less formal physical activity than the England average, and the proportion of primary school children walking to school (whilst high) has fallen year-on-year, with levels of cycling to primary school remaining significantly lower than the national average.

These issues led to the borough being funded (through their Healthy School Project) for the development and training of forest school. It was recognised that forest school would benefit children by going outside regularly, being physically active and becoming more health-aware. It was also recognised that forest school offered the potential for influencing many families unused to the outdoors by sharing their positive experiences.

Within a short period of time, spaces to develop forest school were identified with park rangers, the criteria being accessibility, natural resources and safe management. Park rangers agreed to support forest school staff by providing logs, wood and trees for planting. Nearly 30 forest school leaders have been trained annually in the borough for the last three years and 90 forest schools established.

This case study focusses on a primary school in Bethnal Green that takes 90 children per year in three classes (total school population 650 children). The children are typical of the demographic spread of the Borough. School staff report that children rarely access the outdoor spaces locally. Local parks are perceived to be high risk, as there can be rubbish, dogs and people who may be a threat. Going outdoors is not part of the local culture, and most of the children would only visit local shops as their outdoor experience.

Implementing forest school has been a challenge for the school. Two staff were trained as forest school leaders, with initial priority given to offering forest school to Early Years and Year 1, as well as a number of children identified by the school who would potentially benefit most from forest school experience. It was agreed that each of the three groups would access forest school in a local park area, once a week. The school purchased enough waterproof suits for all the children.

To access the area, children have to walk through a number of minor streets and across a very busy main road. As part of their health and safety management, the forest school staff have sufficient supporting adults and a very rigid routine for the journey so the children and adults know when to stop, how to cross roads and how to manage all the hazards along the way. As a result of taking a regular journey to forest school, the children are safe and confident at crossing roads when they are with their parents too, and staff are aware that these children now access the park with their families and are better at making independent judgements around risk.

The forest school area is a designated area on the edge of the local park. There are a number of trees and natural materials so the area feels like woodland to the children. The area is risk-assessed termly, but also checked by staff before the children go in for each session.

At this forest school, the children have access to areas for mini beasts, digging and tree climbing, a large range of natural resources, den and shelter making and are able to explore the area and take part in a journey of discovery. The children can lead their own learning within the area, and are able to be a part of a forest school session that fulfils the ethos of forest school.

The school reports that, in the two years that the children have participated in forest school, they have identified a large number whose language has improved through the sessions. At forest school, several children feel more confident to use language to describe what they are doing and socialise with others; this and other improvements have been transferred back to school. Staff have seen a dramatic improvement in physical skills: this includes children progressively improving their climbing skills up the climbing tree, getting less tired on the walk to forest school and using fine motor skills to pick things up and examine them. It also includes gross motor skills – using tools, banging in sticks with a mallet and using a peeler to whittle sticks. A large number of children fully engage in the forest school session where they struggle in the classroom environment. Many children have asked parents to go to

FIGURE 14.1 Den building, planning, Ragley Hall, Warwickshire 2013

the forest school area with them outside school, and are definite about explaining the forest school rules to their parents.

So now to answer the question 'Can forest school really work in an inner city urban area?' and address the myths. There are a wide range of urban spaces suitable for forest school, and identification is reliant on local knowledge and good relationships with local parks. These spaces are full of a wide range of natural materials, and additional materials can also be taken in to support and sustain the area. Detailed health and safety management enables positive risk-benefit management of the area, with children being empowered to manage their own risks, too.

Developing forest school for children with learning difficulties (Welcome Hills School, Stratford-upon-Avon)

In the UK, children who have more severe learning difficulties usually attend a 'special school' which is able to meet those needs, whereas children with moderate to mild learning difficulties are usually integrated into mainstream schools whenever possible.

The school in this case study caters for children with multiple and complex special needs, with ages ranging from 3 to 18 years. The children are highly supervised, have restricted independence and their learning experience is closely supervised because of their complex needs: their experience of learning is very structured to minimise risk and promote their safeguarding.

In 2012, we were asked if it would be possible to provide forest school to special needs nursery children (aged 3–6 years) and Year 1 and 2 children (aged 5–8 years). We have had experience over the past 10 years of working with children with special needs, but not on this scale where the children had such complex needs. In order to gain a thorough understanding of the children's needs, I spent two days in the school observing the children in their classroom environment.

The issues we consider when looking at a forest school programme relate primarily to the children's behaviour issues and management, and their communication needs.

The children had a range of learning difficulties – from Down's Syndrome, Autism Spectrum Disorder, Cerebral Palsy as well as many learning difficulties of unknown aetiology. Many of the children had little or no verbal communication, so signing was their main communication method, and also using cue cards. This varied, however, for each child, and it quickly became clear that I would need to create specific signing information on forest school for individual children that helped them understand the routines, safety rules and activities children could choose from.

Many of the children attending would put any item in their mouth to explore or eat it: this clearly had massive health and safety implications, requiring detailed knowledge of plants in the area. Although several children who would be attending had one-to-one supervision, the issue of very toxic plants in the area would require management.

Mobility was another issue. We had two children in wheelchairs, so we needed to think through the access to the site, how activities could be accessed once there and recognise that, in cold conditions, these children – even if well-clothed – may not be able to attend for long due to their circulation issues. Some of the children were very unsteady in their gait, so minimising trip hazards and providing adult support that enabled the children to explore without being restrictive was also essential.

Behaviour management was a challenge for many. I reviewed the school's behaviour management plans and discussed how they could be implemented in a forest school session to ensure continuity.

After careful discussion with teaching staff, it was agreed that the forest school site would initially be on the school grounds in an area not normally used by the children, but secluded and secure: it was more like a garden with a bank and a few trees.

Concentration time was limited for some so it was decided to start off with a very short session that involved establishing the routine of getting ready for forest school and putting on waterproofs. This proved a challenge for some as they had never experienced this and several took a few weeks to learn how to put them on. Then we walked to forest school and explored the area.

Some of the staff were concerned about the children attending forest school, as their perception was that the children would not manage the experience and it would be too dangerous for them. My role was to listen and work in collaboration with staff so that any concerns could be addressed effectively, to create a supportive working environment for staff and to ensure a 'whole team' approach.

Implementation

A meeting with parents was held to give them background information about the concept of forest school, the practical arrangements for sessions and how we were going to support their children in this new learning experience. A really important part of the meeting was listening to and answering the concerns that parents raised. We also held a training session with the staff involved to ensure they had a clear understanding of forest school's objectives.

A detailed risk assessment was carried out and communicated to the staff: this related not only to hazards on the site but also to plans to ensure each child had a risk management strategy in place. The school purchased some waterproofs, and we also donated some to ensure each child had access to suitable clothing. Parents supplied their child's welly boots. There were 8 to 10 children in each session.

The first session involved getting ready, walking to forest school, sitting at base camp on the logs, having an explore and beginning to introduce the rules of forest school and the reasons for these rules. The rules were also presented on cue cards and signed for some children.

The children at this session surprised the staff; they showed great independence on the walk to forest school, and many wanted to explore independently and did find special things to show the adults and their friends. Even at this first session, one boy who has severe behaviour issues showed greater concentration than normally seen, and another tried to use language, which was unusual.

Forest school has taken place in this school now for three years, with those children attending coming every week all year. In total, there are now 60 children coming to forest school every week over two days, and a holiday club runs after school every week from September to October and from April to July, to fit in with daylight hours. The children come to visit our forest every half term to enhance their experience.

What they have learnt

The children adapted quickly to the forest school routine. The introduction of activities and resources for learning – such as spades, paint brushes, buckets for making mud and mud painting, bug pots for minibeast finding and discovery, identification pictures to match what they found – had to take place very slowly as the children gained in confidence enough to try anything new. We learned that it was best to introduce new ideas every two to three weeks to avoid the children becoming overwhelmed.

It took at least a term before the children chose what they wanted to do – this only developed by allowing adults to support the children choosing. After a while the adults felt a bit redundant, but were able to focus on observing the children's learning.

Children who were sensory phobic were introduced to textures and mud at their own pace and given time, and now happily paint with mud and play in the mud and water, and are more able to engage in any learning involving textures indoors as well.

The children love to explore and look for mini beasts and enjoy using the identification cards to match what they find.

One boy who would never eat in front of others will now sit at base camp and enjoy his hot chocolate drink with the others. He also now eats and drinks in the classroom. Many of the children have shown a substantial increase in concentration skill during forest school, and remain engaged in what they are doing for much longer.

FIGURE 14.2 Helping hand, teamwork, Evesham, Worcestershire 2014

The children come out to our forest in Gloucestershire every half term for a half-day session, and this involves a 30-minute trip on a mini bus. We have observed the children transfer their knowledge of forest school routines and rules from their own forest school site to the different woodland area. The children have settled quickly into the woodland environment and, because of this, have chosen and engaged in learning very effectively. We have been amazed at how quickly the children explored the area, showing independence and confidence. The children talk about their woodland experience back at school and to their parents.

What we have learnt

Detailed preparation of the site, briefing the adults and being prepared has been essential. We have focussed what we do on what the children can achieve, not what their difficulties are, and empowered the children to manage risk with adult support. This has required a lot of time, as we know that the children become more dependent if they are scared or unsure.

The steady introduction of resources has encouraged the children to try new experiences. We have also found that supporting and encouraging children to make choices has enabled their independence skills and their confidence to develop.

The cultural change of practice – from close supervision and intervention to being a facilitating adult who encourages and supports – has been a challenge for some of the adults, but the practice has transferred back to the classroom.

FIGURE 14.3 Cooking on the fire, Evesham, Worcestershire 2015

Children with special needs are more affected by low and high temperatures, and we have seen significantly worse behaviour issues on very hot or very cold days. For a few children, the inability to understand why they feel hot or cold and what to do about it has resulted in frustration: we have resolved this by being prepared and, if necessary, allowing the child and their adult to go indoors.

The implementation of forest school sessions in this school has made a substantial difference to the learning experience for these children. The improvement in confidence, self esteem and independence – which is the ethos of forest school – has empowered so many of these children to engage in learning and then transfer those skills to the classroom as well.

We move now from a programmed approach to nature play, to spaces designed in the public realm. In these highly designed spaces, the environment is more controlled, but the way that people use them is less easy to manage. Each has their own challenges and opportunities.

15

CHILDREN'S GARDENS

A tale of two cities

Andrew Laidlaw

Ian Potter Foundation Children's Garden – Royal Botanic Gardens, Melbourne: An Introduction

Modern living has brought increased urbanisation and higher density housing to most modern cities. Children living in Australia today have significantly less opportunity to venture outdoors and enjoy the natural world. The Ian Potter Foundation Children's Garden (IPFCG), which sits within the Royal Botanic Gardens Melbourne, has just turned ten years old and we hope has helped to redefine how children interact with nature. The garden was designed around the premise that 'play is the work of children' and that kids need to be able to dig, build, create, hide and explore as part of their everyday play to learn about themselves and their place in the world.

The Ian Potter Foundation Children's Garden is a safe, interactive environment in which children of all ages, backgrounds, physical abilities and cultures can play, explore and discover nature. The garden aims to link children through their play to the remarkable world of plants. The garden has been scaled for children to create a sense of ownership, learn to care and raise awareness of the environment. It features plants, water, structures and pathways that reflect Melbourne's changing seasons. From the meeting place and ornamental entrance garden through to the 'parterre' styled kitchen garden, the water rill, bamboo forests and the recently added banana forest there is something for every child to enjoy and marvel at.

Design process

The multi-disciplinary design team for this project of five from within the Royal Botanic Gardens and one external person came with expertise in landscape architecture, horticulture, visitor programmes, education and art. The strong internal focus allowed the process to be contained within the organisation, which I believe is very important. Our team was given time to build a strong foundation and develop a clear vision which provided a strong framework for the design process. The mix of design and non-design backgrounds also created a group dynamic that ensured a balanced approach to the project.

Traditionally botanic gardens communicate the world of plants in an adult way. Suddenly the team was presented with the unique opportunity to create a landscape language which was meaningful and interactive for children.

The process began by developing a single, articulate idea for the garden which gave clear direction throughout the design process and beyond. A series of workshops, involving clay modelling and working with form, helped us build a strong team and develop our shared values. The result was a clear vision for the garden that could be written down and communicated to the broader community:

> The Ian Potter Foundation Children's Garden will be a place where children can delight in nature and discover a passion for plants. It will be a garden that celebrates the imagination and curiosity of children and fosters the creative nature of play.

Consultation and collaboration

We had the luxury of a year to gather information and record our data to inform the design process. The team would meet weekly, which included site visits, consultation with specialists and practical sessions with children. Site visits were focused on centres that had strong ideological philosophies such as Reggio Emilia, Steiner and Montessori.

We were determined that children had to play an active role in the design process. Children from both country- and city-based primary schools were involved in activities held both on site and at their schools. Activities varied from drawing their own ideas, to activities

FIGURE 15.1 Overview of Ian Potter Children's Garden, Melbourne Botanic Gardens
Laidlaw & Laidlaw Design

where children were observed during free play with a range of loose materials, flowers, rocks, soil, sand, bark, sticks, cut bamboo and leaves. This research translated into the design creating a variety of sensory and spatial experiences that were largely non-prescriptive (no identifiable focus) in the garden, particularly 'child-sized spaces' which offered group or solo play, quiet and noisy spaces, active and passive areas.

As part of the consultation process we formed an 'Industry Reference Panel'. Panel members offered expertise in landscape architecture, open space management, horticulture, art, journalism, early childhood development and primary and tertiary education. We met with the panel formally three times during the process but sought out individual expertise from panel members on an as needs basis.

The final component of the consultation process was a visit to the United States of America to see what the current trends were and how the children were interacting with the landscape spaces. By and large we were disappointed. What we saw was often large budgets spent on overly intellectual clever ideas that the children would engage with for short periods of time. What was impressive, however, was the cross-generational communication between children and many of the adults that were either gardening or running volunteer programmes in the gardens. On our return we were further convinced that children and their connection to nature had to drive every component of our design and that a vegetable garden should be part of the garden.

Design

Parents' comfort levels are essential to children being permitted to explore and imagine and create their own stories within a space. This is especially true around issues of safety and convenience to toilet and food facilities. The garden was designed with a steel picket fence around its entire perimeter with a single public entry and exit point, which immediately reduces parents' stress around children being lost. The site also sits in proximity to recently renovated toilet facilities with plenty of opportunity to buy good food and coffee. Service access for maintenance staff and a separate access for education officers and school groups is also provided and is essential for the successful operation of the garden. It is not uncommon for over 200 school children to arrive at any one time. The design of a separate area for school children to gather allows them to be corralled and spoken to separately before they enter the children's garden.

> However, now that the Garden has been in operation for a while, we can see that one of our challenges is we do not have a 'Back of House' area for loose materials, tools and equipment to be stored which limits our operation at times.

The Children's Garden entrance is marked by a symbolic art piece which overlays plant and people forms onto stone and flags the gardens entrance to passers-by. Once inside the whimsical gates you enter a meeting place where there are seats and water play. From this single meeting place you can then choose a number of different journeys within the garden. The design deliberately breaks the space into a series of smaller spaces, creating mystery and privacy, with each space having a different plant theme. By creating smaller, intimate spaces scaled for children the site feels much larger than it actually is, and for a child this experience is intensified. The plant themes include a Sea Garden, the Snow Gum Gorge, the Secret

FIGURE 15.2 Stone slabs are available for outdoor creativity
Laidlaw & Laidlaw Design

Ruin and Rainforest, the Wetland, the Bamboo Forest, the Flax and Tea Tree Tunnels, the Grassy Mounds and the Kitchen Garden. Other important elements of the design that are essential to the operation of the garden include a series of water play areas, a potting shed and two purpose built structures: the Discovery Shelter used primarily for delivering education programmes and the Activity Shelter that is used for holiday performance and delivery of a range of public programmes.

> The garden area is small about 1.25 acres and it is full-up, what we lack are generous open areas where loose materials could be left for cubby building and other forms of construction, even the small lawn is often full to brimming with picnickers leaving very little open space.

Water play is a major element in the garden and provides hours of pleasure for the children, especially in the hotter summer months. The garden comprises four main water features: two fountains, a rill running from the rainforest through the grassy mounds and a wetland garden. The water areas are all treated and carefully monitored to ensure public safety. Water at all the fountain points must be constantly maintained at Class A, suitable for human consumption.

> Managing water quality and the risk associated with water play in a children's garden is costly and often requires specialist skills, at the IPFCG this burden falls on the horticultural department that monitors and records water quality every week and purges the system monthly. We had a number of teething problems around water and water quality within weeks of the garden opening, which lead to the shutdown of all the water features over the first summer.

FIGURE 15.3 Water bubblers are the source of the water rill which runs through the Garden
Laidlaw & Laidlaw Design

Plant selection, plant environments and maintenance

In the Children's Garden the plants are the single most important element; they create the walls, the floors, the sounds, the seasonality and the smells of every space in the entire garden. It was therefore absolutely essential to get both the plant selection and the plant environment right. Each plant was selected against a matrix of criteria to ensure the best decisions were made (refer to Planting Design on pp. 116–17). Plant selection avoided any listed poisonous plants and plants with berries and/or dangerous spikes.

Through appropriate soil amelioration, drainage, fertilisation and irrigation the growing environments were optimised to ensure plants thrived in the garden. Issues of soil compaction and poor drainage are major contributors to plant failure in many children's spaces so it was essential to safeguard against compaction caused by over 250,000 visitors each year. To manage the compaction, turf sand was mixed with the site's existing duplex clay loam.

The sand – resistant to compaction – maintains its air spaces and therefore provides a more desirable growing medium for plants. This adjustment of the soil profile, combined with the installation of sub-surface drainage, surface contouring and a well-designed irrigation system, are the main reasons the garden has continued to perform.

Essential to the successful planting was using large, healthy plant stock and providing a generous plant establishment period. Most plants were given at least a year or more to establish, before the garden was open. The bamboo forest, for example, was planted two years prior to the garden opening and watered and fed regularly to promote growth. Finally the entire garden is rested for up to two months every year to give the plants some necessary respite. This closure also allows time for important garden maintenance to be carried out.

> Plant performance and plant selection are continually being monitored in the IPFCG and every year we replant sections of the garden just to maintain the balance of plant cover. This is made easier by having access to an In-House Nursery and a staff member dedicated to the Children's Garden, something that not all gardens have access to.

The result

The garden has achieved remarkable success in a very short period of time and has become a well-known landmark within Melbourne, Australia, winning a Best Landscape Award in 2005 and best Tourism Victoria Best Attraction Award in 2006. It has redefined how children can interact with nature in a designed public space and created a new children's language in Botanic Gardens. This said there is still room for improvement and just recently we have added the banana forest and desert island and are looking at ways to get more loose materials in the garden. As an organisation we must continue to invest in new ideas that improve the connection between children and nature.

Global Gardens for Peace – Gaza Peace Garden: planning and design underway

It was possible to extend the lessons learnt from the Children's Garden in Melbourne Botanic Gardens to a very different setting. From peaceful, wealthy Australia to Gaza, within the Palestinian Occupied Territories. The practical and political challenges in the Gaza Peace Garden are very different to those of Melbourne, but the overarching principle of giving children a safe, green place in which it is acceptable to play are exactly the same.

The Gaza Peace Garden project was started by Moira Kelly AO, international humanitarian, after a medical rescue mission in February 2004. She was struck by two contrasting features: on one hand, her observations of children still playing even within the war torn streets, making playthings from broken metal and other rubbish, and on the other, their families' stories of war, atrocities and death. Most local children by the time they are six will have experienced at least three separate wars.

One of the only green spaces in Gaza is the lush green and manicured lawn of the Australian and English War memorial, funded by the Australian, New Zealand and English governments. This showed Moira what was possible, given the funds and willpower.

In many ways, the project does reflect the Children's Garden in Melbourne. Like Melbourne, there is a diverse (although smaller) team, including myself, Peter Symes from the Royal Botanic Gardens Melbourne, Wendy Clarke from Dirtscape Dreaming and David Wong from DW Design. Again, the space is intended as a beautiful and green oasis within the city, where children can connect with nature from a young age. There is a productive garden, water play, a gorge and spaces for families to gather and meet.

Both Children's Gardens, appropriate to their settings, are overlaid with connection to the local culture. In the case of the Gaza Peace Garden, this is manifested in various ways. After entering through two massive cut stones stencilled with local poetry in a flower garden, tented structures provide visitor facilities, including toilets, a library, picnic shelters with cooking facilities and an education centre. Some of these auxiliary services are not provided within the Melbourne site, but of course there is ample opportunity for Australian children to access these in other locations.

Other differences include the provision of playground structures in Gaza – rope courses, giant slides and flying foxes, and also the extent of the productive gardens, including orchards and livestock. Again, the story running through the whole design is one of the local culture. A maze garden is inspired by Arabic calligraphy; the garden centrepiece is a palm shaded oasis; and the series of raised lawns are set out to resemble an old Palestinian village with

FIGURE 15.4 Concept plan for Gaza Peace Garden
Courtesy: Laidlaw & Laidlaw Design

laneways and a square. By contrast, the Melbourne Children's Garden is inspired much more by Australian landscapes and garden traditions.

Despite these differences, the fundamental focus is to provide a nature-based play experience for all children, with thickets of trees, water rills, sand play and rock mazes. The hope is that the delight that children experience in Melbourne will be echoed, perhaps even more intensely given their circumstances, for the children of Gaza.

However, the practical and political challenges are much greater with this project. Gaza City is the most densely populated in the world, which will bring its own pressures of usage to a green space. That the site is within an ongoing war zone is impossible to ignore. The difficulties of sourcing all the materials required – plants, clean fertile soil, provision of water and energy – are ones which were a good deal easier to address in Australia. The garden has also been designed from the outset to be able to be built and maintained through local labour.

In many ways, it is surprising that there is support on the ground for an ambitious play project such as the Gaza Children's Peace Garden, when so much basic local infrastructure needs repair or is absent altogether. However, the strength of local feeling to get the garden built reflects the respect and hope that Palestinian families have for their children, and for the future. We hope that our experiences in Melbourne will give us a stronger and more informed grounding for the Gaza Peace Garden, as nothing teaches as well as experience.

Finally let's look at a playspace design project in the United States from a more traditional public setting. Its central landscape feature was inspired by the Rocky Mountains, which shaped its unique play elements and iconic form, breathing new life into a well-loved San Francisco Park.

16

REFLECTIONS ON DESIGNING LAFAYETTE PARK PLAYGROUND

Jeffrey Miller

San Francisco's historic Lafayette Park, located atop a hill in one of the city's most upscale neighbourhoods, had declined and was slated for complete renovation including the replacement of the ageing children's playground. Funding for the effort was generated from a large public improvement bond passed by the voters of San Francisco of which $10 million was dedicated specifically for the Lafayette Park project. A neighbourhood support group, Friends of Lafayette Park, proposed to provide financial support for the renovation effort with the infusion of additional funding targeted for the design and construction of the children's playground thereby creating a private/public partnership. Based on the recommendation of an architect colleague, I was asked to discuss the possibility of working with the Friends to design and oversee the development of a one-of-a-kind public playground for the park.

In our initial conversation I proposed a design for the playground where the activity and character of the play experience would be grounded by contact with natural elements. We discussed the potential of creating a place where wonder and mystery sprung from contact with earth and water. We talked about designing a playground where social interaction was encouraged and balanced by the possibilities of more intimate dreamlike experiences. The playground would be a place where adventure and excitement could happen safely in an environment that presented managed risks which would promote a growing sense of accomplishment for children ranging in ages. The more we talked the more we appeared to be on the right track with the aspirations and hopes of the group for the design of the playground.

In my professional career, I have spent 35 years designing many learning areas, playgrounds, and gardens in the context of children's centres, schools, and public parks. I was well prepared to take on the commission and after several interview sessions our company was assigned the task of collaborating with the community and interfacing with the public agency design team in charge of the larger renovation project. Our role was to be focused on the design of this unique playground.

The inspiration for the design of a nature based playground for Lafayette Park was generated from a photograph sent to me from Portugal by my son and his fiancé. The picture evoked a sense of surprise and mystery showing the two of them squeezing through a rocky passage, stones arising steeply on both sides. Their smiling faces, hands in contact with the ancient earth forms, and golden stone walls made me want to create a similar experience.

Our initial studies of the dedicated play area in the context of the larger park led us to believe that the existing play space needed to be enlarged to suit the programme proposed by the Friends. It also became clear that the functionality of the playground would be strengthened by considering adjacent areas for supporting uses including picnic areas, public bathroom facilities, a maintenance office, city views, and large group gathering areas. We looked to the Beaux Arts character of the original park layout and the classical nature of the surrounding neighbourhood architecture in establishing a design language for the area expansion. The plane of the playground area was enlarged to incorporate an extended arching belvedere overlooking the south and an enclosed picnic lawn framed by a curving wisteria covered arbour to the north. Taking careful consideration of user accessibility we proposed a pedestrian route from the neighbourhood into the park and the playground area. We developed concept plans and shared them with agency designers who responded positively, eventually incorporating the expanded areas into the overall park renovation plan.

Having established a context and supporting amenities for the playground we then dove deeply into the issues of the playground design. We wanted the playground to fit into the context while providing a unique sense of fantasy and joy with its own special feeling. We wanted to make use of the existing mature tree canopy as a backdrop to the play area. The idea of centring the playground design on a core built from natural stone was supported by the Friends group. Our initial design studies and sketches depicted two rocky central outcrops with a passage dividing the surrounding playspace into distinct zones dedicated to age specific activities, swings, water play, and social areas where fantasy performances could happen, and groups of children could play, while providing space for enclosures accommodating more secluded interactions. Several trees were to be planted within the central area in our initial design.

Sketches of two stone mountains highlighting viewpoints from several vantage points, and featuring a narrow gorge, were created, and the reaction was quite positive. We presented images of an elevated rock lined creek, featuring several hand pump stations, and they were also well received. Following the meeting, issues of safety and access were raised by the agency designers that led us to consider various alternatives to the rocky central forms including shaped topographic berms and timber structure inclines, none of which were particularly satisfactory.

I began a search for material that would meet our intention of establishing a natural core to the playground. My hope was to find stones that were blocky in nature, material that could be stacked to create a staircase effect which would provide safe access to the upper reaches. I wanted the stone to be warm and varied in colour with the idea that a glowing core to the playground would be an attractive natural beacon. I was directed to a quarry by a crane operator that I had worked with on many other projects where the material for our project could potentially be found. The Friends group supported my travel to the site located on the western slope of the Rocky Mountains to make an initial investigation. Stepping into the quarry, with its expanse of beautiful natural stone, I immediately understood that I had found the perfect material for our playground. I made many photographs of the large stone slabs and returned to San Francisco to share them with the Friends group and the agency designers. Upon viewing our photographs, the excitement for the design of this central feature began to grow.

I returned to the quarry several weeks later with Maya Nagasaka, my design collaborator on the project, to make an initial selection of the material. We identified many beautiful Pritchard Shale slabs that we felt were to our liking, ranging in size from 1 to 8 tonnes. Each stone was tagged and numbered, photographed, measured, and palletised, readying them for shipment to our project site. We selected beautiful stones featuring flat surfaces and warm hues of orange, ochre, and golden tone. Overall, we identified 250 tonnes of rock destined for the park and returned to our office equipped with a list of materials to further the design process.

Back in our studio armed with the photos of our new found materials, drawings were prepared in which individual rocks were located in multiple layers of stacked stone to form the structure with the largest pieces situated at the base to form the foundations. The meticulous stone composition created a narrow passage that we identified as 'The Gorge' between two peaks. Play features were designed to activate the central highpoints including several custom designed stainless steel slides and climbing nets. An arched timber bridge with heavy rope railings connects the two upper areas and an amphitheatre with large stone slab seating was centrally located in the core of the composition. We envisioned that the rock work itself would be an attractive play element encouraging children to clamber up and down and to explore the various outcrops.

Our drawings included other natural rock elements as well, that together formed a linear feature that slithered through the playground. At one end we designed a raised area extending from one of the central outcrops forming 'The Snake's Head' to serve as an overlook to the play area while cantilevering over an open cave below. The platform above is surfaced with black and white stripped pebbles resembling a snake's skin while the walls of the cave below

FIGURE 16.1 Concept sketch for Lafayette Park playground
Courtesy: Miller Company

FIGURE 16.2 Sensory pebble surface of the Snake
Courtesy: Miller Company

feature coral coloured pebble walls resembling the mouth of the serpent. The striped pebble treatment was designed to reappear atop a mounded crawl tunnel that rises from the floor of the play area and extends into the bed of a 60 foot/18.2 metre long raised creek designed for water play.

Design of the natural elements posed challenges regarding issues of accessibility. Numerous reviews of the design documents were undertaken during the design process to assure that the design addressed various codes and regulations. Access to the central rock areas was achieved by incorporating transfer stations into the rock design to accommodate disabled children approaching in wheel chairs. Water pump stations were designed along the raised creek with low pressure pumps and rock work was formed to give space for wheel chair use, allowing all children the potential of touching the water.

Safety concerns were also addressed in the design of the project. The stepping pattern of the rock work and the flat surfaces of the individual stones provide an environment where adventure can happen in a safe manner. The nature of the rock presented challenges during construction. Working closely with the installation contractor, we stacked each rock individually. The large blocks of shale stone had naturally occurring sharp edges which had to be placed or treated. Once everything was in place each exposed rock edge was carefully ground down to ease any safety concern. Open gaps between the stacked natural stones were filled with mortar to guard against finger entrapments as well as to close off spaces where animals could nest.

Maintenance staff provided review and direction at various stages throughout the design process. Our initial presentation to the community included a raised sand play area that was supported by the public but was eventually removed from the design due to concerns regarding wear and tear on the resilient rubber playground safety surface and potential

FIGURE 16.3 Golden stones were hand selected and placed to form the central Gorge
Courtesy: Miller Company

FIGURE 16.4 Water play is a source of much joy at the playground
Courtesy: Miller Company

problems with sand being transferred to the raised creek area. Tree planting in the central rock area was opposed by the park's staff due to the lack of truck access for long term maintenance. Planting at the edges of the playground, however, was accepted by the maintenance team, with new trees providing shade for perimeter seating areas.

Safety issues related to children's contact with water were significant. Balancing the design of the raised creek so that it provided an experience where children could touch and play with water in a safe and healthy way required that there be no standing water in the four inch deep creek bed. We provided a design where the water fell from one pool descending to the next. Drains were provided at each pool that were designed to release water slowly so that the play value remained while providing a system that could eventually fully flush out. Our initial design channelled water from the bottom pool of the raised creek into the landscape of the park. After considerable review by the agency design team and the park maintenance staff it was decided that the water exiting the creek should be directed to the storm sewer instead, which was a disappointment for us.

Maintenance of the water feature has been an ongoing issue due to constant use by children resulting in breakdowns of the hand pumps. Despite our efforts to provide high quality sturdy pump equipment, park staff have been challenged to make timely repairs when they are required. Our three foot/900 mm wide design of the creek bed has proven to be an attraction beyond our expectation. We imagined that water play would occur from the raised creek edges but have observed children of all ages completely immersing themselves, wading back and forth through the length of the water course. Valuable lessons have been learned that have led to us designing similar features for other children's areas with more narrow creek bed profiles where it is less likely to attract full body contact.

Our design team provided several play structures surrounding the natural core area including separate age appropriate swing zones, climbing structures, play towers, and a lengthy overhead feature that we dubbed 'The World's Longest Monkeybar'. For young toddlers a small wooden climber has been provided where children can ascend steps to panelled play platforms connected by crawl tunnels, nets, and outfitted with age appropriate slides. We chose to work with manufacturers that could provide natural materials for the structures in an effort to extend the earthy feel of the playground.

Looking to avoid garish colours that would conflict with the vivid stone core, we selected wooden pole structures with fabricated panel attachments in warm grey, yellow, and golden tones. A raised net tunnel connects the two towers of the older children's play structure, which blends with the branches of the mature overhanging perimeter trees. The resilient safety surface used throughout the playground was designed in a wavy flowing pattern in muted colours of gold and umber, bringing everything down to earth. A change in the surface occurs in perimeter seating areas. Warm toned composite timber decking underlies custom designed integrally coloured concrete bench seating, providing space for parents and care givers inside the playground. Dark brown paint was chosen for the perimeter playground fencing. Two custom hand railings were designed for ascending the outcrops. The 'Cat Tail' railing leading to the highest peak is fabricated to resemble the tall water loving plants and is painted with brown stalks and light tan heads; while the 'Snake's Head Fern Rail' is painted in olive green. We avoided the use of primary colours throughout the playground with the understanding that a more subtle palette would provide an environment where the interaction of the children with the natural materials would prevail.

The playground was completed in 2012 and has been well received by the public. We often hear that it is a favourite destination for children and their families who appreciate the natural experience that the area provides. The playground is actively used and filled with children on weekends, as are the adjoining picnic and lawn areas that were a part of our concept design. We have observed children exploring freely throughout the rocky playground landscape and can see that the design offers opportunities for personal navigation and social interaction that are not available in more standardised structured playgrounds. Children are fully engaged with the variety of elements designed into the playground, and it is a joy to observe the inclusive and free spirited way that they use the space.

Notes

Chapter 10

1 Denise G. Boyd & Helen L. Bee, *The Developing Child*. 13th Ed. 2014, Pearson Education Limited, UK.
2 Ibid.
3 Ibid.

Chapter 11

1 'The Ugly Duckling' (1844) by Danish fairytale writer Hans Christian Andersen (1805–1875). Available at: http://www.hca.gilead.org.il/ugly_duc.html.
2 Kaplan, Stephen, Kaplan, Rachel and Ryan, Robert L. (1998). *With People in Mind: Designing and Management of Everyday Nature*. USA: Island Press.
3 Kaplan, Stephen and Kaplan, Rachel (1989). *The Experience of Nature: A Psychological Perspective*. New York: Cambridge University Press.
4 Helle Nebelong said this first at her presentation in Portsmouth 2002 and has since then been quoted again and again for this statement. Available at: http://www.freeplaynetwork.org.uk/design/nebelong.htm. and/or http://www.sansehaver.dk/asp/side/foredrag/Portmouth.htm.
5 C. Th. Sørensen: Haver – tanker og arbejder. Christian Ejlers. (1975). Forlag. The quote translated into English by Helle Nebelong.
6 Legepladsens betydning for legen. Sammenhæng mellem leg og arkitektur. (2014). Ph.d. afhandling af Lise Specht Petersen, The Department of Sports Science and Clinical Biomechanics, Faculty of Health Sciences at the University of Southern Denmark (SDU).
7 In classical Roman religion the *genius loci* was the protective 'spirit of place.'

Chapter 12

1 Jeavons, M. and Hitchmough, J. 1994, Planning, design and management of open space for children, Chapter 18 in Hitchmough, J. (ed.), *Urban landscape management*. Inkata Press Pty Ltd, Sydney, pp. 521–37.
2 Mårtensson, F., Jansson, M., Johansson, M., Raustorp, A., Kylin, M. and Boldemann, C. 2014, The role of greenery for physical activity play at school grounds, *Urban Forestry & Urban Greening*, 13(1):103–113.
3 Parker, D. B. 2008, Safe and secure, *Parks and Recreation*, April, pp. 47–49.
4 Despard, E. 2012. Cultivating security: plants in the urban landscape, *Space and Culture*, 15(2):151–163.
5 Parker, D. B. 2008, Safe and secure, *Parks and Recreation*, April, pp. 47–49.
6 Chalker-Scott, L. 2007, Impact of mulches on landscape plants and the environment: a review, *Journal of Environmental Horticulture*, 25(4): 239.
7 Hitchmough, J. 2004, Selecting plant species, cultivars and nursery products, Chapter 2 in Hitchmough, J. and Fieldhouse, K. (eds.), *Plant user handbook: a guide to effective specifying*. Blackwell Science Ltd, Oxford.
8 Fjørtoft, I. and Sageie, J. 2000, The natural environment as a playground for children: landscape description and analyses of a natural playscape, *Landscape and Urban Planning*, 48(1): 83–97.
9 Stine, S. 1997, *Landscapes for learning: creating outdoor environments for children and youth*. John Wiley and Sons, New York.
10 Wake, S. 2007, Children's gardens: answering the call of the child? *Built Environment*, 33(4): 441–453.
11 Lekies, K. S. and Eames-Sheavly, M. 2007, Fostering children's interests in gardening, *Applied Environmental Education and Communication*, 6(1): 67–75.
12 Jansson, M., Gunnarsson, A., Mårtensson, F. and Andersson, S. 2014, Children's perspectives on vegetation establishment: implications for school ground greening, *Urban Forestry and Urban Greening*, 13(1): 166–174.
13 Hitchmough, J. 2004, Selecting plant species, cultivars and nursery products, Chapter 2 in

Hitchmough, J. and Fieldhouse, K. (eds.), *Plant user handbook: a guide to effective specifying*. Blackwell Science Ltd., Oxford.
14 Hitchmough, J. 2004, Selecting plant species, cultivars and nursery products, Chapter 2 in Hitchmough, J. and Fieldhouse, K. (eds.), *Plant user handbook: a guide to effective specifying*. Blackwell Science Ltd, Oxford.
15 Mårtensson, F., Jansson, M., Johansson, M., Raustorp, A., Kylin, M. and Boldemann, C. 2014, The role of greenery for physical activity play at school grounds, *Urban Forestry & Urban Greening*, 13(1):103–113.
16 Harvey, M. R. 1990, The relationship between children's experiences with vegetation on school grounds and their environmental attitudes, *The Journal of Environmental Education*, 21(2): 9–15.
17 Moore, R.C. 1993, *Plants for play: a plant selection guide for children's outdoor environments*. MIG Communications, Berkeley.
18 Fjørtoft, I. and Sageie, J. 2000, The natural environment as a playground for children: landscape description and analyses of a natural playscape, *Landscape and Urban Planning*, 48(1): 83–97.
19 Jeavons, M. and Hitchmough, J. 1994, Planning, design and management of open space for children, Chapter 18 in Hitchmough, J. (ed.), *Urban landscape management*. Inkata Press Pty Ltd, Sydney, pp. 521–537.
20 Nelson, L. S., Shih, R. D., Balick, M. J. and Lampe, K. F. 2007, *Handbook of poisonous and injurious plants*. New York Botanical Garden.
21 Ogden, T.L. 2015, *The allergy-fighting garden: stop asthma and allergies with smart landscaping*. Tenspeed Press, Berkeley.
22 Wink, M. and Van Wyk, B. E. 2008, *Mind-altering and poisonous plants of the world*. Timber Press, Portland, Ore., USA.
23 Moore, R.C. 1993, *Plants for play: a plant selection guide for children's outdoor environments*. MIG Communications, Berkeley.
24 Kirkby, M. 1989, Nature as refuge in children's environments, *Children's Environments Quarterly*, 6(1): 7–12.
25 Gibbs, L., Staiger, P. K., Johnson, B., Block, K., Macfarlane, S., Gold, L. and Ukoumunne, O. 2013, Expanding children's food experiences: the impact of a school-based kitchen garden program, *Journal of Nutrition Education and Behavior*, 45(2): 137–146.
26 Parmer, S. M., Salisbury-Glennon, J., Shannon, D. and Struempler, B. 2009, School gardens: an experiential learning approach for a nutrition education program to increase fruit and vegetable knowledge, preference, and consumption among second-grade students, *Journal of Nutrition Education and Behavior*, 41(3): 212–217.
27 Linzmayer, C. D., Halpenny, E. A. and Walker, G. J. 2014, A multidimensional investigation into children's optimal experiences with nature, *Landscape Research*, 39(5): 481–501.
28 Hussein, H. 2010, Using the sensory garden as a tool to enhance the educational development and social interaction of children with special needs, *Support for Learning*, 25(1): 25–31.
29 Dahl, B. and Molnar, D.J. 2003, *Anatomy of a park: essentials of recreation area planning and design (third edition)*, Waveland Press Inc., Ill., USA.
30 Percival, G. 2004, Tree roots and buildings, Chapter 9 in Hitchmough, J. and Fieldhouse, K. (eds.), *Plant user handbook: a guide to effective specifying*. Blackwell science Ltd, Oxford, pp. 113–127.
31 Day, S. D. and Bassuk, N. L. 1994, A review of the effects of soil compaction and amelioration treatments on landscape trees, *Journal of Arboriculture*, 20(1): 9–17.
32 Craul, P. J. 1999, *Urban soils: applications and practices*. J. Wiley & Sons, London.
33 Grabosky, J., Haffner, E. and Bassuk, N. 2009, Plant available moisture in stone-soil media for use under pavement while allowing urban tree root growth, *Journal of Arboriculture*, 35(5):271.
34 Handreck, K. and Black, N, 2010, *Growing media for ornamental plants and turf (fourth edition)*. University of New South Wales Press, Sydney.

Chapter 14

1 Figures from YouGov PLC online survey, published in *Every Child Wild* by The Wildlife Trusts, 2015.
2 A Borough is a defined geographic area, and there are 22 Boroughs in Greater London.
3 Children and Young Peoples Plan for Tower Hamlets, 2015.

Part IV
SPROUTS

Introduction

Children between the ages of 5 and 9 are the focus of this section, and there are two substantial areas of interest that we will examine. Firstly, the place of art in play and playspaces. This is examined through three different lenses: that of permanent art embedded in the playspace; of the creative process as play; and artworks that are in themselves playspaces.

Secondly, children usually start school in this age bracket, and this is a very different and very intensively used environment. We look at the design of school grounds, and how children appropriate every part of a playspace to use it in new and creative ways.

In this section you will find:

17. **Child development – page 167**
    A discussion of the physical, emotional and social development of children between the ages of 5 and 9 years old, including relevant ergonomic information.

Playspaces and art

18. **Colours and materials – page 175**
    Looking at the importance of sensory stimuli in playspace design.
19. **Embedded art in playspaces – page 181**
    A case study by artists who work with the community and build permanent art for play environments.
20. **Child led creativity – page 189**
    An artist's perspective on temporary art installations and children's creativity as an essential element of play.
21. **Art as playspace – page 195**
    Looking at the unique crocheted artworks of Toshiko MacAdam: her philosophy and practice.

Schools

22. **Quintessential play patterns in schools: The interface of space, materials and play behaviour – page 207**
    Revealing the relationships between different activities and the spaces which enhance various types of play in school environments.
23. **When is a slide not a slide? (Or what if we think differently about and beyond design?) – page 219**
    Looking at a different way of thinking when it comes to play, and embracing children's appropriation of time and spaces.
24. **'This place is like a building site… .' – page 227**
    A case study of a Scottish school which is providing for play in a very different and challenging way.
25. **The stepping stones to many playgrounds – page 235**
    The story of East Africa Playgrounds, and their journey to provide school playgrounds in Uganda.

17

CHILD DEVELOPMENT

Elizabeth Cummins & Katherine Masiulanis

Developmental stages

Following the explosion of skills which occurs in the first few years, the physical and emotional development of children aged 5 to 9 may seem more gradual: a continual honing and refining. Importantly, it is between these ages that most children start school, and this is further discussed in later sections.

Physically speaking, children develop improved flexibility, balance and agility and fine motor skills. There is notable improvement in fine motor skills and hand-eye co-ordination between the ages of 6 and 8.[1] This coincides with the development of a mature grip of tools, allowing for much greater accuracy. Their muscle to weight ratio allows them to do tasks which any adult would struggle to achieve such as scaling a vertical pole, or doing flips on the monkey bars.

During the school years, their running, jumping, hopping and ball handling skills greatly improve. The distance and accuracy of ball throwing and catching increases, as does kicking speed, allowing them to participate more in group physical activities and sports. Often, children of this age can intercept moving objects on the run, but will stop to hit, kick or catch a ball.[2] Skipping is co-ordinated and smooth – either along a path, or over a rope or elastics.

Rough-and-tumble play, while physical in nature, is also important in social development, especially for boys. Contrary to appearances this type of play often results in co-operative games and reduced aggression, as it allows children to learn by risk taking, and also assess the physical strength of others.

Observable patterns and interests

The following section examines patterns in skills, knowledge and interests, which is marked at this age by increased social interaction, peer importance and an understanding of the world and their place in it.

Behaviour patterns

This period of childhood is one of learning to engage and participate in the world. Children of this age begin to develop a strong sense of justice and fairness based on equity. It demonstrates a clear understanding of right and wrong, and clear judgement in relation to their own strengths and weaknesses. They are able to engage in social problem solving, are able to control their emotions better by learning to delay self-gratification and display increasing empathy towards others, both known and unknown. They will now apologise for actions not meant.

Children at this age also begin to understand the difference between diverse authority figures in their lives and their legitimacy, sometimes challenging discipline. They are able to distinguish the difference between fantasy and reality, and understand matters of personal choice and social conventions. The genders tend to separate out at this age in terms of friendships and this is reflected in their interests as well. Related to this, children have increasing self-consciousness and sensitivity, which will reach a peak in adolescence. Conformity with peers becomes more and more important.

Physically they start to specialise the skills related to activities they are involved in such as team sports or creative activities. They can identify their right from their left and are able to learn more complex manipulative skills. They draw and write much more confidently and are able to read words with increasing independence.

Socially they are able to listen competently while others speak and respond, engaging in conversation with both peers and other adults.

Interests

Popular culture is discussed within their increasingly important peer groups with more dedicated following of TV, movies, technology and professional sports. Celebrities associated with these activities also start to become role models, and their behaviour observed and mimicked.

School is a dominant influence and as reading skills improve, an interest in the wider world, both geo-political and natural, develops. Science becomes of interest, as children seek an understanding of how the world works. This is reflected in close relationships with pets or animals.

For many children creative pursuits such as art, dance, music and theatre become important, often related to interest within the family or participation with friends. Many children become involved in developing finely tuned skills at this age and willingly engage in competition with others.

Social ergonomics

Socially, as children start school, they are required to be more self-reliant, and have greater self-management of their behaviour and emotions. Attention spans increase markedly in middle childhood, and the ability to concentrate selectively.[3] School is in itself a great tester of these skills, but also is the increasing trend to play with many children of the same age.

Friends (and enemies) start to have greater significance to children than the few important adults of their infancy.

Learning how to make and keep friends is an important part of this stage. There have been suggestions that the development of Theory of Mind (that is, understanding that others do not think as you do) typically becomes more advanced between the ages of 5 and 7, and that this is necessary in the creation of strong friendships. With empathy and understanding comes a deeper appreciation of others. Some studies suggest that siblings can be more important in the development of a Theory of Mind than interactions with peers: dubbed the 'sibling advantage'. At this age, peers are the primary playmates, but family is still very important.

The dramatic play which may have started from about age 3 continues in strength during this period, and becomes more complex as language and relationships with others develop. Through this type of play, children develop co-operation, negotiation and problem solving of all sorts. A social understanding of fairness and equity comes about during this time.

The ability to understand complex rules and an improvement in both physical skills form a necessary developmental step that allows children to play group sports.

At this age, children also begin to enjoy inventing their own games as it gives them a position of power. There also starts to be an internalising of the moral code. Previously right and wrong and appropriate behaviour were dictated by adults. Children at this stage develop the independence and responsibility which underpin these behaviours. A section on the importance of risk taking later in this book has more to say on this subject.

Towards the end of this period, about 7 years onwards, children stop talking to themselves out loud. Theoretical reasoning, planning and evaluation start to develop at this time, and this is reflected in the complexity of their play and creativity. Primary school aged children are good observational scientists, but their deductive logic may still be weak. By about 6, most children recognise colours, letters, numbers and shapes, although these will usually have been learnt through play rather than pedagogical teaching. From about 7 onwards children also often start to develop an intrinsic motivation – that is, valuing learning for its own sake. Knowledge allows them to create and understand the world.

Common affordances for play

Places and spaces that are independent of adults characterise environments that stimulate children in this age group. Common environments for play and recreation include: playspaces, sports fields and open space (such as gardens, local streets, parks and environments such as the beach or forest). It is important to note that children's access to these environments is varied depending on their cultural circumstance.

Surfaces

Surfaces at this age have both a formal and informal purpose for guiding movement and affording activities. Circulation around and within a playspace that avoids conflict between activities and draws children through an environment 'uncovering' different activities in various ways is valuable. Hard or paved surfaces allow for cycling, skating and scooters, art/creative activities and both formal and informal games. Line-marking can be made on hard surfaces for basketball, netball and other less formal games like four-square and hopscotch. Grassed open space enables both formal games such as football or cricket and informal games such as chasey and other ball games, etc. A balance of even and irregular surfaces is also valuable for challenging co-ordination.

Levels and heights

Heights and levels are as important as surfaces for climbing and viewing out, providing for various social interactions. Different opportunities to climb on mounds, steps, rocks, ladders, cleated walls or rope nets test skills and give children a goal or destination. Seats, platforms, decks or small perches of different levels afford children the chance to 'sit back' from the bustle of physical activity and rest, reflect and observe what is happening around them. For many children this is important to help them regulate emotion, build up social confidence at their own pace or just be present during play.

Loose materials

Children of this age group tend to use loose materials 'within' the construct of flexible structures. Loose materials such as bark, pebbles or stones, sand, dirt, seeds, leaves and flowers can be collected and assigned a particular purpose. Children utilise the sensory properties of the materials (ie. colour, smell, texture and sometimes even taste) in their play. Endless uses mean that these items can be creatively re-invented. What starts off one day as pretend bread crumbs, can become eggs in a birds nest or money the next. With a growing interest in science children of this age also begin to appreciate the seasonal changes that affect these materials, and their purpose and function in the natural world.

Flexible structures

There are similarities between loose and flexible structures, in particular the abstract qualities that allow for creative interpretation. Flexible structures, however, are about frameworks for play. Children of this age tend to use items such as branches, logs, rocks, planks, bricks, pavers and sheets that can all provide a valuable platform for play. A growing interest in science and engineering, the opportunity for creative construction and problem solving can occupy children for hours as they build cubbies, forts and other structures.

The natural world

The natural world affords endless opportunities for play, imagination and problem solving. Loose and flexible materials are part of the reason why beaches, waterways, forests, bushland and parks are ready-made playspaces. The relationship goes deeper, however, as the natural environment affords concept learning as well. A healthy curiosity for science and nature builds interest and respect for the natural world. Opportunities to learn not only about flora and fauna, but marine life, seasonal change and climate all contribute to a deeper understanding for children of themselves in the world.

Physical activity and variety

One of the primary functions of play is physical activity. This is especially important to this particular age group as they move into more formal learning at school and spend less time being physically active outdoors. Most outdoor environments afford some opportunity for physical activity, but a large amount of space and a variety of elements and structures are critical for ensuring that children develop and fine-tune all the physical skills they need to master. This should include opportunities for graduated challenge.

Journeys and destinations

Part of engaging children at this age is exploration. Giving children journeys to discover and explore in a playspace is highly important. This extends the duration of play and fosters the desire to return to the playspace. At the end of these journeys are destinations. Destinations are points or goals that encourage children to cross the bridge, climb the tree or cycle across town. There are macro-destinations, such as the local creek bridge or skatepark, and there are micro-destinations within the playspace such as the top of a tower, the centre of a maze or a cubby or den.

Ergonomics

Please find below an illustration of the range of physical dimensions which might be expected among 5 to 9 year olds, of both genders. For more information on interpreting this information, please refer to Seedlings.

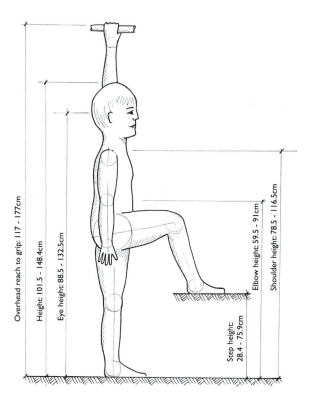
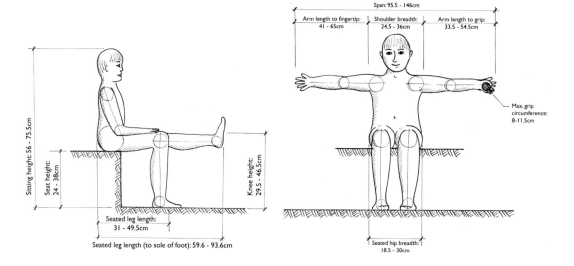

FIGURE 17.1 Ergonomic data of 5th percentile 5 year olds to 95th percentile 9 year olds
Data from: Beverly Norris & John R. Wilson, Consumer Safety Unit, Childata, The Handbook of Child Measurements and Capabilities: Data for Design Safety, Institute for Occupational Ergonomics, Department of Manufacturing Engineering and Operations Management, University of Nottingham

PLAYSPACES AND ART

Art is hard to define. However, whatever form the creativity takes, it can add both a layer of sensory interest and give a space its own unique story and character. Looking first at the effect of colour and texture in playspaces, we then look at three different approaches to art and creativity: embedded art, art as play, and art as playspace.

18
COLOURS AND MATERIALS

Katherine Masiulanis

> We differ, blind and seeing, one from another, not in our senses, but in the use we make of them, in the imagination and courage with which we seek wisdom beyond the senses.
>
> *Helen Keller, The Five-sensed World (1910)*

If childhood is about developing an appreciation of the world we live in, then the sensory information we gain from our environment is crucial. When a space is designed specifically for children to play in, arguably we have a responsibility to carefully consider the sensory experiences we offer them, as we are giving them not only a deeper and richer understanding of the world, but also affecting the actual structure and chemistry of their brains.

If we look solely at colour, then a scientist might note that the actual colours we see are simply a biological response to electrical signals from the cones in the retina. Interestingly, these cones perceive one of three colours: red, which makes up 64% of the receptors; green, 32%; and blue at only 2%. The blue receptors are thought to be especially light sensitive. However, beyond that electrical signal is a layering of language, social expectations, cultural factors and experience which all shape our preferences and perceptions of colour.

For example, a study which looked at the way in which English children and children from the semi-nomadic Himba tribe in Namibia learn and categorise colours found that language actually shapes the way colour is perceived.[1] Whereas in English, 11 basic colour categories are widely accepted (white, black, grey, red, yellow, blue, green, pink, purple, orange and brown), the Himba people use five categories (*Serandu, Dumbu, Zoozu, Vapa* and *Borou*), perhaps influenced by the need for different colour definition and description in our daily lives as adults. Interestingly, despite the widely held belief in western cultures that red, yellow, blue and green are learnt first, this did not prove to be the case with either group.

It has been suggested that newborns are more interested in the contrasts between colours, than the colours themselves, although by about two months of age, their colour discrimination is as acute as that of an adult.[2] For this reason, strong black and white patterns may be the most stimulating and engaging for this age group, and placing them within the focal range of small babies is important.

As children grow and their experience of the world increases, their preferences change. As a generalisation, infants up to the age of four like red best, followed by yellow. As we get older, a preference for blue develops, fascinatingly consistent between genders and cultures. Both as adults and children, we generally like colours such as brown the least. Another notable change in the way we perceive colour as we mature is in the emotional response we have to it. Yellow and red are seen as happy colours by preschoolers, but adults tend to associate red with anger. Similarly, blue is seen as sad by children, whereas adults are more likely to associate black with this emotion.[3] It has been suggested that these changes develop as associations with particular colours are formed, and it becomes increasingly difficult to separate innate colour preferences from societal expectations, as most parents of female preschoolers know: pink fetishism seems to be as much about peer pressure and advertising than anything else. It is also important to note the effect of culture on colour preferences, particularly when discussing the emotional associations of colour. One of the starkest examples in perhaps that of death: firmly associated with the colour black in western cultures, but with white in China and India.[4]

There is a widely held popular belief that children like bright colours, but as acceptable responses are reinforced by our cultures, it is hard to know if this is really the case. There is some research to suggest that this is indeed true, especially for girls.[5] However, by the time that children are able to articulate for themselves their desires, they are steeped in the knowledge that brightly coloured toys, clothes and spaces are more likely to be playful: that within a primary coloured structure it is acceptable to play, for example. In an adult world which is often not really child friendly, these cues can be valuable hints, but are perhaps something on which we need to reflect more deeply.

That said, colour must be used carefully if it is to promote the types of activity, social interactions and opportunities for development that we hope good playspaces will. The relationships we have with colours are both internal and external. Externally, a playspace is an area which has a wider audience than just the people who use it. It may be part of a wider cityscape, a workplace or part of the crucially important public open space available to everyone. For example, a playspace within a new estate in the UK was fenced off for the best part of a year after residents complained that the equipment, which was painted red, blue and green, was 'too brightly coloured and not in keeping with the local colour scheme'.[6] In this case, by not considering the wider audience, the reaction to the choice of colours deprived children of the chance to play in their local park.

Internally, it is widely accepted that different colours actually do have a physiological effect on humans. Generally, warm colours are thought to promote activity and 'happier' feelings. Exposure to red, orange and yellow environments seems to raise our heart rate and blood pressure, and experimentally people in these environments are energised, alert and more creative – at least in the short term.[7] Blues and green are more calming and relaxing, and these cues may be used to suggest the type of activity appropriate for a particular area within the playspace. A cubby or den painted with a glowing yellow and orange interior may not promote the quiet, social play which is intended in this space. Anecdotally, I know of one childcare operator who had a synthetic bright orange surface installed in her outdoor space. The result, she said, was a disaster. The children were completely overstimulated, unable to concentrate, and poor behaviours resulted.

In playspaces, colour often seems to be used somewhat indiscriminately – a 'playful' primary palette which is more like a visual cacophony than anything deliberately designed to give a particular feel. In adopting this approach, arguably we create a place where children feel that it is 'acceptable to play', but we are also selling ourselves short. Certainly, playspaces have the opportunity to be one of the most interesting and beautiful parts of our landscape, for everyone who experiences them. We can change the apparent size and scale of a built project with colour: warm colour and pure hues tending to advance, and large areas of a single colour seeming bigger again. To dumb it down to a random mix of bright colours is to deny ourselves a power of persuasion, and is disrespectful of our audience – both children and adults. To quote Jill Pilaroscia:

> Architects are not always taught to see colour as a tool that has its own integrity. Sometimes architects look at colour as a last resort, and may wait until the last moment to throw colour at a problem, instead of integrating the colour into the design to enhance spatial relationships or the experience of a space.[8]

However, if colour is used skilfully, it can not only direct the types of activity within a space, but also promote a certain mood, in the same way that a different collection of plants does. Imagine two spaces, one planted with coastal species, the other with rainforest plants. The feel of the space, the imaginative games that immediately suggest themselves, are quite different.

Colour, having both physiological and psychological effects, is an even more powerful tool in the right hands. When designing a playspace, it is worth considering not only how

FIGURE 18.1 Finely graded colour is used to divide horizontal 'Swiss Cheese' walls from clean monochrome structures. Carlton Gardens Playspace, Melbourne

Courtesy: Taylor Cullity Lethlean

but when to wield that tool. Does the design ask for broad swathes of colour, or are natural finishes enhanced by carefully selected touches of a particular hue? There is no doubt that which you choose will have a major influence on the ambience of that space, and the experience that people have within it.

Likewise, the relationship between colour and texture is one which requires careful consideration. Would, for example, painting a recycled timber remove its sensory qualities? The subtle variations of natural colour within the grain of the wood would be removed, but perhaps the undulations in the surface brought more clearly into focus. The colour variations of the real world, both natural and constructed, are more subtle and richer when combined with texture.

The importance of genuine sensory experiences for children's development cannot be overstated. If playspaces are where children 'practise life', then we need to try to give them as many opportunities as possible, which includes the changeability of those materials over time and season. A plastic and rubber environment, while attractively safe to adult providers of play, may not always provide a high degree of material interest. When interviewed, artist Andy Goldsworthy said:

> When I began working outside I learnt about the weather, the materials. And through touching the materials and working with the materials I think I get an understanding of those materials that you can only do through touch.[9]

There is a wealth of research which points to the neurological importance of sensory input to children, particularly in the first three years of life, but continuing into later childhood.[10]

To quote Carl Gabbard and Luis Rodrigues:

> As early as 15 years ago researchers believed that the wiring diagram for each person was primarily 'programmed' by one's genetic blueprints, much like the wiring of a new house before being occupied. However, the contemporary view is that while the main circuits may be prewired, such as for breathing, control of heart beat and reflexes, other basic pathways are quite rudimentary, containing trillions of finer 'un-programmed' tentative connections. These connections are dependent upon stimulation from the environment and experience in the environment. It is this stimulation that completes the architecture of the brain.[11]

In the design of playspaces, we have then an enormous weight of responsibility: we are offering opportunities to enrich children's brains in a way which will impact on them throughout their lives. Impoverish the environments to which they are exposed, perhaps with an eye to keeping them absolutely safe, and we risk not allowing them the potential to be the best they can be.

That said, there are so many opportunities to make more interesting sensory places. Colour we have already discussed. In outdoors spaces, weather, planting, loose and natural materials create and change the sensory experiences on offer on a daily basis. As designers, we can embed so many materials and textures within our playspaces, keeping in mind that each space we create need not contain the whole world: it is one of many places a child will visit, and there is some value in repetition to emphasise the flavour and character of a particular place or material. Too many textures, like too many colours, can lead to a type of sensory overload. Clever design allows each to shine and be truly explored and experienced.

Writing about the textures of bricks, flagstones, wooden floors, and the balance of texture against regularity and order, Alain de Botton says 'and yet these features are gracious, rather than threatening, reminders of complexity, for they are neatly contained within a series of calm parallel lines and right angles … '.[12]

There is good evidence to suggest that the brain learns best when exposed to multi-sensory environments – that is, combining sight with roughness, smell with sound or temperature with colour. The human brain has evolved to operate in natural environments where integrating information across multiple senses is essential.[13] Maria Montessori, who developed her teaching method before the First World War, recognised this in her creation of materials which simplify and correlate sensations, such as sandpaper letters. Using the roughness of the item to make the shape memorable, she was building on her idea of the hand as 'organ of intelligence': that is, the sensation of touch will amplify the visual stimulus of the shape.

FIGURE 18.2 Embedded marbles in paving provide inspiration for traditional games and sensory interest. Castlemaine Botanical Gardens 2012

Photo: Katherine Masiulanis

Consideration of the sensory qualities of a playspace may be particularly important for some children with autism, perhaps especially when combined with some sort of legible order. Research which compared children who had been deliberated exposed to highly sensory environments (and interestingly, smell appears to be particularly important) to those in an ordinary environment 'found that environmental enrichment ameliorated autism symptoms for many children both in terms of overall severity and their cognitive performance'.[14]

To summarise, in selecting colours and materials for use within our playspace, we need to look beyond the undoubtedly important issues such as durability and safety. There is the chance to create spaces which encourage certain types of activity or emotion; which are genuinely beautiful contributions to our landscape; which increase the opportunities for children to learn; and, most importantly, which give the greatest potential for the creation of great brains.

19

EMBEDDED ART IN PLAYSPACES

Dorelle Davidson

Most people would appreciate how difficult it can be to make a living as an artist, but for nearly 30 years James Cattell and I have managed to do that – one way or another. In 1988, we formed the partnership Honeyweather & Speight to produce artworks for the design industry, combining James's skills as an artist with mine as a former teacher, interior designer and retailer. Over this time we seem to have developed a specialty in children's playgrounds and would like to present some of our personal experience and observations here.

With the limited market for art sales, artists might reasonably view playgrounds as a potential vehicle for their work, and certainly play can be a means of introducing art to the general public. Writing about playgrounds as part of the modernist art movement of the twentieth century, Gabriela Burkhalter observes 'Playgrounds became lively, interactive and imaginative public spaces … they provided room for art outside installations and away from bureaucracy'.[1]

James and I applaud any opportunity to create art outside of bureaucracy, but feel that some artists have designed playgrounds using sculptural forms that offer limited play opportunities. By contrast, some public artworks have playful forms, and may unintentionally encourage interaction with children by inviting them to touch or scramble over their surfaces. This phenomenon appears to make art more accessible to the public, but when we design work specifically for playspaces, we endeavour to maximise opportunities for open ended play. We feel that artworks should not only present opportunities for sensory and physical interaction, but also encourage imaginative activity.

Our work is generated in a number of ways. Sometimes we conduct community workshops where participants create components that will eventually be incorporated into the playspace. Occasionally, if we are really lucky, we are commissioned directly to design and build a work for a public outdoor space. On a recent trip to India we visited the Nek Chand Rock Garden in Chandigarh, with its 25 acres of crazy concrete and mosaic sculptures, built largely by one man from discarded and recycled products. We would dearly love the opportunity to create such an extensive and total art environment, but unfortunately our works have so far been more modest in scale.

FIGURE 19.1 Sculptures at Nek Chand Rock Garden, Chandigarh
Photo: Rod Waddington from Kergunyah, Australia

In most cases we collaborate with the landscape architects to flesh out the detail of a concept that they have already developed in consultation with the client. Like most construction projects, playspaces are designed to meet a budget, and when there is a blowout, often the art components are cut. This makes us both question and wish to clarify the purpose served by art in playspaces and the value it provides.

Art by and for the people

In the case of community projects, there is firstly the benefit of participation and ownership. Allowing the community to make elements for their playspace literally imprints their fingerprints and character, making it unique. We work with a variety of materials, including ceramic, concrete, metal and timber, but find that clay is a particularly good material to use with community groups. Participants, working either individually or in groups, can create units that are then embedded into a larger installation. It is a wonderfully tactile material that can cater to a wide range of skills and still produce a satisfying product.

Back in 1995, James worked with artist Anne Riggs on a project in a geriatric hospital, where participants were often bemused and sometimes mistook the clay for biscuits. Despite these early challenges, Anne has continued to work as a community artist, undertaking studies in grief and going on to specialise in art therapy. She now lectures in Community Mental Health at Chisholm Institute and feels that art can provide a rare opportunity for 'pleasure' for people who are grappling with difficult lives. She notes that both children and

FIGURE 19.2 James working with students at Seville Primary School
Photo: Dorelle Davidson

adults 'find the acts of painting and drawing and rolling and manipulating clay relaxing'. Pleasure and relaxation are experiences that can be a little elusive in today's busy world and can't be underestimated.

We also find that clay workshops can yield some often surprising results, providing the more unassuming students an opportunity to shine. Because our workshops are generally designed to develop three- rather than two-dimensional skills, we find that the best products often come from the quieter students – not the student best at drawing horses or Bart Simpson, as might be predicted. James endeavours to include all children, not just the adept ones, and it's often the outsider kids who become most engaged. At one school for children with special needs, there was a student who became quite obsessed with the rubber tool used for smoothing clay. He elected to spend his lunchtimes smoothing all the insides of the other children's work – an activity that proved to be quite beneficial to him in its calming and meditative nature.

More ongoing interest in a project can be generated by working with family groups. The workshops can be very sociable, and most people are happy with their end results. Clay is such a malleable and forgiving material that participants are almost always able to produce something satisfying, given enough time. The actual participation provides great opportunities for community building. Landscape architect Fiona Robbe confirms this view: 'Playgrounds offer their local communities a perfect outlet for creative and collaborative artworks, inspired by a common storehouse of shared experiences and stories. Nothing beats everyone joining forces to make something together.'[2]

We have found that rejuvenating public spaces through art provides an excellent opportunity to garner support from the local community for a new project. After having developed a masterplan with Jeavons Landscape Architects, the City of Albury commenced work in 2009 on a dedicated children's garden within its Botanic Gardens. Children were invited to be involved in the process through a series of public workshops to create ceramic troll heads, which would later be incorporated into the rocky base of a troll cave.

This was the first of a series of features that James helped to design and build over the next six years. Apart from its existing planting, the garden consists almost entirely of artworks and includes a giant dinosaur entry with baby and eggs, a fairy temple, mural, assorted fantasy seats and now a lizard castle toilet. Paul Scannell, the director of the gardens, has an office backing onto the troll cave and often overhears people pointing out the troll heads that they'd made 'so many years ago'. He reports that 'definite pride and ownership is displayed, and very little vandalism is occurring, which was a big concern initially'.

Ownership is a theme that keeps recurring throughout our public works. In 2012, we installed a 3D ceramic mural on the side of a toilet building adjacent to the playspace in Victory Park, Chelsea. The local council was feeling rather anxious about potential mischief from a group of drinkers who regularly congregated in the park. However, the group took

FIGURE 19.3 Sunlight illuminates the troll cave at Albury Botanic Gardens

Photo: Dorelle Davidson

great interest in our activity and often chatted with us as we worked. We can only assume they have become self-appointed guardians of the artwork, as there has been no damage at all since. The potential for vandalism is often a concern expressed by stakeholders, yet we have experienced very little within spaces that are liked and embraced by the locals.

Identity and interpretation

Just as art can engender a sense of ownership, it can also define the character of a space by giving it a context or identity. In 2009, Zoe Metherell from Jeavons Landscape Architects designed an adventurous public space that included a climbing wall in the form of a dragon-head profile. James rendered the shaped wall to look like dragon scales and embedded ceramic teeth, claws and a large eye. Officially titled the 'Garden City Reserve', it has become known as the 'Dragon Park', giving the feature a mythical local identity that challenges kids in a way that a standard wall never would.

Likewise, we collaborated with Tract Landscape Architects to create a 'grotto shelter' for a park in the outer eastern 'Circa 1886' housing development by Pask Group. The park design was informed by the original Victorian homestead overlooking the estate, and incorporated sculptural features and exotic planting. Our grotto design was themed to reflect the prevalence of eels in the area, and we embedded ceramic animals throughout to signify other early fauna. By making reference to the built and natural environments of the past, we have added an additional layer of history for park users to contemplate while enjoying the shade and other play experiences that the structure affords.

It is quite unusual for a private developer to fund a recreational space that goes beyond what is required by law, but this park has not only assisted sales of house blocks – it has

FIGURE 19.4 Garden City Reserve playspace

Photo: Dorelle Davidson

enhanced Pask's image within the community. We have noticed that new homeowners will congregate in the park while they follow the progress of their house build. This way, they meet prospective neighbours and can begin to forge relationships that may last many years.

Beyond physical challenge

We have often supplied art features to enhance the quality of playspaces within schools for children with special needs. Various studies suggest that broadening the range of sensory experiences for these children can be of great assistance in their development.[3] Most elements will have an interactive component and stimulate the senses of children who have limited mobility or intellectual ability. We hope that any small trigger might make a real difference to their lives.

Art structures in public, private and institutional playgrounds provide opportunities for open-ended play, where users can creatively interact and develop personal stories. They can cater to solitary children by creating a space for quiet and intimate play, adding an unexpected layer of discovery, or they can enable groups of children to play co-operatively by developing imaginative scenarios together. Artworks not only extend the nature of play for children, they can also enhance the experience for their carers. Creative playspaces provide more opportunities for parents and grandparents to watch, talk and interact with their children in the environment. What a relief this presents compared with the rather tedious act of continuously pushing a swing in the playgrounds of the past!

Albury has estimated that visitor numbers to their Botanic Gardens have increased by 50,000 per year since the children's garden has been added. Paul Scannell informs us that many families take relatives and visitors there as a 'must see' while in town, and consistently fill in surveys with the word *'Wow!'* Here are some of his personal observations:

> Younger children love running, exploring, climbing and water-play. Parents and grandparents' interaction with the younger ones is to accompany and chat about how to interact and stories that can be made up to go with each of the art pieces.
>
> The older the child, the more time is spent investigating and discussing the art pieces and their intricacies – coloured light, beetles, butterflies, bugs, etc.
>
> Imaginative and creative play is most seen in the five to nine year olds. Pretending to be brave around the scary items is very popular. Pretending to be characters from their favourite books and movies is always fun to hear.

Returning to the site to complete later stages has allowed us the opportunity to watch people at play in the gardens, just as they enjoy watching us work and new features emerging. We have seen how entranced children are by small details such as choosing which animal identity to assume when they are sat on their selected seat to eat lunch. While we were eating our own lunch one day, we watched a family arrive excitedly and set up their picnic blanket next to the giant dinosaur. The father delighted in surprising the kids with sounds he created through the hidden speaking tube. Then they all proceeded to do handstands and sit-ups against the dinosaur's tail. The art feature had become an unanticipated exercise station. A local concreter who assisted with the works told us that his grandson was initially frightened

FIGURE 19.5 Albury Botanic Gardens' resident dinosaur
Photo: Dorelle Davidson

by the troll cave, but learning to control his demons has become a rite of passage, so that now he is proudly able to scamper in and out and around this feature.

Lifespans and timelines

Of course there will always be issues associated with art elements in playspaces, and not just being scared by some particular detail. Often there is a lack of continuity of staff or other interested parties to keep a project alive. When James installs children's work in a school playground, he hopes that the school community might extend its life by adding new work on their own accord. Realistically though, curriculums are crowded, teachers often feel overworked or their roles may change. New students may not be interested in a previous project that lies languishing in the school ground. We are inclined to believe that sometimes a short shelf life is sufficient – after all, the process of production can often be of greater value than the actual product.

Sometimes, though, old projects can find a new life. At Vermont South Special School, we incorporated some tired and unfinished artworks from previous projects into a new scheme. We built old ceramic pieces into new totems and extended a 3D wall mural with synthetic grass, mirrors and rendered sky. New tiles, made by children, were embedded into the pavement to extend these works, along with a concrete and ceramic village made by James for miniature toy play.

Even though we try to design our work to require minimal maintenance, sometimes there is no money allocated for this, and deterioration might limit the feature's function or even render it dangerous. Water features can be particularly problematic in this way, despite the fun and wonder that they provide. One of the earliest public art installations we created was an interactive shade structure for a children's sculpture garden next to the Linden Gallery in St Kilda, Melbourne, which was operated by our local council. It consisted of a series of abstracted figures that doubled as seats, holding metal umbrellas to support a vine. Families enjoyed exploring various interactive elements, and children were happier to visit the adjacent art gallery as a result.

After some years, the management of the gallery was leased to an independent operator and neither the gallery nor the council had a budget for maintenance. The garden became neglected and the concrete cracked, so the pool was drained and the entrance gates were permanently locked. Locals were disappointed by the lack of access, though it did take on some romance as an urban ruin. Eventually the council decided to divest itself of this artwork and a major operation was mounted to dismantle it. Fortunately we have found a new home for our structure on a country property, so the figures now stand like sentries looking out over cows and paddocks, and visitors can once again enjoy its charms.

Inadequate time frames can also limit a project's full potential, forcing compromises to the end result. Anne Riggs facilitated art workshops for the multi-layered Wombat Bend playspace in Templestowe, which was designed by Ric McConaghy and also incorporated some elements made by us. She rates it as the most successful project she has worked on, as it was a collaborative process all the way through, with various schools and community groups having input into the space. It was well funded and not constrained by financial year budgets, so she believes that this lack of pressure on timelines contributed significantly to its ultimate success.

When asked how she feels art can contribute to a playspace, Anne says 'the inclusion of art creates a place that people want to be in. Reflecting this human input makes a space warm and dynamic.' She describes James's work as 'quirky' and feels that children benefit from their exposure to imagery and ideas that are unusual and outside of the usual mainstream media.

James, himself, enjoys having families as an audience for his art. Even though he still likes to escape into the studio to produce paintings and sculptures of his own invention, he does not envy artists grappling with the conventional gallery and academic career pathway. On worksites, he regards himself as a trade artist, and feels that tantalising a playground user with his work is preferable to writing obscure art statements about his intentions. We hope that the demand for art in playspaces continues so that we can keep indulging in playful activity, and a new generation of kids can do the same.

20
CHILD LED CREATIVITY

Matthew Shaw

I've been an artist for nearly 15 years. When I started out my main focus was on sculpture, but as my practice developed my work moved towards the creation of large installations. To this point, a key element of all my work is the way people interact with the pieces, and my aim is to engage them physically as well as mentally.

It was therefore a natural step to move this practice towards the creation of creative and playful environments. At this time I was lucky enough to be involved with the brilliant project *Second Skin* whilst also being employed as an artist in residence at a nursery school. Both these projects focussed on the use of play and creativity in learning, with a strong emphasis on using the environment to inspire creative play and development. *Second Skin* especially worked with creatives from a range of disciplines: Music, Visual Art, Dance and Theatre. It was strongly influenced by the 'Reggio Emilia' philosophy from northern Italy, where the child is seen as the expert in their play and creativity.

These projects led to the creatives designing and realising many interesting spaces for children to play and learn in schools and nurseries, and although most of these spaces were temporary the project did offer some valuable lessons for what makes a great playspace. Being ephemeral, they were often dynamic and engaging to children. In addition, the team of creatives supported these spaces, and were able to adapt and respond to the children's actions.

Very quickly it became very clear that regardless of the planning and design that went into all the various aspects of these spaces, it was almost impossible to predict how the children would use the materials and spaces to play. The 'cardboard box' effect comes to mind, where when a child is presented with a new toy they will often find far greater interest and possibilities in the box in which the toy came. The skills that we, as the creatives, therefore developed were not to predict what children would do with a given space or material but instead to build a knowledge of what spaces or materials would encourage the greatest number of creative and playful outcomes. Terms such as 'open ended', 'loose materials' and 'child led creativity' became the key phrases when thinking up what to offer children. Likewise the realisation that providing opportunities for the children to guide their own play and make their own choices was key to a rich and diverse playspace.

FIGURE 20.1 Loose materials at *PlaySpace*
Photo: Matthew Shaw

These findings led directly into the creation of the Arts Council Funded project *PlaySpace*. *PlaySpace* transformed a gallery over a period of six weeks in direct response to the play of those who visited.

The emphasis of *PlaySpace* shifted from the previous projects described where environments were developed by the adults, to providing children with the materials and resources to develop their own spaces and environments. In this project the gallery was continually changed in direct response to the play of each and every visitor. Over the six weeks that the project ran, the space transformed from an empty shell to an intricate maze of structures, materials and spaces that reflected the hundreds of playful interactions that had occurred. Evidence that the space had been created through the decisions and choices of the children was clearly visible.

Making Play at the South London Gallery (SLG) of which I was the fifth artist in residence was a similar project. This made use of a disused shop on a housing estate in South London that was offered to children from the estate. A decision was made early on in this six month project to hand over the control of how the space and materials within were used to the children involved. This project explored a wide range of issues: the focus was on the connections between children's play and creativity and the artistic process. Due to the location of the residency, an inner city London estate, and the children who participated, all from lower socio-economic backgrounds, it raised important questions around children's right to and access to playful and creative activity.

This project ran very close to two other projects that I was involved with: one in a community in Madagascar; and the other in India. It became possible to draw comparisons between the play of children in these three different countries. The visits to Madagascar and India were through Kinship, at the time a fledgling charity whose aim was to nurture friendships with communities around the world to exchange and share ideas around play and creativity. This comparison formed the basis for an essay contribution to the publication by SLG, 'The cat came as a tomato', a collection of essays and conversations on play and contemporary arts practice.

The strongest similarities came from the fact that practically all the children's play at all three of these locations existed in the total absence of any adults. Play was entirely child led and was strongly influenced by the local environment and resources available. In most cases these resources were few, but this just seemed to push the creativity and resourcefulness of the children. This was highlighted by an experience in Madagascar. The aim of that visit was to make a film on behalf of Kinship that documented the playspaces of children in a rural town of what could be termed a less developed country. One day when in search of one these places, we followed some kites that were flying above the town. There were quite a few flying, and even though they were at a height, we could see that they were made from various materials. When we eventually reached the kite flyers we found a large field and a large group of children of all ages playing. There were obviously the kite flyers but the other children were playing with sticks and old bicycle tyres and toys that they had made themselves. The field was slightly terraced so the children were running and jumping, and also just hanging out in what was essentially a playspace. We talked to the kite builders and asked them what the kites were made from. We could see a number of non-flying kites too: experimentation in action. The materials were simple: sticks, paper, plastic bags for the kites and string around tin cans for the spools. All found, scavenged and pieced together.

In Madagascar there were other instances where we saw the simplest of materials being used in the most creative and beautiful ways: such as small stones being used to represent a family group in a game where tapping one stone against another represented the conversations between a child and a father, or the wonderful use of a large leaf made into a plate with thorns and tiny flowers being used as the food.

Back in the UK, and as a result of the work at the SLG, my work took a new direction. Exploring the connections between children's play and art and the processes that artists use became a more explicit aim of my practice. This exploration became a rich source of ideas and one that I was lucky enough to be able to continue exploring through my work at Tate Britain.

At Tate Britain I was taken on as one of a team of freelance artists working with the Early Years and Family Team to devise, design and deliver various residencies, workshops and family days. Obviously the aim of this work was to engage young children and their families with the collections in the gallery, but additionally it was about encouraging them to feel comfortable in the gallery environment. This was an important element to the work in that it allowed the workshops to have the freedom to explore and use the art in quite a free way. As a result, instead of a workshop being along the lines of sitting in front of a piece of work and drawing it, elements of the work would be used to inspire an interactive play based session. Other times it was simply about being surrounded and inspired by amazing pieces of art, and providing materials with which children could do their own thing.

FIGURE 20.2 Flower 'food' on leaf 'plates', Madagascar
Photo: Matthew Shaw

The set up at Tate Britain had a very different balance of factors to previous work, in that access to space was not an issue, but these spaces often contained very valuable pieces of art. Workshops mostly lasted a few hours to a day, and for those participating it may have been their only visit to an art gallery.

Numbers of participants were very high, sometimes hundreds through a day. As a result, ideas for the set-up of the space and the resources provided had to be severely simplified. This turned out to be an advantage, as it was possible to test out ideas and materials literally to destruction. If something can be done with a piece of cardboard and lollipop stick then the children discovered it. Also with these numbers of participants, when one child came up with a good idea or way of fixing materials, then this idea would spread through the space.

As a consequence, the 'design' went into deciding which materials and spaces to use, but also on creating an environment in the gallery where children and parents felt comfortable to play and explore. Decisions on materials were strongly influenced by the art, allowing the participants to experience and use the materials present in a piece of work.

I ran a large number of workshops in my time at the Tate, and there was a real development in my practice through this time. This manifested itself both in terms of how materials were offered, and also in the set-up of spaces. From the days of *PlaySpace* the provocations were vastly simplified, but this never seemed to diminish the quality of play and creativity present.

FIGURE 20.3 Child constructing a wall at the 'Big and Small' Family day at Tate Britain, Duveen Galleries, 2012

Source: Courtesy of Tate Images

Through the provision of simple materials I was always amazed at how this influenced the direction of the workshop and the types of activities the children chose to follow. It also became very apparent how resourceful children were when deprived of a certain material such as tape or glue. They would find ways of 'doing without' by coming up with other ways of fixing, or the play would change into something that was possible without the need to attach things.

Children's playful and creative responses have guided the changes that have occurred in my personal practice over the last ten years. From the other end, it's interesting to observe what my role has been in their playful experiences. Over the years I have been lucky enough to be part of projects that have harnessed the innate ability present in children to play and create and taken it to a fuller potential. I've been able to see what happens when a group of children are offered 1,000 cardboard boxes or 100 metres of paper alongside a Henry Moore sculpture or a Pre-Raphaelite painting. From these experiences I see that it really doesn't take much to get children going. It does feel that the key is how this play is initiated. Choosing the right material in the right quantity and setting up a space in a certain way is a good starting point – if done correctly this will not only inspire, but also provide an environment where the child feels confident to play. This becomes about offering permission to the child to do what they want but also about making them feel comfortable to explore, make mistakes and follow their individual creative process.

FIGURE 20.4 The 'cardboard box effect' Whitnash Nursery
Photo: Matthew Shaw

In all the projects described the spaces were always full of energy and led to a vast array of creative and playful experiences for those involved. However, in terms of design they were often the very opposite. Obviously much thought went into observing what the children did and how they used the materials, plus what and when materials were provided, but essentially these spaces were allowed to organically and often chaotically grow into something that could never have been conceived at the start of the project.

These ideas and projects could perhaps never be used as the basis for a permanent playground or playspace. However, there are many valuable lessons to be learnt where the ideas that have emerged from this very free play could inform more permanent designs.

One of the most important considerations is how to maintain the essence of play: free, unhindered creativity. Children are able to subvert even the most uninspiring material or emptiest of spaces to serve their playful and creative needs, if allowed to do so. However, there is a limit to this. Any design needs to accommodate the flexibility and freedom of children's thought but also has to do this over a prolonged period of time. Children are inherently creative: we can support that, rather than directing it.

21

ART AS PLAYSPACE

Interview with Toshiko & Charles MacAdam

BY ELIZABETH CUMMINS

Toshiko Horiuchi MacAdam and Charles MacAdam of Interplay based in Bridgetown, Nova Scotia, Canada, have been creating amazing playspaces for children for the last 40 years. Born out of Toshiko's love of textiles and in particular 3D crocheted works, her discovery of the 'missing element' to her work happened in the early 1970s when two children climbed onto one of her artworks on exhibition in a gallery and a connection between child and sculpture was born.

Toshiko and Charles spoke to me about their work, the significance of the structures to children's play and development, the many challenges they have faced and some of the fascinating insights into what they have learnt along the way.

EC: How did your childhood growing up in Japan influence your work?

TM: As a child, I was a tomboy. I had four brothers and learned how to fight with boys. I understand how they play. I have a strong memory of Tokyo after World War Two; there was nothing but we played on the streets and had a lot of freedom to be creative. I look at Japan now and for children it's all so organised. I think my God there is no creativity. The only way to solve society's problems is through imagination and creativity, so it's important to develop it from a very early age.

I come from a family of doctors and always planned to study medicine, but the arts were also important culturally to my family and I loved to paint when I was quite young. I attended a very competitive high school but when I graduated I really wanted to do something that I loved, so I made the unusual decision of going to art school (the prestigious Tama Fine Art University in Tokyo) and studying textiles. Japan has a long cultural history of textiles, but it is dying; most students wanted to study graphic or industrial design.

EC: Why textiles?

TM: I have always been interested in the structure of textiles and how the character changes with each type of material. I began learning to crochet at about five years old.

At art school and afterwards I began to create 3D textile works using tension and flexibility as my tools. At the same time, I realised that textiles are made for the human body and move with it and protect it. This flexibility comes from its porosity because it has many, many 'holes'.

In 1971 I created a piece with another artist that was based on connecting holes in abstract space. It was called 'Cell'. One day two children came to the exhibition and jumped inside. The piece had been quietly beautiful in the dark space but now it started to move like a living thing. This was a revelation to me. This 'cell' had come to life!

EC: What was the catalyst, the shift from your sculptures being just works of art to interactive playspaces?

TM: Although I exhibited my work both in Japan and internationally, it was not enough just to satisfy my own ego. Having many doctors in my family, part of me wanted to be more directly engaged. I wanted to connect with people and to work with contemporary materials and help solve problems in contemporary lives. If I could do that then it would personally satisfy me.

CM: Through a combination of observation, experimentation and intuition Toshiko had arrived at the perfect technique and the perfect mesh size (the interstitial 'hole' in the crochet). Japan has a long history of designing solutions to human scale. I think because it was isolated for so long it found its own solutions in reference to the human body and this is deeply engrained in the culture. (Think of the modular construction of the kimono or of architectural space based on the tatami, which was originally a sleeping mat.) Toshiko developed a textile that was perfectly shaped and constructed for children to grab hold of and move over. Later, as we began working in other countries and with various national safety standards, we realised the mesh size was also perfectly sized for avoiding entrapment.

FIGURE 21.1 Spiders Nest, Takino Suzuran National Park, Sapporo, Japan 2000
Design & Fabrication: Toshiko Horiuchi MacAdam with Interplay Design & Manufacturing Inc; Engineer: Norihide Imagawa, T.I.S & Partners; Photo: Masaki Koizumi

EC: What is it about children's play that so inspires your structures?

TM: After the 'Cell' exhibition, when I was teaching at Bunka Institute in Tokyo, I decided to do my own research, going out every weekend with two of my students to investigate virtually every playground in Tokyo – observing, talking to parents, teachers and children. It was quite depressing and I thought 'I don't want to raise a child in this situation'. At this time, no one was playing in the street anymore and more and more people were living in apartments. There was no total humanity there.

Children need their own space that isn't controlled. In this environment children learn to use many skills they need in society, they learn to deal with others. I wrote an article to the newspaper, but no-one was listening to what I was saying.

Previously, I had taught textiles at the University of Georgia in the United States, and one of my students was a graduate student in landscape architecture from Japan. After he returned to Japan and became established, he got in touch to say there was a chance to work on a new national park under construction in Okinawa. This was to be my first public project and I proposed two types of net – the crochet-type (AirPocket) and a large expanse of multi-layered machine-knotted nets stretched under tension (SpaceNet).

My idea was to make a space where children can interact and influence each other through movement. With these nets anyone can get in and choose their way of playing, using their imagination.

I want to make works for people who are alive today. One day the work will be gone and that's fine.

EC: Do you mean that your playspaces are designed to only be there for a limited time?

CM: It doesn't have to be in a museum; anywhere that kids are is the right place. Toshiko always says that 'art seems trapped in a museum, that it seems dead'.

TM: I think of the net playspaces like flowers. When I was working on the Showa Memorial National Park project in Tokyo (an ex-military air force base, turned into one of Japan's largest national parks), the government officials were difficult about the budget; this is often the case in Japan.

The biggest challenge was to change the established way of thinking. There was a lot of opposition to my proposal – in particular because the nets need maintenance and eventually will wear out and have to be replaced. Until that time, all of the play equipment in these parks had been made of steel or concrete and required little or no care. There was not even a budget for maintaining play equipment in Japan's national parks.

I suggested that the park's administrators consider their investment in landscaping. The park's trees and flowers are care-intensive – planting, weeding, pruning. I tried to get them to see how they were spending money to maintain the gardens that would grow and die and this was the same thing.

As the largest national park in Tokyo the Showa playspace sometimes gets 2,000–3,000 children on it each day. That's a lot of use and eventually the structure will wear out. In Japan we have a tradition of using shoji (translucent paper screens) in our houses. As children, we would moisten a finger and rub the paper to poke a hole through. Then at New Year's, the paper would be replaced and made new again. This was our tradition. Why couldn't we use a soft material like this instead of a hard one and replace it when it wears out?

In my early experimental projects I used a material called 'vinylon'. I knew that nylon was superior but it was expensive and out of reach since these projects were self-financed. The project in Okinawa gave me the chance to work with nylon. In this extreme environment – beside the ocean with intense sunlight and heat year-round – it performed well. About ten years later, when we were working for another national park, in Tokyo, we wanted to use another type, nylon 6-6, which was better still. Because it was not readily available in Japan, we would have to produce the nets in Canada, which was when Charles joined me and established Interplay in 1989.

CM: We effectively doubled the lifespan from four to five years for the earlier pieces to an average of eight years in Tokyo where they see very heavy use – some days as many as 4,000 children play on the nets. It has not been without difficulties. There were technical issues with the solution-dyed nylon 6-6 we used at first so now we purchase the fibre and process it ourselves, dyeing and braiding all of it in-house, except for the heavy rope which is specially braided for us by an outside contractor using our material. We use high-grade marine hardware as well.

TM: Because of the huge numbers of people using the nets at this park, our Japanese staff check the structure each month and make repairs once or twice a year. This means we are using government money but I believe it is worth it because of the amount of physical activity the children get and how they use their imaginations. There are many levels of play but everyone interacts with each other. Local kids come to play every week and show off for each other.

EC: How have you experimented with the material for both the AirPocket and SpaceNet structures over time?

TM: The first piece I made for a kindergarten near Kyoto. I learned by watching how children interact, how they played, how the piece wore and broke – that way I learnt to make it stronger and better.

For the next piece, which I exhibited in 1973, I changed the shape and construction so the energy is distributed more evenly throughout the net. Finally, with the Okinawa piece I had a clear idea of the form and construction and added the swinging balls for the two crochet pieces I made there. For this project, I also proposed the knotted net multi-unit hammocks; I knew I would be limited in how much I could create with my own hands and this would allow me to work with assistants.

We planned to install the piece in three weeks but it took three months! There were many problems. The nets sagged more than I expected and had to be completely remade. The bureaucrats were not happy but there was still time before the opening and we worked day and night. I remade all the nets and we modified the height of the external attachment points to solve the problem.

CM: This type, which we call SpaceNet, is deceptively complicated in its design. Because nylon will continuously stretch over time (referred to as creep) you have to be able to adjust the tension to ensure the nets clear the ground and the other nets below them when they are loaded with children. We do this by tethering one or more of the corners with ropes, which can be shortened as necessary. Ideally, the individual units should approach a hyperbolic paraboloid shape (like a saddle), which makes them stronger and gives better tension throughout.

It was about this time Toshiko applied for patents to protect her inventions for both types of play structures in Japan.

TM: In 1979–80 I received a commission from the Hakone Open Air Museum to create a sculpture for children – not just to look at but also to touch and feel, to be experienced with their whole bodies. It was a very large work, weighing about 650 kg produced entirely by hand. A structural engineer who admired this work was intrigued by its complexity and asked me how I had done the mathematical calculations. I could not give him an answer; it was all in my head. I had not studied math since high school.

The engineer, Norihide Imagawa, offered to help me in the future especially on government projects. He and his firm, TIS & Partners, have worked with us since 1989, developing solutions, which are often unique to each project. The Rome piece at MACRO in 2013, for example, was in a courtyard space in the museum where we could only drill a certain number of holes. So we did testing on the building to find the best attachment points and TIS & Partners designed light 'string' beams (hybrid tension-compression beams), which blended invisibly in the space to provide the necessary attachment points.

CM: We get many enquiries for installation in spaces that are the wrong dimensions – too high or long or just too big. Think about a spider constructing its web; it carefully chooses the twigs on which to build. Like the spider's web, the net has to hang freely in space from the tensioning ropes. It has to be stretched tight enough to take shape with just the right amount of sag, which is important in calculating the load on the support structure. We can make the net in all different kinds of shapes, but still have to work within these parameters.

EC: Why is movement so important in play do you feel?

CM: It's thinking about the logic of the structure, rather than its application. We find that many people don't understand this. Nylon has tremendous elasticity, and is capable of stretching 18–24% before it breaks.

It therefore has a tremendous capacity to absorb energy, which is why it is used in applications like automobile airbags. Unlike other fibres, such as polyester, for example, it doesn't recover its original shape immediately after being stretched. Its recovery is slightly drawn out to minimise the rebound and by various means we can enhance this. There are other materials that do fantastic things but not like this. By adjusting the tightness we can control the amount of resiliency so the effect is kind of like when you are floating on the sea, when the wave lifts you up and then down – a reciprocating movement.

We have found that the motion in the net (bobbing/rhythmic motion) actually has a certain frequency like a wave. It turns out that this motion is very close to the floating motion of the foetus inside the mother's womb. We believe that is why kids respond to the net structures (though they have not undertaken conclusive research). You can see children doing this repetitive 'up and down' bouncing motion and they'll do it continuously for half an hour with this 'other-worldly look on their face'. You can tell there is a deep connection there in the brain – that is more than just having a good time.

FIGURE 21.2 Banyan Tree, Okinawa Memorial National Park, Okinawa, Japan 1979
Design & Fabrication: Toshiko Horiuchi; Photo: Masaki Koizumi

TM: My brother is a paediatrician (and professor of neo-natal medicine) working with and researching premature babies. On bringing his grandson to Takino he said to me 'all these years we have been working in the same direction'.

CM: One of the issues with putting premature babies in Incubators (humidi-cribs) is that they get little physical stimulation. This is very important for brain development and as a result many premature babies have developmental disabilities. In his research Toshiko's brother learned that in South America (where resources were limited) they were putting premmies onto the mother's or someone else's body to get skin contact and most importantly feel the rise and fall of the breath and the heart beat. These were shown to be very effective in helping the babies develop because it was as close as possible to putting the baby back inside the mother's womb.

We have noted that children with cognitive problems respond and play on the net really well. We would like to do more research on this. We have talked and worked with people involved with kids with autism and autism spectrum. We feel there is a connectivity opportunity there.

EC: You spoke earlier about creativity in play. How do you think that your playspaces encourage children (and adults) to be creative in their play?

CM: As a kid I remember empty lots. You could roam and slide down a hill on a cardboard box if you wanted. There were little open, unused spaces in the city and now there is none of this – everything is designated or dedicated for this purpose or that purpose. For kids to feel this is ours, this is our place, that's a really important thing and if designers and planners could just think less about trying to make an impact with their designs and more about 'giving' – that's the essence.

A sense of freedom – just the space, the physical space. Give it to them and they'll find something to do. There's a place for programming too, but just give them space and they'll take possession of it.

You only have to look at the violence that you see with young people – acting out. The profile is one of a person with no emotional outlet and suddenly all this anger comes out. There's no empathy. There are some unusual trends emerging in Japan presently, which is a result, I believe, of a society where children are not encouraged to feel and manage their emotions. Kids have to work out how to do this effectively with other kids – that's how you learn.

In Rome the project was open to both adults and children, so there were kids and adults playing together. We didn't need any promotion or to indicate that this was for children. Many adults we work with can't see that there is enough there, but the physical structure is so striking that immediately and intuitively kids interact.

We feel that we need to advocate for kids because they don't have a voice. If you can't remember what it was like as a child then you are going to get off track.

EC: Tell me more about the project at Enel Contemporanea at MACRO in Rome in 2013?

TM: We installed the Rome piece in a glass-covered courtyard with a gate to the street at one side. When we were doing the installation, people would stop to look. Kids out with their parents (even quite late, at 10 o'clock) were glued to the gate watching the net take shape. They knew it was for them.

At the opening, the organisers had a photographer come to take photos and as he was climbing up through the net a child said to him 'oh you can't come on, this isn't for you, this is for us'.

CM: At the end of the project there was this grandmother banging on the gate as we were taking the net down. She spoke good English and she had to tell us how upset she was with us that we were taking it down. She told us just how much it had changed the local neighbourhood – she saw people interacting in ways that she had never seen in all her life.

The passion she felt was really impressive – that's the payback.

EC: What other stories do you have about how your nets have changed people's lives?

CM: Toshiko can tell you lots of stories of how the nets have changed people's lives. As long as we can make the structures we will do it. These kids will do something in life and their experience may have some influence on the direction they decide to take.

TM: I created the Hakone piece in 1981. After 28 years' use, in 2009 we replaced it for the Museum's 40th anniversary. We brought our 24 year old son along to help with the installation and at the opening he was introduced to a couple that first met when they were children on the earlier piece. They liked each other and their families kept up for a while but

FIGURE 21.3 Knitted Wonder Space II, Hakone Open Air Museum, Kanagawa, Japan 2009
Design & Fabrication: Toshiko Horiuchi MacAdam with Interplay Design & Manufacturing Inc; Engineer: Norihide Imagawa, T.I.S & Partners; Architect: Takaharu & Yui Tezuka; Photo: Masaki Koizumi

later lost touch. Then one day when they were attending the same university they recognised each other, after that they started dating and then they married and had children who they had now brought with them to the opening. Our son said 'I have never heard a story like this and now I understand why you are so passionate about these pieces'. He was not quite clear until then.

CM: Since the Okinawa project, we have met and heard of several people who became Landscape Architects because of their experiences playing on our nets. We heard the martial arts actor Jackie Chan (as an adult) played on both the Hakone and Okinawa and there's a scene in one of his movies where he bounces on nets in a pachinko (Japanese pinball) parlour, which we heard he based on this.

EC: Are there other instances where the net structures have influenced popular culture?

CM: There is a famous comic strip and anime character in Japan called Sazae-san, by artist Machiko Hasegawa who wrote many books, one of which is set in the piece in Hakone. The cultural influence is wide, we have also heard about a video game set on the Takino project.

We do as much as we can do. It's not always easy, but what we are doing has satisfied us. We even have copiers now. Mostly they aren't very good and cannot see the difference between their products and their 'inspiration', but we continue to forge on.

EC: What other projects are you currently working on and do you have any dream projects or places you'd like to work on?

CM: We're at a certain point in our lives where we are not at that age where you are really ambitious, we tend to be selective. What's really important is the relationship we can develop with the other members of the team (we are working with) and getting insight into the culture by going there and working with people to make something.

That's the pleasure we're looking for, so we are selective of the projects we work on. We've seen a lot of projects just evaporate after we've put a lot of effort in. We're working on a project in New Zealand right now for a client who did well in the IT world and has started a media production company specialising in kids' programming and is also developing a play park. Along with that we have a condominium project in Miami and the SpaceNet at Showa Memorial Park in Tokyo needs renewing, which will be a two year project.

If we can communicate the 'value' of our work, then any place is fine, we just don't want to be limited to doing some rich person's backyard. The interaction among kids is very important, so unless you have different groups coming to use it, it won't realise its true value.

SCHOOLS

We move now from the art world to the school world: a place where most kids in this age bracket spend a good part of their waking lives. The challenges and dynamics of a school environment are quite different to those of a public space, early childhood centre or gallery environment, and good design is especially important in these spaces. However, as we will explore, we cannot always predict how those designs will be used.

22

QUINTESSENTIAL PLAY PATTERNS IN SCHOOLS

The interface of space, materials and play behaviour

Mary Jeavons

Play has its own intrinsic value to every human being, and especially to children as they develop. Quality physical play environments, and adequate uninterrupted time for play, should be provided for this reason alone, regardless of all the other benefits outdoor play provides.

Children in developed western countries are becoming increasingly indoors, sedentary and time-managed.

Many authors have described the negative effects on children's health and well-being from the lack of exposure to the outdoors and its opportunities for independent play. Issues such as the increase in myopia in children who spend a lot of time indoors, and the importance of load bearing exercise in childhood as one of the few ways of building bone density and preventing osteoporosis later in life reflect the benefits to children's health of playing outside.

Schools remain one of the few places where most children can more or less be expected to play out of doors on most days. How schools support (or deny) quality outdoor play opportunities for children is therefore of the utmost importance to many aspects of children's well-being.

As 'captives' for many years within the one school environment, children frequently develop a unique and intimate relationship with the outdoor spaces at their school. This kind of intimacy with an outdoor place is less likely in other settings such as urban parks and play spaces, and even at home now as (modern western) children spend less time in such places, often superintended by adults.

Children's familiarity with every centimetre of their school grounds, on the other hand, enables them to develop their own activities that respond to the details of that unique micro environment, and then pass on a rich culture of play behaviour to the next generation: '*This is what we do here.*'

School grounds are the ultimate multi-purpose space. They need to cater for all weather circulation, for assemblies, fetes, community gatherings, sport and physical education, for outdoor learning (climate permitting), gardening and environmental education, out of hours care, emergency access, environmental education and for social interaction, eating and performances. They are a workplace for staff and a focus of community life for many families. Over and above all of these functions they need to cater for the daily needs of children who depend upon them for their play.

Play behaviour – one constant across a diverse system

Schools vary enormously across the social spectrum. The approach to outdoor play, and an understanding of its importance, therefore varies considerably. A few things remain constant, however:

- Children's outdoor activities are complex and diverse and respond to the physical and social environment of the school.
- Children demonstrate a highly detailed appreciation of their environment and its qualities and affordances.
- Children are highly inventive in finding or creating their own opportunities for play in school grounds; however…
- Many types of play are vulnerable and easily threatened or stifled by overcrowding, a lack of time, overly rigid rules or the lack of suitable qualities in the environment.
- Of particular importance are small scale, complex spaces; loose manipulable settings; and spaces dominated by natural elements. These are frequently missing, especially in new schools.

School grounds have to arguably be the most robust of any public space: they usually have to survive 'tsunamis' of children at one time, often with minimal maintenance.

Regardless of the school, it is possible to look more deeply and objectively into the relationship between the physical environment and children's play behaviours and some **critical characteristics of spaces** that children value for various types of activities. It is hoped that this may influence the design of school grounds and also encourage adults to adopt a supportive attitude towards play at school.

This section presents a brief selection of play 'patterns' (the interface of activities/spaces and materials) that are commonly demonstrated by children in their play at school. It is not comprehensive and for brevity has had to group numerous activities together into categories that should ideally be sieved out with a finer grain. Broadly speaking, these can be divided into play with balls, children's imaginative play, play on play equipment and nature.

Because children's needs and interests are so diverse, and because their interests also change over time, each school should ideally offer a 'package' that caters for each of these essential activity types, to ensure that each child's needs are likely to be met.

Ball games affect all other play at school

Ball games in schools are amongst the most easily recognised outdoor activities and are usually acknowledged as a fundamental requirement for a school. These activities are highly valued by many children.

If they are not carefully integrated into the overall site plan, ball games can dominate the outdoor spaces in a school, with balls and fast-moving children providing a daunting obstacle to those who are younger and more vulnerable, and to their games. In many schools there is little else to do and the 'small' games are pushed to the very edge, both physically and figuratively.

Briefly, ball games are themselves diverse and complex and require a variety of surfaces and dimensions suitable to the type of game. The brief points below are not focused on specialist sports facilities and sports surfaces in schools, but on free flowing and independent play. Organised sport is an entirely different topic, with different requirements which may overlap ball play spaces at scheduled times.

When planning for particular types of ball games in schools the following matters must not be ignored:

- suitability of the surface for the type of game
- adequate size and dimensions
- orientation (usually north–south preferred)
- placement in relation to buildings, paths and other elements to avoid conflicts
- benefits of adjacency with other spaces/activities (such as seating).

Ball games in schools can be loosely categorised as follows.

'Big' ball games on grass

- Typically these are *kicking* games such as various types of football, and *hitting* games such as cricket and baseball in summer (sometimes all at once).
- They need large spaces away from roads and windows.
- It is ideal if a large oval or soccer pitch size field can be supplemented by a smaller grassed area that provides for other types of play activities.
- De-compact, aerate, rest, irrigate and feed living turf regularly to maintain some grass cover.

Hardcourt games

- These provide for *bouncing games* such as basketball and netball, and are frequently used for tennis and volleyball.
- They need a smooth, nonslip bouncing surface (not synthetic grass) and multiple line-markings.
- They work best configured as two courts located side by side and away from windows and roads.
- Courts must have adequate run-out space around them.
- Seats nearby provide for others to watch as well as for teaching and instruction.
- Their all-weather surface can provide for many other school activities such as performances, markets, fetes and events. The surface and base should be engineered for vehicle loadings.

Small ball games

- These include games such as four square, handball and other small games typically involving very small groups of children; smaller, softer balls such as tennis balls; and on hard surfaces and also against walls.
- Children often appropriate small paved spaces and corners for these games.
- They need to be planned for so that circulation can still move safely around them across courtyards and around buildings.
- They need enough room not only for the bounce but for children to step back and run to get the ball.
- Soft surfaces adjacent will frequently become worn out if the paved area is not large enough.

Ball games, plants and vulnerable activities

Any gardens or plantings close to intensively used ball play areas will inevitably be placed at risk from damage and soil compaction as children run after balls. Site planning needs to take this into account, ideally separating these elements.

If planting is immediately adjacent to ball play areas, then careful consideration needs to be made of elements such as fencing. Typically, low fences will stop children running across planted areas but they don't prevent balls entering. Children then have to enter to retrieve the balls. This also contributes to soil compaction and plant failure. By comparison, taller mesh fences do contain both balls and running children, and allow smaller eddies of planting and small games to flourish, particularly if they are open on one side.

Pretend/imaginative/role play activities

This kind of play occurs in many places across a school ground if the environment is suitable.

The play involves fantasy, role play, imagination and pretend games. It often has a strong emphasis on language and communication, and children may use small toys and dolls, and loose materials such as flowers, leaves, pebbles, twigs and the like. Sometimes the emphasis is on the pretend activity directly (such as families, cooking and mothers with babies), but it frequently evolves in older children into the construction of the house itself, using various materials as a setting for the game. For this play, children often appropriate small spaces and they incorporate very small physical details of the landscape into their games.

Imaginative play is very common amongst girls but is certainly played by many boys when they have the opportunity. It evolves through primary school, frequently played in very small groups of younger children with group sizes becoming larger and more complex as they get older.

These games, however, are vulnerable. Frequently small scale, detailed spaces are simply not available to children at school and especially in new schools where mown grass is the most common physical feature. Pretend and role play games are frequently fairly sedentary and may have delicate arrangements of toys and materials. Busy running and ball games conflict with them.

Quintessential play patterns in schools 211

FIGURE 22.1 Small scale imaginative play with pebbles, Merri Creek
Photo: Mary Jeavons

For this play to flourish, schools need:

- a generally complex physical environment that is not flat, completely open or completely devoted to ball games and running,
- small 'eddies' out of the flow of traffic, where children can find clusters of useful planting, boulders, terrain, logs, tree stumps, edges and overhangs,
- corners and niches between buildings; steps, stairs and doorways; the more complex the better,
- to plant small forested areas, along fence lines, with trees in groups, circles and lines, defining the right small scale spaces,
- tough shrubs with overhanging/weeping habit; configured to form clusters of cubbies that relate to one another,
- loose materials for children's use,
- a sympathetic attitude that values and fosters this type of play.

Play equipment in schools

Play equipment is one of the more visible (and expensive) demonstrations that adults provide for play in a school, usually with hard earned funds. As a result, adult concepts such as a theme, bright colours and terms such as 'wow' factor become confused with children's requirements. An expensive imported play structure might actually provide less play value than a well-chosen log.

FIGURE 22.2 Children at primary school use some native shrubs as their cubby where they develop rich dramatic play scenarios

Photo: Mary Jeavons

Many activities that are provided for by play equipment can occur in equally beneficial ways in the landscape – especially climbing (up rocks, logs and trees), balancing, jumping, stepping and hanging. Others are well provided for by purpose-designed structures. Each setting has its benefits. Ideally a school will offer both a choice of landscape elements for play, as well as thoughtfully designed equipment set in the right location.

The tricky aspect to play equipment is that it has to provide for a complex combination of activities. These may look purely physical but will frequently have complex social, imaginative and role play games integral to them. Frequently there will be many different types of activity going on at once on any given play structure.

Some design considerations on the different purposes for play equipment are offered below. For all equipment, though:

- provide **a choice of functions, properly designed** for usability, to accommodate each purpose in order to maximise play value,
- provide for different sizes, ages and abilities of children; **different degrees of challenge** and opportunities to opt out,
- aim to **minimise conflicts** between the fast moving games and those that are quiet and more sedentary,
- as equipment is often used by many children at once, consider **adequate space and refuge** within a structure,

Quintessential play patterns in schools   **213**

FIGURE 22.3 Children seek out intimate spaces for imaginative/role play wherever they can find them

Photo: Mary Jeavons

- in large schools, at least three different arrangements of play equipment, ranging from small scale for the youngest children and more challenging for the older ones, need to be provided simply to accommodate the numbers who will use it. These don't have to be segregated according to age group but it is important to make sure that children can find equipment that suits their size and skill level.

Agility/upper body activities on play equipment

This typically encompasses activities on equipment such as horizontal ladders, rings, turnover bars, chin-up bars and the like ('upper body equipment').

Sometimes these are purely physical, with children challenging themselves and each other to develop a series of skills. For example, milkshake; how far; how fast; one handed; backward; rings vs bars. Each has its own subtleties.

Frequently these games also have a social aspect – for example older girls often 'hang out' and hang upside down on the tops of bars, talk and play other games (rhyming and clapping, for example). Being up high and being able to look around are also integral to the experience.

- Provide a choice of heights and lengths of bar type equipment. Young children must be provided with easy ways to master this challenge before they are exposed to the higher, longer equipment.
- Link these items in a circuit with other balancing items if possible so that children can incorporate them into a range of games.
- Bars for gripping and turnovers need to be circular section steel tubing, welded or pinned to prevent the bars turning dangerously.

- Swinging rings need to be large enough to grip comfortably.
- Regular spacing is ideal as there is considerable rhythm involved in this type of movement.
- Avoid conflicts at landing zones by providing decks large enough for landing as well as for the queue waiting.

Chasey games/tiggy on play equipment

These fast-moving group games combine running, chasing, climbing up, balancing along, jumping off and sliding down equipment and other elements in the landscape. Sometimes, variations of these games develop into circuits.

Chase games need:

- a variety of ways up – climbing rungs, nets, bars, holds, walls, chains, stairs, ramps, etc. (allowing less able children to participate),
- choices in direction to foil the chaser – through tunnels, across nets, across a balance beam or bridge,
- fast exits of different types – choice of slides, sliding poles and openings to jump out and off,
- when looking at circuits, linked items with choices of direction and challenge, with balance and movement built in.

These activities can compromise the smaller sedentary role play games often played by younger children, so consider any potential conflicts that may be driven by the configuration of the equipment.

Hiding/chasing games around play equipment

Many games require something to hide behind. Play equipment that is very open doesn't cater well for this type of game.

- Complex spaces with changes of level, planting, walls, large boulders, logs and trees provide for good hiding games.
- Play equipment comprising some semi-solid walls at ground level provides more options for hiding games and role play games than structures that are completely open.

Pretend/imaginative/role play activities and play equipment

This kind of play has been described earlier in this section. Play equipment with multiple activity types is not always optimal for this kind of play (especially when the other busy activities are in full swing), but sometimes it is all that is available for children so they adapt their games to suit.

Standard play equipment frequently incorporates a small doorway or shop counter into spaces under decks in an attempt to cater for this type of play. These are frequently so open and soulless that they miss the point.

FIGURE 22.4 Many different games exist simultaneously on play equipment

Photo: Mary Jeavons

In order to optimise this kind of play on play equipment consider the following design points.

- Provide some small scale, partially enclosed (cubby) spaces that are not easy to run through as part of the structure. This minimises the conflict with the busy running games. These spaces might be at ground level and/or elevated. If they are elevated make sure they are easy to reach for young, timid or less able children.
- Make sure there are some 'open ended' features in the cubby space that can be adapted for the children's own games. A timber shelf, a rock seat, a stump with a hole in the top, a wall made of vertical bars, a short tunnel or a cave-like niche will be put to use as a pretend doll's bed, a witch's brew, a kitchen, a prison or a pen for baby animals. These can be incorporated into under-deck spaces and will add to the play value.
- Position 'cubby' type spaces (especially those at ground level under equipment) where they relate to other interesting elements in the adjacent landscape (such as near other small scale spaces; near rocks and logs, planting and loose materials for play). The play will broaden and these elements will be incorporated into the games, helping to deliver better play value from both equipment and landscape.

Social inclusion and the design of play equipment and surfaces

All children want and need to engage with their friends in play and social activities at school. Play equipment can cater for children with physical disabilities/limitations to their mobility through simple design interventions. Even if well-graded ramps can't take children in wheelchairs to the top of a high structure, the under-deck spaces can easily be designed to provide imaginative/role play for children who use wheelchairs and other mobility aids. The surfaces need to provide for easy access and manoeuvring, and design features such as shop counters should provide for front-on use from a wheelchair.

Simple additions such as an easy stairway, and good hand grips and rails, will make it easier for ambulant children who may have a balance or vision impairment to reach higher parts of the equipment.

Nature, loose and rough

The ability of children to engage hands on with loose materials is fundamental to their play. Christopher Alexander et al.[1] sum up the idea in their seminal work *A Pattern Language*:

> Any kind of playground that disturbs … the role of the imagination and makes the child more passive, more the recipient of someone else's imagination … cannot satisfy the fundamental need which play is all about.

Play with loose materials is very challenging for many adults and managers of institutions such as schools in particular. It requires a sympathetic approach to management and sensible location of loose elements so that they do not end up out on the road or in the way at the school entrance.

This kind of play crosses over with some of the activities already discussed, especially pretend/imaginative/role play activities which frequently use whatever loose elements can be found as props in their games.

There are indeed many different ways that children incorporate loose elements into their play, and this section can only draw attention to the value of the quality of 'looseness' as an exceptional tool in self-directed play, however it manifests itself. It provides some examples and some ideas for providing loose elements even when this is challenging.

Natural materials especially lend themselves to imaginative/creative play activities because they are inherently 'open ended', with no particular purpose, so children can self-direct their use.

Some highly successful loose play materials include sand, dirt, water (provided or as natural puddles), rocks and pebbles, lawn clippings, mulch, leaves, pine needles, flowers, pods, twigs, bark, tree prunings and branches. They may also include re-purposed items such as building materials, tyres, fabric and old cooking utensils.

In conclusion

There are many important play activities and settings that have not been mentioned in this chapter. There has not been space here to discuss wilder natural spaces; food gardens;

Quintessential play patterns in schools 217

FIGURE 22.5 Flowers, grass clippings, sand and trees all provide valuable loose materials
Photo: Mary Jeavons

activities such as elastics, hoops, marbles and yo-yos; routes and trails for nature exploration and observation; platforms for dancing, music and performances; or design for activities like chess, table games and the social play of older children.

It can only be recommended that designers and managers of schools take the opportunity of closely observing children's self-directed play at school. Consulting children about the details of their activities in the school ground inevitably reveals useful information for designers. This needs to be done in very small groups and ideally children should be invited to guide adults around their spaces and discuss what they do there, and what they would like to be able to do.

In this way designers can cater properly for this rich type of human behaviour that is so critically valuable to the well-being of children.

23

WHEN IS A SLIDE NOT A SLIDE?

(Or what if we think differently about and beyond design?)

Dr Wendy Russell

I remember reading some time ago about a research project in the USA that used video footage to examine the causes of accidents or near accidents in a school playground.[1] The researchers reported that the most frequently viewed cause of accidents was improper use of equipment. As someone who has spent almost 40 years working with, or studying, children at play, this struck me as a revealing statement and it has stayed with me ever since. So I have returned to it here in order to explore some of the assumptions that lie beneath this concept, not to dismiss it, but to look differently at our common sense understandings, habits and practices to see what more can be said about children, play, space and design.

The chapter opens with a look at the power of language, and our fondness for using words to do with **tree** to describe how the world works; in particular how they may be applied to our understanding of the nature and value of playspaces for children. Drawing on the work of Gilles Deleuze and Félix Guattari, an alternative of the **rhizome** is offered that can help shift our focus from narrow cause and effect for specific future benefit. This may help to develop an appreciation of how spaces are always in the process of becoming through the entanglements of material objects, bodies, feelings, histories and so on, in fluid and continually changing ways that mean space is never 'finished'. The chapter closes with the proposal that alongside design's focus on specifics, appreciating space as relational and never 'finished' – and by implication accepting the future as uncertain – might be useful principles that can help leave space open for children's own play productions.

Calling a slide a slide

When we design spaces, we give names to the elements 'within' them. Play equipment manufacturers have to call the items they sell something. Landscape architects also have a technical language that describes particular landscape features. This naming is useful, since it means we can communicate to others in a way that is largely (although never uniformly) understood. Yet it also has a power to affect how we understand and act in the world.

When playground designers design something called a slide, the focus is on its 'slideness'. They enhance its features for sliding, perhaps making it steeper, longer, twistier for older children (to be age appropriate), or wider (to be inclusive), or making it in the shape of an animal (to encourage imaginative play). They consider safety and maintenance issues. These design features all rest in a particular understanding of the nature and value of childhood and of play, as well as assumptions about how the equipment will be used. The function of a slide is to be slid down; this is 'using the equipment properly'. And much of the time, this is what children do.

Yet anyone who has watched children at play will know that once they have used the slide in this way and have a feel for it, they will often then explore its potential beyond just sliding. Coming down in different positions, maybe, or climbing up the chute, coming down on roller blades, sending different objects down the slide, sitting on the end chatting or building a den underneath. Not limited as much as adults to predetermined ideas of what constitutes a slide, children seek to actualise whatever the space affords at that time.[2] From an adult perspective, because the purpose of a slide is to be slid down, these alternative uses could constitute 'not using equipment properly'. It may be that calling a slide a slide closes down possibilities for it being something other than a slide.

Language is often understood as an accurate representation of a pre-existing world in order to communicate it; however, what this slide story shows is that language also frames the way we make sense of the world and how we act. Nouns turn much of life's ongoing and emergent experiences into things (play, fun, risk, for example), fixing them as something to

FIGURE 23.1 Slide in public playground in Tower Hamlets, London, UK
Photo: Marc Armitage (www.marc-armitage.com)

be known and therefore predictable and controllable. Verbs mean that independently existing subjects act on objects, in a cause-and-effect manner. What's more, we can never capture the whole of human experience in language. There is always something that escapes, an excess of the senses that cannot be captured through representation in words.

The sense we make of the world is about the reciprocal relationship between meaning and doing. Merely using the word 'slide' to represent the material object does not on its own fix its meaning or potential. Meaning, for adults and children, arises not only from language but from the whole entanglement of what can be done with that slide in that place at that time and all 'that' entails. In another time and place, those meanings may shift – and so may we – to become something different. How we make sense of 'slide' emerges in different ways depending on each situation and what combines to make each situation. And how we make sense of 'slide' matters because it affects what we think can or should be done with it.[3]

A powerful metaphor for how we understand the world is that of trees, what Deleuze and Guattari call 'arborescent thinking'.[4] Indeed it informs the overall framework for this book on growing a playspace. What follows here is a critique of this conceptualisation, again, not to dismiss it, but to explore its influence and limitations and to see what a different conceptualisation might offer. Arborescent thinking goes something like this. From the acorn of an idea grow roots, sinking themselves into the soil to fix a position, producing a trunk and branches with leaves and finally, with maturity, fruit (more acorns). This mode of thinking is widespread and pervasive; think branches of knowledge, seeds of hope, roots of a problem, fruits of labour. It represents a logical, linear, fixed and predictable progression through time. Although the branches may go in different directions, they emanate from one tree anchored by one tap root.

This mode of thinking can exclude other ways of understanding the world. Deleuze and Guattari offer an alternative, that of a rhizome, and this has great promise for the idea of growing a playspace. Rhizomes are underground stems; ginger and iris are examples, as are some bulbs and tubers. They have no fixed beginnings (so everything starts in the middle of everything else, a lovely way of looking at history, development or activity), they can spread in any direction; new plants can grow from broken pieces. It is about movement, connections, diversity, multiplicity and rupture, with the capacity to disrupt, start again in a different way, go off in unpredictable directions.

All this may sound rather abstract, so I asked playworkers for stories of children using slides. Many came back, all stories of children using slides in ways that adults could not have predicted. The simple story below illustrates how children are not restricted by categories of toys and make use of whatever is to hand in whatever ways come to mind:

> The slide in my garden got used for a marrow racing track. The kids took marrows that were over-produce from the allotment – added KNEX, cocktail sticks, flowers and wheels – and then raced them down the slide.[5]

What's a playspace for anyway?

What is a playspace? Well, it's a space where children play, isn't it? Or perhaps where they can, or should, play. Does this mean children don't play anywhere else? Of course not. Experience tells us that children play anywhere, with anything and everything, sometimes to the annoyance of adults, often in ways that adults may not even notice. Play is not only a

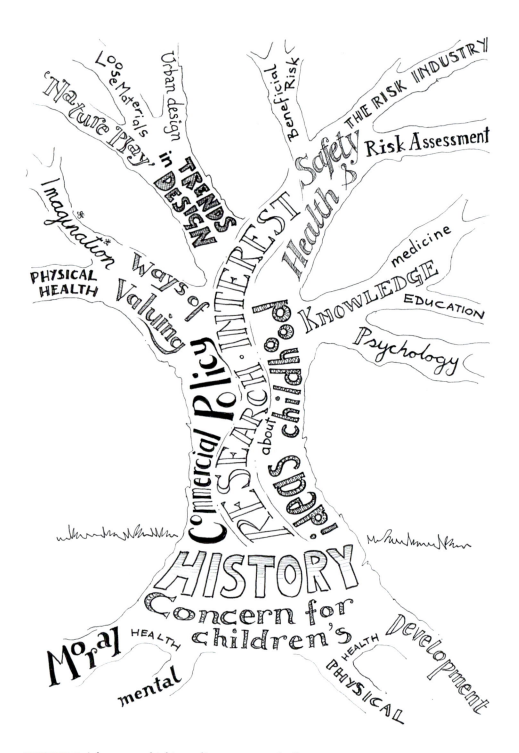

FIGURE 23.2 Arborescent thinking – linear, cause and effect
Copyright Katherine Masiulanis & Wendy Russell

FIGURE 23.3 Rhizomatic thinking – starting from the middle
Copyright Katherine Masiulanis & Wendy Russell

separate time and space bound activity, it is also a disposition to the world (playfulness) that can arise whenever conditions allow.[6]

Designated spaces offer the potential for encounters children may not easily be able to experience elsewhere, or the space and time to be relatively free from constraints and demands of their everyday lives, and this is highly significant; but they are not the sum total of children's play experiences. Sometimes, because we have developed a habit of thinking in particular ways about the concepts of 'play' (as a thing) and 'playspace' (and all that entails), we conflate play and play provision; yet 'play is not a public service, much less a commodity'.[7]

Since industrialisation, separate spaces for childhood, together with their associated material objects, have come into being, including nurseries, schools, clubs and playgrounds. These spaces 'became the means by which adults set out and put into effect their objectives for modern children and their childhoods'.[8] The history of designated spaces for children's play, whether in parks, schools or dedicated play projects, is wrapped up in the history of adult desires and of social policy, where the provision of special places to play was a response to whatever social problems were identified at the time.[9,10,11] Often focusing on working class and poorer children, these have included concerns about socialisation and citizenship;[12] physical fitness as a route to moral fitness;[13] encouraging school attendance and attention in class;[14] keeping children off streets that were deemed morally dangerous[15] and dangerous because of traffic;[16] physical activity and combatting obesity;[17] and lack of contact with nature.[18] These desires have spawned industries of playground design, manufacture and research, often branches of the same 'tree' of knowledge about the nature and value of childhood and play.

From this perspective, playspaces are designed to encourage the forms of playing that will address social concerns and support the development of desirable and promoted cognitive, physical, emotional and social skills. Returning to the opening discussion about slides and arborescent thinking, the assumption is that the space, its features and material objects, will be used in particular ways that yield the desired outcomes. Within the current framework of evidence-based policy and practice, research is commissioned to gather evidence of what works. It is a technical, universal, linear, cause-and-effect way of understanding the world that obscures issues of complexity, justice and power.[19]

These approaches are so pervasive, so powerful, that it is often difficult to think differently about them; they appear to be common sense. What might a rhizomatic approach offer to this conundrum? Again, it needs to be stressed that this is not a complete dismissal of current policy and practice, more an exercise in stepping aside from dominant and habitual mindsets to see what more might be possible.

Design, stuff and growing a play space

If we move from thinking about trees to thinking about rhizomes, the straight line from design to outcome disappears, as does the separation of playspaces from all other elements of children's everyday lives, since playspaces do not operate in isolation. There is no beginning or end, only a middle. Attention shifts from a predictable process to idiosyncratic and spontaneous patterns, flows and movements in the here and now. Rhizomatic thinking intentionally disturbs habit and linear cause-effect thinking in favour of emergence and entanglements.[20]

Space, from this position, is no longer a neutral container to be filled with stuff and in which things happen. The type of play which is likely to happen in a space is not a pre-existing and fixed entity, but is constantly evolving with the ongoing and shifting entanglements of material and symbolic objects and features, bodies, senses, feelings, desires, movements, histories and so on. Although there may be similarities, no one moment in a playspace will be repeated in exactly the same way.

The rhizome contains aspects of planning, organisation, control and so on – the design of and adult intentions for playspaces – and these are necessary. It also contains lines of flight from this 'plane of organisation',[4] moments when children disturb these intentions and appropriate time and space for their own play creations. The great play scholar Brian Sutton-Smith said that in their play, children take aspects of their own everyday lives and turn them upside down in ways that make them either less scary or less boring.[21] Playing has also been described as the deliberate creation of uncertainty,[22] in order to experience the thrill of raw emotions (like fear, joy, surprise, disgust) and of overcoming that uncertainty within the relative safety of something 'as if', an alternative version of 'reality'. Playfulness becomes a state of vitality; more than just fun, it is what makes life worth living for the time of playing.

Children's experiences of space are radically different from adults', and it is difficult for adults to perceive what a space has to offer children.[23] Special spaces emerge through use over time, sometimes in places and ways not apparent to adults, and often named by the children. This is what June Factor calls the 'play lines' of a playground.[24] Marc Armitage's research in apparently barren school playgrounds reveals a rich cultural history of such special places, passed down through generations of children.[25] One example is the 'long black pole', a drainpipe used in hiding and hunting games as a counting pole and home base.[26]

If a playspace is to support the spontaneous eruption of playfulness, what might this mean both for design and for growing a playspace beyond the design process? Stuff matters: physical features and material objects play their part in the ongoing production of playspaces, they are part of the assemblage. And so does everything else: people, movements, flows, emotions, atmosphere, relationships, histories, power relations and so on. No one element of a playspace pre-exists independently of any other; all are in a constant state of flux, of becoming, in each unique entanglement.

The paradox is that if playing represents a flight from adult organisation of time and space, then an adult designed and organised playspace becomes a plane of organisation. We cannot design and plan children's 'flights'. However, design is not fixed only in organisation.

In Deleuze and Guattari's practical philosophy, the plane of organisation is necessary, and interwoven into this is the plane of immanence, of open-ended, uncertain possibilities. Thinking of both allows for the practicalities of design and the openness of playfulness, of possibility, of what might be. We can shift our end-goal, future-oriented focus on the straight line from purpose to design to 'proper use' to outcome; and look instead at the way the space works in the here and now, the flows and movements of bodies that both affect and are affected by everything else. Attention is paid not only to the properties of materials but also to relational qualities.

FIGURE 23.4 When is a slide a slide? Reappropriation of slides by Bellemo and Cat at Wombat Bend, Yarra Valley Parklands, Manningham, Victoria, Australia

Photograph by Wendy Russell

We might perhaps still call a slide a slide (because it has to be called something). What might be different about rhizomatic thinking is that the thing called slide is but one phenomenon amongst everything that contributes to the continuous and ongoing production of a playspace, including adult expectations and children's appropriations. As one playworker said, when talking about the many different ways the slide was used at his playground:

> I can't list all the games, because the children haven't decided what they are yet.[27]

24
'THIS PLACE IS LIKE A BUILDING SITE... .'

Judi Legg

WILDSIDE, SCOTLAND

In 2012 Thornlie Primary School created an adventurous and engaging school playground that might just be the most exciting school playground in Scotland.

With £35,000 from the Scottish Government funded 'Go Play' programme, a 'play landscape' was designed by landscape design practice Wildside Scotland, as part of a Natural Play Project co-ordinated by school grounds charity: Grounds for Learning. A further collaboration between the school and Wildside, funded by the local North Lanarkshire Council, focused on developing practice around 'free play' opportunities – particularly of working with 'loose materials'.

The Thornlie project provided an opportunity (although certainly not the first) to explore to what extent free play is actually possible within a school when, for example, the children have no choice over being there, or the play resources available to them. It was also an opportunity to explore how play could support the ambitions of the curriculum and the implications for policy, management and maintenance.

School grounds in Scotland

The project took place within a context where schools, local authority and Scottish Government were starting to create big changes to school grounds and to the culture and attitudes that have conspired in many cases to ensure that school playgrounds in Scotland are too often sterile and rule bound environments that constrain rather than encourage children's play. Often the playground and what children do there goes unnoticed. Generally they are among the most used yet impoverished environments: monoculture tarmac and/ or grass deserts; flat, exposed and often intimidating spaces with high and complex fencing which frequently keeps children separate from adjacent woods or quality green space. And the factors which shape these conditions are often structural and institutionalised: attitudes to mess, anxieties around litigation, grounds maintenance budgets which focus on grass cutting on a massive scale, lack of land management experience within schools, the need to protect property from damage and procurement routes which offer 'off the shelf' rather than bespoke solutions. Whilst both play and outdoor learning are now clearly valued within the Scottish

'Curriculum for Excellence', it can be difficult for schools to follow through in poor physical environments and with competing formal and administrative curriculum demands.

Co-operation, collaboration and mess at Thornlie

Changing the space and the play practice at Thornlie was further made possible by the seismic changes the school had achieved in the preceding years for its 150 children. Located in a disadvantaged area of Wishaw in the post-industrial Central Belt of Scotland, what already existed was a clear staff approach to equality of opportunity and empowering children through giving responsibility.

> We live in a tough area. Children who come to us haven't always been well guided in how to sort out conflict... . I never get my hopes too high, and teaching children how to emotionally problem-solve remains high on our agenda; but we have had zero exclusions this session, and we have a vision of the 'new' playground not as a source of anxiety but as a source of resolution – as well as fun.[1]

The ambition and ethos was evident in their application for natural play:

> We would like the children to build and to explore and to climb and to jump. We would like them to be immersed in and in contact with natural materials, wood, water, grass, plants, mud. If possible we would like them to make decisions, to take risks, to work together and to test themselves.[2]

From 20 years' experience of working with schools, we knew that the most important factor in 'growing' and sustaining an engaging play environment is the presence of an influential

FIGURE 24.1 The more they use the materials the more they know how to use them, Thornlie Primary School, Scotland

Photo: Sue Gutteridge

champion/leader who wants to drive the project and is convinced of the power and importance of empowerment and free play. Without this, effort is usually wasted. Appointing head teachers committed to this ethos – and without anxieties about mess – would also be supported by an increased remit for head teachers in facilities management (totally separated in Scotland), and the encouragement of head teachers to manage external facilities and resources as well as internal.

What are loose materials?

Of course children have always understood loose materials as the raw materials of play, and the concept of materials that are open to manipulation employed at Thornlie is broad.

> You need to make a mess. It's actually getting stuck into stuff – because when you actually get stuck into stuff is when you learn.[3]

Children now enjoy the infinite possibilities of play with pebbles, timber discs, guttering and pipes, moveable stumps, branches, mini world figures, animals and construction vehicles. No suggestions are made about how the materials 'should' be used and no part of the grounds is out of bounds.

Rods, tarpaulins, picnic blankets, crates, planks and hay bales are often used for den building and the children demonstrate how with these materials they can continuously shape and re-design space: from the beginning there were nomadic dens, wall dens, steps and ramp area dens and sand area dens. Other dens incorporated benches, picnic tables and a basketball post. The presence of particular features in the grounds and a range of materials mean that the concept of a den can expand beyond being a structure to being a space of one's own, of self-expression and play. A den can be a nest. 'Pennies' can be a path into it. Chalk sticks can

FIGURE 24.2 Sand and water engineers, Thornlie Primary School, Scotland
Photo: Sue Gutteridge

become gardens, places can be named and signify ownership. The variety is as limitless as the children's imagination.

A play landscape

The playground itself was designed to support and inspire this kind of play, meaning that elemental natural materials such as *mud, water and sand* are freely available, on a large scale, and that the playground has become a varied natural landscape that changes and develops over time. *Digging and construction tools* are provided in a large and deep bespoke sandpit with adjacent water, *decks and posts with pulleys*. Robust and rustic boulder and timber features and edges suggest routes and perches, and challenging elements such as at the fallen tree give opportunities for climbing and leaping. Trees, shrubs and willow structures yield play contexts as well as *seeds, berries, cones, bark, flowers, sticks*, etc. for play and learning. A landscape of *dips and hillocks* frames the grounds, and a designed grass mowing regime of pathways, nests, running lanes and open spaces are fringed with opportunistic wildflowers.

The absence of any pre-decided or imposed end product or outcome is fundamental to the lack of competitive tension and the authenticity and power of self-discovery. Also fundamental is that adults resist a well intentioned desire to pre-empt or share knowledge, which can be powerfully discovered.

A productive overlap

So how far play (essentially an anarchic[4] activity) can be championed within an educational institution is a debate worth having, and it frames the reality of the compromise required in this kind of approach in a school setting. However, a productive co-existence or overlap between 'play' and 'education' existed and developed at Thornlie, and the work focused on what was achievable. For example, the perceived marathon task of tidying up was solved with a tidy up bell, and access to the new features was achieved by allowing mixed age play (children in Scottish schools are routinely age segregated often with a view to supervision or managing challenging behaviour).

Going against the traditional route of buying 'off the shelf' play equipment (which allows a client to 'offload' safety responsibilities), there was a strong commitment to the design of bespoke and non-standard features, offering greater opportunities for children to experience and manage risk and challenge. New government guidance on managing risk in play provision supported this approach, including a practical Risk/Benefit Assessment tool[5] that allows play providers (i.e. head teachers) to make judgements about acceptable and desirable levels of risk. This was further supported and communicated with parents via a simple play policy.

The role of adults

The training programme included a mix of presentations and discussions about non-prescriptive and self-directed play, the nature of loose materials and the role of adults in such a setting. A series of practical hands on sessions took place at play times, lunch breaks and class times with regular review informing how sessions were set up. Materials were set out in inviting ways,

'This place is like a building site... .' 231

FIGURE 24.3 Left: The role of the adult – observing and scaffolding and making hay bale constructions, right: Constructing with 'pennies', Thornlie Primary School, Scotland
Photo: Sue Gutteridge

and staff supported the children to sort them into large storage bays with a dynamic fleet of trolleys for loading and unloading. The support staff (non-teaching school staff who are with the children at play times) were encouraged to actively support play, rather than merely supervise, whilst at the same time not intervening, from a basis of awareness of what children could manage or resolve for themselves. Aspects of risk management, staff organisation and policy were also covered in sessions with the senior management team.

Keeping children at the centre of design and provision

Keeping children at the centre of your thinking when designing requires the observation of children playing – a delightful obsession. Where are the nooks and crannies that attract them? Why are they doggedly digging away at a 'child resistant' bit of hard landscape? What is it about a broken down garage that is so attractive? And what is it that pulls children to stay on beaches and woodlands for days at a stretch? This ongoing focus is a necessary part of supporting the use of loose material, and observation became one of the main activities of the adults, informing their understanding of possibilities, potential new resources and children's developing aspirations. For example, when straw bales were introduced, this presented the children with new challenges as they experienced their weight, texture and bulk, requiring them to think and plan ahead. So for the following session, trolleys and barrows were made available and the children quickly devised collaborative methods of moving and stacking the bales, building challengingly high towers, immersing themselves in the material and using it for the most energetic and thrilling play, and for rest and reflection. As ever the possibility of combining materials led to increased creativity and invention.

Consulting with users is an intrinsic part of the design process, resulting in children gaining insight to these processes. This has a different aim from that of designing a quality space and the generation of ideas in this way can create tension. At Thornlie the children were invited to comment on the design and responded enthusiastically. Part of the plan had been to repaint steps used as a stage for dancing to the children's favourite tracks, facilitated by the excellent janitor/DJ. We had chosen a subtle colour for the steps in keeping with the more naturalistic elements of the scheme, but the children had other ideas. Many colour combinations were suggested and eventually the children put this to the vote – the outcome: a rainbow! And should anyone care about the designer's sensitivities when it is obvious that the children's 'voice' and engagement in the decision was important? It is an interesting example and genuinely one with no 'right' answer.

Starting to work with loose materials

Unsurprisingly there were anxieties at the outset – thoughts of the entire school marauding around armed with sticks and stones, supervised only by two support staff, understandably gave rise to fears of anarchy and riots. In school playgrounds, support staff are in 'the front line' and can feel vulnerable and relatively powerless – even in more egalitarian schools. Sometimes this is due to a lack of definition of their role. Also the value of their skills in dynamic risk assessment, making a hundred decisions a minute about proportional interventions in children's play, can be relatively unrecognised and unsupported.

At Thornlie the play ethos is well articulated and support for the development of this 'playworker' role was tangible, along with the encouragement to support children to take proportionate risks and meet challenges. Teaching staff helped to introduce the materials, discussing ground rules and establishing a regime for sorting and storing materials at the end of the day. The training programme clarified the role of adults to best support free play, encouraging close observation, using post-its to capture and remember unexpected play moments or issues to address and planned sessions where these reflections were shared, feeding into practice.

As usual it was the actual 'getting on with it', with the right management support, which did the most to boost confidence and allay anxiety. Some schools embarking on this process can become overwhelmed with 'what ifs' and end up strangling the potential energy with complex overplanning. We have found this attitude can be common amongst teachers who do not have the experience of supervising free play as playground staff and who can be fearful of the implications of children having so much control. It can come as a surprise that by and large the activity is focused, purposeful and calmly self-managing.

> We believe playgrounds should be places of experiment and invention, creativity and construction, dreams and surprise … nothing less will do.[6]

This place is like a building site

'The Theory of Loose Parts,'[7] published in 1971, proposed that 'in any environment, both the degree of inventiveness and creativity, and the possibility of discovery, are directly proportional to the number and kind of variables in it'.

This in turn was built on observations about the quality and engagement of play happening on bomb sites after the blitz. And of course many parents are anxiously familiar with their children's fascination for the taboo attractions of building sites and their play possibilities. So when a parent at Thornlie commented that *'this place is like a building site…'*[8] (now also the title of a report and video of the project), we knew we were pushing the boundaries and achieving some of our goals and we expected that we would probably face some resistance or enquiry from staff, parents and local authority providers with a remit for maintenance or health and safety.

Just playing

In fact, the anticipated resistance did not materialise, perhaps because the energy of what was happening was so concrete. Children were experiencing the throb of their own power as they took charge of their play with every material on offer; they set conscious and unconscious objectives, delighted in experimentation, expressing their uniquely personal perspectives through what they did. The enthusiasm and energy quickly spread through the staff and families in the school community.

Although this buzz of activity is infectious there is also space for calm and reflective moments. We are reminded of the cyclical think-do, do-think creative and cognitive processes where ebb and flow of human consciousness is never linear, and motivations, experimentations and understanding constantly spark off each other. An authentic sense of empowerment being experienced by the children can be read in the purposefulness of activity, through children's focus, determination and body language. Moments of sheer surprise and delight, fundamental to human wellbeing, can be rare in schools. Perhaps this is because such experiences are rarely delivered through planned or pre-determined outcomes.

> The children needed mud and they just loved making it and playing with it, discovering how central mud is for building and binding things together, what its properties are and what happens when you add water.[9]

FIGURE 24.4 Tools, materials and skills for the job. Thornlie Primary School, Scotland
Photo: Sue Gutteridge

Of course children developed skills and understanding (all the usual justifications for play), but what educationalists are noting is the fundamental importance of hands on experiences as the building blocks in the lives of future engineers, architects, planners, physicists, environmentalists, chemists, etc. Although 'active learning' has held theoretical currency in the curriculum for over a decade, the self-directed use of loose materials is necessary for this activity to truly take off – all achieved with little adult intervention. Adult attitudes and actions are key to achieving this activity; what is realised is the value of naturally chosen activity (which is perfectly tailored to children's individual needs), driven by an innate desire for challenge and natural enquiry.

Building connection

The playground and play practice at Thornlie has been shaped by, and supports, a humanist approach, which emphasises relationships: empathy, compassion and the value and agency of the children. Features such as the sand area not only invite co-operation, but also allow isolated children to participate alongside other children and suggest a positive flow in and out of each other's play. Conflict (which inevitably arises) is seen as an opportunity for children to negotiate and suggest resolutions. And the development of positive relationships goes further. The possibilities for children to drive change and deliver change through their own hands strengthens the connections with each other as well as connections to place and community. The children now have a strong and intimate relationship with the soil beneath their fingernails, with their new native woodland and the ecosystems it supports. They have a relationship with the materials and tools they use and the cultural history of their community and the wider world.

> The children have really shown me. The children have shown me how to do it. The more they use the materials, the more they know how to use them.[10]

Many of the features of this project have informed practice in school grounds across Scotland. Rather than a formulaic approach to 'cultivating' replica projects, what seems to be important for the future is a wider appreciation of the kinds of places and materials, often unexpected and sometimes chaotic, that yield such possibilities for children and a very practical commitment to ensuring such resources remain replenished and valued.

> When as a head teacher, you catch the aroma of barbecued sausages cooking in your own playground, then you know you've made a difference.[11]

If Thornlie seems a very different sort of school ground, then working in Africa is another step again. However, in this environment, providing physical structures for play is more of a challenge than the mental hurdles involved in using loose materials.

25

THE STEPPING STONES TO MANY PLAYGROUNDS

Carla and Tom Gill

FOUNDING DIRECTORS OF EAST AFRICAN PLAYGROUNDS

>Bursting water pipes, that you were assured were not below that foundation hole. Transporting 10ft long playground parts on the back of a motorbike through a busy town centre. The lorry that we hired getting impounded after the driver trying to eat his fake driving licence in front of a police officer. These are just a few amazing situations we have found ourselves in through building playgrounds in Uganda, East Africa. Anyone who has worked in Uganda will reliably inform you that a dull day in Uganda does not exist.
>
> Carla Gill 2010

Uganda is a wonderfully playful society where singing, dancing, climbing trees and chasing tyres down the red dust paths are something you will see on a daily basis. 55.4% of the Ugandan population are under the age of 18,[1] so everywhere you look there are children. When the children are not busy working in their families' gardens, collecting water or crammed into classrooms learning by rote, they are out exploring their surroundings, returning home at sundown covered in mud after having had a wonderful time.

So if children's play is so rich in natural and explorative play in Uganda why build playgrounds at all?

- A playground symbolises the importance of childhood, providing a platform to discuss the importance of break time at school and interactive lessons.
- A playground brings communities together, especially in a refugee settlement where you have eight-plus nationalities living together, some of whom have been at war with one another.
- Although in the rural areas there can be endless space to play, in the city there is very limited and minimal safe space to play.
- Play is how children learn and therefore it should be recognised and valued; by building a playground, this value is shown as a fixed asset.

Every child has the right to play, as it is just as important as other human rights issues, as stated in Article 31 of the UN Convention on the Rights of the Child.[2] This chapter will give you an insight into play in Uganda through the journey of our charity, East African Playgrounds (EAP).

Step one – understand your surroundings

Our playground-building journey began at Walakuba West Primary School, Jinja, Uganda. Having both travelled and volunteered, building a school and a small playground, in East Africa, we knew the basics of the culture and a little of what we were letting ourselves in for. What we hadn't counted on were the complex logistics of managing a group of volunteers, a community team that wanted everything and welders with a lot to learn.

On arrival, we were greeted with huge smiles, big hugs and long handshakes; the schools put on a wonderful welcome assembly, where introductions were made. The children all repeated our names, struggling when it came to Phil (due to his thick accent). The school, complete with special needs unit, was used to visitors, via its partnership with a local charity, Soft Power Education. We were instantly made to feel at home.

To help fund and build the playground we brought eight volunteers from our University with us. They were very patient and supportive, particularly when we were asked to build a huge fence around the school, as well as mark out a football pitch and concrete a netball pitch alongside the already growing playground!

From the beginning, we knew if we were going to be successful we needed to involve the community in the design and playground build, so they would take ownership, look after it after we had gone and take pride in what they had created. A wonderful idea, but in practice trying to get a group of eight Ugandans to meet together on time was our first challenge, not to mention keeping their ideas realistic. Our first experience of managing a community

FIGURE 25.1 Animals in playground, Nakivale Refugee Settlement, Uganda 2015

group was a steep learning curve. We really wanted to take on their ideas, but couldn't work out how to say no when the brief expanded to include the fence, football/rugby pitch and netball pitch alongside the playground which also had a specific accessible area as well. We did manage to draw the line at the swimming pool through!

Over the years experience has taught us that before starting any community-based project, an understanding and appreciation of the local culture, history, traditions and aspirations is key. We had to quickly learn to manage not only the physical build and material durability, but also work ethics, skills of others, as well as community expectations.

Step two – learning to say no!

We explored and researched many other charities and in turn they inspired us to stay focused on what we were good at, building playgrounds, rather than making water wells or trying to start a school, as so many charities did.

Focusing on one country (we discovered in hindsight) was a good idea too, but the offer came to work on another project in Kenya so off we went. Packing our welding generator (which caused a few border issues on the way back), our playground designs and build team of three Ugandans who had never left the country, we set off east, to Kenya.

Despite Kenya and Uganda bordering one another, there are vast differences in culture and history between the two countries. Kenya is a much more developed and busy country with much more infrastructure. At times you felt like you were in London. Kenyans also tend to be more straight to the point and keen to get the right deal, whereas Ugandans are much more relaxed.

We arrived in Thika at a tiny slum situated next to large, high-rise, modern gated apartment blocks. Feeling like the Pied Piper,[3] we excitedly took a walk around the area set aside for the playground followed by the local children. We knew this was going to be a fantastic spot for these children to access, but the stumbling block was that the NGO that we had partnered with were unable to purchase the land. The agreement to buy the land had been approved for some time, until the owner heard that we were coming to build a playground for the children in the slum. Being situated close to a wealthy area the owner did not want the children of the slum to have something that the more wealthy children did not. With no other option we had to leave that location and build elsewhere.

Building a playground in the slum could have had a significant social impact upon the area and we learnt that though these stumbling blocks cannot always be avoided (especially in a country where rules are often flexible), taking time for further research could have avoided disappointment. Learning to say yes to the right things would have allowed us to spend more time researching a suitable location to be transformed into a playspace for all to enjoy.

Step three – building the team

One of the most challenging parts of growing EAP was developing our building team in Uganda. There are organisations around the world that import and install playgrounds in developing countries from the US, with no follow-up. They are often expensive to purchase and impossible to maintain (as they are not made out of local materials), and do not involve local communities or children at any stage. To a degree, it is a much more straightforward process than training your own local team of playground builders, but we have found the long-term rewards for everyone concerned is far greater.

Our team development started in 2010, when we were asked to build a playground at the Good Sheppard's Fold Centre. They had the money, the location and a specific timeframe to build it. It was a time when finances and study kept us back in the UK, so instead of turning down the opportunity, we asked the three guys we had been working with if they felt they were up for the challenge. A swing, a slide, a seesaw, endless international correspondence later and Good Sheppard's Fold playground was built. It was an important milestone for East African Playgrounds.

We haven't spoken much as yet about community design, consultation or accessibility. This is because we needed to start with the basics first. In Uganda there is a very *laissez faire*[4] attitude to work, poor problem solving skills (due to limited teaching methods) and a lack of highly skilled labour. The end product of the Good Sheppard's Fold playground may not have been an accessible, community designed playground (although they did choose the paint colours); however, it was a safe, strong and fun space for the children to play. A couple of years later Good Sheppard's Fold also received a 'playground extension' for their growing school!

So that was our beginning and all of it took time and patience. Today we have an amazing team of over 30 here in Uganda. They include welders, builders, cooks, play workers and administrators. These local people now drive EAP forward, giving EAP a reputation for building the best quality playgrounds in Africa.

Step four – building robust playgrounds

Having learnt to focus on play, and narrowed our focus to Uganda, we now started to worry about our long-term impact. What if our playgrounds broke on the opening day? What if a child fell off the playground and injured themselves, or worse cannot afford hospital treatment? What if the communities look grateful for the playground at the opening day but then cut the playground down and sell if for scrap when we are gone? These were the questions we asked ourselves constantly before, during and after every playground build.

Every opening day became a mix of emotions; behind the smiles, we didn't feel pride, elation, or excitement – there was worry and anxiety. When the teachers shouted '3, 2, 1, Go PLAY!' and the children stampeded to the playground, covering every inch of it for the first time, our staff and volunteers would all congratulate each other, take endless photos, go play themselves and generally have a wonderful time, as we also did. But at that time the opening day was the worst day. Of course eventually to our delight these things did not happen, but the fear was always there.

We have always been big advocates for challenge-based play with a good dose of risk. Your attitude does, however, change slightly when you are in a country where people cannot afford health care nor have grown up playing on equipment like this. Yes, we know Ugandan children climb more trees than the average child in the UK, not to mention have learnt to use a machete to cut the grass since they were old enough to walk, so they have a level of judgement around risk. To this day this is something that fascinates us, as there is a huge amount of research into children's ability to manage risk in cultures such as the UK,

FIGURE 25.2 Experimenting with play equipment makes us nervous! Kitengesa Primary School, Masaka, Uganda 2011

but what about places like Uganda where their upbringing is so different? Did Ugandan children actually need the same type of challenging play to those in the UK, given their daily challenges are slightly different?

We decided to do a lot of research, studying the *British Playground Safety Standards BS EN 1176* (2008) from front to back many times over and ensuring every piece of playground equipment we built met these standards. Determined to use local materials we hunted out the most robust metal and how to paint it to provide the best protection. Timber is completely out of the question (even though we get endless requests to build out of it) because the termites would eat the whole playground in a week, and the timber is not a fan of the wet and dry seasons. Another stumbling block was undersurfacing. Fancy rubber matting was expensive, chippings encourage snakes and sand turns solid in no time. So we decided that instead of placing flooring down we would consider what we built. We made sand pits at the bottom of the higher equipment and then no surfacing below the lower equipment.

We also looked at our designs. At the time every playground had a brand new element in it. Our favourite was a flying fox. We had attempted roundabouts so many times and simply could not get them to last, due to the intense use the playgrounds got and dust getting into the bearings. As lovely as it would be to have so many different designs for a playground, at this time we decided to limit it to a select few to ensure the longevity of the playgrounds and safety of the children. We removed any moving parts of the playground (apart from the swing bracket, as we imported them in from the US), as we could not guarantee the maintenance and longevity of these elements. We were then left with an adventure complex (including slide, climbing wall, fireman's pole and tyre bridge), swing sets and seesaws.

FIGURE 25.3 Left: Consultations with children about their playground designs, Uganda 2015, right: Building at Bwenda Primary, Jinja, Uganda 2014
Photos: Emily Ward

Step five – developing our consultation process

We began our consultation process in the right direction, involving the community within the design process at Walakuba West Primary School and other future projects. The need to sieve through the community requests, work with the capabilities of our building team and the constraints of safety and long-term enjoyment, meant our community consultation meetings were becoming less active and more of a process.

Aware that the most important (yet difficult) part of the playground build is community involvement, we knew we needed the right process in place. We met Elizabeth Moreno in Gulu, North Uganda, where she had just helped her centre build a creative playground. She came on board to help us develop our community consultation and developed a way of engaging with the community to provide us with the information we needed for our projects, without being bombarded with outlandish requests.

Over time the consultation process has developed and now includes many steps; whole community assemblies/meetings, discussions of play, maintenance visits, community involvement requirements (collecting tyres to use in the playgrounds) and site visits. The steps focusing on the playground designs comprise two vital sessions:

Consultation with children – Playground Reporter

To avoid the 'we want this' scenario Elizabeth designed the 'Playground Reporter' programme. The two oldest classes in the school (P6 and P7) are set an assignment to be Playground Reporters. The groups of reporters are divided up into the number of classes within the school and asked to observe the children from this class at break time. Armed with a pencil and a Playground Reporter sheet, the children observe and fill in the questions. The following day the class share with us what they have found. These sessions are always full of shy smiles to start with, but interesting discussions as well as great games that include everyone in the room are taking place by the end.

Consultation with parents/teachers

These meetings often commence with uninterested adults. 'The playground is for the children, why are we involved?' By the end the adults are usually stretching their hands high in the sky, like their students, waiting for their turn to show off the games they used to play as a child. The room is always full of laughter and rumination, everyone with a playful mind.

We ask the adults to draw a map of where they grew up and draw what they used to play in which location on the map. We ask them to explain what might have changed from when they played as a child to how children play now. Many of you may be surprised to hear the same old 'it was better back in my day' is also heard in Uganda. We ask them what their aspirations for their children are. And finally to show us the games they loved to play as well as the games the children play here.

Adding Fasial Kapeli into the mix was the final piece of the puzzle. A newly qualified teacher at Imam Hassan Primary School, where we were working, he was fascinated by the process. Elizabeth took him on as her assistant and now he runs all of our consultations and is a wonderful play advocate.

The Ugandans run all of our consultations now, and this avoids us coming to the table as outsiders with preconceived ideas. In Uganda many people are used to receiving aid support, not taking ownership of projects and therefore not bothering to maintain them. We work in a way that discusses the playground as the community's own from the start, getting them involved in the build and providing some of the materials, which all helps. Community ownership is so critical to any project, and we have found by starting our working relationship off with an engaging, fun consultation, allowing the children and adults to see their designs come to life, really cements that ownership and supports the projects into the future.

Step six – diversifying our designs

Our consultation only works when we have flexibility in our design process. Having laid down good foundations, it was now much easier for us to be flexible. We knew which materials worked and met local requirements (link chain, metal and plenty of tyres). We knew the safety precautions to assess within every new design. We had also developed six elements of play to include in all of our playgrounds (rest, imaginative, creative, active, obstacle and free).

This is when it became fun!

Working within this basic framework we were confident our designs would be able to meet the needs of these wonderful communities. Our staff also became involved in altering our designs to make them more fun and we began to play around more and more with the layout of the playground. So it wasn't just putting things where they fitted.

A fantastic example of creative implementation was in Gulu, where the elders of the community explained their fantastic history of storytelling to the children. Apparently after the war[5] the community was so dispersed that this tradition had disappeared. In answer to this, together we built a fantastic storytelling area and encouraged them to paint their stories on the walls around. This reignited an old tradition that the children and elders enjoyed together.

At Valley View Primary School, a school on a main road, the children talked a huge amount about being boda (motorbike) drivers and matatu (bus) drivers as this was the career of many of their fathers. So adjacent to the main road (visible from the playground) we built matatus and bodas. On the opening day the children role-played for more than 20 minutes by getting on the matatu and going to the capital city, playing bus driver, passengers and conductors. This type of play is ever present whenever we drive past, reinforcing to us the importance of apparatus to inspire imaginative role-play within a playground.

Recently a child drew a fantastic aeroplane and along with the excitement of the other children we went about making this into an element within their playground. None of the children had ever seen an aeroplane up close, but the school was on the flight path from the nearest airport and so they often saw them fly over. The joy of finally playing in that aeroplane that they designed was simply incredible.

With the help of New Zealand playground designer Amy Church, and Playground Ideas, a playground design not for profit organisation, our repertoire of playground elements grew from about 15 pieces to over 150, and we are still designing more. Using computer design we are able to show the communities their playgrounds before the build starts. The benefits of building in this way are that everyone feels like their ideas have been listened to when they

FIGURE 25.4 Bwenda Primary School, Jinja, Uganda
Photo: Emily Ward 2014

see the designs. We can now also build playgrounds that cater for specific needs, an example being a playground we built at a Centre for the Blind that enabled us to utilise our creative skills and introduce fantastic sensory items that have now made their way into most of our playgrounds, and are very popular.

Step seven – playgrounds and the wider community

Improvements can always be made, and every year we build upon another part of EAP. The current development focus is to integrate our playgrounds more into the educational environment. We have been showing school teachers that learning does not just happen in a classroom by children repeating what the teacher says, but can happen through exploring and experiencing the world outside.

We are currently developing training sessions for teachers to show them how to include a more play-based teaching style in the playground. By encouraging teachers to use their playground to teach science concepts such as gravity and friction (which goes down a slide faster, a stone or a leaf, and why?), storytelling, counting and letter finding, the opportunities are endless.

Exploring the ways in which our playgrounds are painted has opened up further possibilities for creativity and learning. By simply painting numbers on the steps, the children are able to explore in their own time the concept of individual numbers.

Another move forward for EAP is building playgrounds in refugee settlements. The consultation and design process here is even broader, with children coming from quite diverse backgrounds. We have built playgrounds in the pre-schools in Nakivale Refugee Settlement, the eighth largest in the world. Working alongside a very diverse cultural group means there is not one identity that defines them; it is a combination of many. Making the playground more visually appealing has encouraged the children to engage together in conversation around the playground elements. For example, sitting on the tyre cow, they can make the noise of the cow and talk about what they call a cow in their own native language. This is a programme where we wish to extend and develop our designs into the future to bring displaced communities together through play.

Conclusion

Growing a playground is about the whole process, not just sitting on the swing at the end of the build watching others play. We aim to achieve the highest possible impact for everyone involved in the process, from our fantastic team, to the materials we use, to the energy put into the consultation and design and the long-term maintenance of the playgrounds. This is what has made our playground projects successful.

Play to us is more than an incidental activity to fill in time; it is an extension of what it is to be human, part of everyone's identity. When we start to play during our consultation sessions the room comes alight and the conversations had through play are far more than the words you could ever speak. Sharing play with everyone around you is really vital, not a secondary need after shelter and water.

Play stands alongside all of our basic human rights.

Notes

Chapter 17

1 Boyd, Denise G. and Bee, Helen L. *The Developing Child*. 13th Ed. 2014, Pearson Education Limited, UK.
2 Ibid.
3 Ibid.

Chapter 18

1 Roberson, D, Davidoff, J, Davies, IRL and Shapiro, LR. *Colour Categories and Category Acquisition in Himba and English*. University of Essex, Goldsmiths College, University of Surrey and University of Warwick, 2005.
2 Charlesworth, R. *Understanding Child Development*, 7th Ed. Thompson Delmar Learning, USA, 2008.
3 Zentner, M. Preferences for Colour and Colour-Emotion combinations in Early Childhood. *Developmental Science* 4(4), 2001: 389–398.
4 Feisner, EA. *Colour*, 2nd Ed. Laurence King Publishing, London, 2006.
5 Boyatzis, CJ and Varghese, R. Children's Emotional Associations with Colors. *The Journal of Genetic Psychology: Research and Theory on Human Development* 155(1), 1994: 77–85.
6 Children's playground in Cotswolds fenced off for being 'too colourful', *The Telegraph*, 8th February, 2013. Sourced 21/02/15: http://www.telegraph.co.uk/news/newstopics/howaboutthat/9857513/Childrens-playground-in-Cotswolds-fenced-off-for-being-too-colourful.html.
7 Feisner, EA. *Colour*, 2nd Ed. Laurence King Publishing, London, 2006.
8 Pilaroscia, J. from website 'The Architect's Take' sourced 04/01/2015: http://thearchitectstake.com/interviews/jill-pilaroscia-give-color-chance/.
9 Interview with Terry Friedman. *Hand to Earth: Andy Goldsworthy*. Thames and Hudson, London, 2004.
10 Charlesworth, R. *Understanding Child Development*, 7th Ed. Thompson Delmar Learning, USA, 2008.
11 Gabbard, C and Rodrigues, L. Optimizing Early Brain and Motor Development Through Movement. *Early Childhood News*, 2008. Sourced 13/4/2015: http://www.earlychildhoodnews.com/earlychildhood/article_view.aspx?ArticleID=360.
12 de Botton, A. *The Architecture of Happiness*. Penguin Books, Australia, 2006.
13 Shams, L and Seitz, AR. Benefits of Multisensory Learning, *Trends in Cognitive Science* 3(1), 2008.
14 Woo, C and Leon, M. Environmental Enrichment as an Effective Treatment for Autism: A Randomized Controlled Trial, *Behavioral Neuroscience* 127(4), 2013: 487–497.

Chapter 19

1 Gabriela Burkhalter, 'When play got serious', Tate Etc essay, Issue 31, Summer 2014. Available from: http://www.tate.org.uk/context-comment/articles/when-play-got-serious
2 Fiona Robbe, 'The Knitting Tree – Community Art in the Playground', Playground News, Kidsafe News, November 2011. Accessed from: http://www.kidsafensw.org/imagesdb/wysiwyg/playgroundnewsissue382011final.pdf
3 Hussein, H. Using the sensory garden as a tool to enhance the educational development and social interaction of children with special needs, *Support for Learning* 25(1), 2010: 25–31.

Chapter 22

1 Alexander, C., Ishikawa S. and Silverstein, M. et al. 1977, *A Pattern Language – Towns, Buildings, Construction*. New York, Oxford University Press.

Chapter 23

1. Coppens NM, Gentry LK. Video analysis of playground injury-risk situations. *Research in Nursing & Health* 14, 1991: 129–136, cited in Ball, DJ. *Playgrounds: risks, benefits and choices,* Health and Safety Executive Report Number 426/2002.
2. Please refer to Chapter 4 of this publication for further discussion.
3. These ideas are drawn from the work of philosopher and theoretical physicist Karen Barad, mainly from Barad K. *Meeting the universe halfway: quantum physics and the entanglement of matter and meaning.* London, Duke University Press; 2007.
4. Deleuze G, Guattari F. *A thousand plateaus: capitalism and schizophrenia.* Translated by Massumi B. London, Continuum; 2004.
5. Thanks to Rachel Murray for this story.
6. Lester S, Russell W. *Children's right to play: an examination of the importance of play in the lives of children worldwide.* The Hague, Netherlands, Bernard Van Leer Foundation; 2010.
7. Shier H. IPA Global consultations on children's right to play summary report. *IPA*; 2010.
8. Gutman M. The Physical Spaces of Childhood. In Paula S Fass (ed.) *The Routledge history of childhood in the western world.* Abingdon, Routledge; 2013, pp. 249–266.
9. See Carla Pascoe's chapter for more details on the history of play and playspaces.
10. Woolley H. Watch this space! Designing for children's play in public open spaces. *Geography Compass* 2(2), 2008: 495–512.
11. Cranwell K. Towards playwork: an historical introduction to children's out-of-school play organisations in London (1860–1940). In Fraser Brown (ed.) *Playwork theory and practice.* Buckingham, Open University Press; 2003, pp. 32–47.
12. Gutman M, de Conick-Smith N. Introduction: good to think with – history, space and modern childhood. In Marta Gutman and Ning de Conick-Smith (eds.) *Designing modern childhoods: history, space, and the material culture of children.* New Brunswick, Rutgers University Press; 2008, pp. 1–19.
13. Anderson LM. 'The playground of today is the republic of tomorrow': Social reform and organized recreation in the USA, 1890–1930. *The encyclopaedia of informal education*; 2006. http://infed.org/mobi/social-reform-and-organized-recreation-in-the-usa (accessed 11 April 2015).
14. Pellegrini AD, Bohn CM. The role of recess in children's cognitive performance and school adjustment. *Educational Researcher* 34(1) January/February, 2005: 13–19.
15. Brehony K. A 'socially civilizing influence'? Play and the urban 'degenerate.' *Paedagogica Historia* 39(1), 2003: 87–106.
16. Stallibrass A. *The self-respecting child: a study of children's play and development.* Harmondsworth, Penguin; 1974.
17. Dotterweich AR, Greene A, Blosser D. Using innovative playgrounds and cross-curricular design to increase physical activity. *Journal of Physical Education, Recreation & Dance* 83(5), 2012: 47–55.
18. Louv R. *Last child in the woods: saving our children from nature deficit disorder.* Chapel Hill, Algonquin; 2005.
19. Edwards R, Gillies V, Horsley N. Early intervention and evidence-based policy and practice: framing and taming. *Social Policy and Society* 15, 2015.
20. Lester S. Playing in a Deleuzian playground. In E. Ryall, W. Russell and M. MacLean (eds.) *The philosophy of play.* London, Routledge; 2013.
21. Sutton-Smith B. *The ambiguity of play.* Cambridge, Ma., Harvard University Press; 1997.
22. Spinka M, Newberry R, Bekoff M. Mammalian play: training for the unexpected. *The Quarterly Review of Biology* 76(2), 2001: 141–168.
23. Pascoe C. *Spaces imagined, places remembered: childhood in 1950s Australia.* Newcastle-upon-Tyne, Cambridge Scholars; 2011.
24. Factor J. Tree stumps, manhole covers and rubbish tins: the invisible play-lines of a primary school playground. *Childhood* 11(2), 2004: 142–154.
25. Armitage M. The ins and outs of school playground play: children's use of 'play places'. In J.C. Bishop and M. Curtis (eds.) *Play today in the primary school playground: life, learning and creativity.* Buckingham, Open University; 2001, pp. 35–37.
26. Armitage M. The influence of school architecture and design on the outdoor play experience within the primary school. *Paedagogica Historica* 41(4/5), 2005: 535–553.
27. Playworker John Hale, Somerstown Adventure Playground, Portsmouth, UK.

Chapter 24

1. David Hughes, Head Teacher, Thornlie Primary School.
2. David Hughes, Head Teacher, Thornlie Primary School.
3. Andrea Sella, Senior Media Fellow, Engineering and Physical Sciences Research Council and Professor of Materials and Inorganic Chemistry, University College London.
4. The term 'anarchic' in this context refers to a situation with no controlling rules or principles to give order. In terms of 'free play' this becomes a liberating factor where anything could happen.
5. This tool was introduced by PLAYLINK and Grounds For Learning in the form of an assessment form for schools to use to support their programme.
6. Wildside Scotland Mission Statement.
7. Simon Nicholson, 'How Not To Cheat Children: The Theory of Loose Parts', *Landscape Architect Journal* 62, October 1971: 30–34.
8. *This Place is Like a Building Site! A Report on the Introduction of Loose Materials to Three Primary Schools in North Lanarkshire* by Sue Gutteridge and Judi Legg, Wildside Scotland. Published by North Lanarkshire Council, 2012.
9. Teacher, Thornlie Primary School.
10. Primary 1 Teacher, Thornlie Primary School.
11. David Hughes, Head Teacher, Thornlie Primary School.

Chapter 25

1. Uganda Annual Report 2014. UNICEF Published June 2015. Total population in 2015 was 363,459,000 and those under 18 years was 201,593,000.
2. UN Convention on the Rights of the Child (CRC). Adopted and opened for signature, ratification and accession by the UN General Assembly. Resolution 44/25 on 20th November 1989. Entry into force 2nd September 1990 in accordance with Article 49.
3. Definition: A charismatic person who attracts followers.
4. Definition: The *laissez-faire* leadership style is where all the rights and power to make decisions is fully given to the worker. This was first described by Lewin, Lippitt, and White in 1938, along with the autocratic leadership and the democratic leadership styles. https://en.wikipedia.org/wiki/Leadership_style
5. Recent war/civil conflict in Uganda from 1996 onwards initiated by the Joseph Kony led Lord's Resistance Army (LRA) rebels in Northern Uganda.

Part V
SAPLINGS

Introduction

In the final developmental section, we look at children and young people aged between 9 and 14, and the particular challenges and opportunities which exist for this age group. Often, these children fall between the cracks in playspace provision, because the definition of a playspace can be so narrow in the mind of those who commission these spaces. Understanding the social and physical needs of this group is paramount to providing useful spaces for their continued development. One fundamental need at this time is the search for identity, and part of this is taking risks. This is discussed in more detail, as are more unusual ways to provide play opportunities.

In this section you will find:

26. **Child development – page 251**
    A discussion of the physical, emotional and social development of children between the ages of 9 and 14 years old, including relevant ergonomic information.
27. **Beyond 14+ years – page 257**
    Discussing the attitudes and needs of young adults, and the provision of appropriate spaces for this age group.
28. **Technology in playspaces: A snapshot – page 265**
    Thinking about the future interface between technology and playspaces.
29. **Lima and the ever-postponed electric train – page 267**
    Case study of a community movement to reclaim unused public space for play and recreation in Peru.
30. **Be not afeared: Embracing the need for risk in play – page 275**
    Looking at beneficial risk taking, and its importance for children's positive development. Includes discussion of Standards, and the ambivalent role they play in managing risk.
31. **Not in my front garden! Play Streets: A doorstep controversy – page 287**
    Closing streets in London for children to play is not a new idea, but one which is still challenging for many.
32. **We are such stuff as dreams are made on: Paraphrased conversation with Mark Halden, Senior Playworker, Glamis Adventure Playground – page 297**
    Discusses the importance of spaces for free play in disadvantaged communities.

26

CHILD DEVELOPMENT

Elizabeth Cummins & Katherine Masiulanis

Physical development

Although most physical skills, both gross and fine motor, are well established, a continued process of honing occurs. Fine motor skills improve noticeably over this time, particularly in girls. Which skills are the most refined will depend on the interests of the child.

By age 10, children can usually throw a ball with accuracy. Between the ages of 9 and 12, children learn the ability not only to intercept an object on the move, but to hit, catch or kick on the run. They will run, skip, swim, bike and skate with confidence. Team sports become important for those interested, especially if those activities form part of their identity.

From a neurological perspective, there is typically a growth spurt in the frontal lobes between the ages of 10 and 12 years, resulting in the development of clearer logic, better planning abilities and better memory function.[1] Children are able to plan and organise themselves without the need for adult intervention. A second growth spurt at 13–15 results in improved spatial perception, as well as sensory, language and motor skills development.

During this period, sudden growth spurts re-emerge as adolescence kicks in, leading to huge variations in physical growth. Muscle mass and strength increase, although rapid changes in physical size can lead to temporary clumsiness. Girls usually experience a growth spurt earlier than boys. Girls often reach their maximum strength and muscle-weight ratio at about 12, while by 17, boys typically have considerably higher physical strength than girls.

Observable patterns and interests

Often referred to as the 'tweens', between childhood and adolescence, this is an age group that as its name suggests isn't quite one or the other. The following section examines patterns in skills and knowledge, and interests in an age group marked by increasing independence, peer identification and growing self-identity.

Behaviour patterns

This is the final stage of childhood as it merges into adolescence. Children of this age group are highly coordinated physically, able to throw and catch a ball with one hand, skip with alternating feet and attempt complex fine motor skills such as tying shoelaces. Demonstrating competence at this age is very important as a distinct shift of focus away from parents and towards peer group occurs.

Engagement with popular culture grows, in particular sports and celebrities, as children begin to experiment with their own identities. This age group often develops personal or fashionable social speech patterns that continue into adolescence. This coincides with the beginning of puberty and a new found interest in romantic relationships.

Conceptually, children of this age group are high-functioning, abstract thinkers, understanding both hypothetical scenarios and having the capacity to systematically problem solve. They show a high level of aesthetic appreciation in artwork and other cultural fields. They understand complex maths problems and abstract science concepts. With a vocabulary of around 50,000 words, they can now express past, present and future events competently.

Emotionally they continue to push boundaries, challenging authority and social norms, but also begin to demonstrate the confidence to take on leadership roles.

Interests

Technology becomes an important tool, not just with friends, but also with the world, as social media allows for a 24/7 connection, whilst video gaming enables an escape into a fantasy world. Curiosity around adult subjects such as sex can also be found here.

Despite concerns over the passive nature of technology and how it affects children's lives, children are active at this age often using technology to support their activity. This age becomes a turning point for organised sport as children tend to decide to either pursue activities more seriously or give them up altogether. This age is marked by a need for more challenging physical activity such as skating, rock climbing or Parkour.

A burgeoning interest in popular culture leads to growing interests in fashion, movies and music. This is the era of 'hero worship' and imitation as children begin to test self-identity. This can often be played out by creative expression in how children dress, make or listen to music and creative projects.

Growing independence sees an interest in demonstrating competence in adult skills. Looking after pets can be highly therapeutic for many children, as can other more domestic tasks such as cooking and gardening.

Social ergonomics

Generally, the start of this period is a socially stable one for children. Family, friends and siblings form a stable base from which they can explore the world. They are less likely to use physical aggression than previously, and think they are invincible.[2]

At 10 or 11, they can organise group games, but may change the rules during play.

By about 13, self-esteem and self-identity can be shaken, and exploration can become more internalised. The judgement of self-competence gets less positive as children get older. A skill must be valued by the individual to contribute to self-esteem.

Physically, the onset of menstruation in girls typically occurs between 12.5 and 13.5 years, and this can mark a big change in their social dynamics. 95% of girls will experience this change between 11 and 15. Sexuality begins to become part of identity leading to additional confusion. For both genders, trying out different ways of doing things, different looks and groups of friends are important during this period. This continued development of a self-identity will take them into adulthood. Risk taking can be an essential part of this development. Generally, by 14, self-esteem is starting to be revived.

Many of these self-concepts are defined by peers – either by talking with a close group of friends, or by close comparison. Teenagers often have more friends than ever before, but these will not necessarily be close. While these peer relationships might be hierarchical, they still provide a stable base from which adolescents can explore their self-identity, replacing the base parents provided when they were infants. Sometimes peer pressure is positive, and peers become confidants, rather than parents or other family members.

There is generally little tolerance for crossing of perceived gender lines during this period,[3] although this may be changing as societal attitudes change. There are gender differences in the way that friendship groups are formed. Boys often have an extensive group of friends, which is inclusive, and often play outdoors in a wide ranging manner. Girls tend to congregate in smaller groups or pairs, and play closer to home,[4] with these relationships being more intense.

Interestingly, self-concept can become self-perpetuating, so that a child who identifies as sporty, for example, will concentrate more on training. One considered clever or 'nerdy' may take more difficult electives at school. Whatever the internal dialogue going on, older children in this age group require spaces where they feel comfortable to gather with their peers, not necessarily in a 'playground', and not under close adult supervision. Spaces for lone reflection and retreat are also important, as is the world of social media.

Often, adolescents show 'naive ideation': that is, by comparing the real world to a conception of what it might be, they are inspired to make changes. Unfortunately, adults rarely permit them the opportunity to do so, as reflected in a number of sections of this book. They resent being treated as children. However, this greater social consciousness is reflected in a sense of civic responsibility and an eagerness to contribute to the community.

Suggested affordances for play

Between childhood and adolescence, this age group look for opportunity in their environment to 'launch themselves' and if necessary 'retreat', testing the waters in their own way. Spaces and places for play and recreation can be difficult to nail, so keep in mind the following affordances.

Independent neighbourhood mobility

Children's own sense of freedom and competency is intrinsically linked with their ability to explore broader environments on their own or with peers, free of adult supervision. It is important to note that spaces and connections in our cities, towns and suburbs (particularly our local streets) that predominantly support children to cycle or walk around – whether it be to and from school or during leisure time – are highly valuable and should always be part of any planning conversation.

Physically challenging/risky environments

With growing independence comes opportunity to test and push boundaries. Confidence and peer dependence in children of this age begins to challenge the norm of what is deemed acceptable or safe by the adults around them. Danger and the unknown become exciting and engaging, with children seeking out environments more remote, secluded, high-up, fast-moving or difficult to physically access, searching for something with 'edge'. Roofs, creeks and rivers, skatebowls, high posts and beams, climbing walls or rock escarpments, high earth mounds, giant slides and swings are some of the many afforded opportunities for more challenging play. It is important to note that where environments don't legitimately prove challenging enough for this age group, challenge is invariably sought in other non-intended ways.

Environments for creativity

Self-expression during this age becomes central to the development of identity. Influenced by peers, children begin to differentiate themselves from their parents and adult figures of authority. The opportunities for public/outdoor spaces to afford dance, performance, art and theatre bring children in touch with the world and their place in it. This can be tackled through fixed physical structures in the form of a stage, event and temporary exhibition spaces. Flexible environments that can be shaped by children also create diverse opportunities for self and collective expression.

Hang-out spaces

Social connection and gathering is important to this age group and therefore should always be front and centre with any planning and design of public/outdoor spaces. It is important to remember that this is an age group usually without income and as such places that are free of charge and adult intervention are highly prized. Increasing children's physical activity levels, encouraging more face to face social interaction and less screen time need to be considered. Elevated or stepped mounds and slopes allow for viewing the surrounding activity. Clusters or pods of seating where children can sit side-by-side or face each other, and sheltered, tucked away spaces are important. It is often a common misconception that children are less interested in 'playing' in a traditional sense and more interested in physical recreation.

Children still enjoy 'playing' but in a more social sense. This can be supported in a play environment, for example by including multiple activities side by side (such as swings or slides) or activities that children can do together (such as a basket swing).

Sports facilities

The design of sport environments is not the purpose of this book, but these environments should be mentioned, as children of this age group move from unstructured games and activities to more formalised games with rules. Many children derive huge physical and social value from organised sports and the surfaces, spaces and environments they require are usually guided by the particular codes associated with them.

Digital space and interconnection

Whilst not a physical space, technology and its power to connect are part of the world of contemporary children. We often address this as something opposed to physical activity, but there are ever increasing opportunities for it to become a mobile catalyst to play and recreation in open space. Providing structured information and instruction, as well as locations for gathering, an activity such as 'geo-caching' is an example of children tapping into a digitally supported orienteering course in their local neighbourhood. This not only encourages physical movement from site to site, but connection to their local neighbourhood.

Ergonomics

Please find below diagrams to assist with the design of appropriately sized structures and spaces for children between the ages 9 and 14. Refer to Seedlings for more information on how to use these dimensions.

256 Elizabeth Cummins & Katherine Masiulanis

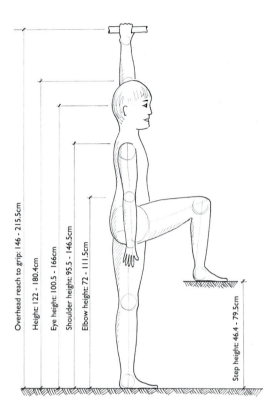

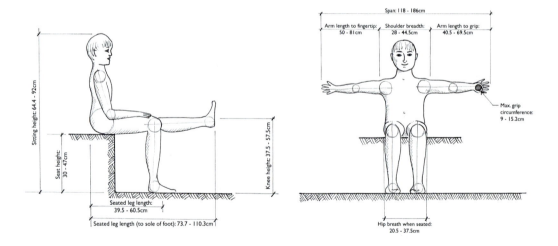

FIGURE 26.1 Ergonomic data of 5th percentile 9 year olds to 95th percentile 14 year olds
Data from: Beverly Norris & John R. Wilson, Consumer Safety Unit, Childata, The Handbook of Child Measurements and Capabilities: Data for Design Safety, Institute for Occupational Ergonomics, Department of Manufacturing Engineering and Operations Management, University of Nottingham

27

BEYOND 14+ YEARS

Gabrielle McKinnon and Alasdair Roy[1]

The concepts of 'play' and adolescence are not often linked, and little attention is given to the needs of young people for public spaces that are welcoming and allow them to grow and develop through recreation and social activity. While adolescents do not play in the same way or for the same developmental reasons as younger children, their unstructured leisure activities serve an equally important role, often focusing on exploring and constructing their identities through social relationships, and testing their own abilities and limits with peers.

Although playspaces for younger children seem to be becoming increasingly homogenised and risk averse, their play and recreation activities are still acknowledged as socially valid, and thought and attention is given to meeting their needs. By contrast, adolescents occupy a more tenuous position, frequently regarded as interlopers both in spaces designed for younger children, and in spaces designed for adults.

The social construction and fear of adolescents presents a challenge to the creation of inclusive public spaces for recreation. To better meet the needs of young people, it is important to understand their perspectives, and to engage them in planning and design processes. In this section we consider some of the insights from the literature, and what young people have told us about how they 'play', and how to develop public spaces that meet their needs.

Listening to young people

Talking with children and young people about issues that affect them is an important (and enjoyable) function of the ACT Children and Young People Commissioner. From our consultations it is clear that young people have views that they would like to express on issues that affect them, and that they are aware of being marginalised in public debate. In a survey conducted by the Commissioner of just over 250 children and young people in 2012, about the best and worst things about being a young person in Australia, almost a quarter said that the worst thing was not being listened to or taken seriously by adults.

Responses from young people aged 12 to 17 included:

"Not having adults take your opinions seriously and treating you as just a kid"
"Being underestimated"
"Not being taken seriously"
"Being discriminated against by adults"
"Not being seen as responsible"
"Being patronised by adults"
"Adults think they are more important than kids"

Or, as one 13 year old girl wrote: "People not really listening to you because you are young".

On the topic of play-spaces for young people 14 and over, we drew on the literature about young people and public space, but we also wanted to test these ideas with young people themselves, and seek their views. In May 2015 we facilitated a focus group consultation with 15 students aged between 14 and 15 at a local public high school in Canberra. The group comprised 8 young women and 7 young men. We asked the young people about 'play' and what it means to them; about the spaces they like to hang out in, and why they choose those spaces; and what an ideal 'play' space for young people their age would look like. The students provided a range of useful insights on these issues and suggestions for designing recreational spaces that are welcoming and accessible to young people. Their comments and thoughts are shared below.

Adolescent 'play'

Adolescent socialising and recreational activities may seem to have little in common with formal definitions of play, which suggest that play is an activity that is actively engaged in (not passively watched), is done just for the fun of it, and involves an element of make-believe or 'non-literal behaviour'.[2]

The young people we consulted unanimously rejected the term 'play' to describe their own unstructured recreational activities. To them the word is clearly associated with younger children, and they consider it patronising to describe their activities as play. As one young person said: "We don't use that word, 'play' is for younger kids. We use the words 'chill' or 'hang out.'" Another young person noted that the word 'play' was relevant to them only in the sense of participation in a structured activity: "You play on the PlayStation, or you play sport, you don't just play."

Although they do not think of it as 'play' it is clear that many of the young people we spoke with still enjoy some of the play activities often associated with younger children, such as using play equipment that challenges them, or having opportunities to create, express themselves and engage with interesting and novel spaces and people. However, there is a tendency for adolescents to be 'designed out' of public play areas, and for spaces built for adolescents (such as high school playgrounds) to become more static, or directed towards structured sports, while providing fewer opportunities for unstructured playful activity. It appears that adults, including designers, may often prematurely remove the opportunity for young people to play.

It is important to recognise that the recreation and socialising of adolescents serves an equally significant developmental purpose as the play of younger children. Developmental theory suggests that a major task of adolescence is developing a stable sense of self, integrating physical and intellectual growth and attaining a degree of independence from family.[3] Young people in this age group generally begin to reason in more abstract ways, seeing themselves through the eyes of others, and relationships with peers become even more important:

> [I]t is during the period of adolescence that there is a slow trial-and-error process of identity resolution. Teenagers test themselves in a variety of ways as they seek deeper levels of self-awareness. ... Quite often it is through relationships that adolescents come to understand themselves.[4]

While children engage in make-believe role play, trying on adult roles and behaviours, in a more subtle way young people socialising and hanging out together are experimenting with and exploring identity. They are working out who they are through interactions with their friends and through engagement with the spaces that are available to them. As one young person noted, "at the mall you can hang out with friends and just be cool, or pretend you are cool." Another young person talked about the identity issues associated with the skate park, stating that "I don't go to the skate park, some kids do – they have a different reputation, I don't want that reputation."

Adolescent 'play' may also include risk taking behaviour. While this behaviour is often of concern to adults, and can sometimes result in serious harms, risk taking is also a valid tool used by adolescents to test and develop their identity. Some young people will take risks to impress others, other risks are taken together as a group and can strengthen bonds between peers through shared exposure to danger or the thrill of doing something that is not approved by adults. Taking risks differentiates the peer group from family and authority.[5] While some risk taking behaviour can be harmful, it is necessary for young people to take risks to develop their abilities and independence, and to improve their abilities to assess future risks.[6] Spaces that allow young people to challenge themselves and take risks may reduce the need for anti-social risk taking behaviour.

Many of the young people we spoke to emphasised the importance of 'adventure', 'excitement', 'challenge' and 'adrenalin' in their recreational preferences. Healthy or beneficial risks may include calculated physical risks, such as those involved in navigating a skate park, Parkour course or climbing wall. It could also include social risks such as interacting with others, or experimenting with and expressing identity, including through creative activity or performance. Appropriate spaces can give young people opportunities to explore and take both physical and social risks that help them to grow and develop as individuals.

Trespassers in a world designed for adults

Young people who are establishing their independence often seek spaces to hang out together without the supervision of family, school teachers and other authority figures. As young people do not usually have access to private spaces outside their family homes, they congregate in public spaces including parks, town centres, public transport hubs and commercial areas.

A clear theme emerging both from the literature and from our consultation is the suspicion with which adolescents are viewed by many adults when they access public spaces, and the subtle (and sometimes not so subtle) ways that young people are made to feel unwelcome. As one young person once told the Commissioner, "Sometimes I feel like a trespasser in a world designed for adults."

In a Western Australian study of adolescent perceptions of parks and playgrounds, Wood et al. reported that young people felt that playgrounds are not 'for them', and that parents and adults perceived them negatively. As one young person in their study stated: "The thing is, what they see on the news, they think we're all trouble – that we're not mature enough you know, and a lot of teenagers are becoming mature, it's only a selected few that do that stuff."[7]

As Malone notes, "Moralists often condemn young people for their risky, self indulgent and anti social behaviour, and identify potential perpetrators by stereotyping youth … these type of accounts often tell us more about the fears and anxieties of adults than about youth."[8]

Young people we spoke with also talked about feeling uncomfortable in spaces where parents took younger children. One young person said that they still wanted to use playgrounds and adventure parks, "but you can feel unwelcome and too old – parents look at you and glare, they think the equipment should be reserved for younger kids." Another agreed, and noted that "They think you're over 10 now you have to act like an adult."

The young people we consulted also described feeling unwelcome in 'adult' spaces such as the mall and the public library:

"They are suspicious of teenagers based on a stereotype that doesn't apply to everyone."
"People glare at you, shops search your bags."
"I don't feel welcome there, I feel like people are judging us because of our age, even though we aren't causing any trouble."

While these young people continued to use these spaces and facilities, they remained conscious of adult disapproval, and their probationary status as users of these spaces. As White notes, "young people rarely gain a sense of ownership when it comes to the use of amenities".[9]

Favourite recreational spaces

Despite often facing suspicion and over-vigilant security, young people are strongly drawn to commercial spaces such as shopping malls. These spaces are intentionally inviting to consumers, combining relative safety, comfort and cleanliness with the interest and aspirational quality of an ever changing commercial display.

The mall was the favourite recreational space nominated by most of the young people we consulted, particularly young women, and some young men. In describing this space, one young woman wrote that "I like it because we sit and chat and discuss popular topics. It's clean, tidy and well designed. We can walk and talk and window shop with friends."

Other young people talked about the importance of the food court where there is a range of cheap fast food, and young people can sit and socialise without necessarily needing to purchase anything. A number of young people said that they felt welcomed at fast food outlets: "it's not too expensive and the staff are the same age as us. They are nice to us, we can talk to them."

These young people also liked movies and arcade games at the mall, although they noted that peers were now generally going to the new trampolining centre in the mall rather than the arcade. Novelty, and being in the popular places, was seen as important. As one young person explained, "it is good to go to the interesting places where everyone is going so you don't feel isolated. Places are good when they are new, but not as cool over time. You want to go to the cool places."

A number of the young women in the group noted that the mall was a safe place, and that parents approved of them spending time there with friends. Although young people are developing independence, parents can still exert a strong influence, and the accessibility of recreational spaces may depend on parental approval. As one young woman stated: "Parents are concerned about safety and getting school work done. They need to be happy with a space too, or lots of young people won't be able to use it." Another young person noted that parents were often more conservative about safety than they were: "The places they let us go aren't that exciting, the places where parents want you to go aren't always where we want to go."

Commercial spaces do have their limitations, and have few options for young people without money to spend. As one young person said, "it's fun to pretend you have money, and look around for a while, but after that it gets boring." Malls provide a safe space, often approved by parents, for socialising, and offer a range of consumer attractions and experiences. However, they offer limited free physical, creative or intellectual challenges to engage young people.

Outdoor spaces

A number of young people talked about local parks and ovals as their favourite spaces, where they could exercise and hang out with friends. Several of the young people mentioned a public adventure park which has some interesting play equipment as being a good place to spend time, but felt that it would be better if it was more challenging for teenagers: "they need more exciting equipment, more adrenalin." They noted that it did not offer the same range of amenities as the mall. "It's good but you need somewhere to get food." The park was not seen by young women as a safe place to spend time after dark.

Wood et al. reported similar findings with adolescents they consulted in Western Australia, where participants favoured adventurous playgrounds, situated outdoors and with natural elements. They preferred play equipment that supported movement, was well maintained and of a suitable size to present a challenge for teenagers. They spoke about having identifiable spaces just for older young people, and spaces where they could 'get away' and not be observed by adults. They also identified a need for amenities such as water and clean unlocked toilet blocks nearby.[10]

Interestingly, while skate parks are often the first option considered in designing a recreational space specifically for adolescents, the young people we spoke with did not utilise the local skate park to hang out with friends. When asked about the skate park, they noted that young people from their school did use it, but were in a different social group. Some believed that the skate park was associated with drug use and felt that they would not be welcome there. One young woman said: "I'm scared of that place, I cross the road to avoid it." A young man stated that he didn't know how to skate well enough to go there, and that it was not a place for beginners: "you have to know what you are doing."

This conversation illustrates that young people (like adults) are not a homogenous group, and their needs cannot be met with a single purpose-built space. It also indicates that as well as sometimes feeling like trespassers in spaces designed for children and adults, young people may not feel welcome even in spaces created for their age group, where these are perceived to be dominated by other groups of young people, or do not fit with their developing identities.

Designing spaces with young people

It is clear that young people encounter barriers to accessing recreational spaces that might enrich their lives and provide meaningful challenges, and opportunities for healthy or beneficial risk taking to help them grow and develop. While the issues are complex, and involve changing adult attitudes as well as improving the design of public spaces, involving young people in discussions and planning new developments is an important starting point in meeting their needs. As White has noted:

> [Y]oung people are bona fide members of the community; however many of them are experiencing problems and difficulties relating to public space that impact on them in substantial and often negative ways … inviting young people into the design and planning process represents a positive and constructive approach towards addressing these issues.[11]

The young people we spoke with were enthusiastic about telling us their ideas for improved public spaces, and the discussion indicated that they were responsive to the constraints and realities of urban planning. While their initial ideas focused on enormous free theme parks with unlimited rides, they recognised that these would be cost prohibitive to operate with public funds.

The young people then developed ideas about expanded adventure parks with equipment designed to challenge teenagers, but with separate spaces for younger children, situated together with commercial hubs with food and amenities, and integrated with running and cycling tracks. These hubs included 'chill out' spaces and access to youth services including mental health support. Other ideas they discussed included spaces that could hold a changing series of events for young people, including music festivals, and outdoor movie spaces with beanbags for young people to relax in.

In considering these ideas, the young people were conscious of issues of safety, parental approval and to have options to appeal to a range of different young people. They noted the importance of avoiding boring static spaces and facilities, and the need for novelty, and active participation in attracting young people to a space on an ongoing basis. Their views support the benefits and possibilities of flexible and user-created elements to allow a space to be re-designed and re-imagined by different groups of young people.

While only a brief and informal consultation, it was clear that young people have a wealth of insight and suggestions to offer about designing spaces that are attractive, accessible and engaging for adolescents, and that they could be involved in planning processes in a meaningful way.

Conclusion

In our society, the needs of adolescents for welcoming and engaging public spaces that facilitate their growth and development are often overlooked. Urban spaces have been designed to cater for the needs of adults, and to a lesser extent younger children, but with little acknowledgement of the importance of young people and the contribution they can make to a vibrant community. Instead groups of young people can be perceived as intruders in both adult and children's spaces, and they are acutely conscious of this perception.

Many young people are drawn to commercial spaces such as shopping malls which are safe and enticing, but focus on consumer activity. While commercial spaces provide a place for young people to meet and socialise, they have limited options available for those young people who cannot afford to participate in commercial experiences.

Where efforts are made to design purpose-built spaces for young people, they may fail to meet the needs of many young people if they assume that all young people have similar interests and identities. While skate parks are valuable facilities for some groups of adolescents, and encourage physical challenges and healthy risk taking, they will not be attractive and accessible to all young people.

The starting point in addressing these barriers, and developing more inclusive public spaces, is to speak with and listen to young people, recognising their diversity and the need to consult with young people from all backgrounds and social groupings. They are the experts in the kind of spaces that would be attractive and engaging to them, and the kinds of healthy risks and challenges that excite them.

We would like to thank the young people from Kingsford Smith School who shared their time, thoughts and enthusiasm with us.

28

TECHNOLOGY IN PLAYSPACES

A snapshot

Katherine Masiulanis

Looking to the future of play, particularly in the context of designed environments, it's necessary to think about the interaction of technology. Many play practitioners, who work hard to get children out from behind screens and into the real world, would recoil at the thought of any sort of electronic element in an outdoor playspace. However, given the increasingly subtle ways in which we find technology now supports and enhances our lives, we should perhaps also be thinking about how it may enrich play outcomes.

Given the fast moving development of technology, it can be a baffling area to enter. Redundancy and lack of robustness are of concern, especially given the lifespan of and hard knocks received by a typical playspace. More insidious is the temptation to sneak in commercial branding, such as currently popular movie or TV characters, which is questionable not only ethically but also in terms of limiting the interest of the product to a particular age group and at a particular time.

Technology also has the potential not only to make play more complex, but also to embrace a wider range of ages than a classic swings and slides playspace. While it's difficult to peer into the silicon crystal ball, there are already products available which take the positive aspects of gaming, but use them to encourage movement and face-to-face social interaction, for example. Key aspects are feedback in some form, the opportunity to improve and achieve success, and the opportunity to 'choose your own adventure' – that is, to effectively develop and program new games.

The opportunity to engage young (and not so young) adults in playspaces may also come through technological means. As already discussed, young adults often do not feel comfortable in these spaces, and their social needs are not well met. Providing free WiFi at an attractive social site is a sure way of attracting young adults. They are incredibly tech-savvy, and are a generation which has grown up within a framework in which every aspect of their lives can be recorded, monitored and supported by technology. For example, there are robust playground elements currently on the market which interact with the user's handheld device to allow DJ style mixing of music, with inbuilt amplifiers and speakers, and places for peers to hang out. While this may not fit into the traditional definition of play, it does invite creativity, social interaction and physical activity through the wonderful medium of dance!

In short, there is an exciting and unseen world of possibilities when it comes to the interface between technology and playspaces. The crucial aspect is to avoid the lure of the bright and gimmicky, and embrace technology where it can genuinely value add to real and involved play outcomes.

FIGURE 28.1 Interactive artwork 'The Pool' by Jen Lewin

Photo: Aaron Rogosin

29

LIMA AND THE EVER-POSTPONED ELECTRIC TRAIN

Basurama

Throughout the twentieth century the urban model has been characterised by the progressive, significant presence of the car. Extensive cities, whose final aim is to provide maximum mobility for road vehicles, leave pedestrians in the background, even in city centres. Lima, Peru, is no exception. Urban planning overwhelmed by the reality of indiscriminate, informal growth and a sub-standard public transport network have accentuated these characteristics. Here pedestrians become a secondary element and public space is in the process of being abandoned and is deteriorating. Most kids in the developing areas of town are used to playing with anything and everything available, as no public services are provided, and the playgrounds in the wealthier areas tend to be boring, typical structures.

In this context of abandoned public space we find ourselves faced with the unused railway lines of an electric train, a great push forward for public transport in Lima, never realised. Construction of the electric train began in 1986 as a projection of a modern Lima, but as yet has not been completed. The eternal promise of each new President of Peru and Mayor of Lima but unfulfilled by all of them. The project is most closely associated with the first government of Alan García. This structure is the most interesting example of urban waste in the city from 1986 to 2011. This is mostly because of its shape (a straight platform made of concrete 9 metres high for several kilometres with no points of access onto it), but also due to its unfinished history – an open wound on the city's landscape.

García, in fact, devoted the economic growth of his second government to finally completing the electric train line and in July 2011 the first track opened (of the entire promised network).[1] Everything that had been built beforehand was demolished – including the area where the 'Ghost Train Park' project was established, and it was built again from scratch,[2] an uncertain situation affecting most residents in Lima.

A raised platform is interesting because it is potentially public space, a great linear promenade, denied to a city where walking at ground level means possibly getting run over, deafened or at least contaminated by the sea of cars that have taken over the city. As the platform passes through the district of Surquillo, its lower part is a strange public space: its lawn fills up with couples and families that wait their turn at a nearby hospital, protected

FIGURE 29.1 RUS LIMA Autoparque de Diversiones Público: Chica art decorates the pillars, Lima, Peru 2010

basurama.orgCCBY-NC-SA 4.0

from the sun under the shade of the platform. This is in contrast to the rest of Lima, where parks are usually fenced in like fortresses and appear as breaches of the urban fabric, rather than connected spaces.

The landscape was completed with 14 huge concrete pillars with the rebar sticking out to the sky. An image repeated all over the city: the steel that protrudes from the pillars of the houses – and everywhere else – pointing to the sky. This urban landscape is the demonstration of a common desire, of a society eternally expecting (and waiting) to 'keep growing'.

A temporary self-built public recreational area. 'Autoparque de Diversiones Tren Fantasma'

This project was part of the bigger Basurama project called RUS ('*Residuos Urbanos Sólidos*' which translated into English means 'Solid Urban Waste'). The Solid Urban Waste project was developed for the network of Spanish cultural centres in Latin America, run by the Spanish International Development Agency (AECID). From 2008 to 2011, we developed 13 on-site, ad-hoc projects with local creators, addressing urban situations and conflicts with interventions, campaigns and public art pieces.

RUS in Lima consisted of the recovery of abandoned public space created by the tracks of Lima's unfinished electric train line, a highly symbolic example of urban waste in the city. It made good use of the already established urban infrastructure and reused it as the basis for setting up multiple public leisure activities. The idea was to recreate a home-made leisure park, with some of the classic rides found at fairgrounds, festivals or amusement parks, like the iconic 'Ghost Train'.

Our crew of local artists consisted of:

- Christians Luna (Performance)
- Sandra Nakamura (Visual Arts)
- Camila Bustamante (Graphic designer of the Lima2427 map)
- C.H.O.L.O. (Local Social Artists)
- Playstation Vagon & EL CODO (Graffiti Collectives)
- El Cartón (An Architecture students collective)

We proposed the transformation of the abandoned platform into 'Ghost Train Park', for the self-made amusement of the local community – a local space to play. The project gained the support of the Council of Surquillo and the participation of its community on several levels, from a group of young environmentalists (called Fuerza Juvenil), to its watchmen, the mayor, its cleaning staff, and the shop traders in the area. Local tyre companies also provided materials. The artists' team, together with Fuerza Juvenil and a number of spontaneous volunteers, built the interventions over 10 days. Using easy-to-use, lightweight tools in the courtyard of the local 'Casa de la Juventud' [Youth Centre], we discussed the designs, uses and possibilities with the neighbours there. We installed the interventions and opened the park with tacit permits from both the electric train and local authorities, which once informed, gave permission, but never really officially supported the project.

Ghost Train Park consisted of the following play structures:

- **The Flying Chairs** – 20.6 metre high swings, made with reused tyres and ropes, hanging from the slab, including swings for couples, lower and higher seats, etc.
- **The Ghost Train** – an installation of a 'favela style' train.
- **The Lookout** – a scaffolding structure that provided a way for neighbours to visit the elevated promenade.
- **Rambo!** – an installation using the rings of reused tyres that connected the ground with the platform slab, as kids love to explore and climb. It was built with the idea of 'conquering' the slab, that far-from-us structure.
- **The Flying Train** – a zip line to complete the trip of the train with your own body, jumping from the slab and landing some 60 metres away. There was also a smaller version for little kids.
- **The Crazy Bull** – a manual version of the mechanical bull that had to be pulled by someone for the fun of the three people riding on top of it.
- **The Pirate Boat and The Viking Boat** – two swinging sculptures made of tyres that allowed groups to ride together.

These rides were completed with three more visual-only interventions that made the space into a meeting place, where local people gathered, lingered and had fun together. The space was at the doorstep of a cancer hospital, so the intervention was even more pertinent when whole families waited outside smiling instead of fearing their visits.

FIGURE 29.2 RUS LIMA, Autoparque de Diversiones Público, Lima, Peru 2010
basurama.orgCCBY-NC-SA 4.0

Tackling a new use involved a clear action of celebrating the public space, while at the same time allowing the citizens to reflect upon the contemporary meaning of public space, getting together in urban spaces and having fun. One of the main goals was to make the 'rides' of the amusement park welcoming for all ages, especially encouraging adults to play. Most playgrounds show that they are meant for kids, because of their colours, size and scale, etc. We made a conscious decision to create some rides that were for adults, in two ways: using them on their own (swings were big enough to be used by adults) or helping their kids 'activate' the rides, thus sharing the experience.

So we had the classic features of a fairground, but operated by people. Together with colourful pillars, a party atmosphere, neon signs and so on . . . the invitation was clear, 'Get on the Ghost Train!' On the practical side many questions arose for the local community. 'Who is paying for this?', 'Why are these rides for free?', 'How can this be happening?' and most importantly 'Why can't we have playgrounds as special as this one everywhere else?'. These questions would eventually resonate and motivate future community action.

The process had two strongly marked features: networking with other local, collective groups and low cost construction. This allowed us to learn and put into practice local graphic and construction techniques in order to adapt them to the built play elements. In turn it also allowed the process to be shared, so that after the first experience it would be owned, repeated and improved by the local people themselves. Community empowerment, with local artists and neighbours learning through doing and demonstrating their right to use local public space freely.

The buzz of debate created around the project intervention because of the delicate political issues it addressed was clear. In order to reflect, a reprint of the 'Lima 2427' map was available on site during the project. The intervention didn't intend to criticise the politics around the unfinished train line, rather to reflect on public transport and the power of infrastructure in town. How is it possible that the biggest urban infrastructure objects have only one non-human purpose? How can we take advantage of their scale, their presence and resistance? The map was a recreation of the original pharaonic strategy for making train lines all over Lima. The map calculated that, according to the building rate of that time, that plan would not be finished until 2427.[3]

Strong ideas and lots of tyres

In order to carry out the project with a very minimal budget (around 1,500 euros for the entire production, excluding artists' fees) a strategy of hands-on construction and recycled materials was decided upon. Relying on the ambition of young local artists, and the desire for experimentation, detailed designs were produced relentlessly, as improvements were made. Car parts, especially tyres, were used as a form of paradoxical reflection on public and private transport. For designing the pieces, we relied on the large number of tyre shops in the area, cutting, drilling, bending and putting tyres together, until we found a way of hanging them

FIGURE 29.3 RUS LIMA Autoparque de Diversiones Público: Ghost Train Park, Lima, Peru 2010
basurama.orgCCBY-NC-SA 4.0

in a fun, stable and cool way. The guiding idea of recreating a fairground/amusement park made the exploration with the tyres easier. Comments from local residents about the designs were received within this framework and discussions more focussed. We also tested some of the mechanisms in the courtyard of Casa de la Juventud, taking some dangerous test rides that ended up being more fun than risk. These demonstrations made the design process more open with the community.

To unify the whole project and at the same time make the action visible (it is difficult to make tyres something vivid, happy), the so-called Chicha graphic art[4] was used. This graphic is the typical signage of Lima, used to advertise Cumbia concerts and parties with folkloric and Chicha music, that is very present in the local imagery. The lettering of the signs was omitted and only the background colours were printed, which were used to decorate the grey concrete pillars. Their bright and fluorescent colours brought a real intensity, radically changing the appearance of the area. The recycled neon 'Desire' (Deseo) sign, of Sandra Nakamura, very clearly symbolised the capacity for desire – to desire again, like when we were children, but also, for example, to desire infrastructure. To desire infrastructure represents in some way the paradigm of the fight between citizenship and power, major cities and citizens, that all citizens carry within: the fight to live our lives and fulfil our dreams and desires within a framework that is given to us, but that we also know that we can and must construct. A string of party flags like the ones used in developing areas of town marked the whole extension of the intervention, around 60 metres long.

We cannot stay here, but we can move

To plan a long-term, self-managed project in Lima, so that it may be maintained and enjoyed in an area already functioning as a quasi-public space, was challenging for all concerned. It was necessary that, as well as offering fun activities, we provided a rich, complex and durable space of high quality, knowing that the neighbourhood children would wear it out. In the end the project only lasted a few weeks on site. It was dismantled by the local authorities with the excuse of 'restarting' the construction works on the railway line. To our knowledge this didn't really occur as expected, until much later on. We will never know how much the project acted as a trigger or provocation to continue building the railway line, what we do know is that the residue of the strategy and process for the project has remained and it has since been replicated in other neighbourhoods on the outskirts of Lima.

The local collective groups participating in and constructing this first initiative of RUS Lima have now created their own network. They have since taken over the project and repeated it in other social contexts in Lima, adapting to each situation and working in direct collaboration with each local community. The project has now taken on a new name, 'Self-Mountable Parks', and is intended to be permanent and multiplied in other locations. The second construction after 'Ghost Train Park' was the Self-Mountable Park with *Nueva Esperanza*[5] recycled material in the shanty-town of Pachacutec-Ventanilla, where C.H.O.L.O., who had participated on the Lima project, usually works. A third Self-Mountable Park was built months later in the town of Canta Gallo-Rimac.

For Basurama, this project served as the prototype for a further number of playgrounds created with the community reusing tyres, especially throughout the Sao Paulo periphery in Brazil, for the project '*O Lixa nao Existe*' (Waste doesn't Exist). From 2011 to 2015 we

FIGURE 29.4 RUS LIMA Autoparque de Diversiones Público: Zip-line, Lima, Peru 2010
basurama.orgCCBY-NC-SA 4.0

created around 20 of these playgrounds, as well as taking those first experiences from 'Ghost Train Park' of hanging swings from tall bridges, that was to be repeated hanging swings from the Minhocao and the Viaduto do Chá, in Sao Paulo.

We feel proud that the 'Ghost Train Park' RUS project now continually transforms itself in this way, as a tool for action on certain social and cultural realities.

30

BE NOT AFEARED

Embracing the need for risk in play

Bernard Speigel

It should be a source of alarm that this chapter needs to be written at all. That one needs to 'make the case' for risk-taking as necessary, inevitable and a broadly beneficial aspect of children and teenagers' play, must mean that too many adults have become decoupled from the common-sense understandings that once formed society's decision-making reference points. This says more about adults, at once generators of anxiety but also its victims, the meanings we impose on childhood,[1] and the nature of our society more generally, than it does about actual children and teenagers.

It is impossible to speak sensibly about risk and play without acknowledging this wider context – and it is certainly impossible to do anything to promote 'beneficial risk-taking' without being alert to the effect those wider factors have on individual and organisational decision-making. Play equipment and surfacing standards form part of this wider context. This section will take a critical look at them to see if, in their current form, they assist or hinder the goal of promoting beneficial risk-taking.

The section aims to connect understanding the importance and unavoidability of risk in play, to the practical business of securing play's potential benefits, weighed against the potential risks that securing those benefits might entail.

I could cast this chapter's intent in more heroic terms:

> This section aims to liberate the judgement-making capabilities of individuals and organisations with responsibilities for children and teenagers' play. To offer a perspective that will assist in freeing them from those restrictions – whether external or self-imposed – that hinder, rather than aid, children and teenagers' beneficial risk-taking and freedom to play.

Why risk?

Children and teenagers want and need to take risks. They do this 'naturally' in the sense that, left to their own devices, they seek out and create encounters that carry degrees of risk, degrees of uncertainty as to what might be the consequences of their actions and projects.

The process of risk-taking necessarily entails exploration, discovery and learning – about oneself, one's capabilities and the wider world. A world that is at once welcoming, resistant and responsive – that responsiveness sometimes causing hurt.

To take a self-chosen risk is to assert one's autonomy and power of agency. It is to *learn* by *doing* what taking responsibility means in practice – that actions have consequences. It is an aspect of moral education.

This connection to moral learning is important and too little remarked upon. Through play a moral universe is formed, encountered and understood – children and teenagers, as agents and choosers, learning through experience how values, beliefs and traditions are transformed into ways of life. This knowledge cannot simply be taught. It is the difference between being able to recite a moral code, and learning how to live by one.

No drill, no handbook, no earnest entreaties by well-meaning, perhaps anxious, adults can equal or replace this form of learning. Fundamental aspects of the world are meaningless until experienced: 'hot' is but a label designating nothing until felt; 'fear' a state of mind that no description can adequately convey in the absence of feeling its grip. Similarly, pain or hurt are not abstract qualities, but understood via experience. Joy, too, cannot be learned by rote.

It follows that a blanket, indiscriminate 'risk-minimisation' policy is potentially a source of harm, not benefit.

Resilience

Much is made of the need to nurture in our children qualities of resilience. An irony perhaps, given the seeming trend to shield or 'protect' our offspring from the possibility of almost any harm. Resilience is an empty term if one has nothing to be resilient about.

To be resilient is to encounter, and then to accept or overcome, difficulty. It is to 'pick oneself up and brush oneself down' after a fall – but first you have to fall. It is to argue with a friend and resolve, or not, the issue at hand – but first you must be in dispute. This strikes me as straightforward logical assertion of the form: if resilience is 'x' then 'y' is the precondition required for it to flourish.

The duty of those responsible for play settings is to ensure that the preconditions for resilience exist – challenge must be designed into play settings, and a supervisory practice must be developed that allows challenges to be undertaken.

Bryce, Heath and Wolf make the point that:

> The duo of deliberation and accident is at the heart of the creative process. . . . Accident or the unexpected during opportunities for being creative encourage flexibility, perception of new possibilities, and discovery beyond the fixed or disciplined.[2]

Vocabulary and language

The phrase 'beneficial risk-taking' seeks to capture by way of a shorthand an entire philosophy and approach. It should help serve as an antidote to the standard, risk-averse, anxiety driven meanings attributed to key words in the health and safety lexicon. These key words have come to have intimidatory force, limiting or closing down discussion about the merits of beneficial risk-taking and what it might mean in practice. A culture of anxiety and defensiveness is the result, one which, to a significant and unacceptable extent, weighs heavily on institutions and professionals that have responsibilities for children and teenagers. Parents, too, both absorb and perpetuate this negative culture of mind.

I want, therefore, to clear up some muddles of definition and language that, in their deployment, impede or prevent children's engagement with beneficial risk-taking in play. The red-alert words are: safe and safety; hazard; harm; risk; injury.[3]

Safe

The term 'safe' is often taken to mean that there is no risk of harm at all (no such situation exists). Other meanings attributed to 'safe' include: that industry standards are adhered to; that the level of risk is below some notional value regarded as broadly acceptable.

Because of this ambiguity, avoiding unqualified use of the words 'safe' and 'safety' – for example, in 'safety surfacing' – is advised.

Hazard

Hazards are potential sources of harm. The word 'hazard' is often used to imply that the source of harm is unacceptable and needs to be mitigated. This can be confusing because, in fact, hazards are everywhere. There is no action and no object that may not be hazardous in certain circumstances, in the sense of having the potential to cause a degree of harm. People may trip over steps, slip on floors or fall from climbing frames.

It follows that the attempted removal or mitigation of all hazards is not only impossible, but also potentially damaging. If the world is, by its nature, full of hazards, children need to learn to recognise and respond to them. Hazards, then, are necessary and desirable to the degree that they create 'acceptable levels of risk' (see below).

Harm

Conventionally, harm is thought of as exclusively negative. Definitions revolve around harm being an injury of some sort. In terms of risk and play, it is unhelpful to always define 'harm' as solely negative. In daily life we respond to the concept of 'harm' in a highly nuanced way – that almost standard parental phrase, 'That'll teach you!', heard so often when a child falls over as a result of their own carelessness or misjudgement, is acknowledgement that self-generated harm is often understood as a valuable form of instruction.

Risk

In general use, the word 'risk' refers to the likelihood or chance of an adverse outcome. In risk management contexts, the word tends to include a measure of the seriousness of the adverse outcome, as well as its probability.

As with 'hazard', the term 'risk' can imply an inherent value judgement that the chance – the 'risk' – is unacceptably high, as in the phrase 'that's risky'. But risks are not as a matter of course unacceptable. Indeed, the task of those responsible for play settings is to determine what constitutes an 'acceptable level of risk'.

Good and bad risks

Good risks and hazards in play provision are those that engage and challenge children, and support their growth, learning and development. In principle, beneficial activities include: tree climbing; jumping on and between boulders; manipulating loose materials, for example leaves, twigs and branches, sand and water.

Bad risks and hazards are those that are difficult or impossible for children to assess for themselves, and that have no obvious benefits: for example, structures where the foundations are weak or damaged and may collapse.

The emphasis here is in the distinction between what children can assess for themselves – for example, height, depth, length, wobbliness or firmness – and what they cannot.

Injury

Bumps, minor cuts and bruises are the stuff of everyday childhood both now and in times past. These type of injuries can occur as the result of children pushing against the boundaries of their competence, making a mistake or being careless. Common-sense parenting has long understood that some mistakes, though causing short-term pain or distress, prompt positive long-term learning through experience.

Crucially, children need from an early age to learn that they must take responsibility for their actions, learn to assess and manage risk for themselves. A play setting's responsibility is to ensure that hazards are available for use (though only by the player's free choice) and that, for example, not every surface is soft to fall on. It is of no benefit to a child to be misled into thinking the world comprises soft surfaces.

Serious injury

There is no one objective answer to the question: what constitutes a serious injury? It is a matter of value-based judgement. This is quickly demonstrated if one considers the number of arm and leg fractures that occur in so many sports, such as football and rugby. There is no suggestion that these activities be banned. Likewise, many parents take their children skiing in the sure and certain knowledge that skiing necessarily entails the risk of falling, and potentially fracturing a limb. And limbs are indeed fractured. Yet there is no suggestion that these parents are being irresponsible.

In all these cases, whether implicitly or explicitly, the responsible adult has determined that these activities are beneficial to children as exercise, for the fun to be had and the sense of achievement once undertaken. It follows that it is not axiomatically the case that activities carrying the risk of a broken limb are automatically to be banned. The questions to be asked are:

- what benefits might flow from the activity?
- and, is the risk worth it?

Grossly irresponsible?

Everything said thus far is critically dependent on how we view children – the scope of their competence, capabilities, understandings, instincts. Coupling 'benefit' to risk-taking, and asserting that resilience comes to life where harm is possible or actual, would be grossly irresponsible if children are understood as weak, fragile, always vulnerable, incapable of learning, with little or no capacity for judgement.

But we know, both from memories of our own childhoods, and by virtue of observing children now, that they do not readily undertake actions that feel significantly beyond their own self-assessed competence.

We can demonstrate the validity of this general view by noting where it does not and should not hold, where special measures need to be taken to protect some children from their incapacity to make informed judgements. An example might be a child at the extreme or severe end of the autistic spectrum, whose capacity to 'learn from experience' is diminished or does not exist.

These personal sources of knowledge have tended to be marginalised and declared of little value. The effect of this limiting ethos has been to degrade the role of individual judgement – that is, trusting adults' capacity to be sensitive and alert to the particular features of a situation – and put in its place the rigidities of rule book and generalised prohibitions.

Searching for assurance in rule book and prohibition are part of a wider malaise: the flight from judgement. This leads to a practice that is essentially self-defensive for both

FIGURE 30.1 Impressive rollerblading skill demonstrates how children will seek challenges
Courtesy: Mary Jeavons

organisations and individuals. More will need to be said about this malaise, for it constitutes a major barrier to securing benefits to children.

The flight from judgement

Total agreement with points made thus far is of little value if the conditions do not exist to turn understandings into practice. The pressures on organisations and individuals to engage in what amounts to a self-defensive, watch-my-back practice cannot be ignored.

These risk minimisation pressures are many. To name but a few: fear of litigation; concerns about potential parental complaint; fear of regulators; potential for reputational damage; insurance issues. These external factors combine with and are reinforced by internalised anxieties about the personal consequences that might follow in the event of an accident: the so-called 'blame culture'.

This can and does lead to a distorted and largely unacknowledged practice known as 'secondary risk management'.

The *primary* task of risk assessing and managing a play space is to judge the degree to which an activity offers potential benefit, balanced against its potential risks. Here the focus is firmly on the welfare and well-being of the child.

However, often decision-making takes a form where the *primary* task becomes focused on, and undermined by, *secondary* questions. Examples of *secondary* questions include, for example, parents' assumed (or known) views, fear of adverse publicity in the event of an accident and insurers' attitudes. Perhaps most worrying is that *secondary* considerations are often justified in terms of benefits to the child, thus masking the true grounds of the assessment. To the degree that the mask remains in place, is the degree to which the *primary* question will be lost or obliterated.

It is, however, not wrong to undertake secondary risk management provided it is undertaken in its proper place, when it can be a prompt for reflection and change. A positive approach to the question of whether or not to allow tree climbing might look something like this:

1. **Primary assessment:** Primary risk assessment's conclusion is to allow tree climbing on grounds that decision-makers believe that benefits outweigh the risks.
2. **Secondary assessment:** It is recognised that the organisation would have concerns about such a decision and not support it.
3. A discussion is initiated aiming to bring organisational policy in line with the values and understandings informing the primary risk assessment.

What this highly schematised and simplified sequence seeks to demonstrate is the need for a clear distinction between primary and secondary assessments, both for the benefit of children, and to create the grounds for positive, embedded organisational change.

Anxiety

Much reference has been made to 'anxiety'. It is a quality that runs through this chapter like a subterranean stream – as it should, for so many decisions about risk, and risk in play in particular, are inflected by anxiety. But the moment has come to put anxiety in its place, to staunch its capacity to distort decision-making.

Anxiety is not a moral quality, nor an ethical position. The fact that we have anxieties about children is simply to describe the territory any parent or adult responsible for children inhabits as a matter of course.

It is the adult's responsibility to interrogate their anxieties, not simply to succumb to them.

In our day-to-day talk we understand that there are 'over-anxious parents'. Our common, everyday understanding is that such parents have made a mistake, have prioritised attending to themselves over attending to their child's *actual* needs and wants. Whilst psychologically understandable and often deserving of sympathy, it is nonetheless not the ground upon which judgements about what is good for children should rest. We become morally culpable if we allow unexamined anxiety to dominate decisions about what is best for children.

Thus we might say that there is also the over-anxious teacher, the over-anxious park department, the over anxious … and so on. There is an easily discernible connection here between this form of anxiety and the tendency to conflate risk management.

Play equipment and surfacing Standards

This chapter would have a great void at its centre if it did not devote some words to play equipment and surfacing Standards.[4] They are currently an integral ingredient in the design, procurement and inspection of play environments. They also have a significant – and many would argue negative – impact on the cost of creating play environments, not least where surfacing is concerned.

There is further discussion of the general principals and requirements of Standards as they stand in the Potting Shed section of this book: please see pages 337–9.

Sailing under the flag of 'health and safety', Standards can appear immune to scrutiny and fundamental critique, both regarding the content, and the decision-making structures and processes that spawn them. There is also a significant, and too often unremarked, 'political' aspect to them, which is the expression of a particular economic ideology and intent. Indeed, as will be shown, this provides a key impetus to what may reasonably be characterised as the Standard-making industry.

Too many of those concerned about or who work in play have treated Standards as a mystery, one cloaked in recondite technicalities, a matter for experts only, and therefore somehow off-limits to critique and, crucially, fundamental change. Even as they prompt bewilderment and frustration at their often negative consequences, increasing numbers of national and local states insist they be adhered to. Yet it is arguable that there are fundamental flaws, both in the Standards themselves, and in the structure and processes that generate them.

Language of entrapment

We need once again to seize hold of language and notice that the very term 'Standard' has implied intimidatory force – and when linked to that word 'safety', can present as a seemingly unassailable edifice.

Thus, dictionary definitions of 'standard' include: 'a definite level of excellence or adequacy'; 'of enduring value'; 'an established or accepted model'; 'an accepted authoritative statement of a church's creed'.[5] Thus the very idea of a 'standard' implies immunity from fundamental critique. Within the Standard-making industry there is always discussion about how a Standard may be changed, or tightened. But such discussion occurs within a largely technical idiom – it does not represent a fundamental questioning of the authority of Standards as currently conceived.

To ensure compliance, Standards have their own guardians – the inspectors whose mission it is to check and enforce their implementation, often down to the last centimetre. In these circumstances, where often so much is at stake – for example, client requirements; budget considerations – who dares to question the findings of an inspection report, no matter how contestable it may be?

Even where not mandatory, Standards are often treated as though they were, banishing thereby the possibility of a more flexible approach to play environment design. Those attempting to create more natural environments for play are only too aware of the often surreal attempts to apply industry equipment Standards to fallen trees, boulders, tree swings and much else.

The possibilities of release

The architecture and the political and economic status of Standards and Standard-making bodies has created a form of self-generated intellectual imprisonment, such that, at every level – political, managerial and among the wide range of practitioners whose work encompasses responsibilities for play environments – they are treated as inherently beyond legitimate challenge and change.

A clarification: it is not argued that Standards are always a bad thing, that they are not in some form required. There is a place for Standards. What I do suggest, however, is that Standards have over-reached themselves, trespassed into territory not properly theirs. What I mean by this, I'll come to a little later, but first it is necessary to notice the political and economic context within which play equipment and surfacing Standards subsist.

Commercial objectives: a key impetus driving Standard-making and their compliance

A key objective of standard-making bodies – for example, the European Committee for Standardisation (CEN) – is to secure the removal of barriers to international trade through a process known as 'harmonisation'. This objective is mirrored and linked to Standard-making bodies across national jurisdictions, as can be seen in the American Society for Testing Materials (ASTM International) explanation as to the purpose and 'benefit' of Standards:

> ASTM standards are passports to a successful global trading strategy. Our . . . market-relevant standards, developed in accordance with the guiding principles of the World Trade Organization, fuel trade by opening new markets and creating new trading partners for enterprises everywhere.[6]

It is difficult to see a meaningful connection between objectives focused on promoting free trade, and those concerned with children and teenagers' play, in particular the sort of values, thinking and knowledge that should inform decisions about risk and risk thresholds. These are civil society matters, not commercial ones.

Misfocused perspective

Playground Standards view complex phenomena through a medical-cum-engineering perceptual prism. This bias leads to a position where:

> Many injury-prevention specialists believe that playground safety can best be realised by advocating for changes in environmental design and product safety standards. The simplicity of this approach is appealing. However, to the extent that children's behaviours also create risk, environmental modifications to playgrounds are not likely to be sufficient to prevent injury.[7]

'Standards are often presented as being technical documents whose content and coverage are matters of objective truth and science. We reject this view, arguing instead that they are saturated with value judgments.'[8] Thus, for example, decisions about what constitutes a 'serious injury', what constitutes an 'acceptable level of risk' in play, are judgement-based questions, not reducible to the technical.

Territory, colonisation and trespass

Where does this analysis take us?

It provides the basis for some cartographical work to be undertaken. Two territories can be delineated: one, where Standards are useful, indeed necessary, and can sustain a claim to be generally applicable; the second, the territory where Standards should not trespass, where claims to be generally applicable are invalid, where, indeed, they are unhelpful, even damaging.

The territory where Standards are useful

It is an objective matter as to whether: a metal or wood platform can take the weight of 'x' number of players; it is an objective matter as to the tensile strength required for the cross-beam of a swing; and, similarly, the depth to which the foundations of a structure should be dug. In these and similar matters, technical knowledge has good grounds to claim authority – this is the territory that Standards should occupy.

The territory into which Standards should not trespass

This is the area where value-based judgements must hold sway. This includes matters that are rooted in what are, at base, value-judgements about, for example, the competence of children and teenagers; and how competence is best engendered. Judgements to be made revolve around key questions such as:

- What is an acceptable level of risk?
- What constitutes a serious injury?
- Where, in any particular case, is the balance to be struck between the potential risk of an activity/feature and its potential benefits?

Questions such as these transcend the merely technical. They are questions of value and judgement, in part responsive to place-specific considerations. The process for reaching such decisions is Risk-Benefit Assessment (RBA).[9] To the sort of questions Risk-Benefit Assessment addresses, there is no Standard-based answer.

Impact Absorbing Surfaces

Whether or not to have Impact Absorbing Surfaces (IAS) around and under play equipment, and if so which type, is a matter of judgement. Therefore the question as to whether or not to deploy IAS in any particular case is, in accordance with the schema proposed here, outside the scope of Standards.[10] It is a matter for place-specific, local judgement.

This has particular pertinence in the case of rubber surfacing as one of the more expensive, but also most convincingly marketed, solutions, which has achieved what can only be characterised as iconic status, such surfacing seeming to represent the very idea of safety. It should be noted, however, that the effectiveness of rubber surfacing is an area of hot contention. There is a significant body of informed, authoritative opinion holding that its utility is significantly overstated, and that it too often constitutes a misuse of always limited finance.[11]

Other areas that, arguably, fall within the scope of place-specific value-based judgement include, for example, fall heights and space around equipment.

The key points not to be lost in the detail are:

- Play equipment and surfacing Standards as currently formulated stray into territory not properly theirs. This has, and continues to have, a detrimental effect on cost and design, and most importantly on children and teenagers' play experiences.
- That the conceptual framework suggested here and in the paper cited[12] is a useful way of thinking about Standards – that is, the distinction between matters susceptible to engineering-cum-medical perspectives; and those matters that are value-saturated and are questions of judgement.

Judgement liberated?

Standards need to become the subject of wider debate. Debate becomes possible, however, only when those committed to the importance of play, and in particular the significance of risk in play, question Standards along with the decision-making structures and processes that generate them.

Vast sums of public money are spent adhering to play equipment and surfacing standards. Many believe that significant amounts of it could be better deployed.

This is above all a civil society matter, not one that should be trapped in the technical committees of organisations concerned to advance the benefits of free trade. In any case, the division of territory suggested above neither questions nor undermines that commercial goal – it simply suggests there are areas of decision-making that should not fall within its purview.

Summary

Play environments should create opportunities for children to engage with 'acceptable levels of risk'. It is not the job of play policy makers to minimise risk, avoid the possibility of all hurt or harm or attempt to eliminate all hazards.

What is an 'acceptable level of risk'? An acceptable level of risk is that which enables the player to gain the benefits of their activity or undertaking but, in the words of the UK Health and Safety Executive, '[T]here must be freedom from unacceptable risk of life-threatening or permanently disabling injury at play'.[13]

That high threshold accords with this chapter's common-sense position: that, in principle, cuts, grazes, bruises, the chance of the occasional broken limb and indeed hurt feelings fall within the bounds of 'acceptable level of risk' provided that it is reasonable to believe that the activity has potential benefits for the player.

Why it matters

To deprive children and teenagers of 'beneficial risk-taking' experiences is to do them a disservice. It is to disable them, to halt, distort or sideline their development into a stagnant backwater of assumed 'safety' – one that will ultimately cause them ill.

That is not your job, nor mine.

31

NOT IN MY FRONT GARDEN!

Play Streets: A doorstep controversy

Paul Hocker

Anyone looking at the extraordinary growth of 'Street Play' projects in London over the last few years could be forgiven for thinking it had all come about with ease. In reality it is a story of hard work and determination by a few pioneers who wouldn't take no for an answer. I want to reveal some of the obstacles that were overcome and the tactics employed that have brought about this play streets revival.

First, however, it is worth describing what a play street is. Simply put, it is an urban residential street, closed to through traffic for a few hours on a regular basis so children can play out. Adult neighbours volunteer to put out and man 'Road Closed' signs to deal with resident traffic coming and going at a snail's pace while the children play. Residents decide how often sessions happen with frequency ranging from a few sessions a week to once a month with most sessions being three to four hours in duration. Local authorities are key partners, as they issue road closure orders and in some London boroughs erect permanent 'Street Play' project signage. The sessions appeal to younger children who are thrilled with the taste of independence a play street offers. Typical play street activities include roller-skating, scooters, cycling, chalking, skipping, hula-hoops, tag and other spontaneous games that suit the space. Activities commonly known as 'playing out'.

Play streets were first established in New York at the start of the last century, in response to a rise in child traffic fatalities as cars began their dominance of local roads. In 1938, for similar reasons, play streets were introduced in the UK through an act of parliament, although up until this point the authorities had been more concerned with keeping children off the streets. According to 1935 crime statistics, over 2,000 children were arrested for playing out in that year alone. The criminalisation of play was nothing new. Nancy Astor, the UK's first female Member of Parliament, spoke on the issue in the House of Commons in 1926: "There is no more pitiable sight in life than a child which has been arrested for playing in the street. … Though these children may be fined, we stand convicted."

By the 1950s, the average residential street had five cars parked on it and there were over 700 play streets in England and Wales, often marked out with apple green painted lines running along their pavements. This was to be their peak. The inexorable rise in car

FIGURE 31.1 Left: Girl playing with cardboard box and Right: Playing noughts and crosses with chalk, London, UK 2015

Photo: Katrina Campbell

ownership meant that by the 1970s the average number of parked cars on a residential street had quadrupled to 20. In 1976 the Bishop of Stepney observed, "Britain preferred motor cars to children and showed it by cluttering up streets with parked cars". In some instances children took direct action to keep cars of their streets. In the late 1960s, one group of young people in east London protested by blocking their street by performing en masse the dance craze of the time, 'The Twist'. Eventually the motorcar prevailed and by the end of the twentieth century, play streets were all but forgotten.

My own awareness of play streets came about by chance while researching a play article in the British Library's newspaper archive. Articles from the not-so-distant-past revealed play streets to be a permanent fixture of British life with no better example of this than the first episode of the long-running TV soap drama *Coronation Street* in 1960, having characters refer to children playing out on a nearby play street.

In 2008 the Big Lottery funded London Play's 'Street Play' project, which aimed to support 100 one-off play street events across the capital over three years. These events awakened residents to the possibility of alternative uses for the space outside their front doors and, in particular, ignited a desire to use their streets for everyday play. With general concern about increasingly sedentary childhoods, the idea of reviving play streets was timely as public health intervention. As we set about supporting the first wave of play streets in the capital it became apparent that they offered more than just a handy new playspace in which children's activity levels can be raised.

It has strengthened the feeling of Community. It is not an unusual sight to see one of the neighbours going in to an other neighbour's house when that neighbour is on holiday to water plants, feed a cat or generally keep an eye on out.

Pien, Haringey Resident

Alongside reports of neighbourly trust on the rise came other unexpected outcomes. The UK's Chief Medical Officer wrote in 2013 that play streets offer "immediate and long-term benefits for children and the wider community".[1] Wider community benefits are also worth acknowledging, as living on a play street can markedly reduce older adult isolation, create safer streets and offer respite from car emissions.

Other benefits are less obvious. One parent emailed London Play to report that her children slept like logs after a play street session. On another play street a parent of a profoundly disabled child, separated from his peers by specialist education and leisure provision, shared how thrilled her boy was to just be one of the local kids once a week at their play street session. A West London councillor told us she regularly attended her local play street to hold informal pavement consultations with residents over a cup of tea, providing a chance to hear what residents really thought about local issues. Bicycle maintenance, road safety workshops, toy swaps, street fitness sessions – the application and benefits were as varied and limitless as the imaginations of those living on play streets.

The 'Street Play' projects this century began as they did during the last, with children's health as the catalyst. It was a road safety measure then, as it is today an intervention into childhood obesity through raising children's activity levels. The University of Bristol's

FIGURE 31.2 Adults socialising while children play, London, UK 2015
Photo: Katrina Campbell

PEACH project (Personal and Environmental Associations with Children's Health) has used GPS receivers and accelerometers to measure children's activity levels while they play out, and among the findings it has shown play streets encourage healthy lifestyles with children three to five times more active outside compared to inside.[2]

In 2011, however, many London councils were wary of children playing out on their doorstep and unable to see the potential benefits. Council highways officers were likely to say 'no' or to ask residents to pay unreasonable fees for road closure orders to be processed. These ranged from £200 to as much as £2,500 and it was suspected were designed to create disheartening obstacles for residents that dared to try to make their street a friendlier, more human place. Another spanner often thrown into the works was Public Liability Insurance (PLI). Most boroughs recommend residents take out PLI but others have insisted on it, thereby creating another hurdle for residents to negotiate. It is these types of obstacles that London Play has found itself in the business of removing.

Meanwhile in Bristol, a group of parents who had been running play sessions in their streets were seeing their grassroots movement spread and set up a community interest company, Playing Out, with the aim of activating a culture of street play.

That summer of 2011 also saw the 'Royal Wedding' of Prince William and Kate Middleton, which helped tip the balance in favour of streets for the community and not just motorists. Hundreds of residential roads across London were closed for street parties. Many councils relaxed the red tape normally imposed for such events and made it easier for residents to celebrate. People saw the potential and the following year jumped at the chance to repeat the experience during the Queen's Diamond Jubilee celebrations, and later that year the Olympics. Londoners, sometimes portrayed as chilly and unfriendly, took to the streets to have fun under bunting like never before. Many wanted more on-street fun, and play streets, now floating into the public consciousness, seemed the perfect solution. We began receiving an increasing number of requests from Londoners wanting help in organising regular play street sessions.

In 2012, the combination of effort and circumstance finally saw Street Play projects get a significant foothold in a few pioneering boroughs. Hackney Council, followed closely by neighbouring Waltham Forest, got behind the idea and provided other councils with a viable, low cost model for delivery. From hereon play streets across the capital spread. In the summer of 2013 only five councils out of London's 33 boroughs were supporting play streets; by 2015 23 boroughs were engaged in projects.

Experience has shown that perseverance pays off with even the most reluctant councils eventually seeing the light (see the Croydon case study following) and getting behind play streets. It might take a change of political administration; or play streets popping up in neighbouring boroughs igniting old rivalries; or simply that the bloke in Highways who thinks streets are solely for cars has retired to spend more time with his carburettors.

A minority of residents can be resistant to the idea of play streets with the common perceived fear being the unknown outcomes that publicly opening up previously peaceful neighbourhoods might bring. Hypothetical drug dealers, roaming paedophiles and homicidal motorists rampaging through innocent games of hopscotch are just some of the misconceptions of play streets.

Often the fearful minority will cite children as the greatest threat to a peaceful existence. A recent story in the *Daily Mail* reported that two children under six playing outside their home had been told by the police to play elsewhere after a neighbour complained about the noise. It's a story often repeated in various forms but essentially boils down to adult intolerance towards children playing in public.

Objections from neighbours on a proposed play street are invariably in the minority and often evaporate once the objectors see a play street up and running. I've attended many meetings with residents meeting for the first time where one or two will air fearful assumptions on the dangers of opening up the street for play. At one memorable meeting a woman got so agitated at the thought of children playing near her flowerbeds a friend had to quietly remind her to stay calm. But by giving the resident a forum to air her fears and receive reassurance from her neighbours, everyone was able to move forward together in a positive spirit.

Other objectors are less easy to deal with. In leafy Enfield, after the first play street planning meeting, residents awoke to find posters taped to lamp posts and trees from an anonymous source. The posters had little impact and the street is now not only a successful play street but the foundation of a network that is helping play streets flourish across the borough.

If it's not the noise or the potential destruction of property that some object to, then it's the sheer inconvenience of a play street. In a well-to-do part of Islington one resident put a block on a play street by claiming her chauffeur-driven car would not be able to collect her from outside her house during a play street. She complained that she could not be expected to walk all the way to the end of her street in heels.

FIGURE 31.3 Boy on bike, London, UK 2015
Photo: Katrina Campbell

At least there's some honesty in that last example. Trickier to counter are the complaints dressed up as concern for child welfare. This tactic often directs scorn on parents that let their child play out and perpetuates the idea that the world is dangerous and all unknown adults are a threat.

Play streets have also revealed the Victorian expectation that children should be seen and not heard is still valid for some in the UK.

'Street Play' project opposition is not, unfortunately, just confined to the general public, as many within the play sector believe that only trained playworkers can provide proper supervision around play. Another view is that play is best provided in a space designed for play and that by endorsing play streets we, the 'play sector', are compromising rather than holding out for funding for purpose-built play spaces.

In my view children need a broad range of play environments, including play streets, in order to stimulate different play experiences. It is unwise for adults to rank play environments, as it invalidates children's own preferences, which are so individual and changeable that they are beyond codifying meaningfully. Play is a creative act with as many characteristics as there are children, and any framework that seeks to support it – be it academic, practical or conceptual – should be mindful of that.

When new funding for dedicated play spaces is not available, play streets offer a low-cost alternative. So while local authorities faced with a shrinking purse might choose to get behind play streets rather than fund playworkers or adventure playgrounds, it at least keeps daily outdoor play ticking over until things change for the better.

Much of the opposition to play streets is fuelled by a fear of change, but when sceptics see play streets in action, their preconceptions often fall away. Indeed in a few cases the most entrenched resisters have become advocates. Clare, a play street organiser in Enfield, posted on Facebook in April 2015:

> Two neighbours who were aggressively anti last time have said 'yes' this time, and the husband of one of them has offered to steward ☺. I guess some people just need to see it in action to overcome their fears.

When children play out they also bring adults out. The shared activity gives adults a sense of wellbeing and kinship with their neighbours. It makes people happy and happiness is infectious according to the *World Happiness Study* commissioned by the United Nations, which reported in 2012 that when "people are in a good mood they tend to help others; helping others in turn fosters a good mood ... good relationships both cause happiness and are caused by it".[3] A chain reaction of community happiness set off by the simple act of children playing out on their doorstep.

It's hard to say no to that.

Croydon: Play Street case study

Each London local authority that supports play streets has a different story to tell about how it reached that point. No two stories are alike, as the variation in residents' determination and council willingness produce markedly different journeys and timelines. The Croydon story is

FIGURE 31.4 Left: Using a template to create a chalk sign on the road and Right: Children playing in the road, London, UK 2015

Photo: Katrina Campbell

one of the more protracted, and one in which London Play was deeply involved throughout, providing a unique insight worth sharing.

2009

South Vale, a small residential street in the London Borough of Croydon, staged a summer street play party funded by London Play. It was one of 100 one-off events that London Play supported across London between 2009 and 2011. The resident taking the lead was Dave Miller, a father of two and husband to Yuko. Dave saw the event as chance to enjoy a day on his street free of traffic and for his family and their neighbours to have some fun together.

> South Vale is a narrow residential street, running between busy main roads, and vehicles speed down every day, most of the time, and even drive on the pavement. The council admits they can't do much about it.

The event succeeded in bringing the community together and providing play on the doorstep for the local children.

> [The children] set up a race track, drew chalk lines on the tarmac all the way down the hill, and out came all the bicycles, scooters, roller skates, even a pogo stick. Soon the word got around the neighbourhood about this amazing racetrack, and children from surrounding streets came along to join in.

As would be the case with other play streets, the road itself worked to break down barriers between families that would not normally socialise. London has many boroughs where household income variance is stark. Million pound houses in Hackney, Islington and Westminster sit alongside social housing, but the tarmac they share is a great leveller. Unlike the expanse of a park or a playground, the very narrow nature of a street pulls people together and the short window of time a play street session provides gives the play urgency. There's simply no time for conflict or the space for exclusion.

2011

In May, Dave and I appeared in a short BBC news film about the South Vale attempt to become a play street. That led to a meeting with a local councillor who at first appeared supportive, but unfortunately declared play streets "would be a bit of a disaster" to a local newspaper.

A row broke out on a local online forum over the matter. "Why should people have their lives disrupted because these kids and their parents are too lazy to walk to the local park?" asked one contributor. Another responded: "Taking kids to the park … is one thing, but giving them that extra bit of independence to play outside 'on their own' with other kids is priceless."

Later that month London Play chaired a public meeting in a church hall near South Vale to discuss the play street idea and take a vote on how to proceed. Around 15 residents attended, and a minority of objectors were won over by the promise of holding a trial play street to see the reality of what they were being asked to agree to. A steering group emerged from that meeting, and their first job was to petition the street on the idea. Despite achieving a majority in favour of the play street, a handful of residents continued to be resistant and Dave experienced a bit of low-level hostility when passing some individuals on the street.

Meanwhile the BBC film was generating interest from other media channels, and Dave and I were caught in a busy string of media interviews. A sense of momentum, despite the objectors, was gathering. But it came to a sudden stop when the idea reached the local council. In October, Dave wrote to Croydon's Highways Department to ask if they would be willing to discuss closing South Vale for a trial play street during the Easter holidays the following year.

2012

The council took five months to respond to Dave, and when they did it was not the answer he'd hoped for. A play street on South Vale, wrote a senior council officer, was not something the council was "willing to support in the current economic climate".

The long list of reasons included anticipated objections from residents, parking, traffic and safety implications for nearby roads, the cost of signage, storage and delivery of 'road closed' signs, access issues for emergency services and a reminder that there were plenty of good parks in the borough for communities to come together. All this and a proposed bill of £2,000 for South Vale residents, to cover the cost of processing the application and advertising the required public notice.

"The attitude of the council is very much that streets are for cars and parks are for children," Dave told a journalist. "All we were proposing was for residents taking it in turns at either end to explain the situation to motorists. It wouldn't have cost anything and provides a place for children to play safely."

Later that day the local councillor who had flip-flopped in his support for play streets made a statement to the local media. "I understand Mr Miller wanting his children to play, however, South Vale is a very well-used road, every day of the week, including Sunday, and is inappropriate for such use, given that the delightfully spacious Westow Park is yards away."

Then unexpectedly the council got in touch to offer to meet with Dave to take another look at South Vale's play street idea. At the meeting a senior council officer promised to push the idea further in the council, with the aim of staging a trial play street in Easter 2013. More correspondence was exchanged between Dave and the council but progress was slow, and Easter 2013 began to look less hopeful for the trial play street.

2013

In March 2013, Dave met with his local Member of Parliament, Steve Reed. Dave explained the idea and the glacial pace of the council and asked if the MP could help get things moving. Then opposition councillor Kathy Bee suggested at a council meeting that play streets could help improve children's wellbeing. If South Vale was ready, she told Dave, they should be included in any plans the council had for play streets.

Dave also met with the flip-flopping councillor who was now firmly a flop. As well as reiterating the old arguments about cost and noise he quite bafflingly stated: "Children nowadays are very different animals to when we were kids."

2014

In May, following the local council elections, Kathy Bee and her party took control of the council and play streets were high on the to-do list. By August, Councillor Bee, now Cabinet member for Transport and Environment, wrote to Dave telling him the council had agreed a play streets policy, and an officer had been designated to help residents set up play streets. In October the council made a small grant available to resident groups establishing play streets in Croydon. Dave's persistence had finally paid off.

In the same year, London Play received funding from the Big Lottery to support play street development in 12 London boroughs over three years – one of which was Croydon.

2015

Not everyone was happy with how things were developing. Dave's neighbours who didn't like the idea in 2011 still didn't like it, and grumbling appeared on the letters page of the local paper. The complainant thought the council's decision to include South Vale in the first wave of play streets would create division on the street. "One lady has already sold up and moved away because of the problems that ensued in 2011 and 2012," the resident warned. "So now, it seems, it will start up once again."

In June, South Vale had their trial play street with more sessions planned and other Croydon Play Streets to follow later in the year. In September, Labour's newly selected hopeful for London Mayor, Sadiq Khan, visited the borough. "I spoke to a mum today about the Play Streets," Khan told a local journalist. "That's a great scheme where kids can play in the street and even kick a ball about."

So from political indifference to political endorsement, South Vale has seen it all. It's only a short strip of a road, but its journey to kick-starting Play Streets in the London borough of Croydon has been long and winding.

32

WE ARE SUCH STUFF AS DREAMS ARE MADE ON

Paraphrased conversation with Mark Halden, Senior Playworker, Glamis Adventure Playground

Penny Wilson

For several years Glamis Adventure Playground in Shadwell, East London, has hosted The Cornucopia Theatre Company, who work alongside the children to stage a Shakespeare production.

This year they are doing *The Tempest*.

Glamis sits in the middle of a swirl of fast moving roads, winds race and tumble around the foot of the cliff of the dull grey tower blocks, the noise and dirt of encroaching new building fogs the air in wreathes of booming, quaking dust.

Despite the attempts to gentrify and tame its undercurrents, the dock-side heritage of prostitution, crime, drugs, violence, corruption, abuse and unkindness still clings like a rash of barnacles around Cable Street.

Two men argue as they walk down the street by the playground, slapping each other really hard.

This is what the children see.

The staple diet of the children seems to be scarily cut-priced chicken and transfat chips. Food that does you harm.

Poverty is ordinary.

Food banks are proliferating, homes are overcrowded.

The tax on bedrooms, as transparently unfair as the ancient window tax, is taxing families and homes that look like perfect show homes are surprisingly often a facade for a turbulent childhood experience.

For a child, life here can be precarious.

Children are given anti-social behaviour orders.

Children are lambasted by parents and grandparents in the streets.

Lives and tempers seem brittle.

The child has no choice.

FIGURE 32.1 Bird's-eye view of Glamis 2014, Glamis Adventure Playground, London, UK
Photo: Mark Halden

They do not choose to be born.

They do not choose poverty.

They do not choose abusive or dysfunctional lives.

How do you thrive amidst the maelstrom of growing up as the child of a prostitute?

It must be horrible to be so helpless.

To be carried along like flotsam and jetsam on the prevailing undercurrents.

Swept away by an invisible riptide.

Situations of conflict here seem to have only the possibility of physical resolution …

Life must seem like one of those shouty soap operas.

Children cannot be blamed for looking for respite from shitty lives, retreating into the world of the screen where unpredictability is a game and horrors are pretend.

If the three generations above you are all addicted to drugs, does that mean that this is your fate too?

If all the adults they seem to meet are arseholes, is that what they have to look forward to becoming themselves?

Children seem world weary and eroded by inappropriate experiences and sporadic attention.

Hell is empty and all the devils are here.

In the middle of this swirl of unpredictability and the tides of change there is a island of something different, something that feels magical. A brilliant landscape, a thing of fantasy and vivid colour like a jewel glimmering against the grey backdrop of the roads and the dust and the looming tower-blocks.

It looks like a thing dreamed up by a child, it is unmistakably a place that is defiantly opposite to everything around it. A looking glass world where children's playing is the priority.

Some adults find it bewildering, it lacks an obvious order. Edges are not straight; angles are not right. To adults who like clean, clear, minimal order, this is an upsetting experience, a tangled jumble of chaos.

To others it feels like a magical homecoming. It brings a sigh of recognition … *this is my childhood* … City, forest, beach, it doesn't matter. This is an embraceable phenomena. Arms of your childhood play wrapping around you. It is a fruitful place for the stuff of creation and imagining.

There are two small buildings – one new one with a green roof that looks like a hobbit home and the other a battered shipping container with the layers of paint of generations of decorating children wearing away into a *wabi sabi* masterpiece.

Not much time is spent inside either of these buildings. Life is outdoors at Glamis.

There is a boat sitting there as bold as brass, as if it belonged, beached and stranded on a sandpit.

There is no level path, no step is predictable. There are swells of ground covered with grass or sand or wood or tarmac. Gaudy shrubbery clashes with gaudy structures in the stunning way that nature clashes with itself and heightens beauty.

Things have been built here, strange Heath Robinson home-made looking structures that stretch into the clouds and are painted in garishly exquisite colours which change and flush from one palette to another depending on the whim of the children and the flow of the donated paint.

The painting of the wooden structures gives permission somehow for the children to manipulate the space, to inhabit it and twist it to their own play needs, to make their mark, to brand it as their own, to paint its face.

FIGURE 32.2 Left: Art can be anywhere, right: Tiger face 2014, Glamis Adventure Playground, London, UK

The structures look as if a breath would blow them away like the seeds of a dandelion clock. Tall, tall telegraph poles, fanned slatted banisters, improbably high bridges and unlikely swings, high rise dens and secretive tunnels undermining them. You get the impression that if you were to lean against one piece of this world, the whole lot would topple in turn like dominoes.

Yet they are rock solid and dependable. Daily examinations for signs and symptoms of rot or decay are as important to Glamis as they are to a farmer tending crops or livestock or a mother her baby.

Children inhabit the structures like wood sprites. They meld into the space and unless they wish it, it is not easy to see them, but you know they are there because you can hear the music of their playing from all around you, high in the air or under the ground.

It is possibly by accident that the fire is right at the centre of the site. There is no firepit, no neat margin to the flames and the embers. No special preparation area for the work that the children do of splitting the donated wood with sledgehammers and axes – a cathartic start to an evening after school is done. The fire pulses, flames and burns the fuel that warms the hands and the faces and the food. It draws adults and children with a primal mesmeric allure. These flames seem to be the focus of a lot of what feels magical here. It is strange to contrast the everyday familiarity and deep affection for the fire at Glamis with the terror and fear that it inspires outside this fence.

The shrieking occult horror conjured up by the juxtaposition of the words 'fire, flames, children, axe' is bewildering when you see the goodness of the relationship that the community of this playground has with the fire at its heart. Fire and children take mutual care of each other.

Every evening, every day, a pot of something bubbling and savoury and fragrant is set on the flames to cook. Here children have learned to become feral eaters as the child immersed in play will be. They may well seek the street cred of an imitation fried chicken (clogger of arteries and bowels alike, quiet thief of the dwindling household budget), but here, should you invite them to taste delicate, subtly sweet flowers from the kale plants that have toughened and seeded in the playground growing beds, they will try. They will eat kale flower pesto with gusto. They have learned to recognise the wild rocket that springs up in clumps around the site and graze absentmindedly on its peppery leaves.

Show them how to grow from tiny specks of seeds, crops that they can someday transform into food, and they will join in, or watch like owls, perched in odd corners of the structure, their arms knotted around them with a wide eyed, wistful empathy, as they watch the tender process of transplanting seedlings, tucking them into beds.

As apparently terrifying and *verboten* as fire and axes, children are cuddled here, hair is smoothed. Touch is not taboo. Here, to hug and to play fight are important ways to learn that conflict can be resolved and touch can be kind.

Playworkers watch each other, offering the support of natural surveillance.

This place has a subtle, tender and delicate side.

There can be great quietness here. An earnest investigation by children – a good deal older than one would textbook expect – into the relevant properties of dry to wet sand and the flow of hand-pumped water spilling into shallow palm-like basins lipping one down into the

FIGURE 32.3 Summertime 2015, Glamis Adventure Playground, London, UK

next, goes un-mocked. No one sneers at the tiny girl in dressing up heels as she navigates the outer face of the high bridge. She is utterly focussed on her own survival.

Narratives weave through the warp and weft of the day. The girl who is sometimes a sweetling princess of flowers and tilty headed smiles, can in a snap shift her persona dramatically to the evil queen who likes all things disgusting and wants to eat rotten eggs, and mouse lungs. Which will she be when your paths cross next? (Stay on your toes.)

There is the child who has stability and food and comfort with grandparents at the weekend and discomfort and instability with Mum during the week, going hungry because Mum has paid for a boob-job. (There's irony for you.) He makes a den a little home of his own. Its small and crowded, but he has control. He needs that.

Dens are being made the whole time, from settees, fabric or planks of wood, they are temporary territory to defend and attack, homes to be made and wrecked.

A group of quarrelsome children decided to make a shared house, marked out their floor plan with rubbly bricks on the grass, then fell out over their plans. The boy stormed out in protest, along the imaginary pathways through the blueprint front door, pausing only to slam it with a resounding silence. How to make the unbearable tolerable.

One of the very first adventure playgrounds was built on homes smashed by bombs, friends with all their faces and stories and quirks, the habits of each home the smells of laundry days and lavender scented beeswax all dissolved in a blistering moment. It was on this site that a group of people in Camberwell chose to reclaim childhood. They knew, and deliberately said, that their children needed to play on the site of this loss to make a psychological recovery. Adventure playgrounds still do that.

Sometimes the emotion spills out and the child has to do something extreme. A child explodes out of the gates into the road and lies down in front of an oncoming bus. It may be true that in this little street the bus moves slowly over speed bumps, and that the child is confident that the driver will be wary of children in the road here and be prepared to stop in a heartbeat. But the gesture is grand. The gesture is terrifying.

This is a place of risk.

Climbing as high as you can so that you feel afraid in every part of you, your bowels squirl. You are at the mercy of the elements, you and gravity in a big old standoff. From way up there you are invisible, untouchable, all-powerful, all-seeing. In this place everything slips away into perspective, so tiny that you can crush the little people with your thumb and forefinger. From up here you can re-write your own narrative, re-invent your story.

You can risk your lifetime reputation with a ballgown and wig over your jeans and tee shirt, brave boy.

You can scramble on to the swing and beg to be pushed, but not too hard, but hard enough to fly. You believe and absolutely know you can fly. From the top platform of the swing you can barely fingertip touch the rope. So you have to leap for it. How certain you have to be of your ability to do this every single time. … But the first time? What fear! There is one child who, bored with this challenge, has developed an acrobatic display on the swinging rope that stops the adult heart and causes bile to rise. … But he knows, he believes… .

A musician sits in an aside place, constructively ignoring the shy child whose curiosity has at last has overcome fear, keeping the invitation to join in unspoken, waiting until all her friends have left the site so that she can finally uncage her voice and let it soar.

I have seen children offered stinging nettle soup, and because they trust, they shrug their shoulders and say 'OK' and take a mouthful without a second thought.

How is this magic made? How do the children sense that they are allowed to try things here? They can unclench and blossom?

Where do you find the wisdom to know that **here** is so different from **there**?

FIGURE 32.4 Left: Climbing to see the world beneath you and Right: Up-cycling from the Glamis Bike Project, Glamis Adventure Playground, London, UK

It is as if a spell had been cast. One that stops time, and puts the rest of the world into a deep sleep far away so that in here that phantasies can be brought to life. A place that suggests with a quiet whisper or an understanding glance, that the things that happen here are important. They are vital.

There are adults, but the site doesn't feel as though it is in adult control. Generally speaking the adults are in the background, often quietly getting on with tasks, repairing bikes with the older kids, gardening on the allotments next door, preparing food. There is something grandparental about the relationship between the adults and children, or perhaps something of an older sibling.

To the child it feels as though they never seem to be supervising you, but they always know what is going on. They are never in your face, but always watching when you want them to 'look at this!' Somehow they know when you want some quiet space, or a hand with some job or another. They crack a joke when you are ready for it, or join in when you want them to clown around. Food magically appears when you are hungry. Adults feel like pillars, uprights strong enough to hold up the structures in the sky, but unobtrusive enough that you play around them without noticing them all the time.

Playworkers should know their craft well enough to appear to be indifferent to whatever the children are doing. It would be hilarious to compare them to swans gliding through the playground, but there is an element of calm that is the public face and hidden beneath the water the feet are madly paddling. Their eyes and ears are constantly alert to everything going on close by and in the farthest corners of the site. They are endlessly mindful of play cues from the children or between the children. They have a finger on the pulse of situations where the pressure might rise from rough and tumble to rumble. They look out for the times when children need help to resolve or alleviate conflict in ways that are new to them and from which pride and friendships are salvageable.

They do not impose their own play desires into the mixture of stuff that is happening around them, but they remember how playing felt and use body/memory to empathise with what the children are doing. They think through what loose parts would expand the possibilities of the play and search them out or scrounge for them.

Every day the whole site needs to be checked over to make sure it is robust enough in every element to withstand the wear and tear that will be played out upon it. And even when they know everything is safe, despite first appearances, they have to pander to the risk averse agendas of other agencies.

As often as they can and in the gaps when they are childless, the playworkers talk through everything that has happened, they winkle away at the things they don't understand, try to find new responses that will open up solutions. They reflect on how their practice is going and how they are working together.

They hold the environment safe and sound.

As a senior playworker Mark holds the team and the site together, advocates for the playground to health, housing, local government agencies and to other charities. He raises money. It is a constant task, going out to earn money to keep all these children and this place. He is at the apex of the very broad based adventure playground pyramid; however, that pyramid is inverted and he bears the weight rather than being borne aloft. The senior takes responsibility but passes praise on.

It is through a combination of all these skills that these playworkers have in their craft that the magic happens, that is, if we understand that the magic that we feel in this place is the playing of the children.

As the play *The Tempest* ends, its performers scrambling over, under and through the structures of Glamis, child and adult actors listen as Prospero has the last word. He promises to explain his magic to everyone, then he breaks the fourth wall, addressing the audience directly, inviting them to applaud and cheer at the content of the play. By doing this they send Prospero in the story, back home, they praise him as an actor, show their enjoyment of the story and encourage the playwright.

By talking to you now we are showing you that there are many ways to see gleams. It is set in a place that is difficult for children, it is like a magical island, and is managed with the craft of playwork as practiced by the playworker team.

Because, here's the thing – children couldn't play freely on the streets of Shadwell. For them to have the experience of their own genius of play, children need this artifice, this stage-managed illusion of freedom.

Glamis is a construct, like *The Tempest*, and for it to work there needs to be a willing suspension of disbelief. But it is a powerful and life changing experience none the less.

Prospero finally allows the sprite Aerial his freedom: *'my Aerial, chick. … Be free, and fare thou well'*.

Mark told me about a very little girl on the playground. He told me how she had paused and had looked around at the site and shouted, 'This is my place of freedom.'

Notes

Chapter 26

1. Denise G. Boyd & Helen L. Bee, *The Developing Child*. 13th Ed. 2014, Pearson Education Limited, UK.
2. Lynn R. Marotz & K. Eileen Allen, *Development Profiles: Pre-birth Through Adolescence*. 7th Ed. 2013, Wandsworth Cengage Learning, California, US.
3. Ibid.
4. Ibid.

Chapter 27

1. Alasdair Roy is the ACT Children and Young People Commissioner in Canberra, Australia. Gabrielle McKinnon works with Alasdair as Senior Adviser to the Commissioner.
2. K.H. Rubin, G. Fein, & B. Vandenberg, 'Play,' in E.M. Hetherington (Ed.), *Handbook of child psychology: Vol 4. Socialization, personality, and social development*. Wiley, 1983.
3. E.H. Erikson (Ed.), *Youth: change and challenge*. Basic Books, 1963.
4. F.P. Hughes, *Children, play, and development*. Sage, 1999, p. 112.
5. C. Lightfoot, *The culture of adolescent risk taking*. The Guildford Press, 1997.
6. L. Ponton, *The romance of risk: why teenagers do the things they do*. Basic Books, 2008.
7. L. Wood, K. Martin, & M. Carter, 'But that's just for little kids' Meeting the needs of older children and adolescents in parks and playgrounds. Paper presented at Open Spaces – People Spaces, Edinburgh June 2011. Available at: www.uwa.edu.au/__data/assets/pdf_file/0004/1857469/but-thats-just-for-little-kids...-poster-Open-Spaces-People-Spaces-conference-Edinburgh-June-2011.pdf.
8. K. Malone, 'Street life: youth culture and competing uses of public space,' *Environment & Urbanisation* 14.2 (October 2002): 157–168 at 163.
9. R. White, 'Youth Participation in designing public spaces,' *Youth Studies Australia* 20.1 (2001): 18–26.
10. L. Wood, K. Martin, & M. Carter, 'But that's just for little kids' Meeting the needs of older children and adolescents in parks and playgrounds. Paper presented at Open Spaces – People Spaces, Edinburgh June 2011; E.H. Erikson (Ed.), *Youth: change and challenge*. Basic Books, 1963.
11. R. White, 'Youth Participation in designing public spaces,' *Youth Studies Australia* 20.1 (2001), at 26.

Chapter 29

1. Electric Train was inaugurated today. Here all you need to know about their use (English Translation) Article published Monday 11th July 2011, Empresa Editora El Comercio, El Comercio SOCIETY, Lima, Peru.
2. Electric Train cost $100 million more than budgeted (English Translation) Article published Monday 18th July 2011, Empresa Editora El Comercio, El Comercio SOCIETY, Lima, Peru.
3. Bustamente, Camila, Lima 2427 issue 7th (March 2015).
4. Quinones, Jimy, El Affiche Callejero: Su Origen Y Su Tecnica, Handy with Technology, Wordpress, (11 May 2015).
5. *Nueva esperanza* means new hope.

Chapter 30

1. I'll use 'children' and 'childhood' to cover the 0–18 year olds.
2. Quoted in 'Jumping off and being careful: children's strategies of risk management in everyday life'. Pia Christensen and Miguel Romero Mikkelsen. (2008). *Sociology of Health & Illness*, 30(1).
3. This section draws heavily from the UK Play Safety Forum's 'Managing Risk in Play Provision: Implementation Guide' of which I am co-author with Professor David Ball and Tim Gill. It is available free, online at www.playengland.org.uk/media/172644/managing-risk-in-play-provision.pdf.

4 In this chapter 'standards' refers only to play equipment and surfacing standards.
5 Definitions drawn from Chambers English Dictionary.
6 Quoted from ASTM International web site at www.astm.org/GLOBAL/wto.html.
7 B. A. Morrongiello & S. Matheis. (2007). Addressing the issue of falls off playground equipment: An empirically-based intervention to reduce fall-risk behaviours on playgrounds. *Journal of Pediatric Psychology*, 32(7), 819–830. Quoted in Children's Play Space and Safety Management: Rethinking the Role of Play Equipment Standards.
8 Ibid.
9 For more on Risk-Benefit Assessment, including examples, see https://playsafetyforum.wordpress.com/resources/.
10 This is distinct from the situation where a product must adhere to its claimed specification.
11 For more on this see BC Injury Research and Prevention Unit at www.injuryresearch.bc.ca/can-we-go-too-far-when-it-comes-to-childrens-injury-prevention/. and 'Observations on Impact Attenuation Criteria for Playground Surfaces' a paper by Professor David Balls at http://bernard-spiegal.com/2015/03/23/824/.
12 Bernard Spiegal, Tim R. Gill, Harry Harbottle, David J. Ball, Children's Play Space and Safety Management: Rethinking the Role of Play Equipment Standards, SAGE Open **DOI:** 10.1177/2158244014522075, February 2014.
13 Quoted from UK Play Safety Forum's Statement 'Managing Risk in Play Provision'.

Chapter 31

1 *Our Children Deserve Better – Prevention Pays*, Annual Report of the Chief Medical Officer, 2013.
2 *Bristol University Outdoors and Active Evidence Briefing*, 2015.
3 Helliwell, John F., Richard Layard, and Jeffrey Sachs, eds. 2013. *World Happiness Report 2013*. New York: UN Sustainable Development Solutions Network.

Part VI
THE POTTING SHED

Introduction

Starting your own play project, even when armed with a solid understanding of developmentally appropriate play, the complex and related issues, and the types of play to consider, can be daunting. This section aims to provide a practical tool box to get your project underway, and running as smoothly as possible. Not everything will be relevant to all projects, but we hope to give you some useful pointers.

First up, it is worth discussing how your playspace will be built, as this affects the skills, resources, team and costs associated with building your space.

Some possibilities include:

Community built
Often a cost effective option, if you have the skills within your community. Playspaces can be long-term projects, though: you need to ensure that there is enough real 'fire in the belly' to sustain the team, and if there are issues down the track, to make changes if required.

Design and construct
Also cost effective, but dependent on a particular supplier. This approach takes a good brief out to the market (often playground manufacturers with a landscaping arm) to see what each of them comes up with. You have less control, but they may also surprise you, and you have the benefit of whatever guarantees, warranties and servicing the company offers.

Tendered
The most complicated option, in that you will need a designer or landscape architect, and a full set of documentation drawings to allow different companies to quote. It is crucial that the documentation is good enough that there is no ambiguity, and contractors are quoting on the same thing. However, you have the most control with this option, can select equipment from different people (rather than everything being from one manufacturer as in the Design and Construct model), and can include many nature-based activities.

However you choose to do it, there are various stages in designing the playspace (or having it designed for you), and the section following discusses in more detail some of the things to consider during the project. It's an exciting one! The better informed you are, the more likely you are to find it a genuinely fulfilling process, although the best part is always seeing the joy of children in your creation.

33
THE TEAM

Katherine Masiulanis

Before your project starts, carefully consider the people you will need to take on the journey. Some should be involved throughout the life of the project – others more periodically. These may include:

Benefactor

The person or organisation funding the playspace. If the benefactor is a government or private agency, check carefully the extent to which they wish to be involved in decision making, and any conditions on the funding, such as sponsorship signage, social inclusion, cultural diversity, community impact or required timelines.

Client

If you are designing for someone else, it may be advantageous to clearly identify both their needs, and those of the 'final client'. For example, a playspace may be built by a land developer to fulfil their statutory requirements, beautify the landscape and make a community a more attractive place to live, and hence buy into. However, in a few years' time, the ownership of that playspace may pass to a local Council or other municipal body, and their maintenance capabilities may not be the same. Most crucially, the space needs to not only look attractive, but provide real and ongoing play value for the children of the area.

Designer

Often projects will have a consulting designer. Care should be taken to ensure that the person charged with this fundamental step really understands play, construction (both methods and costs) and is willing to listen to all the people involved. They should also be adept at communicating their ideas, especially as not all audiences can read and understand architectural plans. Sometimes, a playground manufacturer will carry out the design stage, and this can be a cost effective way of working. There is a specific chapter on manufacturers later on in this section.

Interactors

Teachers, early childhood educators, playworkers, parents and carers will all use the playspace in different ways, and may wish to be involved. They will understand the nitty gritty of what makes a successful play area, such as storage, seating and shade, beyond the exciting play opportunities, but not always the practicalities of construction and cost, depending on their background. The needs of all interactors need to be considered, particularly grandparents and carers with disabilities, in the design of public spaces.

Builder

It is important to have a really clear idea of who will be constructing your playspace before you begin. Will this be built by the community, or through working bees? Will it be tendered out to professional construction companies? Will a playground manufacturer manage the construction? Each different scenario provides different opportunities in terms of detailing, materials handling and speed of construction. It may also alter the degree to which you wish to or are able to include your builders in the design process. Conflict of interest issues may arise if the project is to be tendered publicly. Although working with a single builder allows you to capitalise on their particular strengths, it may not be the most cost effective option, nor allow total design freedom.

Maintenance

There is no point in designing a playspace which cannot be maintained, unless it is intended as an ephemeral play environment. Consider regular maintenance of plantings, replacement when required, topping up of loose materials, general tidiness and the crucial job of regular inspection and repair of any equipment or fixed structures. There may be staff for this, or working bees, but the real abilities of the maintenance team in terms of time, available ongoing funding and physical abilities must be a fundamental part of the design, and included from the outset. Sometimes, maintenance staff can be conservative in their ideas, but it is often possible to work through a problem with them, to achieve the same play objective in a more practical way. Without this input, the design will fail over time.

34

TIN TACKS – BUDGETING AND RESOURCES

Elizabeth Cummins

Where to begin?

Whether your project is large or small, good planning above all else will help assure a smooth process both during and after the project is finished. If you're in local government, education or a community group, it is a good idea to first form a core support group to assist you in the decision-making and management process. These should be interested members of your organisation, hopefully with useful skills and expertise in education, financial management, community engagement, marketing, project management or construction, design and of course play. It is useful to appoint one particular member of that group as the leader or contact person for the project.

To begin with you need to be clear and honest about what you are able to achieve and how this is going to happen. There is absolutely no point designing something costly that you don't have the money to build, unless you're prepared to work hard to source the funds. It is also worth making the point that play can be just as valuable in the low tech as the high tech.

What is needed? (Know your site and audience)

The impetus for playspace projects don't usually commence once a core support group is in place. The seed is often sown much earlier within the community itself and patient lobbying over time has played an important role in bringing your project to this point. At this stage, however, it is important to clearly establish the following:

- Who will be the 'end users' of the project?
- What needs do they have? (Age Specific, Universal Access or Specialised Needs, Intergenerational, Broader Community Activity)
- Where is the project to be located? (Site constraints and benefits, adjacencies to other community, commercial or residential facilities, environmental sensibilities)
- Do you have majority community support for the project? If you don't, how are you planning on seeking it? It is worth noting that community opposition to projects can

be very costly to both time and budget and in the most severe cases completely stop the project altogether. Early planning here is critical.
- Do you have site information around the proposed site (feature surveys, architect's drawings, photographs, maps, etc.)? If you don't, how are you planning on sourcing it? This is one area where many projects fall down and either run into additional unexpected cost in putting together information or wind up with inaccurate or out of date information that causes errors down the track.
- Does your proposal have a time frame of use? Remember communities change over time and playspaces wear out too!

What resources do you have?

It is worth reflecting on the resources required for your project and opportunities you have to draw upon expertise, skill and financial support within your own community. Ask yourself if any of the following are found already within or can be negotiated by your community:

- Landscape/Playspace Designer/Educator with Outdoor Play Expertise
- Landscape Contractor or Specialist Subcontractors
- Supplier of Plants, Surfaces, Timber, Play Equipment, Furniture, Signage, Drainage Supplies, Fencing, Shade Options, Logs and Rocks, etc.
- Project Manager
- Existing Finances or Allocated Budget
- Eligibility to Funding Streams or Grants
- Commercial Sponsor

What resources do you need?

Brainstorming what resources you do have will allow you to see what it is that you need exactly. If you and your group don't have the expertise, then speak to someone who does.

Funding that matches what you are proposing will be extremely important to the success of your project and as such, ensuring that this *will* be available *before* going any further is critical. If you're not sure how much you will actually need, talk to others who have recently built similar projects or a landscape contractor as they can give you accurate guidance. When you think you know your budget, add another 10% for the 'hidden extras' you haven't considered.

The importance of a fundraising strategy

Finances are not infinite. A clear fundraising strategy needs to be established at the outset of your project, if no allocated funding exists.

This strategy needs to clearly state your project's aim and purpose and outline feasible strategies or actions for attaining the finances required. Plot these out in a spreadsheet so you can see everything together.

Appoint someone with experience in this area or the necessary skills (good communicator, confident negotiator) to take this role. Fundraising through events needs to also be targeted, or your project runs the risk of putting all its energies into raising money rather than the project itself. Some events produce a low yield for much work, so focus on those that may yield more profit for less.

Funding grants versus sponsorship?

Seeking larger funding amounts for projects is best sought through grants or sponsorship. So what's the difference, and are there pros and cons to both approaches?

Let's begin with Funding Grants. These are usually made available through government bodies and philanthropic organisations.

Benefits:
- Larger lump sums of money available
- Very little requirement on behalf of funding body (other than reporting) after funding has been secured
- Good support through the application process and feedback given

Negatives:
- Funding is usually one off for a certain period of time
- Qualification for funding can be narrow
- A lot of paperwork and procedure to apply
- Stringent deadlines (if you miss these you may not get another chance)
- Reporting required once project completed

So what about Commercial Sponsorship? This may be through an established programme for sponsors or result from a direct approach. It is usually best to try to target companies with an affiliation or that will benefit from an association with your project. Many companies and banks in particular are keen to be seen as supporting local communities – use this to your advantage.

Benefits:
- Larger lump sums of money available
- Ongoing relationships with a continuing stream of funding may be established
- Wider promotion for your project may be achieved

Negatives:
- Possibly more onerous requirements on the benefactor's part. For example, naming rights, hosted events for staff, etc.
- More difficult sell in terms of the advantages of your project to the potential sponsor

Pro-bono support

This is when you seek the unpaid expertise of a professional for your project. For example, if your organisation has a landscape architect, garden designer or student. They may offer their services to the project free of change or at a discounted rate. This may be with some form of public recognition or skill training in mind.

Another area of pro-bono support worth pursuing would be a team of landscape contractors to construct your project, as labour can be up to 50% of the cost of any given landscape project. You could even try an arrangement whereby the contractor does the hardscape and structural works pro-bono and your community does the planting.

Being clever with material donations

You may also look to approach suitable companies for donations of supplies or materials. This could be anything from plants to play equipment and can cut down your costs significantly. Again, companies participating may expect some form of public recognition or promotion for their company.

Don't forget maintenance and renewal!

Many projects focus on the end result being the opening of the new playspace project, overlooking the fact the legacy left behind that has to be managed over time.

Playspaces take a well-loved beating and wear out: that is a fact. No matter what scale your project is you will need to factor in ongoing care and replacement of parts and the eventual renewal of everything. This all costs money, and without it your project will start to look shabby fairly quickly. This will in turn affect its use.

The advent of 'Nature Play' has seen what many people describe as 'low maintenance' spaces; I beg to argue differently. Trees, shrubs, groundcovers, climbers and other plants in particular require a very high level of attention during their establishment phase and then pruning and cultivation after that to keep them looking their best, especially when they are so well loved.

Factor in the costs of someone to care for the environment (in particular the plants) for at least the first 6 months to 1 year. Then factor in the cost of regular ongoing maintenance on a 6 monthly basis. Finally assume that once the playspace reaches 10–15 years of age it will need a major renewal, which may be equal to the initial cost of construction. Some materials like galvanised steel will last much longer, so always make considered judgements of what is worth retaining before making any changes.

Managing your budget

Lastly manage your budget tightly and effectively. The likelihood is you won't have much room to manoeuvre – so make everything count! Keep revisiting the budget and see how you are tracking; are you comfortable or do you need more funds? It is critical to be across all these aspects for a stress free, successful project outcome.

35

SOCIAL AND ENVIRONMENTAL RESPONSIBILITIES

Katherine Masiulanis

When building a playspace, it is important to think about not only the play value, but also the impact of your proposed space, both socially and environmentally. This impact is measured in terms of the materials which are used to construct it, and also in the messages which are directly or indirectly embedded within the design.

Where possible to lower the impact of construction, consider the reuse of materials from the site. This may extend to sound pieces of equipment (which can also provide a reassuring continuity for the community), or to reinvention. At the very least, if you are refurbishing an old playspace, the loose softfall surfacing, even if degraded for its original purpose, may often be reused as garden mulch. Any tree works required, for example, may bring you logs and steppers, but this reinvention can be much more creative, as we've seen in our Case Studies. If the design involves altering the landform of the site, is it possible to retain or source the necessary soil on site? Adding some small mounds or berms may avoid expensive transport and disposal, and also add to the play value of your project.

There is ample information about various recycled materials, and it is worth delving into these. They often offer new opportunities for design. Be aware that products also change and develop over time. Composite recycled plastic products are a prime example of this: greeted enthusiastically at first, some of the first products suffered from serious warping, which disinclined people from trying them again. Now a well established industry, the materials have been refined, and warping is rarely if ever an issue.

Related to this is the question of longevity. Playspaces, whether through the hard wear they receive, or changing needs and fashions, are rarely long-term projects. It has been suggested by various asset managers that 15 years is about the lifespan of the average public playspace, although some do last much longer. Structures located near the sea are especially vulnerable, and serious consideration should be made of the treatment of any metal components, or they can become maintenance nightmares.

Generally speaking, this relatively short asset life can cut both ways. It offers opportunity for regular review and reinvention, and allows for the inclusion of materials which are not intended to last forever, such as logs. However, you do also need to consider carefully the embodied energy in your play space, and also its disposal. Some treated timbers, for example, must be removed to landfill sites, as the chemicals within them do not allow for their reuse in other ways.

Timber is a large subject in itself, and a hard one about which to obtain really solid information. In many parts of the world, old growth and pristine forests are logged for hardwood, leading to habitat destruction, irrevocable changes to the land, and changes to the local water cycle. Plantation or recycled timbers are preferable, but depending on how sensitive you are to environmental impacts, you may also want to look further into the management of these plantations.

As discussed in the Planting Design section, your choices for the gardens within the playspace (if any) also have an impact. On occasion, and given the available maintenance for a site, it may be most appropriate to use very hardy, drought and cold tolerant planting. Chosen with care, this type of planting can still be beautiful, have seasonal variation, and provide useful loose materials for play. Returning to the question of the messages we send, many playspaces are also considering the inclusion of fruiting and edible plants. These can educate children about food production and increase the sensory experiences available to them. These spaces generally do require higher levels of maintenance, but also perhaps irrigation and regular fertilizer of some sort.

If budget and the structures allow, incorporating elements such as solar panels on shelters or wind turbines can spark discussions about energy generation, and also help to normalise renewable energy. Children will often pick up on the environmental sensitivities embedded in a design, and designers have a responsibility to consider not only the direct effect of their space, but also how it may change long-term thinking.

A socially inclusive playspace suggests that everyone is welcome, and that everyone has the ability to play. Often playspaces become the hub of a community: a neutral meeting place where people with something in common can come together. Hence, by excluding certain people, or making them feel unwelcome, we can marginalise certain sections of society. Obviously this can be an issue for children and carers with a disability, but also for older children and young adults. To this end, it is necessary to extend thinking beyond just the playspace itself, to the amenities which support it. Is it possible to travel from the entrance to the playspace? Are there pram crossings and a decent surface which the wheels of mobility devices and pushers can traverse? Is there shade, and social seating? A careful designer will consider the circulation through the site, ease of supervision, and attractive and varied spots to hang out at a respectable distance from the playground proper. These places will provide teenagers with a little independence, and provide children some respite from the hurly burly.

Consider the wider impact of your proposed space, especially if you are designing a large play area. Playspaces are real honeypots, and news of a good one gets about! Is there adequate transport or car or bike parking near your space? Sometimes, they can become victims of their own success, with angry local residents and traffic snarls as people flock in. Toilets should also be considered, although often budget and local municipal strategies dictate whether it is possible to include these.

Finally, in designing something new, there is the opportunity to make your playspace locally unique. Themes are often flagged as the means to do this, and they can provide great prompts for imaginative and role play. Consider whether there are local stories or history which you can interpret into your space. Interpretation need not be carried out explicitly through signage, especially when the space is designed for younger, pre-literate children. You may wish to provide for people who want details of local history through physical signage or digital support. If the history of the site does not inspire, consider turning the equation around: is there a way you can imbue the park with character in such a way that it becomes a source of local stories? The local playspace is important to children – give it flavour and meaning.

Your playspace does not exist within a vacuum. Messages about environmental and social responsibilities are embedded within it, and absorbed both consciously and subconsciously by the people that use it. This could be seen as a burden, but it is also a terrific opportunity to improve our world.

36

SITE ANALYSIS AND OPPORTUNITIES FOR PLAY

Katherine Masiulanis

A master stonemason will know their stone. They are aware of the feel and character of each piece in a really intimate way. In the same way, to design a new playspace, you need to know your site. A survey will tell you precisely where things are located in space, and this is a crucial tool for carrying out accurate design work, especially if you plan to take the design to quotation or tender. However, a real gut understanding of the nature of the site will only come from being there, and genuinely noticing it. Emma Best from Newcastle Museum in Australia speaks of a game that she asks the groups of school children visiting the museum to do. They look at an object or a picture, and then cover their eyes with their hands. On second look, they are asked to find something new. And they do, and are amazed that they missed it the first time. Our heads are so busy it is sometimes hard to really see what is in front of us. The Victorians on the Grand Tour of Europe, knowing this, but also not graced (or blinded) by the immediacy of cameras or phones, drew by hand many of the buildings and artworks which they came to see.

So, when analysing your site, try to look at it with fresh eyes, especially if you see it every day and it has become mundane. Where are the slopes, and views? What can you see from there? Get down at child level and see what it is like. Are there areas which are particularly hot, cold, windy or sheltered? Do certain areas collect water? Are some spaces secret and hidden, and others exposed? What is the soil like? How will it feel in different seasons, and is it used in the same way year round? Are there things which make moving through the space challenging?

It is worth trying to think like a child to see what really happens on a site, especially if they are not there when you visit. Are there paths through the bushes, or cubby spaces? Are any branches worn smooth by climbing, or collection points? These may be transient, and also well hidden, such as inside fence posts, or in cracks in trunks. Some of these places are precious to children, and may be unwittingly and unnecessarily destroyed by well-meaning people wishing to tidy up, or improve views. Children may often be able to tell you directly about some of these important places, and this is covered in the following Consultation section.

When analysing your site keep your mind open to opportunities, rather than just problems which need to be fixed. A sloping site, for example, may offer the chance for children in wheelchairs to access high spaces without the need to traverse long and boring ramps. Only once you have a really clear picture of what is there, and how a site currently works, are you ready to start thinking about what might be.

37

PLAYSPACES AND COMMUNITY ENGAGEMENT

Elizabeth Cummins

Ownership of public space is important for the success of its future use and maintenance. Engaging with communities is essential for hearing what they value about their existing open space and what they would like to see happen to it.

I would like the discussion in this section to address the tools for making effective assessments of the type of engagement most appropriate to your project.

As each community has a unique make-up, they each have a different desire to input, and also preferences about how that feedback is sought and applied. Therefore engagement with communities can take different forms. Engagement falls into four categories:

- Informing
- Consulting
- Involving
- Empowering

In relation to playspace projects I would like to add a further stage that is 'observing', with which we will begin this discussion on community engagement.

The power of observation in learning about children's play

Keen observers of human life will know that human interaction is complex, and never is this more evident in that little microcosm of the life – play. Where asking questions of people or children is likely to provide a directed (and sometimes limited) response, observation of children's play can open our eyes to the subtleties of space and interaction, allowing us to seek a form of 'wisdom' around what functions elements and spaces serve, and how these can potentially be re-applied in a designed, fixed or flexible playspace.

Play, by its very nature, is a participative process: children empower themselves through playing much more than through any formal consultation process. By observing children's play, responding to children's play cues and reflecting on this experience with our peers we can learn a lot about the value of our play environment.

The limitations of observation, however, come back to the 'to be developed' environment – how does one gain insight on a space which only has a certain capacity and infrastructure, which in many cases may be non-existent or degraded to an extent? I would say that whilst collective observation on how children play on 'other' playspaces should be gathered and stored by designers and play providers as a scrapbook of ideas, this method of engagement is best served for school/early childhood environments where play occurs regularly and over a longer time frame.

Informing

This is about providing information on a particular project to the community, so that they are aware of what is happening.

Consulting

Consultation takes involving the community in a project to a more 'interactive' level (i.e. that information is sought and returned). This may be in the form of question asking or survey taking. This is when particular questions about the project itself or the community's needs are asked, answers to those questions are reviewed and a collective base of information is formed for the project to draw upon. This can be useful both in terms of input into building a project and feedback afterwards to help with ongoing maintenance/renewal or other future projects.

It can also take the form of public meetings or forums whereby information is presented to the community and the community has the opportunity to ask questions about the project or give feedback. This type of community engagement enables the allaying of community fears and opposition to a project, and there is the opportunity for a 'conversation'. Problems can arise when questions are leading or certain community members (who may not be representative of the majority) dominate a forum. This form of consultation can clearly indicate strong support for a project – which can have impact on engagement and empowerment.

Consultation, however, clearly places the decision making in the hands of the play provider, as feedback is merely supporting evidence from the community as to why or why not something should or shouldn't be done. Benefits are the breadth of distribution and the capacity to easily manage the process. Consultation can be tailored for children and young people in the form of activities that seek to teach further educational skills in leadership or civics or prompts for discussion.

Involving/participating

The difference between consultation and involvement is merely the more 'hands-on' nature of the engagement. Involvement shifts the community role from one of a singular question-answer, to one of ongoing questions and answers, as the community participates across the breadth of the project, or at least in the initial stages. This type of engagement usually takes the form of forums or project groups for ongoing reference or management.

The benefit of this approach is that there is much more ongoing community interaction and involvement in the project, which can lead to better use and ownership by the community once the playspace is completed.

Empowering/decision-making

This final type of consultation involves a direct community role in the capacity to 'make' decisions on a particular project. This may involve finances as well as design, implementation and management. Consensus may need to be reached and representation made on behalf of the majority of the community, but empowering allows the community a first hand responsibility in a playspace project.

An example of this is a 'community build' where the community raises the funds to pay for the new playspace and then pulls together an onsite team to 'construct' either a kit form or community led design.

This process can have much broader community building implications than just the project itself, including both skill development and social capital. It does, however, need to have the right team involved and be clear in its terms of reference to ensure successful management and community representation occur.

Consulting with children and young people on their spaces and places

> The idea that children and young people have the right to be consulted about the decisions that affect their lives is so common today that it's easy to forget how recently this mindset has developed.
>
> *(Children's Play Information Service, UK 2006)*[1]

Article 31 of the United Nations Convention on the Rights of the Child and Article 12 of the same convention state 'that all children have the right to be consulted about matters that affect them in all areas of public policy, and to have their opinions taken into account'. Children and young people should therefore always be consulted about the spaces and places they inhabit.

Hart[2] distinguishes four identified areas of young people's participation which he titles the 'ladder of participation':

1. Bogus Participation
2. Informed Choice
3. Consultation
4. Participation

The ladder metaphor used may assume that higher is better; however, with the exception of bogus participation (that should never be used), all other forms are valid ways of consulting with children and young people.

The first rule of consultation is: never do it unless you are genuinely committed to acting on the results. Better no consultation than dishonest consultation.

Consultation is essentially a kind of research. Alderson[3] outlines eight ethical criteria for doing 'social research' with children, which can be applied to consultation with children and young people around play and play environments:

1. Who benefits from the consultation?
2. Are all the children/young people in the group able to take part or are you only hearing certain voices?
3. How will you secure informed consent from children/young people to take part (and from their parents if necessary)? Can children say no if they want? If they say yes, can they change their minds later?
4. How will you make sure that their confidentially is respected?
5. Are they able to choose how they will take part in the consultation or is there only a one size fits all approach?
6. Are the consultation activities interesting and fun, or are they boring?
7. When you summarise the consultation results will you genuinely reflect children/young people's views and allow a variety of voices to be heard?
8. How will you give feedback about what the consultation shows, and about what happens as a result?

It is good practice to draw up a plan for your particular project's consultation that deals with all of these issues in a positive way. Plan enough time for all stages of the process, including analysis of information gathered and feedback to participants. This can take longer than you think!

Good methods for consulting with children and young people may include: observation (as discussed in an earlier section), games (good for under 5s), art or craft activities, photography, songs, poems or stories, pictures, audio recorders, suggestion boxes and worksheets/questionnaires for older children and young people.

Conclusion

Consultation and participation by the community, especially children and young people, is essential for a playspace project to gain genuine insight and understanding. This will help meet the needs of your particular community in the structure of the final project.

With children and young people it can also be a positive learning experience teaching skills like decision making, listening to other points of view, assertiveness, negotiation and problem solving around resource constraints.

> The more deeply they are involved, and the closer they get to actual participation – genuine power-sharing with adults – the more likely they are to learn.
> *(Children's Play Information Service, UK 2006)*

If managed and targeted effectively it will generate better social connection and a sense of ownership over the outcome, which has implications beyond the project itself.

38

INSIGHT INTO PLAYGROUND MANUFACTURERS

Katherine Masiulanis

There is something of a commercial quandary when it comes to sourcing equipment from playground manufacturers. No matter how much research they have done, or what philosophies around play they have developed, at the end of the day, they do need to sell equipment to be able to feed their families. This fact in itself means that even if they know that the best play value will be provided by a bucket, some water and a mound of sand, they must present you with something which you will wish to buy. The playground industry is also quite incestuous, and a new breakthrough is often copied (with suitable levels of design alteration) by other companies quite quickly, and not always with equal quality.

It is a very cost effective option to ask a series of manufacturers to come up with a design-and-construct solution for a particular play space. By doing this, you cut out separate designers, building contractors and sometimes maintenance crew, and this streamlining is a perfectly legitimate approach on some sites.

However, from the manufacturer's perspective, they are in a race to show you how their product is the best of the many you may choose, and the news of one bad experience (despite many smooth and trouble free ones) can spread like gossip. Some clients are uneducated about play. Others will not care about quality, or the product's environmental impact. Some are swayed by the most attractive presentation, while others will read every scrap of information provided.

To help steer through this maze, some suggestions for assessing their proposals follow:

- Educate yourself about children's play and development. There is no point having overly difficult climbers to a toddler slide, or roofs too low on a piece intended for teenagers.
- Visit other sites by the manufacturers you are considering. What is the quality really like? Does it feel flimsy, or is it peeling or splitting? Are joints well executed and considered? Are the colours fading?
- Talk to other people about their post-sales experience.
- Ask the manufacturer all the questions which bother you. If a piece is labelled 'accessible

to children with disabilities', ask how a child would really use it. Is this method playful, socially inclusive and dignified?
- If you are looking for something unique or reflecting the local nature of your site, it may be worth investigating whether the manufacturer is willing or able to customise equipment.
- Does the proposal extend only to the equipment, or to landscaping, furniture and shelters?
- Where does the equipment come from? This has implications not only in terms of the miles of transport and the ethics of local purchasing, but also of lead times to obtain equipment and sometimes parts if they need replacing.
- Think about the feel of the materials they are offering, not just the look. What textures and colours are right for your site, and is excessive heat or cold an issue?

Armed with this awareness, hopefully you will be able to see past the beautiful presentation images, to discern which equipment truly offers appropriate and long-lasting play value.

39
STAGING

Elizabeth Cummins

Delivering new playspaces, particularly on a small budget, is a challenge, and sometimes the best way to manage this is by staging the project.

When staging a project it is important to consider what the key elements of your project are and how this can be delivered effectively in terms of both finance and logistics. Projects within schools or early childhood settings can be complicated to manage during construction, so thinking about how to deliver everything smoothly makes life easier for everyone.

It is also important to remember that the momentum and finance for future stages doesn't always happen even with the best intentions, so stage one should always be conceived of as a 'stand alone' project, otherwise the playspace either won't work effectively or will feel like it isn't complete.

FIGURE 39.1 Construction Works at Melbourne Zoo
Credit: Urban Initiatives Pty Ltd

40
PLANTING MAINTENANCE

Katherine Masiulanis

The management of plants within the playspace is best considered at the design phase, and much more is said on this complex area in the Planting Design section of this book. Please refer to page 115 of this publication.

As a general summary, it is important to consider plant selection, soil compaction, available maintenance (particularly when it comes to plants which require pruning, cutting down, or pest control), and the provision of irrigation.

However good the planting design, unforeseen things can happen – plants sometimes fail for no very obvious reason, children trample unexpected places, or insects or diseases affect plants. As a living part of the playspace, they are more unpredictable than equipment or hard landscaping, and require regular monitoring and, if necessary, replacement. It is important to keep this valuable part of the environment functioning well and looking its best.

41

MAINTENANCE AND LONGEVITY

Elizabeth Cummins

Key to the long-term success of a playspace is the quality of materials and workmanship applied and consistency of maintenance to keep everything functioning.

Use and exposure

It is inevitable that playspaces will wear out because of use. A well-used playspace will wear out much faster than others, parts will eventually fail, ground become compact, plants trampled. It is important to note that while standard parts can be straightforward to replace, this is not always the case with custom items or artwork. With many projects, budgets are raised for the project but no funds are put aside for how the playspace is to be kept up to standard after it opens. This is highly important for the long-term success of the project. It is important to also note that the siting and context of your project will have an effect on its durability. Projects set low on sites, within ephemeral waterways or in coastal areas, will wear out faster than others set in more protected locations.

The importance of regular inspections and maintenance

Regular inspections and maintenance will help to avoid hazardous situations developing in playspaces. Depending on the use or setting, a playspace should be inspected regularly, from daily to fortnightly as needed. This is to ensure that no broken or loose parts, trip hazards, glass or graffiti exist. If your playspace has sand, a daily inspection or the installation of a cover is a necessity. Playspace inspections by an external expert on a six monthly or annual basis are important to comply with Standards.

When to maintain or not to maintain

It is assumed that maintenance in a playspace is a given. However, pruning, limbing up and tree and shrub removal doesn't always support good play. Wild areas are often highly valued spaces where children can hide, imagine, engage in nature play and find mini-beasts and other creatures. By observing children we can learn which environments have high play value and which can be pruned and cut back.

That said, playspaces are often civic spaces with community expectation around how they should be kept. Sometimes wild environments are not always appropriate as universal access needs to be maintained.

Choosing appropriate materials

The quality of materials, workmanship and finish has a big impact on the long-term durability of a playspace. Doing your research and asking questions will assist you, but don't hesitate to also seek expert advice in any way either from suppliers, other designers or engineers.

Some materials are more stable than others. Timber, for example, expands and contracts, over time causing splits or shifts in gaps, and extreme damp will eventually cause it to rot, treated or not. Timber is also vulnerable to being burnt. Steel on the other hand if treated or powder coated stays more stable over time. However, it responds to temperature changes significantly, being cold in winter and hot in summer. Timber tends to regulate its temperature better. There are usually strong feelings about the use of plastic in playspaces. The beauty of plastic is that it is a flexible material that can be easily molded to form different shapes, which is more difficult to do with materials like steel and timber.

Timber should either be a hardwood or treated timber (or don't expect your structure to last long). Timber edges should be chamfered and splinter free, with fixings smooth or sunk below the surface level. Steel and other metals used should also be treated, either powder coated or hot-dip galvanized. The metal surface should be free of burrs or sharp edges.

When using natural materials such as rocks, stones, logs and branches, make sure that sharp corners, edges and surfaces are smoothly finished. The beauty of natural materials is that they are irregular and you don't want to lose this. A little smoothing here and there is common sense to assist these materials to work effectively in the environment.

It is worth noting that any bespoke or unique materials may be costly to acquire and replace. Sometimes it's best to try to use more standard materials and if you want a unique take on your project, use those materials in a unique way.

Succession planning for your playspace

Planning for the eventual renewal or replacement of your playspace is sometimes overlooked, but should be considered before a playspace wears out. Materials and exposure will affect the lifecycle of your playspace, but it's a good rule of thumb that you will get at least 10 years good life out of a playspace. In some cases (and this applies specifically to larger, more bespoke playspaces) you will also need to plan for the replacement of particular elements such as moveable parts more regularly.

42

SUPPORTING INFRASTRUCTURE

Katherine Masiulanis

A playspace does not exist in a vacuum, and the infrastructure which supports it, especially when it comes to public spaces, can make or break a great play environment. These need not be specifically to service the playspace, but may be shared by several activities within a space, or just form the basis of good universal design.

Thinking about this should start at the point when you access the space. However visitors arrive, but especially by car, think about whether there is a safe route into the park or playspace, and whether there are substantial issues to access such as barrier kerbs or gates which are hard to traverse. Remember that visitors may be elderly, have a disability or be trying to manage a stroller or pusher.

When the play area is reached, are there good supervision or time out places? This thinking needs to extend not only to seating, but also to tables or large benches where people can eat and chat. Seats need not always be formal, but a variety of seating, perhaps including edges to perch on, large rocks, logs or even just leaning rails, is always appreciated. Associated with this is the provision of shade in summer, whether natural through tree canopies, or constructed. In many places, concerns about skin cancer have made shading of playspaces a priority. This potentially expensive part of the playspace should be taken into account from the outset.

Likewise, anyone who has ever done consultation for a public playspace will know that the provision of toilets is always mentioned. These facilities need to be taken into account, if the playspace is likely to draw large numbers of people for substantial periods of time. For larger sites, baby and adult change facilities should also be considered, such as the 'Changing Places' initiative in the UK and Australia. This advocates for full size change tables and hoists in public places, to allow people with severe or complex disabilities to be able to use toilet amenities with dignity. The provision of toilets is often a difficult one for local authorities, who cannot provide them at every park, as the cost and maintenance can be prohibitive.

Finally, the knotty issue of fencing. This is not a simply resolved problem, although again there may well be strong policies or guidance in your particular area. On one hand fencing can make a play area safer (for example if it is very close to a busy road), and some children genuinely benefit from a fenced play area. Children with autism, for example, are much more prone to wander or run away from safe areas, causing great stress for carers.[1]

On the other hand, fencing an area can substantially eat into the available funds, and a safe but very dull space serves no one well. There is also the debate around dogs: whether a fence keeps them out, or is a potential trap if a dog gets inside. Fencing too closely or enclosing a small area can make a space feel cage-like and uncomfortable, and also potentially reduces the non-equipment based play that happens in the areas around a playground.

Occasionally, carers have also been known to think that because a playspace is fenced, it is safe, and leave children there unsupervised. Fencing may assist in making a space safe, but it will never replace a caring pair of eyes.

43

STANDARDS AND REGULATIONS (GENERAL AND BEST PRACTICE PRINCIPLES)

Paul Grover

Play design and Standards

The design of playspaces should take into consideration local Standards and guidelines. These are generally not legislated; however, in some jurisdictions there may be legislative requirements in relation to play design. In addition, Standards and guidelines differ between jurisdictions, so a local professional auditor should be consulted.

Standards and guidelines cover a broad range of principles, many of which are common to most publications. This includes materials, structural integrity, hazardous projections, means of access (e.g. stairs, ladders, ramps, climbers), protection against falling (e.g. barriers, guardrails, handrails), ropes, chains, connections, inspections, maintenance and labelling. Standards also list specific requirements for swings, slides, cableways (flying foxes), carousels, rockers and spatial networks. Two of the most important aspects to consider during design are:

- Impact area/use zone
- Entrapment

Discussion on these is provided below; however, note that many measurements relate to European Standards (henchforth referred to as EN) for play equipment, as a local adaption of these is used by the author.

Impact area (use zone)

The impact area (also known as fall zone and use zone) is the area that can be hit by the user should they fall from an item of equipment. The extent of the impact area generally relates to equipment Free Heights of Fall (FHOF). FHOF is taken as the distance from a point of intended body support to the impact area below onto which a user is able to fall freely. As such it is possible, and indeed common, for the overall equipment height to be greater than the FHOF (e.g. a pyramid net can be several metres high but have a FHOF less than 2 metres).

Impact areas typically require impact-attenuating surfacing such as mulch, sand or rubber. The purpose of this surfacing is to minimise the severity of brain injury resulting from a fall. It is important to note that the impact-attenuating characteristics of surfacing may not necessarily reduce the likelihood of long bone injury.

For non-moving play structures, minimum impact area requirements generally range from 1.5 to 2.5m depending on FHOF under EN, and are 1.83m (72 inches) under American Standards. However, some equipment types have specific fall height and impact area requirements such as swings, slides, carousels, cableways and rockers. Note that these are classified as forced movement items, as the users undergo a movement forced by the equipment. There are also Standards requirements relating to overlapping of impact areas.

Under EN, low items (<600mm in EN) do not require impact-attenuating surfacing unless they are forced movement items. Undersurfacing around low items could be warranted should a risk assessment determine that the items require significant balance and or climbing skills hence have an increased likelihood of falling. This should not preclude the use of items in proximity to one another to provide continuity in a play experience sometimes referred to as a cluster (e.g. the use of stepping stones, rocks, logs). This is becoming very common in playspaces with the increased use of natural, sculptural and artistic play elements.

Entrapments

The different types of entrapment to consider include head, neck, torso, clothing, hair, body, foot/leg and finger.

Head and neck entrapment have the worst consequences hence are discussed in more detail. Probes are used to determine if openings have potential head or neck entrapments. The head and neck probes are similar across jurisdictions; however, exact probe dimensions should be sourced from local Standards.

Under EN, the three head probes used essentially indicate that bound openings should be: greater than 230mm wide (America: 229mm/9 inches) in both dimensions; or less than 130mm wide in both dimensions (no 130mm diameter probe used in America); or less than 89mm wide (89mm, 3.5 inches) in one dimension.

The neck probe is fish-shaped and involves multiple steps to determine if an unbound opening is a potential neck entrapment (as such, a brief description of all potential neck entrapment sized openings is not possible). Some dimensions, however, that are not considered potential neck entrapments include openings: less than 45mm wide (America: 47.6mm/1.875 inches); or less than 45mm deep (19.1mm/0.75 inch); or greater than 155mm (155mm/6.1 inches) wide. However, under EN, unbound openings greater than 265mm deep are to be at least 230mm wide.

Openings shall have no parts that converge in the downward direction at an angle of less than 60 degrees (America: 55 degrees).

Standards and risk

It is very important that playspace design is not limited by unrealistic safety concerns. Indeed the introduction to the EN states that "risk-taking is an essential feature of play provision" and discusses the benefits of play. In addition, the Scope of the EN, while recognising that the purpose of the Standard "is to ensure a proper level of safety", does state that its purpose is also "at the same time to promote activities and features known to benefit children because they provide valuable experiences that will enable them to cope with situations outside the playground". More invaluable information on risk benefits assessment is provided in another section of this publication.

Other points to note from the Scope of the EN are:

> "It has been prepared with full recognition of the need for supervision of young children and of less able or less competent children"; and it "specifies the requirements that will protect the child from hazards that he or she may be unable to foresee when using the equipment as intended, or in a manner that can be reasonably anticipated".

Current Standards

Some of the playground equipment design Standards in use (as of April 2016) are listed below. This is not a definitive list, however, of all Standards relating to playgrounds used in these countries/regions. There would also be other countries that have their own Standards. Many countries do not publish their own playground Standards but playground professionals will often refer to some of the Standards below.

> **Europe:** EN1176 set (2008), *Playground Equipment and Surfacing – Safety requirements and test methods.* This Standard has also been adopted in at least the following countries.
> **Australia:** AS4685 set (2014), this is an adoption of several parts of EN1176 with Appendices listing specific conditions for Australia.
> **New Zealand:** NZS5828 (2015), this is an adoption of EN1176 with Appendices listing specific conditions for New Zealand.
> **South Africa:** SANS 51176 set (2010), this is an adoption of EN1176.
> **Asia and Africa:** It is understood that professionals in many countries refer to EN1176.
> **North America:** There has been significant harmonisation between the Canadian and US publications.
> **Canada:** CAB/CSA-Z614-14 (2014), *Children's playspaces and equipment.*
> **United States:** ASTM F1487-11 (2011), *Standard Consumer Safety Performance Specification for Playground Equipment for Public Use.*
> **South America:**
> **Brazil:** NBR 16071 set (2012), *Playgrounds.*

Notes

Chapter 37

1. Children's Play Information Service (CPIS) Factsheet 7: Consulting Children About Play, National Children's Bureau UK 2008.
2. Hart, R.A. 'Children's Participation: From Tokenism to Citizenship' UNICEF International Child Development Centre, Florence, Italy 1992.
3. Alderson, P. *Listening to Children: Children, Ethics and Social Research*, Barnardos Policy Research Unit UK 1995.

Chapter 42

1. Tarkan, Laurie. 'Study Confirms: Autism Wandering Common and Scary.' October 2012. Available from: www.autismspeaks.org/science/science-news/study-confirms-autism-wandering-common-scary. Accessed November 2015.

CONCLUSION

Elizabeth Cummins & Katherine Masiulanis

> It is the child in man that is the source of his uniqueness and creativeness, and the playground is the optimal milieu for the unfolding of his capacities and talents.
>
> *Eric Hoffer*

Having reached the end of our journey, hopefully your ground is now nicely cultivated and ready for planting.

We've established that play is crucial for children's health and that this is a world-wide commonality, whether that be in a school ground, botanic garden or street. An engaging, unique playspace is fertile soil to inspire children. Begin your project by trying to imagine yourself as a child exploring your playspace for the first time; what might cause you delight and wonder, what might get you giggling or make you catch your breath, or make you want to 'go again'?

Playspaces are complex beasts, never just 'built space'. We have discovered they are imbued with cultural history, social interaction, and spatial and temporal parameters. A playspace requires 'possibility' and 'potential', not to be presented on a plate, but something that can be unwrapped and re-gifted with imagination again and again.

We hope that this book will encourage you to make a genuine effort to produce inspiring designs and ideas for your playspace. Remember to think through practicalities and plan for maintenance, and you will certainly have more success at producing a long-lived playspace that's relevant to your community for many years to come.

Play is, after all, about the freedom to experience wonder and explore the world, to be challenged and build resilience, to have fun with friends and build skills. To reiterate the introduction in this book, *the value of play is in the lessons learnt in childhood.*

FIGURE C.1 'Play is an enjoyable journey of discovery...' Ian Potter Children's Garden, Royal Botanic Gardens, Melbourne

© John Rayner, Ian Potter Children's Garden, Royal Melbourne Botanic Gardens

INDEX

Abstract thought 28, 34, 50
Accessibility 19, 74–75, 158, 238, 313, 318, 327–328, 335
Access consultants 75
Acquisition, of knowledge and skills 30
Adventure playgrounds 16–17, 51, 259, 292, 297–304
Adolescents 62, 252–255, 257–263, 318, 327
Adults 169, 176, 178, 189–191, 207–208, 211, 216–217, 224, 230–232, 251–254, 257–261, 263, 287, 289, 292, 297–299, 303, 312
   concepts of safety 254, 275, 277–281
   design of playspaces 19
   directed play 5, 49, 145
   perceptions of play 5, 23, 220, 223, 226, 234, 241, 291, 292
   play 15, 20, 201, 271
Adversity 25, 30–31
Affordances 6, 34, 37–47, 101–102, 169–171, 208, 221, 225, 253–255
Age-appropriate play 160
All abilities 212 *see also* Accessibility, Inclusion *and* Disability
Andersen, Hans Christian 105
Animals 168, 185–186, 220, 229, 243, 252
Anthropometry (Science of) 40
Appropriation 6, 19, 22, 220–221, 224–226
Architect *see* Landscape Architect *and* Designers, landscape
Article 31 (UN Convention on the Rights of the Child) 3, 20
Art 271, 321, 333
   as a playspace 165, 181, 195–203, 338
   by children, or as play 165, 183, 187, 189–194
   living sculptures 122, 124
   permanent 165, 181–188
   sculpture 182, 184–188, 191,193, 338
   within a playspace 80, 149, 181–188, 268–269
Attention
   deficit (ADD/ADHD) 78
   directed 105
   involuntary 105
Attention Restoration Theory 107
Autism 142, 180, 200, 279, 336

Babies *see* Infants
Balance (vestibular sense) 83
Ball skills/games 67, 167, 208–211, 251
Beaux Arts (character) 156
Behaviour 142–143
Benefits of play
   to children 6
   to community 6
Bicycles 169, 287, 289, 291, 293
Blindness (vision impairment) 73, 75
Botanic gardens 147–152, 184, 186, 341
Boulders *see* Rocks
Boundaries 21, 74
Boy Scouts 14
Brain development *see* Psychology
Bubble-wrapping (of children) 25, 106
Budgets 188, 197, 211, 227, 236, 271, 281–282, 284–285, 290, 295, 303, 311–316, 318, 325, 329, 333, 336

Cerebral Palsy 142
Challenge 25, 27, 31, 78, 82, 107–108, 252, 254, 258–259, 261–262, 279, 302, 341
Championing 229–230, 241, 276, 303
Chasey 214, 287
Child-friendly cities 71, 253, 255, 260

Childhood memories (influence of) 114
Children
   agency of 66, 219–226, 232, 234, 240–241, 253, 257, 262–263, 276, 279, 284, 323, 325
   connection with nature 170, 191–192, 207, 212, 234, 240
   consulting with 71, 116, 240–241, 243, 258, 262, 323–326
   developmental stages 6, 31, 97–100, 167–171, 249–255, 259, 278, 308
   insights into thinking 34, 189, 192–194, 321
   mortality 15
   patterns and interests 52, 98–100,
   perceptions of 13
   with disabilities 73–85, 180, 200, 216, 243, 289, 312, 318, 327–328, 335
Child-sized spaces 33, 149
Chippings see Mulch
Choice 189, 212–214, 262, 265, 292, 297
Christensen, Keith 74
Circulation 169, 209–211, 318
Classroom, outdoor see Outdoor learning environment
Climbing 170, 186, 220, 228, 230, 252, 269, 302
   equipment 212, 269, 271
   trees 141, 214, 212, 238, 278, 280, 321
   walls 185, 239, 254, 259
Cognition 31
   children's thinking 27, 34, 37
   in early years 27
   social 33
Cognitive development 30–31
Cognitive play behaviours 41, 42
   behaviour mapping 41, 42
Collaboration 35, 227–228, 231
   with artists/designers 62, 182–194, 269
   with communities 136, 181, 267–274, 311
Colonisation (for play) 19
Colour 115, 175–180, 231, 238, 270, 272, 299, 327–328
Community
   built playspaces 183, 236, 238, 241, 268, 271, 308, 312, 325
   community building/bonding through play 61, 133
   engagement 182, 184–185, 232, 236–238, 240, 268, 272, 291, 311, 313, 323–326
Communication 80
Complexity (in play environments) 52
Compromise (in play) see Negotiation
Concentration 138, 143–144
Concrete thought 34
Confidence 25, 145–146
Conflict 209–210, 212, 228, 234, 276, 291, 293, 297–298, 300–301, 303, 313–314, 318

Connecting with nature see Children, connection with nature
Conran, Terence 52
Consultation 84, 217, 232, 236, 257, 291, 323–326
Construction
   by children 210, 229–234, 262, 297–304
   of playspaces 237–239, 242–243, 308, 312–313
Contested space (and play) 66
Control 24
Cooperation (in play) 31
Costs see Budgets
Courts 209
Creativity 4, 168, 170, 181–203, 230–232, 241, 243, 254, 259, 266, 299
Crime Prevention Through Environmental Design (CPTED) 115–116
Cubby 118, 138, 141, 176, 211–212, 215, 220, 229, 300–301, 321
Cultural influences 169, 175, 176, 191, 196, 202, 227, 234–235, 237, 243, 311
Curiosity 23, 28, 112
Curriculum 227–228, 234
Cyber playspaces see Technology

Dattner, Richard 17
Davis, Erin 51
Deafness (hearing impairment) 73–74
de Botton, Alain 50
Decks 170, 214, 217, 230
Deleuze, Gilles 219, 221, 225
Den see Cubby
Design
   -and-construct contracts 17, 308, 327–328
   by children 189–194, 231, 262–263
   evaluation 76, 84
   landscape 207–217, 321
   planting see Planting, design
   process 41, 147, 177, 189, 191, 196–203, 207–217, 219–226, 231, 238, 240–243, 271–272, 308, 313, 321
   zoning of play 108, 116
Designers
   horticultural 315
   landscape 6, 217, 219, 242, 258, 308, 311, 314, 315, 324
Development see Children, Developmental stages
Dewey, John 13
Disability see Children, with disabilities
Digital media see Screen Time
Digging 141, 230
Discipline 168–169
Discrimination (against children playing) 68
Disneyland 17
Down's Syndrome 142
Drainage 152
Dramatic play see Play, dramatic

Dry riverbeds, creekbeds 132
Duty of care 24

Ergonomics 6, 22, 37
   physical 76, 103–104, 171–172, 196, 255
   social 27, 31, 33, 100–101, 167–171, 252–253
Early Years setting *see* Preschool, Preschooler
Elements (play affordances) 38
Emotions 32, 228, 238, 252, 276, 281, 302
Engineering 199, 209, 283–284
Entrapment 196, 282, 337, 338
Environment(s) 1
   designed 4, 42
   for teaching and learning 80
   natural 78, 105, 138
Equipment 18, 110, 219–221
   fixed 195–203, 211–216, 235–243, 327–328
   for schools 211–216
   movable 334
   standardisation of 18
Experimenting (through play) 28, 111
Exploration 4, 28, 50, 112, 141, 144, 149, 171, 186, 191, 193, 230–231, 233–234, 257, 269, 276

Fabricius, Brita 112
Failure *see* Adversity
Fantasy Play *see* Play, *dramatic*
Feelings *see* Emotions
Fencing 76, 210, 227, 236–237, 268, 335–336
Fine Motor Skills 108, 167, 251–252
Fire, fire pits 138, 300
Fluidity (in play) 24
Food 124, 300, 302
Food gardens *see* Gardens, *productive*
Forest Schools *see* Schools, *Forest*
Fort *see* Cubbies
Freedom 4, 24–25, 304
Friedberg, Paul 17
Froebel, Fredrick 13
Frost, Joe L 17
Fun 22
Funding *see* Budgets
Fundraising 313–315

Gaster, Sanford 19
Gated-communities (and playspaces) 66
Galleries 188, 190–193, 195
Games 169, 208–217, 225–226, 241, 252, 255, 326
Gardens 197, 147–154, 210, 230, 235
   productive 124, 149, 153
Gardening 252, 300, 303
Gender roles 168, 176, 210, 251, 253, 260–261, 302
Genius loci (spirit of place) 108
Gentrification (of the city) 61

Geography (children's) 34
Gibson, James J 37
Gill, Tim 19, 112
Girls (freedom to play) 71
Girl Guides 14
Grass 209, 227–228, 230, 238
Gross motor skills 97–100, 108, 167, 251–252
Groups 169, 183, 207–217, 227–234, 236, 252–253, 258–263, 301
Guattari, Félix 219, 221, 225
Gully cricket 68
Gymnasia (outdoors) 13

Hammocks 198
Hay bales 229, 231
Hazards 277–278, 285, 333, 337, 339
Health 207, 232, 238, 263, 276, 281, 288–290, 300, 341
Hideout *see* Cubby
Hills *see* Mounds
History 4, 13, 223, 237, 241–242, 287–288, 301–302, 341

Identity 31, 251–254, 257, 259, 263
Imagination *see* Play, *imaginative*
Imaginative play *see* Play, *imaginative*
Imitation (in play) 32
Impact area (use zone) 337–338
Inclusion 4, 19, 73–74, 160
   physical 75–76, 220, 328, 335
   social 75, 216, 289, 311, 318–319, 328, 335
Independence 6, 107, 138, 143, 146, 169, 171, 197, 201, 230, 251, 253, 259, 261–263, 294, 299, 304, 318
Infants 97–99, 101–104, 175, 200
Injury 18, 278, 283–285, 338
Insects 141, 144
Interactive environment 148
Intergenerational 19, 149, 186, 201, 269, 313
Interpretation 170, 185, 318–319
Irrigation 152
Investment (in play) 56

Judgement (children's) 21, 24–25, 145 *see also* Children, *agency of*
Junk playgrounds *see* Adventure playgrounds

Kaplan, Rachel 105, 107
Kaplan, Stephen 105, 107
Karsten, Lia 19
Kindergarten *see* Preschool, Preschooler
Kinder-spel (17th Century) 14
Kitchen gardens *see* Gardens *productive*

Lady Allen of Hurtwood 17
Landmarks (in play) 34
Landscaping 212, 215

Landscape Architect 17, 182, 184–185, 202, 219, 227, 311, 314–315, 324
Landscape Designer *see* Landscape Architect / Landscape Designer
Language 111, 219–221, 251, 276–278, 282
  learning/development of 28, 141
Leadership skills 25
Lee, Alison 73
Line marking 170, 209
Litigation, liability 17– 18, 227, 280
Location (importance of in play) 41
Logs 211–212, 317, 334–335
Loose parts, materials 24, 77–78, 110, 115, 152, 170, 178, 189–194, 208, 210–211, 215–217, 227–234, 278, 300, 303, 318
Longevity (of playspaces) 316–317, 333–334
Louv, Richard 5
Lynch, Kevin 19

Maintenance 5, 311–312, 317–318, 323–324, 333–335
  art 187–188, 197–198, 333–334
  gardens, landscape 312, 316, 331
  play equipment 158, 220, 237, 239–240, 243, 272, 312, 327, 337
  schools 208, 227, 232
Materials 5, 112
Mazes, labyrinths 122, 190
McDonalds (playspaces in) 18, 56
Mental maps 34
Mess 50, 216, 227–234
Metal 241, 316–317, 334
Minibeasts *see* Insects
Minimalism 17
Mobility 142
  independence 74, 142
Mobility aids *see* Wheelchairs, wheelchair accessibility
Montessori, Maria 148, 179
Moon bikes *see* Bicycles
Moore, Robin 20, 112
Moral education 276
Morris, Robert 51
Mounds 43–44170, 230, 254, 299
Mud 143, 216, 228, 233, 235
Mulch 239, 317, 338
Multi-sensory environments 98, 179
Music 266, 302, 326

Narratives (construction of) *see* Storytelling
Nature (connection to) 149, 152
Nature deficit disorder 5, 19, 223
Natural materials 106–107 112, 155, 160, 170, 178–179, 211–212, 216, 227–234, 334
Nature nurseries (Scandinavia) 137
Nature play *see* Play, *nature play*
Natural settings 4, 110, 112

Neighbourhoods (and integrated play) 66
Neighbourhood mobility 24, 253–254
Negotiation 32, 34
Nicholson, Simon 50
Noguchi, Isamu 17
Not-for-profit organisations 20, 51, 70–71, 235–243, 267–274
Novelty playgrounds 17
Nursery school *see* Preschool

Obesity 223, 289
Objects (play affordances) 38
Observation
  of children 111, 186, 189, 191–194, 196–198, 217, 231–232, 303, 323–324, 326
  of site 125, 236, 313–314, 321–322
Organisational structures (children's thinking) 29
Outdoor learning environment 137, 208, 243 *see also* Classroom, *outdoor*

Parallel Play 99
Parents *see* Adults
Parkour 252, 259
Parks 20, 56, 60–64, 66–68, 155–160,169, 176, 186, 197, 207, 223, 259–260, 267–274, 293–294
Paths 45, 109–110, 209, 230, 321, 147
Pebbles *see* Rocks
Peers 6, 167–169, 176, 251, 253, 257, 258–263, 266
Pergolas *see* Shelter
Persistence 30
Picasso, Pablo 51
Plans (concept and masterplan) 43, 108–109, 153, 156, 157, 311
Plants 115–127, 147, 150
  design 116, 120, 122, 177, 318, 331
  edible 124, 300, 302, 318
  establishment and maintenance 116, 127, 152, 210, 331, 334
  for cubbies, enclosures, tunnels 120–121, 211
  for play 117, 120, 122, 191–192, 210–212, 214, 228, 230, 282
  lifecycle 111, 115
  selection 111, 125, 116–119, 151, 318, 331
  sensory importance of 84, 124
  toxic, hazardous (to avoid) 119–120
  trees 122, 126, 335
  weeds, weed control 116, 120
Plastic 317, 334
Platforms *see* Decks
Play
  as a natural occurrence 55, 64
  child-directed 51, 80
  city play 56, 176, 200, 235, 253, 267–274
  free play (and lack of) 21–26, 55, 65–71, 76–77, 80, 275, 297–304

influence of 20
in war zones 152–154
nature play 4, 105–114, 130, 137–146, 147–149, 154, 170, 208, 211–212, 216, 228, 231, 282, 308, 316, 333, 338
open-ended 17, 37, 40, 130, 297–304
street play 13, 60, 169, 197, 223, 287–295, 304
Play advocate *see* Championing
Play equipment 211–217, 219, 230, 235–243, 258, 260–261, 269, 275, 281, 283, 308, 327–328, 338
Play types 308
cognitive 115, 170, 224, 261
creative 115
dramatic 32, 115, 156, 210, 212, 214, 216, 242, 259, 301, 318
imaginative 4, 22, 28, 31–33, 37, 40, 81, 112, 149,177, 181–186, 195, 198, 208, 210, 214–216, 220, 230–231, 233, 241–242, 258, 299, 318, 341
physical 140, 167, 171, 198–199, 208–214, 224, 238, 252, 255, 258–259, 266, 269, 288
social 167–171, 201, 210, 212–215, 224, 231, 253–254, 255, 257–261, 265–266
Playground movement 15
Playhouse *see* Cubbies
Playworker 232, 293, 300, 303–304, 312
Pleasure (in play) 22–23
Politics (influence on play and playspaces) 60, 154, 292–295
Portable equipment *see* Equipment, *moveable*
Postmodernism 49
Preschool, preschooler 98, 100, 102, 104, 129–136, 189, 198, 223, 324, 329
Privacy 35, 53
Problem-solving 51
Programming 150, 189–194, 227, 231–233
Proximal development 30
Psychology, brain development 175, 178–179, 200, 251
Public playspaces 57
Public space 49, 52
Purposeful interaction 20

Quotes *see* Tendering

Ramps 76, 81
Rasmussen, Kim 19
Recreation 16, 65
Recycling *see* Sustainability
Refuge 212, 215, 318
Reform movements 14
Reggio Emilia 148, 189
Representation (of objects) 28–29, 34
Resilience 19, 276, 341
Resourcefulness 21–22

Retreat spaces 170, 184, 241, 253, 335
Rhizome, concept 219, 221, 223–224
Risk 27, 31, 106, 169, 178, 228, 231–232, 238, 249, 257, 275–285, 302–303, 338
aversion 19, 50, 139
management, minimisation 138, 142, 158, 280, 285
risk benefit, risk benefit assessment 135, 143, 230, 238, 262–263, 275–285, 338–339
risky play 25, 51, 78, 219, 239, 253, 259–260, 285, 302
Rock(s) 170, 191, 156–157, 211–212, 214–216, 229–230, 232, 321, 334–335, 338
Role play *see* Play, *social* and *dramatic*
Rough and tumble (play) 23, 167, 303
Rubber (undersurfacing) 239, 284, 338
Rules 19, 169, 208, 232, 237, 252, 279

Sand, sandpits, sand gardens 13–14, 129, 216, 229–230, 234,239, 268, 299, 300, 327, 333, 338
Safety 106, 158, 230, 238–239, 254, 261, 276, 281–285, 294, 335–336, 338–339
surfacing 19 *see also* Mulch, *rubber*
Scale 41, 50, 117
School 27, 187, 223, 235–243, 300, 324, 329, 341
Forest 137–146
grounds 6
primary 165, 168, 205–217, 227–234, 253
secondary 253
special, specialist 74, 79–85, 142, 183, 186
special school staff (involvement in projects) 74, 79–80, 85
Science 139, 169–170
Screen time 265, 298
Sculpture *see* Art, Sculpture
Seasons 111, 115, 118, 170, 318, 321
Seating 186, 188, 209, 254, 312, 318, 335
Secret places 321
Self (children's sense of) 28, 31 *see also* Identity
Self-confidence 4, 107
Self-esteem (children's development of) 138, 145
Sensory 81, 83, 108, 111, 115, 149, 175–180,183,186,195,199, 243, 251
phobia (aversion) 143
Settings 5
behavioural 42–47
for play 24, 39, 78
Settings (play affordances) *see* Settings *for play*
Sexuality 252–253
Shade 5, 185, 188, 268, 312, 318, 335
Sharing 101
Shelter *see* Shade
Shopping mall (playspaces in) 56
Simplicity (in design) 52
Site assessment, analysis *see* Observation, *of site*

Site preparation 126, 131, 149
Slides 214, 219–223, 226, 238–239, 254, 265, 337
Skating 169, 251–252, 259, 261–262
Social competence 32, 138
Social connection 33, 167, 169, 252–253, 257–258
Social interaction, ergonomics *see* Ergonomics, social
Social media 252–253, 255, 265
Soil 126, 151
Solitary play 186, 301
Solomon, Susan G 18, 20
Sound 52 *see also* Music
Sorensen, Carl Theodore 16, 107
Spaces 34, 35, 39, 64, 73, 83, 109, 149, 257–258
Spaces and terrains (play affordances) *see* Spaces
Special needs 180, 183, 186, 200, 236
  therapeutic requirements 80, 84
Spontaneity 21, 24
Sport 167–170, 207–210, 251–25, 252, 258, 262, 278
  fields 62 *see also* Courts
  impact on play 208–209
  surfaces 169, 209–210, 236, 255
Staff built 131, 136
Stage 217, 231, 254
Staging 329
Standards 25, 196, 239, 281–285, 333, 337
Standardisation 106, 127
Steiner, Rudolf 148
Steiner, philosophy 148
Steps 211, 229, 299
Stipulations (in play) 28
Stone(s) *see* Rocks
Storage 231, 312
Storytelling 32, 242–243, 304, 319, 326
Steel *see* Metal
Street play *see* Play, street play
Structures (play affordances) 38, 147
Subversion (of environments for play) 50 *see also* Appropriation
Supervised spaces, supervision 35, 149, 287–285, 297–304 *see also* Adventure playgrounds
Suspended reality (in play) 40
Sustainability 50, 112, 317–319, 327
Sustained play 133
Sutton-Smith, Brian 13
Swings 83, 239, 254, 265, 269–270, 274, 300, 302, 337
Symbolism (in play) 28

Tag *see* Chasey
Technology 19, 24, 255, 265–266
Technical drawings 6, 308, 310
Teenagers *see* Adolescents
Tenders, tendering 308, 312, 321

Theory of Loose Parts 50
Theory of mind 31, 101, 169
Texture 178–179, 196, 328
Therapy 182 *see also* Special needs, *therapeutic requirements*
Timber 178, 228, 230, 239, 300, 318, 334
Time 49
  constraints on play 22–23, 25
Toddlers 176, 327 *see also* Preschoolers
Toilets 318, 335
Toilet humour 23
Tool use 138
Toys (for early years) 101–102
Tradition 197, 242 *see also* History
Transfer decks 75
Transference (of learning) 146
Transformation (in play) 28, 133
Trees *see* Plants, *trees*
Tree climbing *see* Climbing, *trees*
Tree, concept 219, 221–222, 224
Treehouse 122
Tricycles *see* Bicycles
Trip hazards 333
Tunnel 45, 83, 214, 300
Tyres 239–241, 243, 269, 271–272

Upper body equipment 213
Urban design, planning 14, 67, 197, 200, 223, 235, 237, 253, 262–263, 267, 272, 287, 297
Urbanisation 55, 66
Urban revitalisation 60

Vandalism 184–185
van Eyck, Aldo 17, 62
Viewing out (importance of) 81
Virtual worlds *see* Technology
Vision impairment *see* Blindness *and* Special needs
Volunteers 236, 287, 292, 294
Vygotsky, Lev 30

Water 147, 321
  collection/harvesting and storage (tanks) 112, 129, 132
  feature 129, 188
  play 129–136, 150, 158–160, 186, 216, 228, 230, 233, 327
  pump 129, 132, 156, 300
  safety 135, 150–151
  waterproof clothing 143
Wheelchairs, wheelchair accessibility 73, 75–76, 84, 216
Whyte, William H 52
Wood *see* Timber

Young, Donald 20
Young people, youth *see* Adolescents